DATE DUE

Jan 19 '67			
Mar 16 '68			
Mar 30 '68			
May. 17 '73			
Feb 18 '76			
24 '76			
Mar 24 '76			
GAYLORD			PRINTED IN U.S.A.

THE FIRST RUSSIAN RADICAL

Also by David Marshall Lang

LIVES AND LEGENDS OF THE
GEORGIAN SAINTS

THE WISDOM OF BALAHVAR
A Christian Legend of the Buddha

(George Allen & Unwin Ltd)

———

THE LAST YEARS OF THE
GEORGIAN MONARCHY

(Columbia University Press)

1 Alexander Radishchev *(oil painting by an unknown artist)*

The First Russian Radical

ALEXANDER RADISHCHEV
1749-1802

❧⟨♦⟩☙

DAVID MARSHALL LANG

M.A., D.LIT.

Reader in Caucasian Studies
University of London

Ruskin House

GEORGE ALLEN & UNWIN LTD

MUSEUM STREET LONDON

FIRST PUBLISHED IN 1959

*This book is copyright under the Berne Convention.
Apart from any fair dealing or the purpose of private
study, research, criticism, or review, as permitted under
the Copyright Act, 1956, no portion may be reproduced
by any process without written permission. Enquiries
should be addressed to the publisher.*

© *George Allen & Unwin Ltd* 1959

PRINTED IN GREAT BRITAIN
in 10 *on* 11 *point Plantin by*
SIMSON SHAND LTD
LONDON, HERTFORD AND HARLOW

CONTENTS

CONTENTS

PLATES

Except for the frontispiece, the illustrations are from contemporary engravings.

INTRODUCTION

If it be true that every nation gets the government it deserves, the Russians must be among the most undeserving or at least the most unlucky of peoples. Absolutism tempered by assassination—that has long been the keynote of Russian political history. The tender plant of liberal democracy has never flourished on the draughty steppe. Scattered thinly over vast tracts of land, exposed to a harsh climate, harried by many foes, the Russian nation was forced in self defence to entrust its destinies to ruthless autocrats, who did not shrink from oppressing their obedient subjects. In so many ways, the history of the Russians since mediaeval times is a chronicle of the suppression of individual liberty, with long spells of inertia and apathy suddenly punctuated by desperate, elemental upheavals.

Yet all the time, the literature, art, music and heroic lays of the Russian people proclaim them a sturdy, virile and talented race. Today, the Soviet citizen away from his commissar is charming, kind-hearted, hospitable, and full of an earthy humour. It is tantalizing to speculate about the qualities of the nation which might have evolved in Russia, had providence shaped its history differently. Indeed, from Russia's conversion to Christianity until the thirteenth century, it seemed that a bright future was in store for the country. Ably led by their Norse Varangian overlords and civilized by the Christian culture imbibed from Orthodox Byzantium, the Russian people formed an effective rampart of Christendom, barring the steppes against Khazar, Pecheneg, Polovtsian, and the other dread Asiatic hordes of Gog and Magog.

All this was changed by the Mongol onslaught headed by Chingis Khan and his successors. The need to survive taught the Russians to cower and humble themselves. To throw off the Tatar yoke at last, the Russians had to adopt the ruthless policies of their barbarous conquerors. The centre of gravity shifted from sunny Kiev and free Novgorod to Moscow, where the Tsars claimed the inheritance of the Emperors of Constantinople and stamped out the proud liberties of their nation. Renaissance and Reformation passed Russia by. Alternately Byzantine and Asiatic in outlook, the rulers of Muscovy left an indelible imprint on the national character. Peter the Great turned Russia's face towards Western Europe; he wiped out that turbulent Pretorian Guard, the Moscow *Strel'tsy*, sheared off the boyars' beards, and tamed the grubby and superstitious monks. Yet the veneer of Western ways did nothing to educate or enlighten the peasant masses, who remained as downtrodden as ever, while their masters took on the outward trappings of the European aristocracy. Peter's legacy was a modern police state, based on serfdom, and well equipped with torture chambers and hangmen to enforce the despot's will. Today, after wars, upheavals and revolutions, the Russian people are still without any right of political self-expression.

Yet Russia has never lacked prophets of freedom, who have not shirked martyrdom for the sake of their convictions. Such a one was archpriest Avvakum, leader of the Old Believers, and author of a famous autobiography, who was burnt at the stake under Tsar Theodore II late in the seventeenth century. Under the 'enlightened' Empress Catherine II, the freemason Novikov, publisher, philanthropist and apostle of Enlightenment, was mercilessly harried and then imprisoned, to emerge from his dungeon a broken man. Ryleev, the bard of freedom, was executed for his part in the Decembrist conspiracy of 1825, while Pushkin and Lermontov knew what it meant to incur the displeasure of Nicholas I and his gendarmes. Chaadaev, who denounced the sterility of Russian life under Tsardom, was certified insane by order of the Emperor. Dostoevsky was dragged before the firing squad. Chernyshevsky, outspoken leader of the radical intelligentsia, spent over twenty years in jail and exile. Under Stalin, writers who refused to toe the party line were shot or tortured to death. Recently, we have seen Dudintsev, the candid author of *Not By Bread Alone*, placed under a ban for exposing the shortcomings of the Soviet paradise, while Pasternak's *Doctor Zhivago* can be published only outside Russia. Rare indeed is the Russian writer of any talent who could bring himself to lend sincere support to the régime in power.

Among Russia's apostles of freedom, Alexander Radishchev is an outstanding figure. Sentenced to death for his outspoken book, *A Journey from St Petersburg to Moscow*, later reprieved and sent off in chains by Catherine the Great to exile in Siberia, his fate set the pattern of what was to befall later critics of Tsarist and communist dictatorship. One of the most noteworthy books in Russian literature, Radishchev's *Journey* was the first great manifestation of the Russian social conscience. 'I looked around me—and my soul was afflicted with the sufferings of mankind. . . . I felt that every man may contribute to the welfare of his fellows.' With these words, as Nicholas Berdyaev has justly said, the Russian Intelligentsia was born.

Nor is the significance of Radishchev's message confined to Russia alone. Many of Russia's problems were also those of Europe. Radishchev was born in 1749 and took his own life in 1802. He witnessed the transition from the old order to the modern industrial age, with all the turmoil produced by readjustment to new social, political and economic conditions. Pressing problems claimed the attention of philanthropists and reformers throughout Europe, as old dominant forces struggled teresting to find Gleb among the 324 nobles who signed one of the rival constitutional projects drawn up in 1730 in an attempt to restrict the authority of the new Empress, Anna Ivanovna. Needless to say, this document, like most Russian constitutional projects, was torn up, and Anna and her favourite, Biron, were soon ruling as despotically as previous sovereigns had done.

Radishchev's grandfather Athanasius, or Afanasy Prokofievich (1684–1746), was one of those rugged veterans of Peter the Great's reign who helped to impose the will of that dynamic potentate on an often recalcitrant people. Under the renowned commanders Sheremetev and Menshikov, Afanasy Radishchev saw active service in Courland, Pomerania, Finland and Poland. In later years, he took part in the *coup d'état* which in 1730 placed Anna Ivanovna on the Imperial throne, and was appointed a member of the Little-Russian General Tribunal. As Colonel of the Starodub ('Old Oak') Regiment, he organized military reprisals against the Old Believers in the Ukraine, and at length retired with the rank of Brigadier. His belated marriage to a wealthy heiress brought into the family the estate of Ablyazovo in the Saratov region, where Afanasy's grandson, the young Alexander Radishchev, spent his childhood years.

Alexander's father Nicholas (1728–1803) received what was for Russia in the 1730s an excellent classical education. While Brigadier Radishchev was serving in the Ukraine, Nicholas was able to take lessons from scholars of the Kiev Academy in several languages, in history and theology. No careerist like his father, Nicholas married young, in 1747. His bride, Thekla Argamakova, bore him no less than eleven children —seven sons, the eldest being Alexander Nikolaevich, the subject of this book, as well as four daughters. But for this numerous progeny, Nicholas Radishchev would have been quite well off, his serfs totalling, according to official records, 3,338 in 1790, compared with 3,453 in 1782. However, even such resources as these hardly sufficed to provide dowries for his daughters and educations and careers for all his sons, with the result that he was constantly in difficulties for ready money. Nicholas Radishchev was a humane master to his peasantry. During the revolt of Pugachev, when all around the serfs were wreaking gory vengeance on their lords and masters, Nicholas Radishchev's peasants concealed him and the older boys in the forests and took care of the little ones, whom they disguised as peasant children. He was a strict churchgoer, to such an extent that one of his grandsons refers to him as being 'extremely superstitious'.

Alexander (Sasha) Radishchev was born on August 20/31, 1749, in the house which his father possessed in Moscow. The infant Sasha soon found himself in the country, where he was given into the care of a peasant nurse, Praskovya Klementievna by name. To the end of his life, Radishchev retained a warm affection for his peasant 'nyanyushka'. —'A great one she was for coffee', he recalled in one of his writings. 'She used to say it helped her get rid of her headaches.—As soon as I have swallowed five cups full, she would say, things seem all brightened up; without it, I should be dead in three days!'

After a year or two, Sasha Radishchev was given a 'little uncle' (*dyad'ka*) or peasant governor, Peter Mamontov by name, nicknamed Suma. 'My dear old *dyad'ka* Suma', Radishchev calls him in his mock-ballad *Bova*, adding that 'he was a cultured man, combed his hair with a real comb, instead of picking his scalp over. He went around in a half-length *kaftan* with beard and moustache shaved off. Snuff would he take, and at cards a great dab was he.'

These peasant *dyad'kas* were a real institution in old Russia, as anyone will remember who has read Pushkin's story *The Captain's Daughter*, with its unforgettable characterization of the faithful and crusty Savel'ich, who rescues his master from so many scrapes. A contemporary of Radishchev, the dramatist Fonvizin, refers to his own 'dear *dyad'ka*, preceptor and tutor, guardian of my cash, my laundry and my doings'. Suma was all these things to Sasha Radishchev; for hours on end he would tell him the old legends of the Russian countryside, recite ballads to him, or teach him to read out of popular chapbooks brought round by the country pedlars, or from the Slavonic Psalter and the Book of Hours of the Orthodox Church. It is a striking fact that all Radishchev's prose works are tinged with the rhetorical and archaic style of Old Slavonic literature, suggesting that with all his later readings in the literature of the Western European Age of Reason, he never quite broke loose from the influence of the church books with which he was imbued in his childhood days.

On one occasion, Suma's intellectual supremacy was put to a severe test. Following another fashion at the time, Radishchev's father decided, like Major Grinev in Pushkin's *The Captain's Daughter*, to get his Moscow agents to supply a French tutor for his son together with the next consignment of Bordeaux wine. This venture ended in much the same way as that of Monsieur Beaupré in *The Captain's Daughter*: young Sasha's new tutor was unmasked as an illiterate deserter from the French army, and had to be unceremoniously dismissed—to the glee, no doubt, of the worthy Suma. A bogus French tutor appears, by the way, in Radishchev's book, *A Journey from St Petersburg to Moscow*, chapter 'Gorodnya', and may well have been suggested by this real character who featured in Radishchev's childhood memories.

At this period, life on the Ablyazovo estate had a patriarchal flavour.

The Radishchev mansion, which was still shown to visitors during the nineteenth century, was no Palladian villa of the type increasingly fashionable in later eighteenth-century Russia, but a plain, square structure standing close to the peasant *izbas* of the village. From the spacious entrance hall, with its store cupboards and massive oak chests at the sides, one walked straight into the living room. In one corner, there were icons hung upon the wall; in the centre of the room was a solid wooden table covered with a rug by way of table-cloth, on which stood a couple of bronze candlesticks. Around this table were a number of heavy wooden chairs with straight, upright backs, carved by peasant craftsmen on the estate. On one of the living-room walls there hung an oil painting of Radishchev's grandfather, Brigadier Athanasius, who died three years before the lad was born. The old gentleman was portrayed heavily bewigged, his left hand on the hilt of his sword, his right holding the *pernach* or gilt staff of office which was the emblem of a colonel in a Ukrainian regiment.

While Radishchev's father was distinguished for mild and humane treatment of his serfs, the same could not be said of grandmother Nastasya, Brigadier Athanasius' widow. It was she who had brought the Ablyazovo domains into the family, and she still exercised matriarchal sway over them. The testy old lady's exactions sometimes provoked her serfs into taking refuge in flight.

This was a period in Russian history when the power of the landowners over the peasants was steadily on the increase. It has been said with truth that under Peter the Great and his immediate successors, the gentry were themselves thralls of the Tsar just as much as the serfs were thralls of the gentry. The great reformer had been emphatic in laying down that land-tenure and serf ownership were tied up with service to the State. The squires and the great nobles must educate themselves and their sons, must fight for their country, must man the civil service—and if they shirked, must be punished like anybody else. This attitude aroused widespread opposition. With Peter safely buried, the disgruntled backwoodsmen looked forward to an easy life of gorging and vodka swigging on their rustic demesnes, while those nobles who had acquired a taste for Western ways hankered after the dignities enjoyed by their counterparts in Poland, Germany, France and elsewhere. The gentry's great ambition was to emancipate itself. There were even movements to limit the imperial prerogative and establish government by aristocratic oligarchy. These were thwarted both by the strength of the autocratic tradition, and by the influence of the petty squirearchy, who had no wish to come under the sway of the great nobles. However, the gentry were successful little by little in consolidating their own privileges, while whittling down the surviving rights still belonging to the peasantry. This trend culminated in Tsar Peter III's edict of 1762, whereby the gentry were freed from obligation of State service, and confirmed in unrestricted proprietorship of their lands and serfs. Many, of course, continued to give loyal service in the army, navy and civil administration. But there were many others who settled down to a parasitic and oppressive way of life, which they enjoyed at the expense of the serfs over whose goods and bodies they now enjoyed almost unlimited power. The feudal principle of lord-vassal relationship was superseded by a system of slave-owning proprietorship.

It was naturally the long-suffering *muzhik* who came off worst. Some landowners developed into regular martinets, who punished every breach of orders with brutal violence. Since they had wide powers of summary jurisdiction, certain landed proprietors evolved their own private law codes, usually of great severity. On Field-Marshal Rumyantsev's estates, a regular tariff of beatings was laid down for various offences. A serf flogged with up to seventeen thousand strokes of the rods (*batogi*), or one hundred of the knout was allowed—if still alive—a maximum of one week in bed to recover. Anyone not back at work after that time was deprived of rations. We hear of a maidservant who accidentally disturbed her master's slumbers being severely beaten, and then denied the use of her own name. Her fellow servants had to address her as 'Faint-Heart' and 'Liar', offenders against this rule being punished with five thousand strokes. Particularly shameful was the case of the Widow Saltykov, known as 'Saltychikha', a sadistic pervert and sex-fiend, who tortured to death scores of her peasants, both male and female. The striking feature in this instance was not the crimes themselves, but the fact that her conduct was notorious throughout the countryside for years without any action being taken by the authorities. Village priests used to bury her victims, 'no questions asked'. It was only when two of her serfs escaped and managed to reach St Petersburg that the Senate took cognizance of Saltychikha's misdeeds, and brought her belatedly to book. Naturally, these are extreme examples. Most landed proprietors, like those described in the novels of Sergey Aksakov, developed a paternalistic approach, regarding the serfs as irresponsible children to be coaxed or chastened as necessary. Scarcely anyone thought of them as fully-fledged human beings, endowed with feelings and basic human dignity.

In 1755, the first Russian University was founded in Moscow through the joint efforts of the great scientist and pioneer of Russian literature, Michael Lomonosov, and the patron of letters, Ivan Shuvalov, and under the patronage of the much-maligned Empress Elizabeth. Since no schooling was to be had in the depths of the country where Radishchev was brought up, he was sent at the age of eight to study in Moscow where a relative of his mother, Michael Argamakov by name, had a house at which Sasha Radishchev could stay as one of the family. This arrangement had special advantages: Michael Argamakov's uncle, A. M. Argamakov, was the first Director of the University and of the affiliated 'Gymnasium and Pension' for children of the gentry. Radishchev was granted permission to attend lectures, as well as sharing with the Argamakov children the private tuition provided by a French refugee, who had been a councillor at the *Parlement* of Rouen but suffered banishment, so it seems, for his advanced political views.

Michael Argamakov had plenty of lively reminiscences to share with his young kinsman. As a young officer in the Guards, he had been suspected of complicity in the abortive plot against the despot Biron in 1740. Arrested and cruelly tortured, he and his comrades were saved from execution only by Biron's fall. Under the brief regency of Anna Leopoldovna, Argamakov was promoted and rewarded for his sympathy with the anti-Biron movement. As a partisan of the Brunswick party, however, Argamakov was not long afterwards once more disgraced and dismissed from the army after yet another *coup d'état* had placed Peter the Great's daughter Elizabeth upon the Russian throne. Thus, Michael Argamakov's reminiscences must have provided his young relative with some food for thought on how Russia was ruled and justice administered under the successors of Peter the Great.

Moscow University was housed at this early period in a handsome building in the baroque style of architecture. The courses included arithmetic, geometry, Russian grammar and 'refinement of style', the elements of history and geography, French, German and Latin, as well as a few other miscellaneous subjects. The Professor of Law was a German named Dilthey, who used as his text-books the legal treatises of Puffendorf. The teacher of French was none other than the dramatist Pierre du Belloy, later famous as author of the patriotic tragedy *Le Siège de Calais*; certainly Radishchev's fluent mastery of French, which he wrote with greater facility than he possessed in Russian itself, can be dated from this period.

Some features of Moscow University life in that pioneer stage were open, of course, to criticism. An amusing account of those days is given in the memoirs of Fonvizin the dramatist, according to whom conditions and academic standards then merited as much censure as they later came to deserve praise. 'During my time at the University,' he adds, 'we studied in a highly disordered fashion. This arose in part from childish idleness, as well as from the negligence and tipsiness of the teachers. Our arithmetic master was drunk as a lord; the Latin teacher, though notorious for bad-temper, intoxication and all sorts of low vices, had a very sharp brain and knew Latin and Russian extremely well.'

Examinations were conducted after a fashion which would hardly satisfy a modern school inspector. On the day before the Latin test, Fonvizin tells us, his teacher arrived wearing a coat with five buttons up the front, and a waistcoat with only four. 'Surprised by this oddity, I asked the master the reason.—My buttons may seem ridiculous to you, he replied, but they are in fact the guardians of your reputation and of mine. The ones on the coat represent the five declensions, those on the waistcoat the four conjugations. And so, he went on, banging the table with his fist, just you listen to what I am going to tell you.—When I start asking you about some noun or other, and what declension it belongs to, then pay attention to which button I shall touch. If it is the second, then you can answer boldly: Second declension! With the conjugations, just keep an eye on my waistcoat buttons and proceed in the same way, and you won't make any mistakes.—And that is how our examination was conducted!'

Nor was the geography test much more searching. Unfortunately, the geography master lacked his Latin colleague's dexterity with buttons, so his three pupils advanced at the examination hall without prior briefing. They need not have worried. The first candidate was asked: 'Into what does the Volga flow?'—'The Black Sea,' came the reply. The question was repeated to the next victim.—'The White Sea,' he answered. When Fonvizin's turn came, he said, with a demeanour of childish candour: 'I don't know,' with the result that he was unanimously awarded the medal.

'All the same,' Fonvizin concludes, 'I am bound to remember the University with gratitude. It was there that I learnt Latin and was grounded in several branches of knowledge. At the University I picked up quite a lot of German, and above all acquired a taste for literary pursuits.'

This, then, was the environment in which Radishchev spent nearly five years of his life, from the age of eight to thirteen. He was by all accounts a well-knit lad, of medium height, with fine hazel eyes, lively and attractive in his manners. He was, above all, highly sensitive and quick to absorb impressions and ideas. Already he was marked by those traits of plain speaking and sincerity so characteristic of him in later life—qualities which were to bring upon his head so grim a destiny.

Radishchev was still with the Argamakovs in Moscow when the Empress Elizabeth died at St Petersburg at the beginning of the year 1762. Soon rumours reached Moscow that all was not well under the new Emperor, Peter III. A fanatical admirer of Frederick the Great, Peter hastened to make peace with Prussia on terms highly favourable to the Germans, in spite of the triumphs won by Russian arms in the Seven Years' War. It was bruited about that Peter was planning to attack the King of Denmark in order to further the interests of his native Holstein, and that the crack Guards regiments, manned by the pick of the Russian nobility, would be posted abroad to serve in North Germany. Even Peter's manifesto freeing the gentry from compulsory State service failed to win their allegiance, since this was followed by widespread uprisings of disgruntled peasants demanding their liberty as well. After the splendour of Elizabeth's reign, with its unmistakable upsurge of Russian patriotism, the nobles were scandalized by the sight of Peter III's court, where 'nonsensical talk was combined with immoderate drinking, the punch bowl was brought in after dinner and pipes laid out ready, so that prolonged tippling and fumes from tobacco smoke produced a scene more fitting for some low tavern than for a royal palace. . . . Praise for the King of Prussia, who had then only just ceased to be our foe, and belittlement of the courage of the Russian armies—such were the means employed in order to win affection for this sovereign!'

Very different was the temperament of Peter's consort, the future Catherine II. From the little German court of Anhalt-Zerbst, she came to Russia as a girl of fifteen to marry the Empress Elizabeth's heir, the semi-imbecile Peter of Holstein. In that uncongenial Russian environment, she consoled herself by cultivating the philosophy of the French 'Age of Enlightenment', as well as the company of men more attractive and responsive than her boorish spouse. Long before the Empress Elizabeth's death, Catherine and Peter were estranged and living on terms of strong mutual hostility. With Peter on the throne, Catherine's position was intolerable. Fortunately for her, she had a good following among the young officers of the Imperial Guard, partly as a result of her liaison with the popular Gregory Orlov. The Emperor's own folly precipitated the inevitable crisis. At the beginning of July 1762, Catherine was summoned to St Petersburg from the country palace of Peterhof; the Imperial Guard swore fealty to her, and a manifesto was published announcing her accession to the throne of All the Russias. After a futile attempt to flee the country, Peter III abdicated and was consigned to the château of Ropsha as a prisoner in the care of Alexis Orlov and another of Catherine's trusties, Theodore Baryatinsky. A week later, news was received that Peter was dead. There had been a drunken quarrel, so it appeared; in the ensuing mêlée, Baryatinsky and Alexis Orlov had strangled their charge.

On the whole, public opinion was disposed to listen favourably to the Imperial manifesto which was sent to Moscow from St Petersburg to be read in the churches and posted up in public places. Peter was

declared deposed, and all Russians were invited to acknowledge his
former consort as the Empress Catherine II. 'The autocratic monarch
Peter III,' Radishchev and his relatives heard it announced, 'through
hatred towards the Fatherland, contempt for the Orthodox faith, a
desire to deliver the homeland into foreign hands, and revulsion from
everything which that sovereign of world renown (i.e. Peter I) had
established in Russia', had brought the realm into so desperate a
condition that it was already tending towards revolt and anarchy.
Promising extensive reforms, the manifesto added, in terms then
somewhat unfamiliar, that 'when not held in check by good and
benevolent qualities, despotism in a sovereign wielding autocratic
power is an evil of such magnitude as directly to bring about many
deplorable results'.

The Coronation of the Empress Catherine II took place in Moscow
in September 1762 and was followed by a series of public holidays and
celebrations. This was judged a good moment to secure for young
Sasha Radishchev an entry into that charmed circle of court life to
which in those days the sons of the gentry eagerly aspired. Here again,
Radishchev's family connections on the Argamakov side proved
invaluable. Young Basil Argamakov had just completed a period of
service in the Imperial Corps of Pages. His place was now reserved for
his kinsman, Alexander Radishchev, and when on November 25th a
decree was issued, nominating forty boys 'exclusively of the gentry
class' to be pages in the service of the Empress and the Tsarevich Paul
the heir-apparent, Radishchev's name was on the list.

Not until June 1763 did the Imperial Court finally leave the mediaeval
splendours of the Kremlin palaces and return to St Petersburg. There
on the banks of the Neva, opposite the forbidding stone mass of the
Peter and Paul Fortress, the architect Rastrelli had just completed the
Winter Palace, which now reared up in grandeur from amongst the
older, single-storied dwelling houses clustered around it. This was the
new residence of the Russian Tsars. Next door, at the mouth of the
so-called *Zimnyaya Kanavka* ('Winter Canal'), was a dilapidated
mansion dating from the time of Peter the Great, abandoned by the
Court, and handed over to serve as quarters for the Imperial Corps of
Pages. This was to be the home of Radishchev and his comrades while
the Court was in residence.

Radishchev was now almost fourteen years old. At first, the pomp of
the Imperial palaces cannot have failed to overawe him. The young
Fonvizin was also about fourteen when he paid his first visit to Court,
and says in his memoirs that he was amazed at the splendour there:
'Everywhere glittering gold, an assembly of people in blue and red
decoration ribbons, a multitude of fair women and finally, an enormous

orchestra, all this astonished my sight and my ears, and the palace seemed to me the dwelling place of some supernatural being.' Again, a traveller received at Court early in Catherine's reign reported that 'the opulence and pomp of the Russian Court exceeds all descriptions. An enormous suite of courtiers is constantly in attendance on the Empress. Many of the grandees are virtually studded with diamonds: diamond buttons, diamonds on their shoe-buckles and on the hilts of their swords.' The British Envoy, Sir James Harris, commented sourly that 'great luxury and little morality seem to run thro' every rank.'

Sasha Radishchev was well placed to see both sides of the picture. The pages were of course expected to perform turns of duty at the Imperial table and at receptions and balls. They were under oath never to reveal the confidences they might overhear in the course of their employment; no doubt they heard plenty of conversations unsuitable for their young ears, for even judged by the standards of those tolerant days, the ménage of Catherine and the Orlov brothers scarcely presented an edifying spectacle.

In addition to providing young retainers for the Court, the Corps of Pages was intended as a finishing school for selected children of the gentry. The curriculum as laid down in 1759 provided that they should learn geometry, geography, fortification, history, French, German, drawing, dancing, fencing and riding; Russian, significantly enough, was not at first included. Later on, the historian G. F. Müller drew up an even more elaborate syllabus, including mathematics, philosophy, ethics, Natural and International Law, history, geography, Latin and Russian, not to mention the elegant composition of Court compliments.

Since only one preceptor was appointed for the pages, a mediocre Frenchman named Morambert, most of this remained a dead letter, and the standard of tuition was not high. But at least Radishchev rapidly perfected his command of French: interesting evidence of this has been provided through the discovery of a programme printed for the Imperial theatre during the season 1764–5, on a night when Philippe Poisson's comedy Le Procureur Arbitre was being given. The programme notes are here described as 'composed by Monsieur Tchelicheff' (Chelishchev, another page and a life-long friend of Radishchev's), and then 'written up by Monsieur Radichoff'.

Basically, however, the pages were regarded simply as rather high-class servants, to be cuffed and clouted by the Court Chamberlains if they failed to perform their duties efficiently. Inevitably, some of these high-spirited youngsters came to cherish rebellious thoughts as a result of the treatment they underwent. In these years were planted the seeds of that contempt for flunkeydom, courtly hocus-pocus and all the outward trappings of royalty which sprout with such violence from the pages of Radishchev's books. Such was the environment in which Sasha Radishchev spent the period from his fourteenth to his seventeenth birthday, dividing his time between Court duties, study, and, very likely, some of the forms of dissipation for which so many opportunities existed in the gay St Petersburg of those days. It is hard to conceive of a school of life which could have afforded our future moralist and reformer a more fruitful field for observation and reflection.

CHAPTER 2

Student Years in Leipzig

Catherine's Internal Policy – Triumph of the Gentry – Philosophy on the Throne – Reform in the Air – A Shortage of Jurists – Catherine as an Educational Theorist – A Grasping Preceptor – Arrival in Leipzig – German University Atmosphere – Sordid Living Conditions – Able Teachers – Impact of French Free-Thinkers – A Sentimental Friendship

To maintain herself in power, the Empress Catherine II needed all the support she could muster. Large sections of public opinion, both in Russia and abroad, were uneasy at Peter's deposal and the indecent haste with which he had been liquidated. There remained too the former child Emperor, Ivan VI, who remained incarcerated in the Schlüsselburg fortress until in 1764 the ill-conceived attempt of Mirovich to liberate the Imperial prisoner provided an opportunity for putting Ivan to death once and for all. There were also those who, headed by the Imperial preceptor and statesman Nikita Panin, regarded Catherine's young son, the future Tsar Paul I, as the rightful ruler of Russia, and would gladly have limited Catherine's authority to that of Empress-Regent. Thus, the scions of the aristocracy among the Guards officers who had carried her to the throne were assured of her gratitude; she and they both knew that the same faction which had raised her up could at any moment cast her down once more.

Upon what other sections of the community could Catherine rely? Here was no robust middle class, from which trained administrators might be recruited to create a bureaucratic absolutism like that of Louis XIV or Frederick of Prussia. In 1762 the urban population of Russia formed only three per cent of the community, and possessed little education and still less influence on affairs of State. Since the Moscow Patriarchate was abolished by Peter the Great, and the Russian Church subordinated to a Holy Synod, or Ministry of Religion, the clergy had lost its former preponderant role in Muscovite politics. In any case, the State was intent on completing the process of secularizing the Church estates. Unless Catherine were willing to let those rich domains slip for ever from her grasp, there was little point in setting up as a champion of Russian Orthodoxy and bidding for support in that quarter. Catherine knew by her own successful experience that the Russian throne, like that of old Byzantium, was neither elective nor hereditary, but occupative. Herself responsible for the death of two Tsars, she was to spend the rest of her life with the feeling that her turn might come next. She knew that the great nobles who dominated the Guards regiments and the Court, and the country squires who ruled the provinces, held the key to the situation. They must be taught to look to Catherine personally as the supreme provider of present benefits and of good things yet to come.

The peasantry, now that their masters were freed from the duty of State service fastened upon them by Peter the Great, looked forward eagerly to their own emancipation. They were to be disillusioned, and kept waiting for a whole century. Russia's new sovereign, a woman, a foreigner and a usurper, realized that she could not let her abstract notions of social justice stand in the way of measures essential for her authority and, perhaps, for her very life. Within a few weeks of her accession, she issued a manifesto declaring her intention of 'energetically protecting the noble proprietors in their lands and properties', and another whereby all members of the gentry in State service were automatically to be granted officer's rank on retirement, whether they had earned it or not. In February 1763 a commission was set up to revise and confirm the list of privileges accorded to the gentry by the late Tsar, Peter III. It recommended among other things that members of the gentry should not be punished by the sovereign without trial, and should be exempt from corporal chastisement; in case of condemnation to death or exile, a squire's estates should not be confiscated, but should pass to his heirs; a gentleman should be free to dispose of his lands at will. The commission's findings were mostly incorporated in the Charter of the Nobility promulgated in 1785, though some of them were put into effect without delay. In 1765 Catherine granted landowners the right to send their serfs to forced labour in Siberia on their own authority, and without reference to any tribunal. In deference to pressure from the squires, she even suppressed in 1767 the traditional right of the Russian peasant or citizen to present a personal remonstrance (*chelobitnaya*) to the sovereign, and appeal for protection against injustice. Any serf who complained to the Government about the treatment he received from his master was knouted and sent back to his lord for any necessary action. Vassalage degenerated over the years into downright slavery, such as had virtually ceased in the rest of Europe since the Middle Ages.[1]

Within her empire, then, Catherine pandered to the most retrograde vested interests. In her relations with the outside world, she showed wonderful flair for winning the support of 'progressive' opinion. Catherine was a consummate propagandist. It was she who created that image of Russia as a haven for depressed Western intellectuals, which has been revived to such effect since the Communist revolution. She had the brilliant idea, copied in our own times, of maintaining in Western Europe a claque of supporters whose paeans of applause would drown the yells of those who were being knouted into submission at home. She fostered the idea that 'Philosophy was now seated on the Throne.' Hearing that Diderot's great *Encyclopédie* was proscribed by the French authorities, she proposed that its printing and production should be transferred to St Petersburg, a gesture which Voltaire glee-fully described as 'this buffet administered from the depths of Scythia to fools and to scoundrels'. It was a pity, no doubt, that Catherine (so it was alleged) had had her husband murdered to secure power for herself. Still, one must take one's friends as they were, and the Semiramis of the North was so generous with gold snuff-boxes and subscriptions to the French Free-thinkers' much-banned publications that misgivings were quickly shrugged off.

In the climate of opinion in the 1760s, to be in the good books of the *philosophes* was to be on the side of the angels. Throughout Europe, rationalism was gaining ground, together with such concepts as 'Natural Religion', the rights of man, and the Social Contract. Men were seeking to find a humane and reasonable basis for the social order. As the educated classes aspired to influence and political power, so was absolutist and theocratic rule on the Bourbon model held up to ex-ecration, even by members of the ruling classes themselves. The ideas of Montesquieu and Voltaire were all the rage, and a woman likes to be in the fashion.

Not that Catherine's enthusiasm for the ideas of the Age of Reason was insincere. She was a clever woman, to whom brilliant and daring ideas made a genuine intellectual appeal. What is more, an alliance with the French Free-thinkers had political uses. When one proposed, as did Catherine, to carve up Catholic Poland, there could be no more useful ally than Voltaire, with his cry of 'Écrasez l'Infâme!' by which he meant superstition, the Roman Catholic hierarchy, and organized religion generally. (This, incidentally, did not deter Catherine from vexing the French Government by granting asylum to the Jesuits, when they were expelled from France in 1764.) If one hoped, as did

[1] For the social and political background, see V. O. Klyuchevsky, *A History of Russia*, trans. Hogarth, V, 1–119.

Catherine, to dismember the Ottoman Empire and set up a Romanov as neo-Byzantine Emperor in Constantinople, then there was no harm in joining with the Encyclopedists in scoffing at Mustafa the Grand Turk, and poking fun at the Prophet Mohammed and the Islamic faith. Since the Government of Louis XV, which persecuted the *philosophes* and burnt their books, was Catherine's chief adversary in her schemes against Poland and Turkey, then obviously conviction and self-interest both encouraged such an alignment. To retain the cheap and effective services of the Paris pamphleteers, it was worthwhile allowing Diderot to slap one familiarly on the knee and hold forth interminably on the art of government, however boring one might find what Catherine later termed his 'arrant babbling'. Philosophy, as the late Paul Hazard remarked, imagined itself to be taking advantage of monarchs; but it was the monarchs who were taking advantage of philosophy.

If Catherine's cultivation of the doctrines of the Age of Reason sprang partly from a desire to bedeck the harsh realities of Russian life with the flowers of fashionable ideology, the same could be said of many of the westernized aristocrats of eighteenth-century Russia. While the mania for Western modes of thought, dress and speech was not altogether a new phenomenon, under Catherine the Great the gulf between the French-speaking absentee landlords who thronged the Court of St Petersburg, and the 'black people' (*chërny narod*, meaning common rabble, working folk) who tilled their fields, grew wider than ever before. Hardly since the days of the Roman Emperors had such a proliferation of domestic servitude been seen in any European country. It extended into the arts and sciences. Serf musicians and serf actors performed for their owners' delectation, and were buffeted if their efforts failed to delight. Serf tutors taught the squire's children to read and write. Serf artists decorated their mansions. Serf butlers decanted choice claret and burgundy, and were well beaten if the wine did not please the palate. Russian *grands seigneurs* with their squads of serf retainers started touring Western Europe, where they found a ready entrée into polite society. Sooner or later, the subject of serfdom was bound to crop up in conversation. However hotly the Russian visitor might defend his native land and its customs, he could not avoid realizing that Russian ideas on personal servitude were not in accordance with those held in the civilized West.

In this way, there grew up a double standard of conduct for the Russian aristocracy. On the one hand, it was necessary to keep up an appearance of Western 'enlightenment' and modern views; on the other, one had to fit in with the backward norms of Russian social conditions. This dichotomy sometimes produced intolerable psychological stresses, as in the case of Radishchev himself. In many instances, however, the gloss of Western sophistication was quite compatible with a taste for barbaric splendour and luxury on an Asiatic scale. There was old Count Stroganov, after whom is named that excellent dish, *Boeuf Stroganoff*. This wealthy grandee had spent much of his life in Paris, and been on intimate terms with Grimm, Baron d'Holbach, and d'Alembert, frequenting the salons of ladies of wit and fashion. Later on, he sent his son Paul to France with a preceptor, Gilbert Romme, who was 'an enthusiastic follower of Jean-Jacques Rousseau, and proposed to turn his pupil into an Émile.' Both tutor and pupil got affiliated to the Jacobin Club and regularly attended its séances, to the horror of the Russian ambassador and of Catherine II. In old Stroganov, there was what Adam Czartoryski described as 'a singular mixture of the Encyclopedist and the old Russian boyar. He had a French mind and turn of speech, but Russian habits and manners, a great fortune and masses of debts, a vast and elegantly furnished house, a fine picture gallery which he had catalogued himself, an infinite number of domestics —slaves, who were very well treated by such a master—and among them, several French valets de chambre. Great disorder: robbed by his staff, he was the first to treat this as a joke.' He kept open house, and anyone could drop in on certain days of the week to dine at a huge table lavishly laid in the old Russian style. The conversation would centre on Voltaire and Diderot, the Parisian stage, or the merits of the Old Masters, while the company was waited on by hordes of serf butlers and attendants.[1]

Alongside such genial scenes, the eye was affronted when reading the Moscow and St Petersburg papers by such advertisements as the following, which are genuine items culled from the *Moskovskie Vedomosti* ('Moscow News') of the time:

'1. For sale: domestics and skilled craftsmen of good behaviour, viz. two tailors, a shoemaker, a watchmaker, a cook, a coachmaker, a wheelwright, an engraver, a gilder, and two coachmen, who may be inspected and their price ascertained in the 4th District, Section 3, at the proprietor's own house, No. 51. Also for sale are three young race-horses, one colt, and two geldings, and a pack of hounds, fifty in number, which will be a year old in January and February next.

'2. In the 2nd District, Section 15, No. 183, near the church, for sale, a maker of shoes for women, entirely expert in his trade; in addition, carries out all domestic duties for his owner, acts as lackey and coach-man and waits at table; has a wife of 32, pregnant, able to sew, iron,

[1] *Mémoires du Prince Adam Czartoryski*, Paris, 1887, I, 152–3.

C

starch, wait on her mistress and prepare meals; they have a daughter three years old.

'3. For sale: Peasant of 35 with wife of same age and three small children. Intending purchaser may ascertain price from the owner personally.

'4. In District 12, a maid of 16 for sale, able to weave lace, sew linen, do ironing and starching and dress her mistress; furthermore, has a pleasing figure and face.'

The statistics relating to the number of formerly protected State peasants given away by Catherine to her favourites and various grandees, and reduced to the lowest grade of servitude, make depressing reading: to Bezborodko, 16,000 souls; to N.I. Saltykov, 6,000 souls; to Ostermann, 6,000 souls; to the brothers Orlov and to Potemkin, scores of thousands each; and so on *ad infinitum*. When there were not enough Crown peasants to go round, Catherine gave away those she had taken over with the newly secularized Church domains; nor did she scruple to enslave the once free yeomen of the Ukraine.

Addiction to the ideas of Rousseau did not always make the country landlords any more humane towards the serfs they owned, bought and sold. The sophisticated squire might superintend the knouting and branding of some delinquent farm labourer, and afterwards be found shedding a maudlin tear over his Russian translation of *La Nouvelle Héloïse*, *Clarissa* or *The Sorrows of the Young Werther*. Russian hopefuls educated abroad often returned home full of Western ideas, but soon developed into even greater bullies and blackguards than their fathers had been. In 1769 the following mock-advertisement appeared in N. I. Novikov's satirical journal, *The Drone*, published at St Petersburg: 'Young Russian porker, who has travelled in foreign lands for the enlightenment of his mind, and having profitably completed his tour, has returned home a perfect swine; anyone wishing to inspect same may see him free of charge in many streets of this city.'—'Never in Russia,' wrote the historian Klyuchevsky, 'has there reigned such cultured savagery as Russia witnessed during the eighteenth century's second half.'[1]

As time went on, there was a tendency, often apparent in Russia both before and since, to blame the shortcomings of Russian ways on evil foreign ideas imported from the decadent West. Thus, Prince M. M. Shcherbatov (1733–90), a historian and aristocratic *frondeur*, composed a tract entitled *On the Degradation of Morals in Russia*, in which he deplored the action of Peter the Great in encouraging the

[1] Klyuchevsky, *A History of Russia*, V, 109.

spread of Western ideas in Russia, the attendant demand for forms of luxury hitherto unknown, and the breakdown of old patriarchal virtues. Of his sovereign, Catherine the Great, Shcherbatov wrote, 'She is intoxicated by the irrational perusal of modern authors. Although she pretends to be pious enough, she really counts the law of Christ for naught. However much she may conceal her thoughts, her deeds speak for themselves. Many books by Voltaire, which contradict the Christian faith, have been translated by her command, for instance *Candide*, *La Princesse de Babylone* and others, not to mention Marmontel's *Bélisaire*, which makes no distinction between pagan and Christian virtue.'

A similar attitude underlies some of the writings of the famous dramatist Denis Fonvizin, who painted a devastating picture of the Russian country bumpkin in his comedy, *The Minor*, fancied himself as 'a watchman of the public welfare', and could hardly be accused of favouring rustic boorishness. Nevertheless, he held trenchant views about the sophisticated decadence of Western Europe. 'I have seen Voltaire,' wrote Fonvizin to his sister from Paris in 1778, 'I have witnessed the ovations which have been accorded him; I have seen all the great writers except Rousseau, who has shut himself up in his room like a bear in his den. I had entertained about them the same illusions as I used to have about France in general. With a few exceptions, they merit contempt rather than respect: envy, pride, perfidy, are the principal traits of their character. They are ready to tear each other to pieces like wild beasts. I cannot convey to you what pitiable wretches those same men have appeared to me, whose writings I used so wholeheartedly to admire.' In another letter from Western Europe, Fonvizin wrote, 'Even if people here started their life before we did, at any rate we who are on the threshold of ours may impart to ourselves whatever form we like, and avoid those incongruities and evils which have taken root here. *Nous commençons et ils finissent*. I deem a man just born to be happier than one who is dying.' Here we have a striking formulation of a basic argument in the great 'Slavophile-Westernizer' dispute which occupied Russian intellectuals in the nineteenth century, and continues, with variations, in the Soviet Union today.

During the opening years of her reign, Catherine seemed to throw in her lot with the 'Westernizers', at least in so far as political theory was concerned, though with due regard to the susceptibilities of the landowning class. Great promises of reform were made. The Imperial mountain was observed to be in labour, though little but the proverbial *ridiculus mus* was ever to see the light of day.

In a State as centralized and regimented as Russia, the great obstacle to any form of administrative progress was the lack both of an efficient civil service and of any coherent code of laws. Judges and administrators had to grapple as best they could with the antiquated code of Tsar Alexis, promulgated in 1649, and since supplemented and often contradicted by a hotch-potch of edicts issued piecemeal by successive monarchs; often, they were reduced to judging ordinary criminal cases by the Naval Statute of Peter the Great, which was supposed to be used exclusively for maintaining discipline in the Fleet. The late Empress Elizabeth had summoned a commission, to codify and redraft the fundamental laws of the Russian Empire. Her death, and the disorders which marked Peter III's brief reign, had brought this plan to nothing.

One of Catherine's first acts was to revive this project, while imparting to it all the éclat of a complete novelty. Deputies were to be elected from all over the country to meet at Moscow in 1767, and draft a new and modern code of laws for the Russian Empire. With the aid of large chunks lifted bodily from such highly regarded works as Montesquieu's *De l'Esprit des Lois* and the Italian penal reformer Beccaria's *Dei Delitti e delle Pene*, Catherine compiled her famous *Nakaz* or 'Instruction', by which the deputies were to be inspired in their deliberations. On paper, the result was generally adjudged very nice. 'Lycurgus and Solon would have appended their signature to your work,' said Voltaire politely, 'and perhaps would not have been capable of composing it themselves.' So progressive in tone was the *Nakaz* that it was at once banned in France, and later on, even in Russia itself.[1]

But where in Russia could conscientious men with educated and well-ordered minds be found, capable of administering and interpreting these new laws, if the time ever came to proceed beyond the realm of fancy to that of hard fact? This was not so easy. Well might the Empress urge the Senate, as she did in 1763, to 'fill Government offices with honourable and worthy candidates'. Since the material simply was not there, ignorance and inefficiency continued to prevail in the public administration: 'I might as well,' said a British representative, Sir G. Macartney, 'quote Clarke and Tillotson at the divan of Constantinople as invoke the authority of Puffendorf and Grotius here!'

With all her native optimism, Catherine could not blind herself to this state of affairs. It was largely to produce a cadre of young administrators capable of carrying out her ambitious proposals that she decided in 1765 to send six of the most promising members of her Corps of Pages, together with six other young gentlemen, to receive a liberal education in one of the Western universities, with special emphasis on the study of jurisprudence.

At this point, the reigning favourite's younger brother, Vladimir

[1] See Klyuchevsky, *A History of Russia*, V, 25–43.

Orlov, returned from Saxony after three years studying at Leipzig University. Vladimir Orlov is portrayed by a contemporary, the Princess Dashkov, as 'a man of shallow mind who had derived from his studies in Germany nothing but a pedantic tone and an entirely unfortunate conviction of his own deep learning'. The Empress promptly appointed him Director of the Imperial Academy of Sciences. In consequence of his favourable report on that seat of learning, Leipzig was chosen as the destination of Catherine's twelve protégés. The Governor of Livonia was charged with finding some Baltic German with Russian citizenship, capable of taking charge of the party and treating in the vernacular with the good people of Leipzig. He eventually supplied a Major Gerhard Georg von Alten Bochum (or Bokum), a person of scant education and less honesty, but in whom the Empress placed her entire confidence.

The interest shown by Catherine in her Russian students' career is illustrated by the instructions, dated September 22, 1766, which she personally wrote out for Bokum's guidance. Their syllabus was to include Latin, German and French and, if possible, the Slavonic tongue, in all of which they were 'to exercise themselves by conversation and through reading books'; they were all to learn 'moral philosophy, history and above all, Natural and Universal Law, as well as a certain amount of Roman Law. Other subjects might be studied according to individual choice'. Several hours were to be reserved every day for recreation, and a full day's holiday was to be allowed from time to time, on which the Russian students could go for excursions in the neighbourhood of Leipzig.

Major Bokum was to see that they attended lectures regularly and punctually; they must observe in their conversation 'courtesy, modesty and well-bred freedom of expression, and avoid rudeness and extravagance; in a word, the rules of humanity and virtue should form the basis of their whole life and conduct'. The young men were to wear clothing of dark or grey material, without silver or gold braid. Two menservants would be hired locally to wait on them all in common, and, no doubt as a concession to local opinion, none of the students was to take personal body-serfs from Russia with him. Any difficulties should be referred to the Russian envoy-plenipotentiary at the Electoral Court of Saxony in Dresden. Bokum was to draw eight hundred roubles a year as his own salary, and a like sum for the maintenance of each of the young noblemen committed to his charge. Thus was every material contingency provided for.

It is worth noting that the Empress Catherine, herself scarcely a pious woman, fully shared Voltaire's respect for religion as an adjunct to discipline. A chaplain, Father Paul, was appointed to the party, with a stipend of six hundred roubles, and a deacon at two hundred to assist him. Bokum was responsible for seeing that Father Paul regularly read morning and evening prayers with the Russian students, together with every necessary exposition of what the Lutheran-born Empress termed 'our Orthodox doctrines'. On Sundays and Holy Days the whole party was to attend the Greek Orthodox Church in Leipzig. Sad to say, this Father Paul, an erudite but absent-minded cleric, was to be the butt of numerous merry pranks on the part of his unruly young flock.

To ensure the party's favourable reception by the Leipzig professors, Vladimir Orlov wrote to his old teacher, Hofrat Johann Gottlob Böhme (1717–80), Professor of History and Constitutional Law, and official historiographer to the Court of Saxony, promising that in those fields of study, absolute preference would be given by the Russian students to Böhme's lectures over all others. This, incidentally, is the same Böhme of whom Goethe, also a student at Leipzig, fell foul at the outset of his scholastic career, and whom G. H. Lewes, Goethe's biographer, describes as 'a genuine German professor, shut within the narrow circle of his speciality. To him, Literature and the Fine Arts were trivialities. . . .' Böhme later became quite a crony of Major Bokum's, with whom he would spend many an evening feeding and tippling at the expense of the student's scholarship fund.

Towards the end of the summer of 1766, the Russian students were assembling in St Petersburg and getting ready for their departure. The lives of several of them were to be closely linked with Radishchev's own. There was Fedor Ushakov, the eldest of the group, who had already begun a promising career in the Government chancery and was distinguished for his ready wit and knowledge of the world; Fedor, whom Radishchev came to regard as his spiritual and intellectual master, was to end his life prematurely in Leipzig. Then there was Radishchev's room-mate, Alexis Kutuzov, the future freemason and mystic. It is to Kutuzov that Radishchev dedicated *A Journey from St Petersburg to Moscow*; under the repressive régime of Catherine's later years, he was doomed to a life of exile which ended in 1797 amid the sordid surroundings of a Berlin debtors' prison.

Another comrade of this period, Peter Chelishchev, shared many of Radishchev's own views on the condition of the Russian peasantry, to the extent of being suspected of complicity in the writing and publication of *A Journey from St Petersburg to Moscow*; in 1791, he composed a similar though more innocuous work under the title *Journey through the North of Russia*.

Sergey Yanov, earlier a page together with Radishchev and now accompanying him to Leipzig, was later to occupy diplomatic posts in Dresden, Venice and Warsaw, and then be assigned to administrative duties in the finance department at Tobolsk in Siberia; it is to Yanov that Radishchev later addressed a controversial brochure, entitled *Letter to a Friend living in Tobolsk*, in which he criticized the policies of Peter the Great and the Russian autocratic system generally.

Finally, we must not forget Andrey Rubanovsky, two of whose nieces, Anna and Elizabeth, were to play so intimate a role in Radishchev's personal life. The elder, Anna, was to become Radishchev's first wife, and with her he lived happily from their marriage in 1775 until her untimely death in 1783. The other sister, Elizabeth, was later to accompany him into exile in Siberia, where she became his second wife, in fact if not in name.

The party left the Russian capital on September 23, 1766. As soon as it was no longer necessary to create a favourable impression upon the students' families and the authorities at Court, 'Hofmeister' Bokum showed himself in his true colours. Let loose into foreign lands with unlimited power over a dozen youths and their annual grant of some ten thousand roubles per annum, the doughty German soon showed that he realized that he was on to a good thing and meant to make the most of it while it lasted.

After the sumptuous farewell dinner given to the students on the eve of their departure, their first meal on the road under Bokum's guardianship consisted of 'bread and butter with some stale meat cut into chunks'. Economizing on winter clothing, Bokum condemned his charges to shiver through their four months' journey along the chilly Baltic coast, in the course of which they passed through Riga, Königsberg and Danzig; the youngest of the party contracted measles and died on the way. Radishchev later commented: 'Having power and money in his hands, our preceptor forgot all moderation and, like the rulers of nations, imagined that he was not with us for our benefit, that the power granted to him over us and the money allotted were not for our use, for but his.' Radishchev also drew the wry conclusion that this and similar situations are a natural result of the despotic system of Government, which makes an underling imagine that he is entitled to indulge privately in the same kind of tyranny that his monarch exercises in public.

At length Bokum and the students arrived in Leipzig, on February 11, 1767. A fortnight later the young Russians' names were inscribed on the University register, where they can be inspected to this day; within a week or two they had already embarked on their courses.

Even after the havoc of the Seven Years' War, Leipzig in the 1760s was one of the outstanding trading, industrial and intellectual centres of Germany. If Dresden was the fashionable capital of the Saxon Electors, it was Leipzig which supplied the life-blood of commerce, as well as the brain-power which stimulated the body politic. Its great fairs at Easter, in September and again in the New Year were attended by merchants from all over Europe, including Russia, as well as by visitors from distant Asia. From the end of the seventeenth century, Leipzig, with its more tolerant censorship, had outstripped the other German publishing centres to become the headquarters of the German book trade.

In the eighteenth century, Leipzig was renowned as the centre of the most influential body of writers and literary men in Germany. From that city, the purist J. C. Gottsched wielded a dictatorial sceptre over the whole evolution of German literature—an influence tempered as time went on by the milder approach of his colleague at the University, the poet and fabulist C. F. Gellert. It was in Leipzig that Lessing, the great protagonist of the German *Aufklärung*, had his first play produced. Leibnitz the philosopher had been a native of the city, and received his early education there. As for music, Johann Sebastian Bach had brought Leipzig undying renown by his long association with the Thomaskirche. The University, of which we shall hear more presently, counted Klopstock and Goethe, and later on, Fichte and Schelling, among its alumni. Not for nothing does Goethe in his *Faust* refer to Leipzig as 'Paris in miniature' (*klein Paris*), for the city bore a decidedly modish, cosmopolitan air.

In Radishchev's time, the city had not yet sprawled out into the surrounding countryside to embrace the outlying villages in a network of suburban development, though elegant villas in their neat gardens outside the old city walls already bore witness to the taste and wealth of leading citizens. The old town was still more or less intact, with its narrow streets and ancient houses with their characteristic high-pitched roofs. The market square, on which the principal thoroughfares converged, was dominated by the Gothic *Rathaus*, dating from 1556, while nearby was Auerbach's *Hof* with its wine *Keller* later immortalized in Goethe's *Faust*. Not far off was the *Königshaus,* which had been for centuries the home of the rulers of Saxony. Elegant promenades, coffee-houses, theatres and assembly rooms added to the city's amenity. Behind the main squares lay a maze of noisome alleys, in which stores and warehouses were mingled with ancient and often insanitary dwellings.

Some idea of how the Leipzig of those days appeared to a Russian visitor is provided by the historian Karamzin, who stayed there somewhat later, in 1789. He found the city proper rather small, though the residential suburbs with their spacious gardens were extensive. Most of the houses inside the city were four stories high, the streets narrow. It was a bustling, crowded centre, trade and the University attracting great numbers of foreigners. 'They say that Leipzig is a gay place to live in, and I believe this. Many of the wealthy merchants here entertain frequently at dinners, suppers and balls. Young dandies from among the students add lustre to these gatherings. They play cards, dance, and flirt with the ladies. In addition, there are special learned societies or clubs, where the latest scholarly or political news is discussed, books are judged, and so on.'[1]

The University of Leipzig traces its foundation back to the year 1409, when four hundred German students seceded from the University of Prague and migrated to their native land with a view to setting up a centre of learning of their own. The Elector of Saxony of that time, Frederick the Belligerent, assigned them quarters in the Ritterstrasse and the Petersstrasse, which formed the nucleus of the budding University. After the Reformation, in 1543–46, Duke Moritz allowed the scholars to take over the former headquarters of the Dominican monks, abutting on to the Paulinerkirche. This cloister, an ensemble of buildings grouped round a courtyard, formed the so-called *Paulinum*; it included a rabbit-warren of verminous and ill-lit students' dormitories which in Radishchev's time still retained their mediaeval character. In course of time, other hostels were founded to cater for scholars hailing from different provinces, the principal ones being the *Bursa Saxonica* and the *Bursa Bavarica*. These, with the various faculty buildings, dominated a large quarter of the old city.[2]

In spite of competition from the rival foundation at Wittenberg, and intermittent 'town-and-gown' disorders, the University grew steadily in renown and wealth. By the eighteenth century it enjoyed substantial revenues from house property in Leipzig itself and rural estates throughout Saxony, inherited or presented by way of endowments. The University was subject to the authority of the electors of Saxony in Dresden, but possessed disciplinary and judicial powers of its own, to the extent of maintaining its own prison for refractory students.

In the 1760s the student body numbered on average between seven hundred and seven hundred and fifty, and was distributed between four faculties, among which the departments of Jurisprudence and Medicine vied for pride of place. Both students and professors were divided further according to regional affiliations into four 'Nations'. The Rector Magnificus was elected, for a term of office of one semester only, from each 'Nation' in turn.

In accordance with the city's reputation as a miniature Paris, it was

---

[1] N. M. Karamzin, *Letters of a Russian Traveller, 1789–90*, trans. Florence Jonas, New York, London, 1957, pp. 72–8.

[2] On Leipzig life in the eighteenth century, see Julius Vogel, *Goethes Leipziger Studentenjahre*, 4th edition, Leipzig, 1923.

claimed with pride that 'in Leipzig a student could scarcely fail to be *galant*' (i.e. courteous and elegant). This applied the more especially to the law students, many of whom came from good professional families; it was noted that they at least listened to the lectures intelligently instead of just scribbling them down verbatim, and that one could enter their lecture-rooms without holding smelling salts to one's nose. The theologians, on the other hand, came for the most part from poor country pastors' families and had to work their way through college; they were often shabby, unwashed and half-starved.

❋

True to his usual policy, Major Bokum hired for himself a spacious residence in one of the main squares, while the students were cheaply boarded out in a squalid house in a back street, overlooking a damp and smelly courtyard. This state of affairs was first exposed by one Michael Yakovlev, a Russian Government courier whom Bokum was foolish enough to lodge with the students instead of entertaining him in his own mansion. 'During my stay in Leipzig,' this courier reported to the St Petersburg authorities, 'having regard to the substantial grant allotted for the maintenance of the young Russian gentlemen committed to Major Bokum's charge, I could not refrain from remarking on the bad conditions in which I observed them to be living, namely the squalor of their rooms, their beds, their linen, clothing and footwear, as well as the quality of their food.' The wooden bedsteads, hired from the landlord, frequently gave way in the middle, while the blankets were dirty and full of holes. The rooms were cleaned out only twice a year.

Some of the young Russians went around in worn out boots all down at heel, others in shoes patched with bits of old leather. As for their diet, Yakovlev describes with unappetizing detail various dishes served up to him and the students during his stay: 'Two dishes with cabbage and little bits of old, tough mutton and rancid fat, almost inedible. As roast, three hares, with the meat so putrid that no one could eat it.' In guise of wine, 'slops mingled with water' were provided.

The room occupied by Radishchev and his friend Kutuzov on the second floor had a niche cut into the wall just big enough to hold their beds, but was badly ventilated and damp. As for Radishchev himself, the same observer reported that 'during my entire visit to Leipzig, Mr Radishchev was ill, nor had he recovered by the time I left; owing to his indisposition, he could not come down to meals, so food was sent up to his room. Through illness and the supply of bad food to him, he is genuinely suffering from malnutrition.'

In the separate quarters occupied by Major and Frau Bokum, things were very different. When it came to entertaining local notables like Professor Hofrat Böhme and Baron von Hohenthal the banker, no expense was begrudged; excellent wine appeared from the cellar and choice dishes were 'served up in great sufficiency'.

The Russian students reacted vigorously against this state of affairs. Indeed, when one reads of the difficulty he had in controlling his flock, it is possible to spare a touch of sympathy even for the scurvy major. The young Russians were of noble birth and reluctant to submit to discipline or chastisement; the eldest, Fedor Ushakov, was a grown man, and did not fail to remind Bokum that he himself possessed a rank equivalent to major in Russian Government service. Besides ragging poor Father Paul, their chaplain, the students had what was described at the time as 'an uncontrollable propensity to flirt with the feminine sex', one of them even getting a local burgher's daughter in the family way.

Bokum and his termagant wife's method of keeping order was to swear at their charges with 'curses scarcely fit to be employed towards guttersnipes', to clout them and have them birched, and even to call in a posse of German soldiers to keep them under house arrest. Finally, the Russian Minister at Dresden and the Leipzig University authorities were called in to settle matters; in his report on these incidents, the envoy could not refrain from paying tribute to the mutual loyalty and high morale of the students, remarking that they treated an insult paid to one of their number as an injury inflicted on them all.

The papers in the case reached the Empress Catherine, who read them with indignation, and at first hotly supported her fellow-country-man, Major Bokum. In the end, a compromise was worked out on the spot, whereby the students, as Radishchev put it, simply carried on as if Bokum's authority had lapsed: 'He looked after his pocket and we lived as we pleased, and did not set eyes on him for a couple of months at a time.' The end of the Bokum régime was heralded somewhat dramatically in 1772, when the Russian chaplain, Father Paul, issued a notice that the Russian party was bankrupt, since Bokum had em-bezzled all the students' allowances and procured supplies on credit. Bokum's German cronies, whom he had entertained so lavishly at his charges' expense, enabled him to make a getaway with his ill-gotten gains. Bokum was indeed a sorry specimen of the type of official to whom the Russian Government only too often entrusted its funds and its authority in the time of Catherine the Great.

✳

The young Russians' director of studies, as already noted, was Hofrat Böhme, the Professor of History and Constitutional Law, and a man of influence at the Court of Dresden—a small, stocky, lively man, reputed 'to have an exceptional fund of conceit which, as a very subtle courtier, he is skilful at concealing'. As Rector Magnificus in 1768, he made himself unpopular by campaigning against traditional student 'rags' and festivities, provoking a regular riot through his misplaced zeal. As a partisan of Major Bokum, he naturally failed to endear himself to the Russians, who soon sought other intellectual guidance.

To start with, they had to take a preliminary course to fit them for their more advanced studies in the legal faculty. A contemporary document gives this schedule for their working days:

7–9 a.m.	German language
9–10	Latin
10–11	Logic, with Professor Seydlitz
	After lunch:
2–3 p.m.	French
3–4	Universal history, with Hofrat Böhme

The rest of the day was spent in optional subjects and pursuits. Radishchev, for instance, took violin lessons as well as dabbling in medicine and the Natural Sciences. In the latter branch, he found stimulus in the experiments carried out by J. H. Winckler (1703–70), the Professor of Philosophy and the Natural Sciences, whose demonstrations in electricity caused a sensation in Leipzig at that time. The Russian students played a practical joke on Bokum by egging him on to wager that he could withstand electric shocks better than any of them, and then administering such a strong one that he nearly passed out.

At the start, some of the young Russian scholars were handicapped by their insufficient command of German and Latin. Most of them, including Radishchev, soon overcame this, so that in 1768 the Russian Minister in Dresden was already reporting to St Petersburg: 'Everyone in general admits with amazement that they have achieved notable results in so short a period, and are not inferior in knowledge even to those who have been studying there for a long time. Special praise for outstanding aptitude is accorded to the elder Ushakov and after him, to Yanov and Radishchev, who have surpassed the hopes of their teachers.' In May of that year, a public debate was held in the University, at which the Russian students replied to questions put to them by their teachers and by other professors; according to the Leipzig almanac of the time, 'their exemplary answers in tongues Classical and modern earned well-deserved approbation'. Individual reports on the students sent in by their various teachers were, as research into the official archives has shown, warmly commendatory. We learn also from a letter written in later years by Radishchev to his patron, Count A. R. Vorontsov, that he was able to tackle Klopstock's religious epic, the *Messias*, as well as savouring Virgil's *Aeneid* in the original Latin.

Later on the Russians embarked on a formal syllabus specially drawn up for them according to the Empress Catherine's requirements by members of the Leipzig faculty. Here is their curriculum for 1769 to 1771:

ACADEMIC HALF-YEAR BEGINNING MICHAELMAS, 1769

Encyclopaedia Juris
History of the Northern States
Mathematics
German and Latin

Second half-year
Practical philosophy
Institutions of Jurisprudence (theoretical)
History of the German Empire
Physics

Third half-year
Philosophy (continued)
Institutions of Jurisprudence (practical)
Instruction on subjects relating to the Northern States
Physics

Fourth half-year
European political questions of the seventeenth and eighteenth centuries
German Constitutional Law
Instruction on letter-writing in German on subjects related to political affairs

The legal faculty, to which Radishchev and his comrades were assigned, had its main lecture rooms in the bustling Petersstrasse. Much of their time was spent in the picturesque old auditorium built in 1641, its ceiling supported by two massive pillars; the scene was dominated by the lofty dais or *cathedra* from which the professor held forth to the graduates and students of noble birth seated on the raised stalls at the sides, and to the general run of students and public on the benches in the body of the hall. In a niche stood an impressive statue of one of the Electors of Saxony, while portraits of successive Deans of the Faculty, who held the title of *Ordinarius*, adorned the walls. Since the beginning of the eighteenth century, lectures were given in German, though some of the textbooks were still in Latin, as was the formidable printed syllabus of lectures and seminars conducted by the faculty's twenty professors and lecturers or *Dozenten*.

In contrast to such pedants as Böhme, there were several really eminent scholars and public figures on the University staff while Radishchev was in Leipzig. Among these was Karl Ferdinand Hommel (1722–81), the Professor of Canon Law, who was noted for his advocacy of the humane legal theories of the Italian jurist Beccaria, of whose progressive treatise *Dei Delitti e delle Pene* he published a German rendering in 1778. Hommel has been described as 'an *epigone* of the theory of Natural Law, a genuine son of the age of the *Aufklärung*. Witty, fearless, energetically striking at the root of what he recognized as abuse, also a man of practical influence, as in the abolition of torture in Saxony, but at the same time lacking in historical perspective and often banal and insipid. His main merit lies in the domain of criminal law, but he also turned his attention to civil law and, as Professor of Canon Law, to ecclesiastical law.'[1]

The standard history of German law by Stintzing and Landsberg gives details of a ceremonial address which Hommel delivered in 1765 before the young Elector of Saxony, Frederick Augustus III, and members of his Court.[2] Hommel held that all monarchical authority is based on law, and that preservation of the law was therefore a prince's highest duty. The object of legislation was to exercise benevolent control over the individual for the benefit of the community, but without interfering with the rights and liberties of the citizen. It was useless to terrify potential offenders by the threat of savage penalties, when the real remedy for crime lay in the improvement of economic and moral conditions. Dealing with the so-called crime of blasphemy, Hommel advocated a policy of tolerance, saying that it was absurd to punish it as an offence in the criminal courts: it would be well to remember the Roman adage *Deorum injuriae dis curae*, that is to say, 'An insult to the gods is the gods' own affair'. Hommel ended his speech by urging the Elector to be humane in administering the law, to ensure that the penalty fitted the offence, and to take into account the circumstances which drive people to commit crimes. Such opinions as these, when

[1] E. Friedberg, in *Festschrift zur Feier des 500-jährigen Bestehens der Universität Leipzig*, Leipzig, 1909, II, 95.

[2] *Geschichte der deutschen Rechtswissenschaft*, München, Leipzig, 1880–98, III, 386–400.

repeated in the lecture hall, must have made a strong impression on Hommel's Russian pupils; it is probable that Fedor Ushakov's essay on punishment of criminals and the death penalty, which Radishchev later translated into Russian and published, was partly stimulated by Hommel's theories.

Classical studies at Leipzig were dominated by the personality of Johann August Ernesti (1707–81), Professor of Classical Literature, of Rhetoric and of Theology. His lectures on Cicero's *Orator* were famous. We read of Ernesti in a letter of the time: 'A man who has an audience of two to three hundred students when he discourses in Latin upon a Latin author, for whom the lecture theatre is too cramped when he gives his commentary on the New Testament—this is something unparalleled perhaps since the days of Melanchthon in Wittenberg and Camerarius in Leipzig.'

Radishchev was just in time to sit at the feet of the poet Christian Fürchtegott Gellert (1715–69), who had held the chair of philosophy at Leipzig since 1751, and was one of the young Russians' favourite lecturers. Radishchev himself recalls that one of Gellert's most cherished disciples was Fedor Ushakov, and that Gellert would himself correct Ushakov's essays in German literary composition. The other Russians also attended Gellert's courses, but, Radishchev adds, 'our imperfect knowledge of the German tongue prevented us from rivalling Fedor Vasil'evich.' Among Gellert's students was numbered the great Goethe. 'The veneration and love accorded to Gellert by all young people was exceptional,' says Goethe. 'Not tall of stature, slim but not thin, gentle, rather sad eyes, a very fine forehead, a moderately aquiline nose, a sensitive mouth, a pleasant oval face: everything made his presence pleasant and agreeable.'

Gellert's untimely death was much regretted throughout Germany. His successor in the Leipzig faculty was Christian Garve (1742–98); Radishchev was also Garve's pupil, and pays tribute to him in the philosophical treatise entitled *On Man, his Mortality and Immortality*, composed in Siberian exile in 1792, where he writes:

'For a long time Garve was prevented by illness from reading and writing, and found it burdensome even to think, but he overcame this and later wrote his outstanding commentary on Cicero. These are his words: "Blessed," said he, "be the very exhaustion of a sickly body, which has taught me so often how the spirit can control the flesh!" '

Radishchev's reference is to Garve's translation, with commentary, of Cicero's *De Officiis*, commissioned by Frederick the Great in 1779 and published in 1783; this allusion shows that he kept in touch with the intellectual world of Germany and the work of his old teachers long after leaving Leipzig. Garve had been a close friend of Gellert and, like him, was essentially a moderate in literary and aesthetic questions. In philosophy, he admired Locke's empiricism and Hume's critical scepticism, but he refrained from developing their ideas in the direction of downright materialism.

Radishchev was also influenced by the ideas of Ernst Platner (1744–1818), a pupil of Ernesti, and a bold and active scientist and thinker. Appointed Professor Extraordinary of Medicine in Leipzig in 1770, he also lectured on logic, metaphysics, practical philosophy and aesthetics. In philosophy, Platner was originally a follower of Leibnitz, but later he took up a more sceptical standpoint. While his courses were extremely popular, his *Philosophische Aphorismen* (1776–82) aroused indignation among the orthodox-minded; however, Platner survived the storm, becoming Professor Ordinary of Physiology in 1780 and Professor Extraordinary of Philosophy in 1801. When the Russian author and historian Karamzin visited Leipzig in 1789, he called on Platner, who still remembered Radishchev and his Russian comrades, all of whom had been his pupils. 'None of the Leipzig scholars,' remarks Karamzin in his *Letters of a Russian Traveller*, 'is so famous as Dr Platner the eclectic philosopher, who seeks truth in all systems without adhering to any one in particular; who agrees, for instance, with Kant on one point, with Leibnitz on another, or contradicts both of them.'

Certainly, Platner's wide interests in the domain of philosophy helped Radishchev to find his way about the intricacies of eighteenth-century European thought; without such a stimulus, it is doubtful whether he would have been capable in his Siberian banishment of composing, largely out of his head and without library resources, so elaborate a treatise as his *On Man, his Mortality and Immortality*. A trace of Platner's ideas may also be detected in the *Journey from St Petersburg to Moscow*, where Radishchev attacks all censorship and insists on the folly of punishing blasphemy as a crime: 'If in his ramblings the fool says, not only in his heart, but even in a loud voice: "There is no God!" then from the lips of all fools rings out a loud and prompt echo, "There is no God, no God!" But what of that?' (Chapter 'Torzhok'). This argument, based of course on a development of Psalm 14, has been tracked down to one of Platner's courses of philosophy in which liberty of speech and conscience is defended; as has been seen, Platner's colleague Hommel also took this attitude.

During his imprisonment in 1790, Radishchev wrote for his sons a moral story entitled *The Holy Philaret*, containing many autobiographical traits, and there is reason to believe that the figure of Theophilus, Philaret's teacher in 'Athens', is really an idealized portrait of Platner. 'Philaret,' wrote Radishchev, 'assiduous in all branches of wisdom, felt most attracted to the science of the mind, that is, psychology, to theology, the science of the knowledge of God, and to moral philosophy.' All things, Theophilus explained to Philaret, are either composite or simple, but only those which are composite, and so subject to disruption and decay, can die. Thought and the spirit which produces it are indivisible and indissoluble, and thus cannot perish. The soul can never cease to exist: 'Recognize, O Man, your glory, for you have a part in the Deity. Although your body is doomed to destruction, thought is eternal and your soul is deathless.' These and other kindred ideas are later worked out in more detail in Radishchev's *On Man, his Mortality and Immortality*. While studying under Platner, Radishchev busied himself also with physics, chemistry and medicine, which studies he later put to effective use: his son, Paul Radishchev, relates that in after years he once cured a young man in Siberia of frostbite, and used to distil brandy and spirits of wine with an alembic which he fitted up himself.

To these influences has to be added that of the startling and brilliant works of the French *philosophes*, already widely circulated in Germany, where they found many eager readers, and even penetrated surreptitiously into the conservative cloisters of German academe. Between 1767 and 1771, when Radishchev was in Leipzig, the struggle between the protagonists of the Age of Reason in France and the champions of the established order had already reached a high pitch of intensity. It was not long since Jean-Jacques Rousseau's *Emile* had startled Europe with its educational doctrines and its cult of passion, while his *Contrat Social* confronted the world with a new presentation of what has been termed 'totalitarian democracy'. Precisely at this period, too, Voltaire's campaign to rehabilitate the memory of the Protestant Calas, tortured and broken on the wheel on a trumped-up charge of murdering his Roman Catholic son, resulted in a spate of brilliant pamphlets denouncing the rule of the priesthood and judicial savagery in France.

These skirmishing forces of the new thought were mightily sustained by the heavy artillery of Diderot and d'Alembert's *Encyclopédie*, which appeared volume by volume between 1751 and 1765 in spite of the persecution endured by the editors from bigots of many kinds. These massive tomes, imbued with the spirit of technological progress and scientific enquiry, found their way into every important library in Europe. In spite of the inoffensive tone of the articles on theology and politics, the Encyclopedists' emphasis on the superiority of useful knowledge over abstract dogma, their hostility to monkish obscurantism, their practical spirit and empirical approach, coupled with optimistic

D

views on the unlimited perfectibility of men from every race and class of society, could not fail to prove destructive of entrenched privilege and effete scholasticism.

To crown all this, there appeared pseudonymously in 1770 a treatise called *Le Système de la Nature*, the work of a Paris financier called the Baron d'Holbach. In this powerful if long-winded work, d'Holbach preached a system of complete atheism, based on an uncompromisingly materialistic view of the universe. The speculative portions of *Le Système de la Nature* are interlarded with the most violent tirades, in which the author proclaimed, twenty years before the French Revolution, that religion was naught but a pretext devised by despots in league with charlatans to keep human society in a state of servitude. In some passages, we seem already to hear the rattle of the tumbril and the swish of the guillotine: 'The only reason why men are everywhere so wicked, so corrupt, so rebellious to common sense is that they are nowhere governed in conformity with their nature, nor instructed in its essential laws. Everywhere they are lulled with useless chimeras; everywhere they are subject to masters who neglect the education of the people, or seek to deceive them. We see nothing on the face of the globe but unjust and incapable sovereigns, softened by luxury, corrupted by flattery, depraved by licentiousness and irresponsibility, devoid of talent, of morals and of virtue; indifferent towards their duties, which often they know nothing about, they are preoccupied scarcely at all with the welfare of their peoples. . . .'

It has been suggested that the Leipzig professors would have shielded their students from 'the evil influence of French radical doctrines'; if they did attempt to do so, it was in vain. On one occasion, it is recorded in the official papers that Yanov, one of Radishchev's fellow students, refused to attend Professor Böhme's course on diplomacy and constitutional law, on the grounds that this subject could be learnt more profitably from the Abbé Mably's treatise *Le Droit Public de l'Europe*, Radishchev recording agreement with this view. It is important to note that this Gabriel Bonnot de Mably (1709–85), a brother of the metaphysician Condillac, was noted as an advocate of utopian communism and republican doctrines generally, based on his conception of the laws of ancient Sparta. 'Wisdom is seldom seated on a throne,' was one of his maxims, and again: 'Ecclesiastics are enemies of liberty.' The following passage is characteristic of Mably's social programme:

'Why are there any rich people, why any poor ones? Are we not all born with the same needs? . . . The law which permits large fortunes to be amassed in any commonwealth condemns a mass of wretches to languish in indigence, and the city is no longer anything but a lair of tyrants and of slaves, jealous and hostile the ones towards the others.' (*Entretiens de Phocion.*)

This was the outlook which underlay Mably's book on the international law of Europe, which Radishchev and his comrades came to prefer to Böhme's stuffy courses. *Le Droit Public de l'Europe*, which contained an analysis of the principal treaties between the States of Europe since the Peace of Westphalia in 1648, was the fruit of Mably's practical work in the French chancelleries of State. It is imbued with the idea that war is the product of human folly and the jealousy felt by one autocrat towards another—an idea which was to reappear more than once in Radishchev's later writings. 'A clear and methodical précis,' it was called by one eighteenth-century critic: 'It is in fact the ABC of modern politics.' It is clear that Mably's republican ideals, combined with personal experience of Bokum's petty tyranny, helped to produce in Radishchev a highly critical if not rebellious attitude towards autocracy in general, and Russian Tsarism in particular.

Of even more significance for Radishchev's mental outlook was the famous and controversial book by Helvétius, *De l'Esprit*, condemned on its appearance in 1758 to be burnt by the Paris hangman, and banned by the Holy Inquisition. Of this book, the French Ambassador in St Petersburg wrote to its author: 'I found on my arrival the Russian *esprit* just as preoccupied with your *Esprit* as all the rest of Europe'; and indeed it was a book which enjoyed a wide diffusion in Russia. The attention of Radishchev and his friends was first directed to Helvétius' book by a Russian nobleman, usually identified as Count Fedor Orlov, who, as Radishchev recalls, on a visit to Leipzig 'aroused in Fedor Vasil'evich [Ushakov] and in all of us a great enthusiasm for reading, and acquainted us with Helvétius' book *De l'Esprit*. . . . Following his advice, Fedor Vasil'evich and we after him read this book, read it with attention, and in it learnt to think.' Radishchev adds that the well-known journalist Baron Melchior Grimm, who happened to pass through Leipzig at the time, informed Helvétius of this gratifying tribute to his work: 'Even the praise of an ignoramus is sometimes flattering to any author, and Helvétius was certainly not indifferent to the news that a whole group of young men had learnt to think from his book. In this connection, his work can always be studied with considerable advantage.' In his article 'Alexander Radishchev', the poet Pushkin comments on the significance of *De l'Esprit* in the mental formation of the author of *A Journey from St Petersburg to Moscow*, and affects to be shocked by the students' addiction to this 'banal and futile metaphysic'. Pushkin added sarcastically that when Grimm—'the commercial traveller of French philosophy'—found those young Russians reading *De l'Esprit*, he carried off this piece of news to Helvétius in Paris as something 'both flattering to his vanity and joyous for all the brethren'.

Pushkin, of course, was writing at a time when the Romantic reaction had discredited eighteenth-century rationalism. There is no denying that the writings of Helvétius did in fact exert a powerful influence on European social thought, especially among Jeremy Bentham and the English Utilitarians. Helvétius' contribution to sociology arises as a logical consequence of his ideas on psychology. He considered man as born without any inherent mental characteristics or 'innate ideas', and followed John Locke in attributing all mental processes to the stimulus of external influences, to the impact of sensations on the grey matter of the brain: 'To perceive, to reason, to form judgements, is to experience sensations.' Helvétius regarded the mind as nothing but a specialized form of matter, moulded by education and modified by environment.

After much abstract reasoning, Helvétius is led to the conclusion that self-love and the pursuit of agreeable sensations are the only valid motives of human conduct, fear of disagreeable sensations the only worthwhile deterrent from crime. Helvétius does not so much deny the existence of God, as Holbach was to do, as ignore it. There was no place for the Deity in his scheme of things; indeed, it was essential to discount religious belief in order to have a clear field for an ethical system which has nothing in common with traditional morality. Man being deemed to possess no spiritual nature, Helvétius sets the criterion of general utility above all standards of personal vice and virtue: 'The love of virtue is therefore nothing but the desire for general well-being.' It was he who gave general currency to the idea of 'the greatest happiness of the greatest number'.

It is easy to pick holes in Helvétius' naïve sociology. If the perfect society is to be created by reconciling the interests of the individual with those of the community, what happens when the dominant human emotion of self-love conflicts with the general interest? Who is to frame and administer these ideal laws which are to harmonize the two? As John Morley objected, 'Helvétius vaulted over this difficulty by imputing to a legislator that very quality of disinterestedness whose absence in the bulk of the human race he made the fulcrum of his whole moral system.'

However this may be, Helvétius deserves credit (or otherwise) as one of the first to formulate the basic ideas underlying the modern 'Welfare State'; in particular, it was he who placed firmly in the forefront of European consciousness the notion that public utility is the essential criterion by which any system of government is to be judged, and not conformity with abstract ideas such as Divine Right of kings or any system of religious dogma. He looked forward, in those closing years of the *Ancien Régime*, to an era when the triumph of enlightenment and the spread of education would ensure that the individual's pursuit of his own best interests would harmonize rather than conflict with the public weal.

While Radishchev was not in agreement with Helvétius' materialist concept of the universe, *De l'Esprit* left a deep and lasting impression on his mind. Twenty years later, when on his way into exile in 1790, he wrote about his family to his patron, Count Alexander Vorontsov, saying: 'What control can reason exercise over feeling? . . . According to the system of Helvétius, the mind revolves round one single idea, and all my reasoning, all my philosophy vanishes when I think of my children!' In another letter, which he wrote to Vorontsov from remote Irkutsk, Radishchev exclaimed: 'A man without any desire would be scarcely more than an automaton, as Helvétius of accursed memory used to say, if I am not mistaken.'

It is not difficult to track down to Helvétius some of the more paradoxical notions expressed by Radishchev in *A Journey from St Petersburg to Moscow*. In the chapter 'Krest'tsy', for instance, a Russian nobleman bids farewell to his sons, including in his parting homily an assurance that they are in no way obliged to feel any gratitude for his paternal care and love: he had begotten and brought them up, he says, simply because 'he found his own comfort, pleasure or advantage in doing so'. This idea is evidently borrowed direct from the tenth chapter of the fourth book of *De l'Esprit*, where Helvétius says it is a great mistake to imagine that parents are actuated by any disinterested motive in bringing up their children: 'This paternal love of which some people make such a parade, and by which they believe themselves to be deeply moved, is most often nothing more than the effect either of a desire to perpetuate their family, of a passion for domineering, or else fear of boredom and being at a loose end.'

This same nobleman of Krest'tsy further urges his sons to avoid attendance at official audiences and levees, which he describes as 'a wretched custom, which signifies nothing and reveals in the visitor the spirit of servility and in his entertainer the spirit of vanity and feeble-mindedness'. A highly similar opinion is expressed by Helvétius: 'What picture more humiliating for humanity than the audience of a vizir when, in an atmosphere of pomposity and stupid gravity, he advances in the midst of a troop of hangers-on, while the latter, serious, dumb, motionless, with eyes fixed and downcast, await in trembling the favour of a glance?' Such parallels are surely too striking to be merely co-incidental.

✳

Apart from amorous escapades and beer sessions in the renowned Leipzig *Keller*, there is nothing to show that the Russian students entered much into the general hurly-burly of German student life. As foreigners, they were not admitted on an equal footing into the closed fraternities of the Saxon or Bavarian *Bursen*. Intensely loyal to one another, they kept themselves much to themselves outside lecture hours, not, perhaps, without that tinge of superiority with which the Russian abroad affects to observe the goings-on of the decadent West.

The great influence upon Radishchev's emotional life at this period was his sentimental friendship with the eldest of his comrades, Fedor Ushakov, a biography of whom he was later to write and publish. Fedor Vasil'evich had been educated in the *Sukhoputny Kadetny Korpus*, a kind of military academy for sons of gentry. His brilliant career there at once secured him a good post in Government service at St Petersburg, which he threw up of his own accord, to the consternation of his friends and protectors, in order to complete his education abroad. Unfortunately, overwork combined with the dissipated way of life only too common in eighteenth-century St Petersburg had already fatally undermined his constitution. In this connection, Radishchev's biographical account provides a curious insight into the backstairs workings of officialdom in that period. Among Ushakov's numerous callers and petitioners, Radishchev writes, 'there were sometimes women, young women who in the heat of pressing their just or unjust claims, occasionally forgot their obligations to chastity, and others who, mindful of the youth of him to whom their petitions were addressed, purposely exploited the magic of their beauty in order to win Fedor Vasil'evich's favour. He used himself to tell of an incident of this nature. Here is his story:

'After staying up well after midnight in gay converse with some people of the category usually described as social friends, he returned home and worked until five in the morning when, exhausted by festivity and toil, he fell fast asleep. His carefree youth was not yet subdued by the prickly thorns of experience, and the visions of his dreams were just as much filled with gaiety as his waking hours. He dreamt that he lay in the embraces of a beautiful woman, intoxicated with that voluptuous passion which reigns with such authority over youthful emotions. In the middle of this wondrous dream, sleep fled from his eyes.—But what met his waking gaze? A hundred times more attractive than the one he had seen in his dream, he caught sight of a girl, a young maiden almost, sitting beside his bed and carefully driving the flies away from his face and moderating with her open fan the heat of the sun, which was already penetrating his bedroom with its beams—it was summer, and already ten o'clock in the morning.

'He did not at once realize that he was awake. Seeing him aroused, and directing towards him a gaze of flaming desire, with a smile of passion and the voice of a Siren—"Excuse me, Sir," said the fair petitioner, "for interrupting your slumbers and depriving you, it may be, of sweet visions of some beloved person." And as she spoke, she penetrated his inmost being with a glance of fire. If I were writing a love story, what an abundant harvest of description would be mine to reap! Sensibility within Fedor Vasil'evich was ready to burst into life, the fair claimant was living estranged from her elderly husband and required the good offices of Fedor Vasil'evich; counting on his ardent temperament, she came to take advantage of it —and succeeded. . . .

'By this and similar adventures Fedor Vasil'evich undermined his constitution; even before leaving for Leipzig, he felt within his body that disorder which is the inevitable consequence of immoderate indulgence and abuse of carnal delights.'

In Leipzig, as we have seen, Fedor Ushakov led the Russian students' opposition to Bokum's tyranny, thus incurring the displeasure of the Empress Catherine. The alarming progress of his syphilitic condition only increased his anxiety to master every branch of knowledge before it was too late. Radishchev tells us that the Latin tongue's expressive quality and the heroic virtues of the Roman republicans, so different from Russian servility, greatly attracted Ushakov: 'Filled with the spirit of liberty, those overlords of kings expressed in their mode of utterance the dauntless quality of their spirit. It was not the flatterer of Augustus [Virgil] or the sycophant of Maecenas [Horace] who attracted him, but rather Cicero thundering against Catilina and the caustic satirist [Juvenal] who spared not Nero.'

Radishchev recalls further that Ushakov would have taken up English, had he lived: 'If death had not snatched you away from among your friends, O dauntless spirit, you would have applied yourself to the language of those proud islanders who, once upon a time, beguiled by the most cunning of their leaders [Cromwell], ventured to take the life of their own sovereign by process of law; who safeguarded the welfare of society by expelling their hereditary monarch [James II] and electing an outsider [William III] to govern them; who, in spite of the most extreme corruption of morals, wherein all things are weighed up on the scales of avarice, even now frequently deem the greatest glory to consist in opposing arbitrary rule [i.e. that of George III] and conquering it by recourse to the law.' It is evident that Radishchev's often expressed loathing of autocracy and his sympathy towards constitutional ideals may be traced back to those Leipzig days in which, under Ushakov's influence, the young Russians imbibed the austere republicanism of ancient Rome, and marvelled at the half-admired, half-dreaded example of the English regicides.

In May 1770, it became clear that Ushakov had not long to live. The advance of his syphilitic condition caused him ceaseless agony. At last, the doctors told him that his case was hopeless. On his death-bed, convulsed with pain, Fedor asked Radishchev and Kutuzov to bring him poison, and put an end to his sufferings. This they refused to do, with the result that Fedor's agony was prolonged by several hours—hours which haunted Radishchev until the end of his life. In after years, Radishchev wrote to Kutuzov, 'If ever again you hear the groans of a friend of yours, if he be doomed inevitably to perish—if it is I who cry out to you for deliverance—then do not hesitate, my beloved friend; you will put an end to an intolerable existence and give relief to one who is disgusted with life and detests it.' (Death by suicide was to be Radishchev's own lot.) Towards the end, Ushakov called Radishchev and entrusted him with his papers, saying, 'Use them as you will. Farewell now for the last time. Remember that I have loved you; remember also that in this life one must have principles in order to be happy, and be brave in spirit to die fearlessly.' Tears and sobbing, Radishchev recalled, were all the answer he could make his dying friend; but Fedor's words echoed in his mind and were for ever inscribed upon his memory.

Among the papers which Ushakov bequeathed to Radishchev was an essay on criminal law and capital punishment, as well as another on love, and a series of letters on Helvétius' book *De l'Esprit*. All these were written in French or German. They were later translated into Russian and published by Radishchev as appendices to his biography of Fedor Ushakov. The first-mentioned essay is interesting as embodying the doctrine of the Social Contract, as formulated by John Locke, and later taken over and elaborated by Jean-Jacques Rousseau in his famous tract. Human society, it is argued, originates as a voluntary association of free human beings who band themselves together for mutual protection and comfort. It follows that no member of the association should be punished or harmed by the community at large, except when he must be restrained for the security of his fellows. Thus, to reform offenders and not to wreak vengeance and retribution on them should be the legislator's proper objective. With the optimism so common among the eighteenth-century rationalists, Ushakov argues that one day an ideal state of society will be achieved, in which the advantage of the individual will coincide with the interests of the State, with the result that crime will automatically disappear. Ushakov concludes that the death penalty should be reserved for murderers, who place themselves outside the pale of civilized society. Ushakov's espousal of French Utilitarian ideas is also evident in his brief essay 'On Love', in which he suggests that 'we should term virtue that which conduces to the pleasure and wellbeing of all, or, since this is impossible, at least to that of the majority'.

Finally, in a series of five epistles addressed to a certain 'F.', evidently Count Fedor Orlov, Ushakov discusses the salient ideas put forward by Helvétius in the opening sections of his famous and controversial *De l'Esprit*, to which Orlov had first directed his attention. While so impressed with the book that he read it through three times, Ushakov admits that he differs from Helvétius on certain questions, though greatly admiring his psychological insight into the motives of human conduct. He begins his commentary by discussing Helvétius' conception of the nature of mind, and his denial of the existence of mental processes on an abstract or immaterial level independent of concrete matter. Helvétius seems to have thought of ideas as exclusively the product of sensations which, after making their impact on a material mind, are retained by memory, to be subsequently formed into new concepts through fusion with other sensations already recorded and stored up in the brain.

Ushakov's approach to this problem is critical, and he has little difficulty in picking holes in Helvétius' rather naïve attempt to create a materialist theory of knowledge by means of an over-simplification of John Locke's *Essay concerning Human Understanding*. In particular, Ushakov proves convincingly that Helvétius' conception fails entirely when it comes to a comparison of two different impressions, and to the formulation of abstract ideas through rational and logical deduction, for which the sensualist explanation is powerless to account satisfactorily. It is a striking thought that almost the first intelligent *critique* of Helvétius' historic book—a *critique* which rejected the shoddy materialist dialectic, but retained and enlarged on its fruitful contribution to social and political progress—came from the pen of a young Russian student in a German university. In this respect, Ushakov may be said to have anticipated by many decades the work of Jeremy Bentham and James Mill.

*

Such, then, were some of the intellectual influences and personal experiences which combined to mould Radishchev's character and outlook while he was a student in Leipzig. In 1771, the Russian Minister to Saxony, Prince Belosel'sky, expressed the view that Radishchev was now fully qualified to return home and take up his official duties at St Petersburg. The professors declared themselves highly satisfied with

Radishchev's achievements, and provided him with testimonials to that effect. Towards the end of the year, he left for Russia together with his room-mate Alexis Kutuzov, and his comrade Andrey Rubanovsky, after nearly five years abroad, in which he had received a sound legal training and entered into contact with the main currents of European thought, absorbing influences which were to have a profound effect on his entire life and career.

CHAPTER 3

Among the Senators

※→⊙ ⊙←※

'Remember what impatience we felt to see ourselves once again in the land of our birth, recall our delight when we caught sight of the boundary which divides Russia from Courland!' wrote Radishchev in later years to his friend Kutuzov. 'If anyone should affirm that we were not capable at that moment of laying down our lives for the sake of the fatherland, then I declare that person to have no knowledge of the human heart.' But recalling the experiences which lay in store for the Russian students after their homecoming, Radishchev added in a different vein: 'I confess, and you also, my dear friend, will confess the same thing, namely that the experiences which followed our return put a decided damper on our ardour.'

When Radishchev and Kutuzov, together with their comrade Andrey Rubanovsky, reached St Petersburg in November 1771, they found a great deal altered in the atmosphere surrounding the Government and the Court. To begin with, the Empress Catherine's flirtation with legislative and constitutional reform schemes had virtually come to an end. The deputies who assembled in Moscow in 1767 had brought with them a mass of petitions and complaints from all conditions of men throughout the Russian Empire, resembling in many ways those which the Estates General were to produce at Versailles in 1789. In Moscow, discussion of these petitions uncovered a vast, alarming sea of discontent, and brought wide out into the open the latent clash of interests between different classes of society—the landed gentry, the urban burghers, the serfs and the few remaining free peasants, not to mention the national minorities. It soon became clear that the bland formulae of Catherine's liberal-sounding *Nakaz* or 'Instruction' were far from adequate when it came to framing a complete new legal and administrative code, and that if the demands raised by the more outspoken deputies were to be met, nothing less than a radical shake-up of Russian society would ensue. Since this would have involved a frontal attack on the privileges of the gentry, on whom the Empress principally relied, such a convulsion would have been fraught with dangerous consequences for the régime as a whole.

And so it was with something like relief that Catherine and her advisers received the news of the Turkish declaration of war, which enabled them in December 1768 to prorogue the assembly without loss of face, and with the promise that it would be recalled at the end of hostilities. Russian jurisprudence was again reduced, as one memoirist put it, to memorizing the numbers and dates of Imperial decrees.

This Turkish declaration of war had been brewing for several years, ever since the conclusion of the Seven Years' War in 1763 had transferred the focus of great-power conflict from Central Europe to Poland and the shores of the Bosphorus. The 1760s were marked by increasingly flagrant interference by Russia in Poland's internal affairs, amounting virtually to complete hegemony. Under guise of protecting the Russian Orthodox 'dissidents' against the Roman Catholic majority, and maintaining in power King Stanislas Poniatowski, Catherine's protégé and former lover, the Russian Government was able to install an ambassador, Prince Repnin, with virtually viceregal powers. In 1767 Repnin and his Russian troops coerced the Warsaw Diet into conceding the Orthodox 'dissident' nobles equal rights with the Catholics, at the same time deporting to Russia some recalcitrant members who refused their agreement, and establishing a procedure for dealing with Polish affairs later copied so effectively by Tsar Nicholas I and by Stalin. The Russo-Polish treaty of February 1768 established Russia's status as 'protector' of Poland, that country being solemnly guaranteed a constitutional régime as well as the maintenance of its ancient laws and liberties.

These developments, which were accompanied by a *rapprochement* between Catherine and Frederick the Great of Prussia, had long been viewed with disapproval by the Courts of France and Austria, to whom the growing power of Russia in Poland and in the Black Sea area appeared as a threat to France's privileged position in the Levant and to Austria's interests in the Balkans. The chancelleries of Versailles and Vienna therefore took the obvious course of stirring up the Ottoman Turks, the Slavs' inveterate foes. Not that the Turks required much stirring up. In spite of the increasing debility of the Ottoman Porte, of which Muscovy in the flush of its vigorous expansion had increasingly taken advantage, the Turks were spoiling for a fight. In the Kuban area, the Cossacks had been pursuing an aggressive line towards the Circassians and other Turkish vassals, while the Crimean Khan, also an ally of the Sultan, had been hard pressed from the Ukraine. These were but minor irritations in the age-old struggle for free navigation in the Black Sea and for control over the Balkans, the Ukraine, the Crimea, the Caucasus and eventually of the Bosphorus straits themselves, a struggle in which the Treaty of Belgrade concluded in 1739 had provided little more than a breathing space.

Early in 1768, the situation on Russia's south-western frontier took on an explosive character. In February, a group of Polish patriots formed the so-called Confederation of Bar to defend Poland's territorial integrity and national rights, and bring to heel the Russian-protected 'dissident' stooges. Thereupon the Russians under Apraksin captured Bar and marched on Cracow. Without waiting for official orders, Russian guerrilla forces started operations against the Poles close to the Turkish border, at one point penetrating into Ottoman territory. Being assured of Western support, the Turks now fondly imagined that they could turn the tables on their Russian enemies, and hastened to declare war.

Catherine's first Turkish War lasted from 1768 until 1774. In Rumania, Jassy and Bucarest fell to the Russians, while other armies kept in check the Polish Confederates. The Crimean peninsula was successfully invaded, though a military diversion through the Caucasus and Georgia towards Eastern Anatolia was less successful. Spectacular naval victories were scored in the Mediterranean by the Russian fleet, leading up to the wholesale destruction of the Turkish navy at Chesmeh in June 1770. Great hopes were set by the Russians on a wholesale rising of the Christian Greeks and Montenegrins against Muslim domination. While still at Leipzig, Radishchev and the other Russian students were kept well informed of developments, since Leipzig lay on the route between St Petersburg and the Russian naval headquarters established at Leghorn in Italy. It is worth noting that Radishchev even turned into Russian a propaganda leaflet entitled 'The Greeks' appeal to Christian Europe', composed by a certain Albanian prince, Anton Ghika or Guica by name, though Radishchev's rendering was not published at the time.

The Prussian and Austrian Courts hardly fancied the prospect of sitting by in unprofitable idleness while Catherine carved up and swallowed the Ottoman dominions in Europe. As it turned out, the enlightened despots of Berlin and Vienna had little difficulty in persuading their colleague in St Petersburg that the best way of maintaining the equilibrium of Europe was for all three powers to adjust their territories at the expense of the kingdom of Poland. The result of their confabulations was the notorious First Partition of Poland in 1772, by which that country was deprived of about a fifth of her population and a quarter of her territory. Whether in the long run Russia gained anything from this piece of brigandage and the two others that followed in the 1790s remains a moot point. In exchange for tempting slices of territory, she lost a useful buffer State and forfeited some of the international esteem which the country had enjoyed since the days of Peter the Great. What is more, she acquired a mutinous national minority whose resentment was to bedevil Russia's internal and external affairs for many years to come.

While the Empress Catherine was casting aside idealism in her foreign policy, the defects in her social programme at home were also becoming apparent and arousing criticism among the more vocal *literati*. The beginnings of a Russian social conscience were already discernible in the literary productions of the 1760s, particularly in the realm of prose writing. It was at this period that the novel, earlier regarded as inferior to the poetic genres, began to develop in Russia as a recognized literary form. It early manifested that tendency towards discussion of current problems and social moralizing in the Dickensian vein which was to be so striking a feature of the Russian novel throughout the nineteenth century, and has reappeared in our own time in such works as Dudintsev's *Not by Bread Alone*. In 1763, for instance, F. A. Emin published his *Inconstancies of Fortune, or Adventures of Miramond*, which contained reflections on agriculture and on political economy based on the views of Jean-Jacques Rousseau and of the French Physiocrats.[1]

Another of Emin's early novels, *Letters of Ernest and Doravra* (1766), contains passages like the following:

'Happy are those peasants who live beneath the authority of righteous masters! But how unfortunate are those wretches whom fate has subjected to the will of men who are ignorant of the character of a good peasant, and indeed of the very nature of mankind! . . . I have seen many of our unscrupulous neighbours refuse to believe their bailiff when he told them that there was nothing to seize from the peasants. They came down to their villages and personally tormented their poor serfs with relentless beatings, to force them to purchase relief with hard cash. I considered such landlords to be tyrants, and their presence near us to be our misfortune.'

Between 1763 and 1770, Emin published over thirty original works

---

[1] A school of economists among whom the most prominent were François Quesnay (1694–1774) and Dupont de Nemours (1739–1817).

and translations of a popular or didactic character, many of which were widely read.

Russian journalism also developed rapidly following Catherine's accession. A pioneer in this field was the formidable Princess Dashkov, who had played a prominent part in dethroning Peter III and securing Catherine's triumph; her interesting memoirs are available in English.[1] One of Princess Dashkov's periodicals, called *Nevinnoe Uprazhnenie* or 'Innocent Exercises', included translated extracts from Helvétius' *De l'Esprit*, one of Radishchev's favourite books.

Of greater bite and topicality were the satirical journals published by Nikolay Ivanovich Novikov (1744–1818): *Truten'* ('The Drone') of 1769, *Zhivopisets* or 'The Painter' (1772–3), and finally, *Koshelëk* or 'The Purse' (1774). 'The Drone', like most other Russian periodicals of the time, started off as a kind of imitation of Addison and Steele's celebrated *Spectator*. However, Novikov, who had worked as a secretary in the commission of deputies at Moscow in 1767, was not content to follow the official line and confine himself to innocuous jokes about old-fashioned prejudices. The directness of the topical comment and social criticism contained in 'The Drone' brought its editor a series of sharp rebukes from the rival organ *Vsyakaya Vsyachina* or 'All Sorts', which was directed by none other than the Empress Catherine herself. In spite of this, Novikov refused to recant, until finally, his paper was obliged to close down altogether in 1770.

One of Novikov's main preoccupations was the condition of the peasantry. By implication, though not overtly, he anticipates Radishchev by striking with his shafts of irony at the bedrock of contemporary society, the system of serfdom. Here, for instance, is an extract from 'The Drone' purporting to be a squire's orders to his bailiff on steps to be taken in respect of a famine-stricken village on his domains:

'To our man, Simon Grigoriev.

You are to proceed to our village of X and on arrival to carry out the following measures:

1. Your journey from here to our estate and back to be at the expense of our village elder, Andrew Lazarev.

2. On arrival, you are to flog the village elder with the utmost severity in front of all the peasants for supervising the peasants slackly and letting the quit-rent fall into arrears, and then deprive him of his eldership; and furthermore to extract from him a fine of one hundred roubles.

3. Discover most exactly how and in consideration of what bribes the elder deceived us with his false report? First of all, have him flogged

---

[1] *The Memoirs of Princess Dashkov*, translated and edited by Kyril FitzLyon, London, 1958.

and then begin the investigation of the matter entrusted to you. . . .
8. Settle the division of land between the peasants as you think fit, but tell them that there is to be no reduction in the quit-rent and that they must pay up promptly without any false excuses. Flog any defaulters pitilessly in front of all the peasants. . . .
16. After carrying out all the above orders, you are to return here. Order the elder in the strictest terms to keep a vigilant watch on the collection of the quit-rent money.'

For its time, the sarcasm of 'The Drone' is devastating. One of Novikov's imaginary characters, the squire Nedoum ('Brainless') is shown submitting to the Government a plan according to which 'no creatures were to exist in the whole world except members of the gentry, and the common people were to be completely exterminated; on which theme he kept on handing in projects.' The moral of all this was clear enough, and indignant reactions from various quarters showed that the cap fitted a large number of heads uncomfortably well.

Undeterred by the suppression of 'The Drone', Novikov returned boldly to the offensive with his new periodical, 'The Painter', which contained essays on problems connected with serfdom, and touched on other burning social questions. In particular, there was a series of wittily revealing letters, supposedly addressed to a young country bumpkin, Faliley, by his family, a collection of clownish provincial squires much resembling the Prostakov ('Simpleton') family and the Mr Skotinin ('Beastly') who figure in Denis Fonvizin's immortal comedy *Nedorosl'* or 'The Minor' (1782). Novikov also pilloried venal judges, fops, as well as extortioners like that officer, now retired to his estates in the country, who 'while serving in his regiment used often-times to exact a contribution from the foe, but here collects dues from his own peasants; there, he used to hack at the infidels, but here, he flogs and torments the believers'.

One of the most outspoken contributions to appear in 'The Painter' was until recently attributed to Radishchev himself, so closely does it foreshadow his view of the serf problem as expressed in the *Journey from St Petersburg to Moscow*. The title of this piece is 'Fragment of a Journey to . . .', and it appeared over the initials 'I.T.' in the fifth and fourteenth numbers of the journal. The 'Fragment', probably from Novikov's own pen, is written in a vehement and somewhat sentimental style, with outbursts of indignation which do indeed foreshadow some of Radishchev's later writings. The first instalment describes the writer's journey through a country district, where he observes nothing but 'poverty and servitude' among the peasantry, unploughed fields, bad harvests—in short, the complete abjectness of 'those poor creatures

2 Catherine the Great in Russian National Costume

3 St Petersburg from the Neva

who should form the wealth and greatness of the whole realm'.—'To my great indignation,' continues the traveller, 'I always found that the proprietors themselves were responsible for this. O Humanity! Thou art unknown in these villages. O Authority! Thou dost tyrannize over thy fellow men. O blessed Virtue, love of one's neighbour! Thou art abused. The imbecile masters of these poor slaves exercise thee towards horses and dogs rather than towards men. With the great compassion of a sensitive heart I begin the description of a few villages and hamlets and their proprietors. Far from me, flattery and partiality, base qualities of vile minds!—Truth guides my pen.'

This tirade is followed by a lurid picture of the squalor found in a typical peasant's hut, or hovel, as Novikov calls it. Finding three infants on the point of death from neglect and starvation, the traveller does what he can to save them, exclaiming:

'Hard-hearted tyrant, depriving the peasants of their daily bread and peace of mind! . . . Cry out, poor creatures!—said I, shedding tears— Utter your plaint! Profit in your youth by this last consolation, for when you grow up even this solace will be denied you. O Sun, lighting up with your rays the village of . . . ! Look down upon these unfortunates!'

These strictures, be it noted, appeared only three years after the Empress Catherine had assured Voltaire, in her letter of July 3/14, 1769, that 'what is more, our taxes are so moderate that there is not a peasant in Russia who does not eat a chicken when he feels like it, in fact, for some time past there are provinces where they prefer turkeys to chickens'.

The second instalment of the 'Fragment of a Journey to . . . ' begins with an ironical description of the waning hours of evening: the idle rich are glad to have rid themselves of another day in their useless existence; the unjust judge rejoices at having caused streams of innocent tears to flow; gamblers prepare to wager the fruits of their serfs' labour and sweat on the hazards of a card table; lawyers are thinking up fresh legal methods of ruining the prosperous citizen. Meanwhile, in the village of . . . the peasants struggle home from the fields, dusty and exhausted, rejoicing that they have completed a hard day's work—but all for the sake of one man's caprices. Reaching their impoverished homesteads, the serfs apologize to the traveller for being absent when he arrived, and explain that they were all out gathering the squire's corn. If the weather holds, they may even succeed in gathering in their own meagre sheaves on Sunday—the only day they are allowed to devote to cultivating their own smallholdings.

The whole episode anticipates the chapter 'Lyubani' in Radishchev's

E

Journey from St Petersburg to Moscow, where the traveller finds a peasant ploughing on Sunday, and learns that he is forced to work all six days of the week on the lord's estate. The sentimental rhetoric of the passages quoted here are unusual in Russian literature as early as this, and show that the influence of Laurence Sterne's *Sentimental Journey through France and Italy*, first published in 1768, was already making itself felt in Russian literature.

As a precaution, Novikov appended to the 'Fragment of a Journey to . . .' the following editorial note:

'I received this satirical article, entitled "Journey to . . ." from Mr I. T. with the request that it might be included in these pages. Had it been at the time when our minds and hearts were infected by the French nation, I should not have dared to serve my readers from this dish, because it is very salty and bitter for the tender palates of genteel nitwits. But nowadays Philosophy seated on the Throne protects truth in all things. And so I hope that this essay will merit the attention of those who love truth.'

This diplomatic paragraph, which was designed as a tactful appeal to the 'philosophic' Empress, did not disarm Novikov's offended readers among the squirearchy. In a subsequent number of 'The Painter', in the course of a dialogue under the title 'English Promenade', the editor is asked by a friend why he does not publish a sequel to the 'Fragment of a Journey to . . .', of which only a portion had been printed. 'I fail to understand,' says this friend, 'why some people imagine that this composition is an insult to the entire nobility—it merely describes one nobleman who abuses his power and aristocratic privileges.' The controversy aroused by the 'Fragment' is further echoed by another item published in 'The Painter', under the title 'Letter of a District Squire to his Son'. This epistle is written in an intentionally crude style which cleverly reveals the outlook of its supposed author:

'Who is this Painter bloke who has turned up where you are? Some German, I suppose, since no Orthodox Russian would have written all that stuff. He says the landlords torment the peasants and calls them tyrants. . . . He presumes to say the peasants are poor! A fine shame! I take it he wants them to get rich, and us—the gentry—to grow poor? Our Lord never ordained that: someone has to be rich, either the boss or the clodhopper. Not every monk can be an abbot. And in the Scriptures it is written: Bear each other's burdens and thus you will fulfil Christ's law. They work for us and we flog them if they start

idling, and so we are all square—I know how to manage the oafs! . . .
If I was a great lord, I'd send the fellow off to Siberia.'

The appearance of these tirades on the peasant question coincided,
ominously enough, with the first rumblings of the discontent which
was soon to burst into the Pugachev rebellion. Although the threats
voiced against Novikov by the imaginary district squire were not to be
fulfilled until his arrest twenty years later, it seems clear that the Government told him to moderate his tone. At any rate, 'The Painter' ceased
publication in July 1773, and his third and last journal, 'The Purse',
turned out to be a very innocuous affair. Gradually, Novikov turned his
attention to another sphere of activity—the publishing business which
contributed so much to the spread of learning and of literacy in later
eighteenth-century Russia.

※

It will be recalled that the Empress Catherine's intention in sending
Radishchev and his comrades to Leipzig University had been to form
a cadre of trained jurists to serve on the secretariat of her grand legislative commission of 1767–8. This body no longer existed, and there
was little prospect of its being reconvened. A fitting use had somehow
to be made of the talents of Radishchev and his friends Kutuzov and
Rubanovsky, and so the three young men were given the rank of
Titular Councillor in the Civil Service and detailed for service in the
St Petersburg Senate as 'Protocolists' under the Procurator-General
or Minister of Justice, Prince A. A. Vyazemsky.

The Russian Senate, as set up by Peter the Great, was not a deli-
berative assembly, as its name might imply, but rather a central judicial
and administrative body, combining the functions of a Government
chancellery with those of a Supreme Court. The Senate drafted
administrative orders according to instructions from the sovereign,
despatched them and was responsible for their enforcement. It was
called upon to see that the *ukazes* were rightly interpreted and applied
to specific instances, and thus acquired the status of a Court of Appeal
for both civil and criminal cases. It was also supposed to manage the
fiscal apparatus and exercise what one would nowadays term 'Treasury
control' over the various ministries, or 'Colleges' as they were then
called, and other Government departments. The provincial governors
and finance bureaux were under the Senate's supervision, and were
supposed to submit to it regular reports and periodical returns.

The Minister of Justice was the real source of power in the Senate,
through the direct access he enjoyed to the sovereign. The Senators

themselves were often retired men who had won distinction as Generals or Viceroys, or else hangers-on of the Court or relatives of the reigning favourite. The permanent staff of the Senate's six departments included five Chief Procurators and a number of Secretaries and Chief Secretaries, all Radishchev's superiors in the hierarchy. Below him were the dozens of copy-clerks, scribes and chancery secretaries, busily copying out *ukazes* and other documents passed down from the higher levels.

Though great stress was laid on observance of the letter of the law, members of the Senate and its permanent officials did not enjoy a high reputation for either efficiency or honesty. In his memoirs, Prince Adam Czartoryski refers to that body as 'full of incapables and chronic failures, of all the invalids and idlers in the Empire'. When a man showed himself incapable of action, the same writer goes on, when he was good for nothing and no one knew what to do with him, they made him a Senator. Since the most trivial cases rapidly accumulated round themselves a vast mass of papers, composed in a long-winded and obscure verbiage, it was easy for the Procurators and their staff to lead the Senators by the nose. As Czartoryski puts it, the permanent officials (that is to say, Radishchev and his superiors) chewed up and pre-digested the dossiers before they were dished up to the Senators. The latter were usually happy to append their signature to what was put before them, without burrowing into the jungle of reports and affidavits that lay beneath.

The spirit characteristic of the bureaucrats in this and other Russian Government institutions was pungently summed up in the dramatist Kapnist's classic comedy, *Yabeda*, or 'Chicanery':

> Grab, it needs no learning crabbed,
> Grab what lets itself be grabbed;
> What were hands hung on us for,
> But for grabbing more and more?[1]

The First Department of the Senate, to which Radishchev was assigned, was the most important of all. Headed by the Minister of Justice in person, it was concerned with broad questions of political and economic policy, with local administration and civil service personnel and promotions. It supervised foreign trade and home industries, controlled the St Petersburg and Moscow banks and authorized the issue of banknotes. The First Department also occupied itself, admittedly to little effect, with questions of health and public hygiene.

The main job of Protocolists like Radishchev was to be present at sessions of the Senate and of its separate departments, for which they

[1] English rendering by the late Sir Ellis Minns.

helped to prepare the agenda; they then wrote up the minutes, checking decisions against the relevant *ukazes*. It also fell to them to sort out all kinds of petitions and complaints submitted by private citizens, summarize them and bring them up for discussion either in the Protocolists' own department, or in the weekly meeting of Senators of all departments combined.

The researches of the Soviet scholar Makogonenko have lately resulted in the discovery of a number of dossiers actually dealt with and signed by Radishchev during the fourteen months he served in the Senate. It would be hard to imagine a better apprenticeship for a would-be reformer than this forced familiarity with reports sent in by provincial governors on the local situation in the far-flung provinces of the Russian Empire in Europe and in Asia, on harvests and trade, on runaway peasants and rural uprisings, on the plague epidemic then raging in the Moscow region; with complaints about the corruption and extortions of local magistrates and governors; with petitions from soldiers, merchants and common folk seeking redress against the treatment meted out to them by the hard-bitten landed gentry who controlled the Russian provincial administration.

In the deliberations of Radishchev's department, the grim and the trivial featured alongside important affairs of State. Within three days of Radishchev's appointment, he found himself involved in the sentence passed on the mutinous indentured serfs at the Petrovsk factories, who were condemned on December 12, 1771, to be knouted and have their nostrils torn off; since there was no executioner available on the spot, one was to be sent from St Petersburg, 'equipped with all instruments required for public chastisements'. Another day, it was the affair of a certain Captain Izedinov, who had thought up a fraud subtly different from that practised by Chichikov in Gogol's famous novel: namely, to enter his live serfs as 'dead souls' in the census returns, thus avoiding payment of poll-tax on them. The ingenious captain was sentenced to a fine of two hundred roubles per soul. Then there was the business of the merchant Pogodin, who had defaulted on his contract for the milling of rye and the supply of flour to the capital. The erring contractor was sentenced, aptly enough, to be kept three days under arrest in theSenate building on a diet of bread and water.

Again, Radishchev had to deal over a period of several months with the case of the soldier Alekseev, illegally beaten up by the landowner Mordvinov of Novgorod. The Senate sentenced Mordvinov to pay Alekseev fifty roubles by way of compensation, whereupon the irascible squire had the luckless Alekseev again flogged by a posse of his landowning cronies. Hearing of this, the Senate told the Novgorod authorities to make the culprits pay Alekseev further damages. The Novgorod bureaucrats being, so it seems, very much in the pocket of Mordvinov and his party, they prevaricated for months on end; finally, the Senate deducted the sums in question from the personal salary of the Novgorod officials—not a bad procedure, one might think. In cases like the last mentioned, a great deal depended on the initiative of permanent officials like Radishchev and his colleagues, for it was to them that the Senators left the carrying out of their verdicts. But for Radishchev's love of justice, cases like that of Mordvinov and the Novgorod bureaucrats would have gone by default and been conveniently buried under mounds of chancery papers.

While serving in the First Department, Radishchev was also involved in the drafting of measures to cope with the growing distress and dissatisfaction felt among the common people, increasingly disillusioned with the reality which followed the bright promises of Catherine's accession. As a result of the burdens of serfdom, the war with Turkey, and the plague outbreak in Moscow, riots broke out in the old capital. Elsewhere, obscure pamphleteers and agitators found a ready hearing among the disgruntled populace.

In March 1772, it was found advisable to reissue an earlier proclamation, in which stress was laid on the Empress's 'maternal' care for her subjects' welfare. Regret was expressed at the continuing existence of 'persons of corrupt morals and thoughts, who think not of the general weal and tranquillity; since they are themselves infected with strange delusions about matters which do not in the least concern them and about which they have no direct knowledge, they try to infect other feeble-minded individuals as well, and extend their propensity for senseless agitation to the point of impudently animadverting in their rantings, not only upon the civil power, upon the Government and upon the measures decreed by Her Imperial Majesty, but upon the very laws of God.' In the revised version of this proclamation, it was found necessary to add that 'if this maternal admonition and exhortation by Her Imperial Majesty fails to take effect in the hearts of the perverted and does not make them return to the path of true felicity, then let every such ignoramus know that Her Imperial Majesty will thereupon act with the full rigour of the law, and offenders will inevitably be made to feel the full weight of Her Imperial Majesty's wrath'.

While the Senate was thus trying to bolster up the prestige of Russian autocracy, there can be little doubt that it contained, in the person of Radishchev, at least one of those 'impudent' sceptics whom it was desired to suppress. We have spoken already of Novikov, the outspoken satirist who early in the 1770s found it safer to transfer his literary energies from journalism to publishing. It was Novikov's company which commissioned Radishchev to translate into Russian one of the provocative treatises by the Abbé Mably, the French utopian socialist whose writings the Russian students at Leipzig had preferred to Hofrat Böhme's dreary dissertations; for his translation, Radishchev was promised one hundred and five roubles.

The work in question, Mably's *Observations sur l'Histoire de la Grèce*, was first published in 1766, and represents a revised version of the same writer's earlier *Observations sur les Grecs* (1749). At that period, Mably's views on Greek history had much topical interest, since he took full advantage of the scope afforded by his theme to praise the 'democratic' republics of ancient Hellas, and to criticize the system of monarchy which dominated eighteenth-century Europe. Although the late Professor Laski felt that there was 'an air of stucco villadom about his new Sparta',[1] yet Mably's political ideas were not without force and originality, and exerted a great influence on French legislators during the Revolution, as well as on Polish patriotic reformers during their struggle against Russia, Austria and Prussia.

The Sparta of Lycurgus, Mably considered, was the ideal political organism, a masterpiece of constitutional planning which the human race has never since managed to equal:

'For almost six hundred years, the laws of Lycurgus, the wisest ever vouchsafed to mankind, were observed there with the most religious fidelity. What nation was so attached to all the virtues as were the Spartans, or ever gave such great and constant examples of moderation, patience, courage, magnanimity, temperance, justice, contempt for riches, and love of liberty and of the fatherland? When reading their history, we feel ourselves inflamed: if we still bear in our heart any seed of virtue, our spirit is exalted and seems to aspire to soar beyond the narrow bounds within which the corruption of our century confines us.'

The revolutionary implication of this tirade is made even clearer when Mably goes on to remark how fortunate the Spartans were in being preserved for a long time from the corrupting influence of luxury and riches, and from the tyranny of vicious kings and venal bureaucrats such as had become the curse of modern Europe, 'where everyone is a subject and nobody a citizen'. It was the pernicious example of voluptuous and ambitious Athenians like Pericles and Alcibiades which later brought ruin to Greece and caused her to fall an easy prey to Philip of Macedon. This energetic prince had, in Mably's opinion, a number

[1] H. J. Laski, introduction to E. A. Whitfield, *Gabriel Bonnot de Mably*, London, 1930.

of excellent qualities, which he owed to his upbringing in a republic where monarchy was held in scorn and there was nothing of the 'pride, pomp and flattery which besiege palaces, intoxicate princes with their power and persuade them that they are great enough by their rank to have no need of any other kind of greatness'.

When Mably comes to discuss Alexander the Great, he uses him as a symbol of all dynastic conquerors, including those of Mably's own time. With gusto and verve, Mably denounces Alexander's selfish ambition, his lechery, his projects for subjugating his own and other nations: 'What name,' he asks, 'is odious enough to be given to a conqueror, who looks always in front of him and never casts his eyes behind, who marches on with the sound and onrush of a torrent in flood, flows away and vanishes in the same manner, and leaves nothing but ruins in his track? What did Alexander hope to achieve?' If, Mably concludes, Alexander realized the impossibility of retaining his conquests and yet persisted in his acts of aggression, then he was 'a mere detestable lunatic'. It is worth noting, incidentally, that Radishchev later imitates Mably's condemnation of Alexander and of other military adventurers in the *Journey from St Petersburg to Moscow*, chapter 'Khotilov', where he enquires: 'But what is it that the conqueror thirsts for? What is he seeking, to devastate populous lands or to subdue deserts to his sway? . . . Madman! Look upon your career. The precipitate whirlwind of your onrush, passing through your Empire, involves its inhabitants in its vortex, squanders the vigour of the State in its course and leaves behind it wilderness and desolation.' In this way, Mably's implicit condemnation of the predatory policies of Louis XIV and later 'enlightened despots' of Europe was turned under Radishchev's pen into an implied criticism of Catherine and her favourite Potemkin's grand strategy of carving up Poland and the Ottoman Empire.

Thus, Radishchev was not slow to grasp the inflammatory conclusions which could be drawn from Mably's treatise. He appreciated that the French writer, in praising the virtues of antique Sparta, was in reality condemning his own era. Not content with rendering Mably's text into Russian, Radishchev makes his views clear in a special footnote which he added to his translation on his own initiative. Where Mably refers to the enervating system of despotic rule which prevailed in ancient Persia, Radishchev rendered the French word *despotisme* with the Russian *samoderzhavstvo* or 'autocracy' and added the following comment of his own:

'Autocracy is the condition most repugnant to human nature. We cannot give anyone unlimited power over ourselves, and even the law, the expression of the general will, has no other right to punish criminals than that of self-preservation. If we live under the authority of the laws, it is not because we are bound irrevocably to do so, but because it is to our advantage. If we resign to the law some part of our rights and natural powers, we do this in order that the part which we renounce may be turned to our own good; in this we conclude a *tacit* contract with society. If it is broken, we are released from our *obligations*. Injustice on the part of the ruler gives to the nation, as his judges, a right over him which is just as great as, and yet greater than that which the law gives the ruler over criminals. *The ruler is the first citizen of the national society.*' [Italics Radishchev's.]

This remarkable passage is, of course, largely a statement of the main principles of the 'Social Contract', one of the basic elements of eighteenth-century political thought. The doctrine had been worked out to its logical conclusion by Jean-Jacques Rousseau in his famous tract, *Du Contrat Social, ou Principes du Droit Politique*, which appeared in 1762. In the fourth chapter, Rousseau points out that it is absurd to imagine a person giving himself up unconditionally into someone else's power, and without any advantage to himself, adding that such an act on the part of a whole nation would be null and void, as presupposing a race of lunatics. Rousseau explains in the sixth chapter how a violation of the 'Social Pact' by the sovereign power entitles each individual to resume his primitive natural rights and liberties. Radishchev's assertion that the preservation of society is the basis of criminal law also derives from the *Contrat Social* (bk. II, 5), where Rousseau says, 'The only individual whom one is entitled to put to death, even as a deterrent, is one who cannot be left alive without peril.'

If we trace them back a little further, these ideas which Radishchev borrowed from Rousseau can be plainly seen to derive from English political philosophy of the Whig school, as elaborated by John Locke in his *Two treatises of Government*; this work, published in 1690, was one of Rousseau's primary sources. For instance, Radishchev's sentence beginning, 'We cannot give anyone unlimited power over ourselves . . .' resembles Locke's contention that 'a man, not having the power of his own life, cannot, by compact, or his own consent, enslave himself to any one, nor put himself under the absolute, arbitrary power of another' (*Of Civil Government*, paragraph 23). Radishchev's claim that autocracy is repugnant to human nature is foreshadowed by Locke's remark that absolute monarchy is inconsistent with the very existence of civil society, for in absolutist systems there is no security against 'the violence and oppression of this absolute ruler' (*ibid.*, paras. 90, 93). Locke's conception of the basis of human society is similar to Radishchev's:

people unite themselves into a community, says Locke, 'for their comfortable, safe and peaceable living one amongst another, in a secure enjoyment of their properties. . . . The power of the society, or legislative constituted by them, can never be supposed to extend farther, than the common good' (*ibid.*, paras. 95, 131). Political power, concludes Locke, 'has its origin only from compact and agreement, and the mutual consent of those who make up the community' (*ibid.*, para. 171). Furthermore, Radishchev's assertion that injustice on the part of the ruler releases his subjects from their obligations of loyal obedience had also been developed by Locke in his treatise *Of Civil Government*, in the nineteenth chapter, entitled 'Of the Dissolution of Government': 'Whenever the legislators endeavour to take away, and destroy the property of the people, or to reduce them to slavery under arbitrary power, they put themselves into a state of war with the people, who are thereupon absolved from any further obedience, and are left to the common refuge, which God hath provided for all men, against force and violence.'

There is thus a striking resemblance between Radishchev's note on the evils of absolutism and the arguments used by John Locke to justify the bloodless revolution of 1688 which drove James II from the throne of England. We know from the extracts earlier quoted from Radishchev's life of his comrade Fedor Ushakov that the Russian students in Leipzig were keenly interested in the history of the English parliamentarians and regicides of the seventeenth century. This enthusiasm is further evinced in the 'Ode to Liberty' which Radishchev wrote some years later for insertion in his *Journey from St Petersburg to Moscow*: the twenty-third stanza of the ode invokes the shade of Oliver Cromwell, who haled King Charles I to the scaffold and thereby 'taught every race and age how nations can their wrath assuage'. In this way, the example of Cromwell and the English parliamentarians constituted a standing challenge to political systems like Russian autocracy, even in the form of the 'enlightened despotism' of Catherine the Great. Only two years after Radishchev's return from studying in the West, his translation of Mably, with its outspoken condemnation of the absolutist system of Government, contains the seeds of the *Journey from St Petersburg to Moscow*, the most forcible protest against the established order to be found in all Russian literature of the eighteenth century.

It is worth comparing Radishchev's early concept of the 'Social Contract', as borrowed from Rousseau and Locke, with the more complex theory of society which he later put forward in an unfinished essay entitled 'On Virtues and Rewards'. Here, Radishchev joins issue with such thinkers as Rousseau on the question whether men originally entered society exclusively for the preservation of their individual rights and liberties. In Radishchev's view, it would be truer to say that they joined forces to present a common front against any attempt to infringe the general welfare of mankind: 'Summoned into society by the powerful voice of their own weaknesses and deficiencies, men soon realized that in order to resist wanton aggression there was need of an executive force which, rising above the whole social confederation, should serve as a defence for the weak, a support for the downtrodden.'

Radishchev develops this idea further by saying that ideally, the social organization does not restrict the citizen's rights and liberties, but rather arouses in him latent energies, and favours the development of qualities which enrich his personality. The solitary state, in Radishchev's view, is pernicious: 'Formerly shrouded by the fog of inertia and encompassed by dark ignorance and insensitivity of self, those human faculties which earlier drowsed in isolation, slumbered rather, remained indeed dead, in social intercourse blossomed out and were mutually strengthened, extended and elevated. After comprehending not only all things which existed, but also everything which could exist, men went on further yet, to conceive of that which is beyond their scope, touching even upon the realms of the Godhead.'[1] Radishchev felt that it was not enough to think of the social order as merely a kind of police force to prevent individuals and Governments from exterminating one another; society fails in its function if it does not provide stimulus for the fullest development of human potentialities, and scope for their maximum deployment and utilization. Radishchev is led to draw the conclusion: 'The more closely the interests of the individual are made to coincide with the interests of the community, the happier a society may be called.' (Obviously, according to this criterion, a country where most of the population remained in servitude could hardly be placed high in the scale.)

Radishchev's independent approach to such classics of eighteenth-century political thought as Montesquieu and Rousseau is further evinced in a brief fragment found among his posthumous papers, in which he criticizes Montesquieu's doctrine of the division of powers in the ideal State, as well as Rousseau's idea that democratic government is possible only in a small country. 'Montesquieu and Rousseau,' says Radishchev, 'have done a lot of harm by their theorizing. The former discovered the so-called division of powers, having in view the ancient republics, the Governments of Asia, and France. He forgot about his neighbours.' (By this, Radishchev evidently means that Montesquieu omitted to make any practical recommendations for reform in East European autocratic States like Russia, whose political

---

[1] Radishchev, *Polnoe sobranie sochineny* ('Complete collection of works'), vol. III, Moscow, Leningrad, 1952, pp. 28–31.

evolution had proceeded on lines different from the Greco-Roman and Western European traditions.) In this same document, Radishchev goes on to challenge Rousseau's negative view of the prospects for progress in Russia, and his idea that sound government is possible only in small, compact countries where every citizen can have a voice in the counsels of the State; Radishchev objects to the fact that Rousseau, 'without making any reference to history, imagined that good government is possible only in a small realm, whereas in large ones, despotism is inevitable.' Rousseau's additional assumption, namely that the Russians were in any case a barbarous people incapable of running their affairs in a civilized fashion, also appeared to Radishchev as an offensive generalization.[1]

This fragment, which dates from the 1780s, shows that Radishchev had not yet lost hope in Russia's political future. Even in autocratic Russia under Catherine the Great, he evidently felt that reforms might still be introduced to mitigate the effects of absolutist rule, without necessarily having recourse to revolution or to artificial schemes devoid of any basis in Russian national tradition. The document also shows that with all his Western affinities, Radishchev was enough of a patriot to resent Rousseau's supercilious strictures on the Russian character.

Part of the price Radishchev had to pay for his espousal of the radical ideas of the Western 'Age of Reason' was a gradual estrangement from his friend and room-mate, Alexis Kutuzov, who was still working with him in the Senate. Already Radishchev's reaction to social injustice was to take up the cudgels on behalf of the underdog. Kutuzov, while as humane in outlook as Radishchev himself, took refuge in an attitude of passive non-resistance combined with pious quietism. 'There is no virtue higher than resignation and patience,' he would say in reply to some tirade of Radishchev's. On Kutuzov's table, there appeared more and more frequently books of an ethical and mystical tendency, including the tracts of the 'Martinists'[2] and kindred Masonic sects who were making great headway among the nobility and middle-classes of eighteenth-century Russia. Philanthropic discourses were mingled in such works with admonitions to submit to legally constituted authority, and with cryptic allusions to secret rites revealed only to the chosen few.

Freemasonry in Russia had little of that anti-clerical and revolutionary flavour which characterized parallel movements in France and other Roman Catholic countries. With leading Masons like Novikov, its main feature was active philanthropy based on a genuine religious

---

[1] Radishchev, *Polnoe sobranie sochineny*, III, 47.

[2] A branch of the Masonic movement which followed the teachings of the Marquis de Saint-Martin (1743–1803), often known as 'le Philosophe inconnu'.

sympathy for the poor and needy. This aspect of Freemasonry, however, served only to make the movement increasingly odious to the Empress and her ministers. Catherine could not stomach any encroachment on her much-advertised personal monopoly of social reform and enlightenment in Russia, and the zeal shown by the Freemasons in the field of welfare and popular education formed an invidious contrast to the Government's inertia. Having herself a rational turn of mind, Catherine felt an instinctive distrust of Freemasonry's secret ceremonies, and always imagined them to involve some sinister plot against her throne.

At the same time, the Freemasons came under fire from the Russian 'Voltaireans', who formed a powerful body of opinion at this period and resented the Martinists' adherence to what the rationalists looked on as simply one more manifestation of religious mumbo-jumbo. 'If you open the latest mystical writings,' complained Radishchev, 'you imagine yourself to be back in the age of scholasticism and theological disputation, when the human mind busied itself with preachifying, without stopping to reflect on whether there was any sense in what was preached.'

In 1773, Kutuzov left St Petersburg to fight the Turks and Tatars as a captain in the Russian army. In after years, he recalled when thinking of Radishchev that 'although by the time of our separation, our ways of thought had become entirely different, and at times we used to quarrel, yet we loved one another all the more, since we saw clearly that our differences lay in our heads and not in our hearts'.

Later on, in 1774, Radishchev was invited by some of his comrades to visit the 'Urania' Masonic Lodge at St Petersburg, which, besides its properly Masonic functions, served as a club for some of the smart set. After one or two visits, the atmosphere of the Lodge palled on Radishchev, and he tended more and more to part company with his friends in Masonic society.

CHAPTER 4

Lost Illusions

❧❧❧ ❧❧❧

Farewell to the Senate – Break-up of a Comradeship – A Scion of the Bruces – Russian Military Law – The Cossacks in Revolt – Triumph and Downfall of Pugachev – Radishchev's Retirement and Marriage – Financial Worries

Radishchev's work in the Senate, combined with his status as a former member of the Imperial Corps of Pages, opened to him the doors of the best St Petersburg society. 'His manners,' Radishchev's son later recalled, 'were simple and agreeable, his conversation engaging, his countenance handsome and expressive.' This agrees with the reminiscences of the German diplomat G. A. W. von Helbig, whose book *Russische Günstlinge* ('Russian Favourites') provides such fascinating insight into the private lives of Catherine II and her admirers: according to this observer, Radishchev was liked and respected in St Petersburg for combining in his manner and conversation 'a veritable hoard of learning' with 'a modesty such as is not commonly met with'.

Among the houses which Radishchev frequented at this period of his life was that of General-in-Chief Yakov (James) Aleksandrovich Bruce, an officer of Scottish descent in the Russian service. Bruce required a trained lawyer on his staff to deal with administrative and court-martial work; Radishchev for his part was tired of slaving away among the bureaucrats in the Senate, and imagined that army life might prove more congenial and provide better hopes for promotion. (He had, in fact, set to work on translating a training manual for officers which Novikov's publishing company wanted to bring out in Russian.) When General Bruce suggested to Radishchev that he should transfer from the Senate on to the roll of the War Office, and join his personal staff, Radishchev readily accepted. This transfer, we learn from a personal letter from Bruce to the Minister of Justice, Prince Vyazemsky, was arranged in May 1773, little over a year since Radishchev started his career in the Senate. In the same month, both Kutuzov and Rubanovsky were also moved from the Senate to the military branch, both of them being posted away from the capital as captains in the army.

It may well be that the break-up of this long-standing association of the three comrades was the occasion for Radishchev's first original work of literature, a brief, rhapsodical fragment entitled *Dnevnik odnoy nedeli* or 'Diary of One Week'. This composition purports to describe the emotions of a man 'afflicted with sensibility'—that 'fatal gift of Heaven' celebrated *ad nauseam* by Rousseau. The hero's friends depart, and leave him for a week all by himself. The emotional tension which he experiences and records in this 'Diary' suggests the atmosphere of Goethe's *Werther* and the other sentimental best-sellers of the time. Here is a typical extract:

'Monday.—But where can I seek even a momentary relief from my afflictions? Where? Reason says: Within myself. No, no, there I find doom, anguish, hell; let us go . . . into the garden, the public promenade —hasten, hasten, unfortunate one, they will see all your anguish upon your cheek.—So be it.—But what of that? They will not sympathise with you. Those whose hearts feel with yours are absent.—Let us pass on.'

In search of distraction, the hero of our 'Diary' visits the theatre, where they are presenting *Beverley*, a Russian adaptation by I. A. Dmitriev of Edward Moore's sentimental drama *The Gamester*. (This play was actually put on at St Petersburg in 1773 with great success, which gives a clue to the date when Radishchev wrote the 'Diary'.) But the theatre brings no solace to Radishchev's hero, and so he goes on to the Volkov Cemetery: 'In this place, where silence eternal reigns, where the reason has no more aspirations, nor the spirit desires, let us learn in advance to look calmly towards the end of our days.—I sat down upon a gravestone, took out my frugal meal and ate with complete tranquillity.—Let us accustom our gaze to decay and ruin, let us look upon death. . . .' Echoes of Gray's *Elegy* or Young's *Night Thoughts*? This may well be the case, especially as Paul Radishchev, in his biography of his father, mentions that he was well versed in English poetry.

This morbid tone is repeated in the entry for Sunday in Radishchev's 'Diary': 'If they have forgotten me, forgotten their friend, then come, O Death, and be most welcome! How can a man exist alone, solitary amidst Nature?' In the middle of distracted outpourings, Radishchev still finds time for a reminiscence of the Sensualist philosophy of Helvétius. Addressing the human species, he exclaims: 'O proud insect! Tremble, and recognize that you can reason only because you feel, that your reason has its origin in your fingertips and in your nakedness.'

For all its lack of literary merit, Radishchev's 'Diary of One Week' is interesting as an early Russian example of the hysteria and subjective emotion characteristic of *Werther*, *La Nouvelle Héloïse* and other works of the European pre-Romantic movement which burst forth in the late eighteenth century. The 'Diary' establishes Radishchev as one of the pioneers of this movement in Russia; it antedates by many years Karamzin's celebrated tale *Poor Liza*, which came out in 1792, and has often been regarded as the first example of the sentimental genre in Russian literature.

*

James Aleksandrovich Bruce (1732–91), General-in-Chief, and Count of the Russian Empire, was descended from an officer named James Bruce, of the line of the Scottish kings, who migrated to Russia in the time of Cromwell, and became a Major-General in the army of Tsar Alexis. His descendant, Radishchev's patron, was the last male representative of the Russian Bruces of this branch. Though not a man of outstanding intellect, James Aleksandrovich was noted for dourness and courage. He owed his rapid advancement in part to the good offices of his wife, a sister of Field-Marshal Rumyantsev, and one of Catherine the Great's boudoir intimates. In addition, he was remembered for his bravery in the battles of the Seven Years' War. In 1771, when plague spread from Turkey and was killing thousands of victims daily in Moscow, Bruce set up a *cordon sanitaire* to protect St Petersburg from the epidemic, and succeeded by his energetic measures in saving the capital from the raging infection.

When Radishchev was appointed to his staff, in 1773, Bruce was not yet Commander-in-Chief at St Petersburg, a post to which he was promoted some years later. He commanded at that time the Finland Division, which was based on St Petersburg, and responsible for the Karelian Isthmus sector and for the defence of the capital against any attack from Finland and Sweden. Russia was still nominally at war with Turkey; had Gustavus III of Sweden, an ally of the Ottoman Porte, shown the same initiative he was to display in Catherine's Second Turkish War some years later, a situation very grave for Russia might have ensued. However, things remained comparatively quiet on this front, so that Bruce's military skill was scarcely put to the test.

Bruce evidently liked Radishchev, since it was he who some years later recommended him for the Directorship of the St Petersburg Customs House. It is hard to conceive that the intellectual young official could have had much in common with the gruff General, though,

4 St Petersburg: Customs warehouses

The Road from St. Petersburg to Moscow

as often happens, the hard-bitten man of battles may have felt a protective regard for his sensitive, thoughtful subordinate. It is worth
noting as one point of agreement between them that Bruce, like Radishchev, had no time for Freemasons and mystics. As Commander-in-
Chief at Moscow later in his career, he was detailed by Catherine to
make a raid on Novikov's printing office, and subsequently declared
the Masonic literature produced there to be little to his taste. Bruce
was noted for his persecution of the Moscow 'Martinists', the most
active of the Masonic sects in late eighteenth-century Russia. In the end,
Bruce told the Empress that the 'antiquated customs and murk of prejudice' which he found among the Muscovites was more than he could
stomach, and petitioned to be transferred back to the more rational,
westernized atmosphere of St Petersburg.

Such was the chief under whom Radishchev served for the next two
years. The post assigned to him was that of 'Ober-Auditor' or military
procurator. His duties consisted, in accordance with the system established by Peter the Great, mainly in supervising the proceedings of
regimental courts-martial and making sure that their verdicts agreed
with the military code. The procurator passed on the verdicts of these
courts-martial to the divisional commander for confirmation or rejection. In view of the lack of legal training among Russian junior officers
who constituted such courts-martial, a great deal depended on the
vigilance and knowledge of the military procurators.

The reminiscences of a contemporary of Radishchev, an adjutant
named I. M. Dolgorukov, provide an illuminating insight into the
functioning of Russian military law at that period. One of Dolgorukov's
duties was to supervise the infliction of corporal punishment when
ordered by court-martial: 'The first time I saw a soldier forced to run
the gauntlet, I felt sick and had to be carried off parade. Later on I got
so used to this that I often walked along the ranks when an offender
was running the gauntlet, and even used to scold soldiers who beat the
air with their rods instead of the body. That is what automatic habit
does to a man! . . . It is fortunate for the sake of humanity that the
sentences of the Guards' courts-martial were sent up for revision to the
Adjutant-General, an officer always selected from among experienced
jurists, and who did not permit either mistakes or excessive brutality
to be authorized. But for that, what reliance could have been placed on
our verdicts? We were all young men, without any knowledge of the
laws, either of their severity or their substance. Admittedly, we used to
give judgment impartially, that is to say, without any bribery or
personal favour to anyone, and without besmirching ourselves with any
concession to avarice. What could we have got out of a common soldier
anyway? But with the most honourable intentions, how much harm

F

were we not able to inflict on an accused man out of sheer ignorance!'

The researches of G. P. Makogonenko into the Russian military archives have brought to light a whole series of verdicts confirmed or modified by Radishchev while on the staff of the Finland Division under General Bruce. Many of them relate to deserters, who presented a special problem. Cases of desertion by serf recruits as a result of ill-treatment by their officers were frequent, one case on Radishchev's files involving, for instance, a grenadier mercilessly flogged by a captain whose knapsack (with his shirts inside) had fallen off a cart over which the grenadier was standing guard. As Russian officers could apparently beat their soldiers whenever they felt inclined, such cases were not uncommon. One instance, in which this licence was abused to the point of deliberate murder, is worth quoting for the light it throws on eighteenth-century military mentality. In August 1773, Radishchev received from the War Office an *ukaz* giving its verdict in the case of a certain Colonel Stahl von Holstein, an officer of German origins in the Russian service:

'The colonel, being at Pskov for the enrolment of recruits, after completing this assignment proceeded to Riga, taking with him the soldiers Ivan Vakhonin and Trofim Dorokhin of the First Battalion, and the recruit Alexis Fadeev, who acted as coachman to the colonel's carriage. . . . While passing over a pond by a mill on March 26 of the current year, owing to the weakness of the ice, the colonel himself whipped up the horses so as to pass over quicker. On reaching the far side, the bank, as the soldiers testify, turned out to be precipitous, and on reaching it, the vehicle tipped over underneath the colonel. The latter was sitting on the coachman's seat and toppled off it, while the recruit was hurled off the box; all three soldiers picked up the carriage immediately, but the colonel ordered the recruit Fadeev to be beaten with a stick, as thick as a finger or even larger in diameter. The soldier Vakhonin accordingly beat him, and the recruit in question, holding his arms aloft, begged for mercy, so that the blows fell on his hands as well. When the stick broke over the recruit, the colonel told them to beat him with another one, whereupon the recruit fell on to the ground. However, he went on striking him lying down until he stopped crying, after which the colonel ordered the recruit to get up and put the carriage in order; but owing to fright and the beating, he was unable to do anything. Then the colonel got angry with him and told them to cut some rods, while the colonel struck the recruit two or three times on the shoulders with a thin cane. When the rods were brought the colonel had him stripped and flogged with the rods, in compliance with which command the soldiers flogged him severely, taking five turns at it each.

These beatings were witnessed by the local miller with his wife and others, who begged him, the colonel, to have mercy. However he refused to listen and went on urging: "Beat harder!" And when the recruit no longer made any sound, the colonel told them to stop beating him, but the recruit died on the spot within an hour.'

For this sickening display of sadism, the colonel was let off with a church penance and cashiering from the army.

As documents like this piled up on his desk, Radishchev must have groaned, and wondered if all his personal idealism would ever make any impression against such a dead weight of brutishness and cruelty.

Radishchev's duties also included examining candidates applying for the post of regimental procurator, as well as supervising the transit of convoys of recruits assigned to the Finland Division and paying their travelling expenses to the front. This task gave him insight into the press-gang system often employed to fill the quota of serf recruits levied on every village or estate. This is a theme on which Radishchev was to discourse with emotion in the *Journey from St Petersburg to Moscow*, but he was already concerned about it at this period in his career. A recently discovered memorandum drafted by Radishchev, entitled 'Concerning abuses during recruitment levies', contains observations like the following: 'In the enrolment of recruits who have been purchased [to act as substitutes]; in the conscription of free foreign citizens and others; in forcible recruitment from among the State peasantry; in the enrolment of drunkards, vagrants, idlers useless in their own trade—what a mass of opportunities for abuse!'[1]

The burden of recruiting levies undoubtedly played a part in provoking the Pugachev uprising, which broke out in 1773. It was then that Catherine's retrograde social policy came home to roost. The early years of her reign were, as already noted, marked by a series of measures in favour of the landed aristocracy and rural gentry on whom she depended for running the country and maintaining her personal power. The downtrodden state of the serfs became a frequent topic for comment by foreign travellers, who described with surprise and pity the wretched ignorance of the common people and the filthy squalor of their hovels. An English visitor, the Reverend William Coxe of Cambridge, deplored the abject state in which the masters kept their serfs, which 'renders them humble, cringing, obstinate, careless, and in a manner insensible'. 'We have every reason,' declared Coxe, 'to conclude that the generality of boors must still be cruelly oppressed.'[2] A Frenchman,

[1] Radishchev, *Polnoe sobranie sochineny*, III, 47–8.
[2] William Coxe, *Travels into Poland, Russia, Sweden and Denmark*, London, 1784, I, 436–9, and II, 114–15.

C. F. P. Masson, who spent some years in Russia, remarked in his memoirs that the Russian peasantry, brutalized by centuries of servitude, detested work, because they had never known what it was to work for their own advantage. 'They have not yet even grasped the idea of private property: their fields, their possessions, their wives, their children, their very bodies, belong to a master who can and does dispose of them at will. They have no interest in anything, because they possess nothing.' In spite of all this, the Russian peasant was recognized as being cheerful, kindhearted, gay, honest and brave. 'He possesses in short all those inherent virtues which recall to us the manners of patriarchal times, and his vices are but those of servitude itself.'[1]

This is not the place to embark on a detailed account of the economic and social reasons for the impoverishment of the peasantry under Catherine the Great—the increase in the number of days of *barshchina* or forced labour on the landlord's own fields, the rise in the rate of *obrok* (the commutation payment levied on serfs who went away to work elsewhere than on the lord's estate), the lack of initiative in improving methods of agriculture, the low level of capital investment, and the higher standard of living demanded by the new upper classes. The solid researches of Semevsky in Russia, of Engelmann in Germany, and, more recently, of G. T. Robinson of Columbia University in America, provide abundant documentary evidence of this deterioration in the status and standard of living of the Russian masses throughout Catherine's reign.[2] The promise held out to the peasants in the summoning of the great Moscow assembly of 1767 was not fulfilled, and it was not long now before the inevitable explosion took place.

Soon after Radishchev had joined General Bruce's staff, this smouldering discontent of the common people burst into flame in the most terrible *Jacquerie* witnessed in Russia since the uprising of Stenka Razin in 1670. The revolt originated in a series of disputes between the central Government and the Ural or Yaik Cossacks over such matters as fishing rights and exemption from military service, and was exacerbated by the repressive policy pursued by the Russian authorities against local Turco-Tatar tribes such as the Bashkirs and the Kalmucks. Disorders had already broken out when early in 1773 a born leader appeared on the scene in the person of Emelyan Pugachev, a Don

[1] C. F. P. Masson, *Mémoires secrets sur la Russie*, Amsterdam and Paris, 1800–2, II, 8–9, 47.

[2] V. I. Semevsky, *Krest'yane v tsarstvovanie Imperatritsy Ekateriny II* ('The peasants in the reign of Catherine II'), St Petersburg, 1901–3; J. Engelmann, *Die Leibeigenschaft in Russland*, Leipzig, 1884; Geroid T. Robinson, *Rural Russia under the Old Régime. A History of the Landlord-Peasant World and a Prologue to the Peasant Revolution of 1917*. Second printing. New York, 1949. See also Klyuchevsky, *A History of Russia*, V, 60–109.

Cossack who had served in the Russian army and been flogged more than once for indiscipline. While leading a vagrant existence, Pugachev was befriended by some monks who, discontented at Catherine's anti-clerical policy, suggested that Pugachev should give himself out to be the Tsar Peter III, miraculously delivered from the fate planned for him by the Empress and her lovers, and returned now to claim his own. Pugachev readily agreed to this plan, and, in his new character as Tsar of All the Russias, proclaimed his intention to abolish serfdom (a project with which Peter III had long been credited by the common people), partition landed estates among the peasantry, and establish universal freedom of religion.

By the middle of 1773, Pugachev was strong enough to launch his campaign in real earnest, taking several forts and besieging Orenburg. Preoccupied as she was with Turkish and Polish affairs, Catherine tried at first to laugh the uprising off, poking fun in her letters to Grimm and Voltaire at the 'Marquis Pugachev' and his ragged followers. But this was no laughing matter. The countryside was swiftly turning into an inferno. Landlords' mansions were set alight, the masters and their families slaughtered, and towns and factories plundered. The *muzhiks* everywhere were responding eagerly to the call to rebellion. Every day lost by the Government was a month's gain for Pugachev. The first general sent against him by Catherine proved incompetent. Guerrilla warfare, lack of supplies, ignorance of local geography and the sullen hostility of the peasant masses all hampered the imperial forces. As Pushkin wrote in his account of the Pugachev rising, 'All the "black people" [i.e. the common folk] were on Pugachev's side. . . . The nobility alone was openly on the side of the Government. . . . Examining the measures taken by Pugachev and his associates, one must admit that the insurgents adopted the course which was most reliable and effective to achieve their goal. The Government for its part acted weakly, slowly, mistakenly.' As the British Ambassador reported to his Court, discontent was not confined to the immediate theatre of revolt: disaffection was universal and growing daily in force.

By December 1773, Pugachev had fifteen thousand men and over eighty guns. The price set upon his head rose from 500 to 28,000 roubles. His name dominated every conversation in St Petersburg and Moscow, which were crowded with panic-stricken squires fleeing from the countryside. Radishchev had many anxious moments, thinking of his own family down in Ablyazovo, near Saratov, one of the main centres of the rising. Fortunately, as we know, his father Nicholas Radishchev was a humane master to his serfs, who kept the family hidden until danger was past. Elsewhere, hardly a mansion was left standing and scarcely a landlord or official spared; in those areas of south-eastern Russia dominated by Pugachev and his marauding bands, thousands of acres of forest lay smouldering, blanketing the country with smoke for miles around. The great city of Kazan fell to the rebels, and the merchants' quarter was gutted by fire.

In his uncouth way, Pugachev set about forming a regular 'shadow government'. In his capacity as the 'resuscitated' Tsar Peter III, he appointed sundry of his ragged followers to be ministers, even giving them the names of Panin, Orlov and so on, after the members of Catherine's own Government. A number of strongly worded *ukazes* formulated the insurgent leader's social policy. The landowners were declared pernicious to society, ruinous to the peasantry and traitors to the Empire. The serfs were exhorted to treat their masters just like the latter, who were persons devoid of all Christian feelings, treated their peasants. Following the extermination of the squirearchy, Pugachev promised that 'everyone shall enjoy the feeling of quietness, a tranquil life, which will last for all time'. The self-styled Tsar granted the serfs freedom and liberty: no more recruiting levies, no more taxes, peasant ownership of the land, unrestricted access to meadow lands, fishing rights, use of woods and timber, and general deliverance from the 'imposts and burdens previously imposed on the peasants and entire nation by the villainous gentry and corrupt city judges'.

The peace treaty with Turkey, signed at Küchük-Kainarji in July 1774, set free the main forces of the Russian army to crush the movement once for all. A famine on the Volga damped the insurgents' enthusiasm and the peasants' sympathy with their cause. After several defeats at the hands of Russian regular troops, a sense of doubt and fear demoralized the rebel bands. Pugachev's closest associates were either captured, or began to desert him. Finally, the great Suvorov himself was sent in pursuit of the Cossack leader, who tried to beat a retreat towards the Urals. In the end, the defeated pretender was betrayed for a handsome reward by one of his last supporters. Pugachev was brought in an iron cage to Moscow, where he was executed in January 1775.

The bankruptcy of Catherine's peasant policy had been demonstrated. The memory of Pugachev lived on among the peasantry, and remained a nightmare vision in the heads of the gentry. Unfortunately for Russia's destiny, the Empress and the landed aristocracy seemed as incapable as the Bourbons either of learning or of forgetting anything. To a sovereign and an upper layer of society nourished on the doctrines of the Social Contract and the 'Rights of Man', it should have been clear that to eliminate Pugachev without removing the country's basic social disorder, serfdom, would merely postpone the day of reckoning. Deep down in her heart, Catherine herself sensed this quite clearly. Soon after Pugachev was executed, she wrote to the Minister of Justice concerning the peasant question, 'If we do not consent to diminish cruelty and to moderate a situation which is intolerable to the human race, then sooner or later they will take this step themselves'—that is to say, the serfs would resort to revolution to improve their unbearable conditions. In the event, nothing was done. Vested interests were too strong, official inertia was too great. It was reserved for Radishchev in his *Journey from St Petersburg to Moscow* to wave the battleaxe of peasant revolt before the noses of the landed gentry, and to make a lone prophecy of the course of events which led up to the Russian Revolution of 1917. Although Radishchev affected to regard Pugachev as nothing but a 'crude pretender', he made it abundantly clear that if the root causes of peasant misery were not removed, then some future cataclysm, even more terrible in its impact, would inevitably result 'from the very burden of slavery itself'.

It should not be supposed that preoccupation with social problems prevented the young and brilliant procurator from making his mark on St Petersburg society. In 1774, Radishchev was elected a member of the exclusive English Club, an institution so often mentioned in memoirs and novels relating to that epoch. Later, the St Petersburg English Club, like some of its prototypes around St James's Street, was to become the closed preserve of important officials and testy old Generals. At this time, however, it was still a favourite resort of smart young men of the capital, who met there to dine, play cards or billiards, and read the latest newspapers and gazettes from Western Europe. While most of the members belonged to the middling class of army officers and serving nobility, the list of Radishchev's fellow clubmen included also such eminent names as Yusupov, Meshchersky and Odoevsky.

The main event of these months was Radishchev's courtship and marriage. We have more than once had occasion to mention Andrey Rubanovsky, Radishchev's old comrade at Leipzig University. Andrey had an elder brother, Vasily, a middle-aged family man serving in the bureau of the Imperial Court with the rank of State Councillor. Vasily, his second wife, and three daughters lived in a house of their own on the *Gryaznaya Ulitsa* ('Dirty Street'), later the Nikolaevskaya, and now Marat Street. The two younger daughters, Liza and Dasha, were still at the Smol'ny Institute for Young Ladies, but the eldest, Anna, was already a girl of marriageable age, of attractive features and pleasant ways. Andrey introduced Radishchev to his brother soon after the students' return from Germany, and the young procurator, captivated by Anna's charm, soon found himself a frequent visitor to the Rubanovsky household. According to family tradition, Radishchev first encountered opposition from Anna's stepmother, who entertained an inflated idea of the family's grandeur and her stepdaughter's matrimonial prospects, and hoped that Anna might wed some young prince or count about the Court. Radishchev, as one of his sons records, was not looking for a wealthy heiress to be his bride: 'His wife, the daughter of a member of the Court Bureau, was not rich, but she possessed every quality that could make for a good man's happiness.' The young pair's mutual affection finally broke down parental resistance, and Radishchev was accepted as Anna's husband-to-be. Towards the end of 1774, the Imperial Court and various Government departments moved for some months to Moscow in connection with the celebrations marking the peace treaty with Turkey and the suppression of Pugachev's revolt. Bruce and his staff accompanied the Empress's party, and it was in Moscow that Alexander Radishchev and Anna Rubanovsky were married in the early spring of 1775.

Nowadays, a young man's first thought on contemplating marriage is to find himself a good job, or, if he has one already, to make sure of his security of tenure and future prospects. It is therefore somewhat surprising to find Radishchev submitting his resignation from the post of divisional procurator, and leaving Government service altogether. On March 20, 1775, the War Office accepted his resignation from army service, at the same time granting him the next rank above that of captain (his rank hitherto)—namely that of Second-Major, retired.

It may be that Radishchev's reason for taking this step was the same as that of the honest Krest'yankin, a character who features in the chapter 'Zaytsovo' of *A Journey from St Petersburg to Moscow*. When taking up a post in the Russian criminal justice department, Krest'yankin believed that there was open to him, as he put it, a broad field for the satisfaction of his dearest aspiration—the pursuit of mercy and the suppression of 'the sceptre of cruelty which so often weighs down the shoulders of innocence'. However, the idealistic official's zeal soon 'turned to gall and worm-wood'. On referring to the law books, says Krest'yankin, 'I found therein instead of humanity a savagery which had its origin not in the nature of law itself, but in its obsolete approach. The lack of proportion between punishment and crime often wrung tears from my eyes.' It is probable, therefore, that the sensitive Radishchev, with his ideas about human dignity and the 'Rights of Man', felt as disgusted as did his fictional character Krest'yankin with a job which often involved ordering floggings and mutilations, or sending mutinous recruits off to Siberia.

Like many young couples, Radishchev and his bride dreamt of an idyllic life in some sylvan nook, far from the vices and distractions of the big city. However, discussions with his parents soon cured Radishchev of any notion that the family fortunes would permit him the leisured life of a country squire. Nicholas Radishchev, it is true, possessed over three thousand serfs; but he also had eleven children to provide for—younger sons still to educate, daughters to marry off with an appropriate dowry. In addition, the Radishchev estates down at Ablyazovo had been ravaged by Pugachev's marauding bands, as well as being in part mortgaged. As eldest son, Radishchev's patrimony was the original family domain at Nemtsovo, in the Malo-Yaroslavets district not far from Moscow. But Nemtsovo counted only about three hundred peasants, and it soon became clear that in throwing up his Government post Radishchev had entertained all too rosy a picture of his immediate financial prospects.

A year after Alexander and Anna were married, their first son was born; he was christened Vasily, after his Rubanovsky grandfather. Another year passed and a second son came into the world; this time, they called him Nicholas, after grandfather Radishchev.

The arrival of a family, with all its attendant joys, also posed financial problems. For the first year or two of their life, Alexander and Anna had been living contentedly in Moscow with various relatives. But this was no permanent solution, and Radishchev now became impatient to stand on his own feet and provide for the needs of his wife and children. Luckily, his reputation was good, and his friends in St Petersburg had not forgotten him. In December 1777, an *ukaz* of the Senate announced Radishchev's appointment to the post of Ministerial Assessor in the Board of Trade, and by the New Year of 1778 Alexander and Anna with the babies were settled in St Petersburg with a home of their own.

CHAPTER 5

At the Receipt of Custom

⟿⟿⟨⟨⟵⟵

*A New Protector – The Expansion of Russia – Catherine in Her Hey-
day – Potemkin the Enigmatic – Catherine Viewed by Pushkin –
Seditious Reading – The Bronze Horseman – Family Sorrow*

In the Imperial College of Commerce (or Board of Trade, as we should
term it nowadays), Radishchev's superior was the young Count Alexander Vorontsov, who had been appointed the College's President four
years previously at the early age of thirty-two.

Though not of ancient lineage, the Vorontsovs were one of the most
distinguished families of career nobility in eighteenth- and nineteenth-
century Russia. They first emerged into prominence in the troublous
times that followed the death of Empress Anna in 1740, when they
gave their support to Peter the Great's daughter, the Princess Elizabeth.
For services to the winning side, Alexander Vorontsov's father Roman
became an imperial chamberlain or *Kammerherr* and a senator; Roman's
brother Michael rose to be Chancellor of Russia.

Count Roman's children were all in some way remarkable. Alexander
Vorontsov, Radishchev's protector, was also to become Chancellor of
Russia under Tsar Alexander I; Simon Vorontsov, for many years
Russian Ambassador at the Court of St James, was a friend and admirer
of the younger Pitt, and so well known in England that a London street
—Woronzow Road, near Regent's Park—was named after him; Eliza-
beth Vorontsov, though described as a plain and stupid girl, was the
mistress of Tsar Peter III. At that very same time, in 1762, her sister,
Princess Dashkov, was conspiring with Peter's estranged consort, the
future Catherine II, to procure that monarch's downfall. This Princess
Dashkov was a redoubtable blue-stocking; she later became Director
of the Imperial Academy of Sciences and President of the Russian
Academy founded by Catherine the Great to encourage the study of
Russian language, history and literature. She lived for some years in
Edinburgh while her son was being educated at the University there,

and had a truly Scottish attitude to money matters, combined with an obstinate temperament which led to quarrels between her and the Empress; under Paul I, she was subjected to rigorous banishment. In a later age, Simon Vorontsov's son Michael, a hero of the Napoleonic wars, was Viceroy of the Caucasus shortly before the Crimean War; another member of the family, Count Vorontsov-Dashkov, also governed the Caucasus as Viceroy not long before the Russian Revolution of 1917.

As a young man, Alexander Vorontsov spent some time in France, at the officers' academy of the *Chevaux légers* at Versailles. He early entered the Russian diplomatic service, and was Minister in London when hardly more than twenty years of age. He was one of those sophisticated grandees so common in the Courts of Europe during the eighteenth century, tenacious in safeguarding their own status and privileges, and yet increasingly disillusioned with the autocratic system, with its inefficiency and rampant favouritism, and secretly attracted to the liberal ideas spread by the precursors of the French Revolution. A rich bachelor of independent character, he disdained to pay homage to the Empress's reigning favourites and so was usually under a faint cloud of suspicion, as being a 'superior person' not quite in sympathy with prevailing trends in public affairs. He was a confirmed misogynist, and had no time for boudoir politics. In later life, he enjoyed a great reputation as a far-sighted statesman and a partisan of alliance with Great Britain. In a despatch in the Public Record Office, we find the British Minister to St Petersburg under Alexander I writing in 1802: 'If however His Imperial Majesty should appoint Count Alexander Woronzow to the Post of Great Chancellor of the Russian Empire, I shall have to congratulate Your Lordship on the solid advantages which must result to publick affairs, from the great talents, wisdom and experience with which that Gentleman would fill so honourable and exalted a station.'[1]

In commercial policy, Vorontsov was an avowed protectionist, and an advocate of balanced budgets and sound, orthodox finance, so un-fashionable in the inflationary era of Catherine the Great. The French Envoy, Ségur, who knew him well, described him as 'able, but thrifty and self-opinionated—austere and opposed to luxury; he would have had the Russians drink nothing but hydromel, and dress themselves exclusively in home-produced fabrics.'[2]

Radishchev soon attracted the personal notice of his distinguished superior. The Government Colleges or departments of eighteenth-

---

[1] British Foreign Office archives, Public Record Office, London: *Russia*, F.O. 65/51. B. Garlike to Lord Hawkesbury, No. 8 of September 19, 1802.

[2] Comte Louis-Philippe de Ségur, *Mémoires*, in *Oeuvres*, Paris, 1824, II, 396.

century Russia operated on the principle of collective responsibility which Peter the Great had imported from Sweden. All decisions were approved and signed, not only by the President, the Vice-President and the councillors, but also by the relatively junior assessors, of whom Radishchev was one. It so happened that soon after Radishchev's appointment, some officials concerned with the grading and valuing of hemp were accused of malpractice. Vorontsov and the higher officers of the department were for punishing the individuals concerned. Radishchev, who had made a detailed study of the matter, declared them to be innocent of the charges brought against them, and refused to sign the verdict on the case. Vorontsov demanded to see this obstinate novice on his staff, whom he imagined to have some private interest in the matter. Radishchev, however, so impressed his chief with his clear-cut arguments that the enquiry was reopened, and the officials acquitted of the accusations made against them.

From this time onwards, Vorontsov never faltered in his kindness towards Radishchev. In 1780, when old Senator Roman Vorontsov was going on a tour of the south-eastern provinces of Russia where the Radishchev estate of Ablyazovo and some of the Vorontsov property were situated, he received a note from his son: 'Dear Sir and Father! On your passage through the Governorate of Penza, should you see there our neighbour Nicholas Afanasievich Radishchev, I beg you not to omit to extend your favour to him. I am very fond of his son. . . . Nicholas Afanasievich may be glad to have such a son.' Having no family of his own, Alexander Vorontsov treated Radishchev with almost avuncular affection.

In that same year, Radishchev was appointed deputy to the director of the St Petersburg Customs House, the elderly State Councillor Dahl, who was happy to leave the day to day running of that important office to his young and efficient lieutenant. At the same time, Radishchev retained his links with the Board of Trade, to whose President he submitted reports direct. As well as containing data on Russia's foreign commerce, these deal with the usual events in a customs official's life: seizure of contraband, the absconding of a dishonest employee, the burning down of a warehouse and so on. Radishchev's personal friendship with Vorontsov is reflected in the informal, almost intimate tone of certain of these reports, which are more like private letters than official documents. In due course Radishchev was awarded the order of St Vladimir, 4th Class, and the rank of Ministerial Councillor; early in 1790, he was promoted to succeed Dahl as head of the St Petersburg Customs administration.

During the twelve years Radishchev served under Vorontsov, the ports of St Petersburg and Kronstadt gained increasing importance as centres of international trade. This was the period when Russia's international prestige reached its somewhat precarious apogée, not only as a result of Catherine's own statesmanship, but also through the prodigious personality of the greatest of her favourites, Gregory Potemkin.

To the Orlov brothers, Gregory the lover and counsellor, Alexis and Fedor, the men of action, belonged the first decade of Catherine's reign. In 1772, Gregory Orlov fell into disgrace because of his liaison with Princess Golitsyn, and Catherine took on as her favourite the handsome but boring Vasilchikov. But Catherine—and this was one of her great political talents—always required a partner rather than a mere paramour, and the insignificant Vasilchikov was soon eclipsed. At this juncture Potemkin came into his own.

One of the most intriguing and bizarre personalities in Russian history, Potemkin was a poor gentleman from Smolensk who played a modest part in Catherine's *coup d'état* of 1762, and later distinguished himself in Marshal Rumyantsev's campaign against the Turks on the Danube. While at Court he gained a footing in Catherine's entourage, and soon captivated her by his ingenious mind and caustic, earthy sense of humour. He was a man of massive stature, one-eyed and far from handsome. His intimate relations with the Empress lasted hardly two years; but until his death, while she consoled herself with a procession of handsome ninnies, handsomely paid for caressing her shrivelled charms, there passed between her and Potemkin a flow of letters in which affectionate endearments alternated with serious dissertations on affairs of State. Catherine had great faith in his resourceful energy and drive, and found his turbulent, moody character a congenial foil to her own calculating Germanic temperament.

Psychologically, Potemkin presents a curious case. Extravagant and lavish to a fault, he would indulge in fantastic excesses of sexual or alcoholic indulgence or amazing feats of physical endurance, only to relapse for weeks on end into a morbid torpor, when he would lounge about his apartments in a filthy old dressing gown and refuse to see or speak to anyone. Of recent years, it has become fashionable to discount the many anecdotes that circulated during and after Potemkin's lifetime, illustrating his wayward and often outrageous conduct; however, these have at least the merit of showing the impression he made on the Russian public of his day and on foreigners who knew him personally. A typical story, retailed by Pushkin, relates to one of Potemkin's morose phases, when his staff despaired of bringing him to sign some important State papers. A young official called Petushkov ('Cockerel') cheerfully volunteered to secure the great man's signature and boldly entered Potemkin's sanctum, where the favourite sat barefoot, his hair uncombed, biting his nails and apparently sunk in thought. Silently the prince stretched out a hand for the papers and appended a signature to them one by one. 'Signed!' exclaimed Petushkov jubilantly as he emerged with the documents into the antechamber. Then someone had a look. What a surprise! Instead of Potemkin's signature, at the foot of every page: 'Cockerel, cockerel, cockerel. . . .'

Potemkin was no respecter of persons. Many a gilded magnate, many a renowned field-marshal had to endure his snubs. He was one of the few people in Russia to be on familiar terms with the sinister S. I. Sheshkovsky, head of Catherine's dreaded Secret Chancellery. 'Now then, Stephen Ivanovich,' Potemkin would say to him, 'how is the knouting and bashing getting on?'—To which the inquisitor would answer with a low bow: 'Quite nicely, thank you, Your Serene Highness.'

Haughty towards the grandees of Catherine's Court, in his dealings with ordinary folk Potemkin could be kindness itself. It is told of him that once he woke up in the middle of the night and rang for an attendant. No one answered. Potemkin jumped out of bed, opened his door and caught sight of his orderly officer asleep in an armchair. To avoid waking him, Potemkin took off his slippers, and tiptoed through the hall in his bare feet. On another occasion, some young man about the Court offended a certain Prince B., who threatened to denounce him to the Empress. Hearing of this, Potemkin one day called the young man to the table where he was playing cards in Prince B.'s company.— 'Tell me, brother,' said Potemkin, holding up his cards, 'how am I to play this hand?' The young man, tipped off beforehand, retorted: 'What do I care, Your Serene Highness? Just play them as best you can.' 'Heavens above,' said Potemkin in mock dismay, 'a fellow cannot say a word to you without your going off the deep end!' (Hearing this familiar exchange, Prince B. decided it would be wise to cancel his complaint.)

Potemkin was notorious for his extravagance, to which Radishchev makes caustic allusions in the *Journey from St Petersburg to Moscow*. He treated the Imperial Treasury as his private purse. He once sent an adjutant there with orders to draw out a huge sum of money. The cashiers demanded written authority. Informed of this, Potemkin scribbled on a scrap of paper: 'Fork out, you scum!' The money was promptly forthcoming. According to a contemporary observer, Masson, author of the *Mémoires secrets sur la Russie*, Potemkin had in his suite a senior official called Bauer, who was regularly employed as a courier to travel to remote parts of Russia and even to countries abroad in search of exotic dainties for the prince's table or dancers for his amusement. Radishchev makes a direct reference to this in the chapter 'Spasskaya Polest'' of the *Journey from St Petersburg to Moscow*, where he introduces a courier who has won high promotion by his skill in producing succulent oysters for the Great Man's dinner table.

In 1774, at the conclusion of her first war with Turkey, Catherine was a mature woman of forty-five. The first dozen years of her reign had been a period of stress and trial, from which she had emerged triumphant in a way which amazed Europe, and must have exceeded her fondest hopes. Pugachev and sundry other pretenders liquidated, large tracts of Poland annexed, the Turks tamed, and Russia recognized as protector of all Orthodox Christians in the Ottoman Empire, herself hailed by brilliant French writers as the Minerva, the Semiramis of the North—this was no mean record for a little princess from Anhalt-Zerbst.

Another might have been tempted to relax and enjoy what had already been gained. Not so Catherine. To the day of her death, her restless energy drove her on towards fresh, ambitious adventures in international politics, in the same way that her sexual appetites found their outlet in fresh amorous affairs. Not content to be Mistress of All the Russias, she must need set herself up as arbitrator of the destinies of all Europe. The English Envoy, Sir James Harris, was only expressing a commonly held opinion when he commented in 1778 that 'the incredible vanity of the Sovereign gets the better of her fine parts; she is willing to give credit to any assertion that she supposes to be in consequence of her own greatness and power'.[1]

The role of Potemkin in the events of Catherine's later years continues to arouse keen discussion among historians. Was he the initiator of those grandiose schemes of expansion and world domination which led to such uneven results, or simply the willing executant of his mistress's behests? No doubt he filled both these roles. Catherine raised him from insignificance, for she saw in him her man of the hour. Once established in favour, Potemkin cajoled, coerced and influenced his sovereign to a marked degree. So long as his ambitions coincided with her own, all was well. And yet, there was never any doubt in whose hands ultimate authority lay. Finally came the inevitable show-down. In 1791 the mediocre, arrogant Zubov won his way to favour, and Potemkin, hastening to St Petersburg to protest, met with rebuff. After that, there was nothing for him to do but go away to die on the plain of Jassy.

But in 1777, when Radishchev returned to St Petersburg to join the Board of Trade, this crisis lay far ahead in the future, and Potemkin and his Empress were engaged in unison on their far-reaching plans of imperial dominion. The great scheme at the Russian Court in those days

[1] *Diaries and Correspondence of the 1st Earl of Malmesbury*, London, 1844, I, 181.

was the 'Greek Project', involving the total expulsion of Turkey from Europe and the setting up of a Greek Empire in Constantinople under Russian tutelage. One of Catherine's grandsons was christened Constantine, in openly declared anticipation of his one day occupying the throne of Constantine the Great. In 1780 took place the interview between Catherine and the Austrian Emperor Joseph II at Moghilev; Austria was to be rewarded for her co-operation by the acquisition of Serbia, Bosnia and Herzegovina. Even the Persians were to be brought in: in return for granting free passage to Russian troops invading Anatolia and Mesopotamia, Persia would receive large slices of Kurdistan.

As should have been foreseen, these undertakings alarmed public opinion abroad. The French Foreign Minister, Vergennes, intent on 'preventing the alarming revolution menacing the Ottoman Empire', combined with Frederick the Great to dissuade Joseph of Austria from sharing in the proposed partition. Nor were Russia's long-term interests much served by Catherine's ostentatious declaration of 'armed neutrality' in 1780, directed against Great Britain's domination of the high seas, and aimed at protecting the maritime commerce of neutral States in times of war. London naturally regarded this as a hostile act, and Anglo-Russian relations were subjected to unnecessary strain.

Behind this smoke-screen of diplomatic activity, Catherine and Potemkin proceeded apace with the consolidation of gains already won. Having taken from the Turks the outlets of the Dnieper and the Bug rivers, as well as Kerch and the Sea of Azov, the Russians proceeded in 1783 to annex the Crimea, to the Turks' great indignation. Further eastwards, Catherine established a protectorate over the Christian Kingdom of Eastern Georgia, as well as embarking on a sanguinary offensive against the Muslim tribesmen of Daghestan in the Caucasus. On the Caspian, Count Voinovich with his flotilla attempted unsuccessfully to set up a Russian trading colony on Persian soil.

As Viceroy of the new Black Sea provinces, Potemkin displayed boundless resource and ingenuity in colonizing vast areas till then sparsely inhabited by a few Tatar nomads with their flocks and herds. Kherson and Ekaterinoslav (now Dnepropetrovsk), the latter town named after the Empress, were founded in 1778, Sevastopol in the Crimea in 1783. Often propaganda outstripped achievement, as in Potemkin's stage management of Catherine's famous procession through the Taurida, with the pasteboard villages and their joyous, specially imported inhabitants. However, his title of Prince Potemkin-Tavrichesky was by no means undeserved.

The Vorontsovs, in common with other aristocratic families, disliked the upstart Potemkin. As President of the Board of Trade, Count Alexander was painfully aware of the price which Russia had to pay for the favourite's grandiose enterprises, which resulted in a chronic balance of payments crisis and running inflation. From London, Simon Vorontsov sent reports of the unfavourable effect which the 'armed neutrality' declaration and Russian imperialism in the Balkans and Near East were having on English public opinion. Radishchev's intimacy with the Vorontsovs helped to confirm him in his critical attitude towards Potemkin's policies. The fate which befell him as a result of his book, *A Journey from St Petersburg to Moscow*, was, as we shall see, partly due to the fact that he could plausibly be regarded as a mouthpiece of an important faction hostile to the reigning favourite.

Despite the alarums of foreign wars, Catherine found time to carry through a number of important administrative measures. In 1775, she published the 'Edict on Provinces', whereby Russia was re-divided into fifty governorates or provinces. A regular system of provincial administration was set up, depending on the central Government in St Petersburg. Ten years later, in 1785, the concessions already made to the gentry class were consolidated and supplemented by the 'Charter granted to the Nobility', whereby the squirearchy were confirmed in their prerogatives and encouraged to hold regular provincial assemblies. In addition, the 'Charter granted to the Towns' accorded the urban bourgeois class certain encouragements and safeguards. Thus was shaped the provincial administration of the *gorodnichy* or mayor, with his attendant Bobchinskies and Dobchinskies, which Gogol was to portray with such hilarity in his comedy, *The Government Inspector*.

Despite the cruelties which marred the epoch of Catherine the Great, there is no denying the change in Russian society which took place between 1762 and 1796. New attitudes, manners, habits of thought and dress kept seeping in from Western Europe. No longer was it thought seemly in the best circles to spit on the floor in public, pick lice from the scalp, eat with one's fingers, or beat one's wife into a jelly. Under the lead of the Empress, drama, music, art and architecture made great strides. Catherine was a playwright and a literary satirist of distinction. Her mania for building created many splendid edifices in and around St Petersburg, which are to this day the pride of the Russian people, although their cost crippled the treasury and hampered long overdue urban development in the provinces. She encouraged foreign scholars and scientists to accept posts at the Imperial Academy of Sciences and at Moscow University. While Russia could not replace the great Lomonosov, who died in 1765, yet mathematics, physics, geography and geology, history and philology all made great progress. With un-

G

stinting, if tiresomely paternalistic Government support, the great Russian academic school of the nineteenth century was able to build on a firm tradition of scholarly achievement.

Useful foundations such as the College of Medicine (1763), the Free Economic Society (1765) and the School of Mines (1774) made their contribution to the improvement of professional standards and physical conditions generally. The 'Statute on Popular Schools within the Russian Empire' of 1786 laid the basis for a system of elementary education. In 1782, there had been only eight State Middle Schools in the whole of Russia, with a total enrolment of 518 pupils, and teaching staffs totalling 26. In 1796, there were already 316 such establishments, extending into remote Siberia, and catering for 17,341 pupils with a staff of 744 teachers.

Side by side with this went a spectacular increase in the number of books printed and sold in Russia, disregarding the substantial flow from France and Germany. In 1762, 95 titles were published, including 43 in the field of belles-lettres, 7 novels and 5 periodicals. Through the energy of the Freemason publicist and journalist N. I. Novikov and his Typographical Company, these figures were raised by 1788 to a total of 439 titles, including 248 in the belles-lettres category, 88 novels, and 19 periodicals. The increased severity of the censorship which resulted from the outbreak of the French Revolution culminated in Novikov's arrest and the break-up of his company. Only 256 titles were published in 1796, and 165 in 1797, the first year of the reign of Paul I.

The progress of education in Russia, however, could produce but limited effect on a society where some nine-tenths of the population remained in servitude. There was little incentive for self-improvement where a serf, by learning some art or science, simply raised his market value for the benefit of his owner. In the West, this was the age of the industrious apprentice, a class which often managed to rise by 'self-help' to affluence and distinction. Very different was the position in Russia. We read for instance of one Nicholas Smirnov, arrested in 1785 on charges of attempting to flee the country with a false passport to complete his education abroad, with a view to qualifying as an architect and entering Russian Government service. This Smirnov's father, though a serf, was steward to the Golitsyn family and a man of substance; he had employed a private tutor to teach his son French and Italian. Sentenced to be knouted, have his nostrils torn off and be sent to hard labour, young Smirnov was later reprieved by the Empress and despatched as a private soldier to Siberia, for which 'unspeakable act of mercy' Smirnov expressed his most humble thanks. With such deterrents affecting the vast majority of the population, it is hardly surprising that Tsarist Russia laboured under a constant lack of trained minds and skilled manpower.

The aggravation of serfdom during this period had a distinctly retarding effect on the Russian national economy, both agricultural and industrial. In Western Europe, these years saw the beginnings of the Industrial Revolution and the opening of a golden age for the bourgeois entrepreneur, to whose manufactures depressed agricultural labourers were free to flock in their thousands. In Russia, the supply of free labour for industry was infinitesimal, only rising as late as 1825 to the modest figure of 210,000 out of the total population. Many factories, including the great Demidov metallurgical works in the Urals, were operated largely on a forced labour or 'possessional' basis, being manned by serfs attached to the factories in the same way that their fellows were attached to the glebe. Other enterprises were operated by peasants released by their owners for a certain season of the year in return for a cash commutation payment or *obrok*, while yet others, including many small wool and linen mills, were operated by landed proprietors on a manorial basis.

The industrial policy of Peter the Great had depended to a great extent on the creation of State-operated industries, combined with the granting of monopolies and concessions. Catherine the Great, on the other hand, declared in a decree of 1767 that she was in favour of the freedom of trade and industry. A low cost of living, she affirmed, was achieved through a large number of competing sellers and an unimpeded increase of goods on the market. The manifesto of 1775 proclaimed the freedom of industry and trade throughout Russia, permitting everybody and anybody (serfs naturally excepted) to start any type of mill and produce in those mills any kind of handiwork, apart from vodka distilling, which was a monopoly of the aristocracy. Although internal customs duties had been abolished under the Empress Elizabeth, it was still found necessary for the protection of home manufacturers to resort to high tariffs and occasionally outright prohibition of the importing of certain categories of foreign goods.

In spite of all this, the lack of mobility of labour and of personal incentive among the working class continued to put a brake on industrial development on a massive scale. The reinforcement of the régime of serfdom and the intensified exploitation of serf labour resulted mainly in an increase in the small-scale manorial enterprises of the nobility, this latter category tending to rival in number the undertakings of the merchants. While industrial technique and *per capita* output showed little improvement, both classes of enterprise increased substantially in number during the period. It has been reckoned that on Catherine's accession, there existed some 984 factories, whereas in 1796, excluding the mining industry, there were 3,161. According to figures quoted by the economist Lyashchenko, there existed in 1780 just over three hundred really large industrial establishments, apart from mines and Government arsenals. The most substantial of the private companies had capital resources of 150,000 to 300,000 roubles, with perhaps three thousand workers each, though there were many more with only a few score workers and a few thousand roubles' capital. The foreign trade figures show a large increase during our period: in the 1760s, exports averaged 13,886,500 roubles per annum, more or less, imports about 12,000,000; in the 1790s, these totals had risen to 43,266,000 and 39,643,000 roubles respectively. It has to be remembered, however, that the population grew during the same span of years from nineteen to twenty-nine millions, an increase due in part to extensive annexations and partly to natural operation of the birth rate. Nor must it be forgotten that this was a time of chronic inflation and consequent devaluation of the rouble.

This inflation stemmed to a great extent from the mounting deficit in the State budget, caused by lavish expenditure on the army and fleet, an extravagant programme of public buildings, the malversations of swarms of corrupt officials and favourites, and the cost of policing and administering great tracts of unruly territory. The deficit was financed by foreign loans, as well as by reckless issues of *assignats* or banknotes by virtue of an ordinance of December 1768. Inflation was also aggravated by the higher standard of living now affected by the nobility. The boyars of olden days had been content to live on their estates in patriarchal fashion, surrounded by their vassals, who spent part of their time in tilling the lord's land and the rest in looking after their smallholdings, or engaging in crafts and trades around the village. Each manor largely sufficed for its own needs. Surplus agricultural products were sold or exchanged for luxury goods as required. But now that his lordship lived in a house in St Petersburg, rode in a gilt carriage, entertained smart friends from Court, and sent his son off on the Grand Tour, he could not manage without a substantial income in cash. This was an age when enormous estates were granted to various grandees. A sort of manorial 'collective farming' system developed, the serfs being herded to work in gangs on the squire's or the magnate's broad acres. Agricultural tools and methods remained about as primitive as ever, and *per capita* production failed to show any significant increase. The result was that the peasants often had to work six or seven days a week on the lord's estates, their own little plots suffering accordingly. So outrageous did such exploitation become that one of the first acts of Catherine's son, the autocratic Paul I, was to forbid forced labour on Sundays and Saints' Days, recommending that the serf should do three days' *corvée* on his master's land, and three days' work on his own holding. This and other measures directed against the privileges of the gentry helped to lose Paul his throne and his life.

The progressive growth in the population of central Russia meant that a more or less fixed area of arable land had an increasing number of mouths to feed. Following the crushing of Pugachev, landlords exercised stricter control over their serfs, and flight to the under-populated Cossack or Siberian territories was made more difficult. At the same time, wars abroad and the suppression of unrest at home made necessary a huge standing army. The strongest, fittest young men were dragged off by the recruiting sergeants, leaving women and children to fend for themselves. By the 1780s, large areas of Russia were reduced to a state in many ways similar to that of France at the close of Louis XIV's reign, with regular famine conditions in bad years. In 1787, things were so bad that even the hard-bitten courtier, Prince Shcher-batov, was moved to write, in a memorandum entitled 'The Condition of Russia with regard to Bread and Money': 'Private persons cannot feed them all, and occasional alms-giving can serve only to increase the number of the indigent. The Government is deaf, blind and insensitive to this. If posterity believes my words, what will it say about our century?'

It is worth recalling in this connection that some of the severest criticism ever levelled at Catherine and her policies comes, curiously enough, from the pen of Russia's great poet, Alexander Pushkin. In an early historical essay, which he composed under the influence of his friends among the future Decembrist conspirators, Pushkin wrote: 'The reign of Catherine II exerted a new and potent influence on the political and moral condition of Russia. Elevated to the throne by the conspiracy of a few insurgents, she degraded our restless aristocracy whilst enriching them at the nation's expense. If to govern means to know the weaknesses of the human soul and to take advantage of them, then in this respect Catherine merits the admiration of posterity. Her magnificence blinded, her graciousness attracted, her munificence attached. The very sensuality of this cunning woman strengthened her régime. Provoking but a faint murmur in a people accustomed to venerate its rulers' vices, it excited in the upper classes an obscene form of competition, since neither wit nor merit nor talent was necessary in order to attain the second place in the realm. Many were called and many chosen; but in the long list of her lovers, doomed to incur the contempt of posterity, the strange Potemkin's name will be marked out by the hand of history. He shares with Catherine a part of her military glory, for to him we owe the Black Sea and the brilliant, albeit fruitless victories in northern Turkey.

'Sweden subdued and Poland annihilated—those are Catherine's great titles to the gratitude of the Russian people. But in time history will weigh up the influence of her reign upon morals, will reveal the terrible activity of her despotism beneath the mask of mildness and tolerance, the common folk oppressed by her governors, the treasury pillaged by her lovers, and will show up her important errors in political economy, her insignificance in legislation, her repulsive buffoonery in her relations with the philosophers of her century—and then the voice of the captivated Voltaire will not save her renowned memory from the execration of Russia.

'We have seen by what means Catherine degraded the spirit of the gentry. In this she was zealously seconded by her favourites. . . . Catherine was aware of the swindles and malversations committed by her lovers, and was silent. Emboldened by such weakness, they set no limit to their avarice, and the distant relatives of a favourite profited greedily by his brief reign. This was the origin of those vast estates which came into the possession of families completely unknown, and of the entire absence of honour and probity in the topmost class of the nation. From the Chancellor to the humblest secretary, all stole and all were for sale. In this way the immoral Empress demoralized even her Empire.

'Catherine abolished the term *slavery*, just designation though it is, but distributed as gifts about a million State peasants (i.e. free yeomen), and enslaved the free Ukraine and the Polish provinces. Catherine abolished torture—but the Secret Chancellery flourished under her matriarchal rule. . . . Catherine made a parade of harrying the clergy, which she sacrificed to her own unlimited love of power while pandering to the spirit of the age. But by depriving it of its independent status and limiting the income of the monasteries, she dealt a massive blow against popular education. The seminaries, which used to be attached to the monasteries but now depended on the bishops, fell into a complete decline. Many villages lack priests. The poor and ignorant condition of that class of persons, so essential to the State, debases them, and renders them unable to fulfil their important vocation. Hence arises our people's contempt for priests and their indifference towards the national creed. It is a mistake to regard the Russian as superstitious: perhaps nowhere more than among our common folk can everything ecclesiastical be heard held up to ridicule. A pity! for the Greek faith, all else apart, gives us our specific national character. . . .

'Contemporary foreign writers showered Catherine with exaggerated praise—very naturally: they knew her exclusively from her correspondence with Voltaire and from the accounts of those individuals to whom she granted travel facilities.

'The farce of our deputies, played out with such indecency, had its effect in Europe; her *Nakaz* was read everywhere and in all languages. It was enough to cause her to be set up along with the Tituses and the Trajans; but when reading over that hypocritical *Nakaz* it is impossible to refrain from just indignation. It was excusable for the sage of Ferney to laud the virtues of a Tartuffe in petticoats and crown; he knew not, he could not know the truth, but the sycophancy of the Russian writers I find incomprehensible.'

❋

Advancing years and established success made Catherine increasingly impatient of criticism, however well meant. Potemkin's heady flattery caused her to regard even the most innocuous comments on her régime as impudence and potential subversion. This attitude made itself felt, for instance, in the case of Denis Fonvizin, author of the great comedy of manners, *The Minor*. In 1783, Fonvizin sent in to the *Sobesednik Lyubiteley Rossiyskogo Slova* or 'Mouthpiece of the Lovers of the Russian Tongue', a periodical edited by Princess Dashkov in collaboration with Catherine herself, a rather searching questionnaire, in the hope of eliciting replies from the editorial board. It was rather like those sets of topical questions addressed by newspaper correspondents of modern times to Stalin or Khrushchev, and answered usually in mellow tones. There was nothing mellow about Catherine's replies to Fonvizin's queries, as the following specimens show:

'*Question:* Why do people here vigorously dispute true principles, which everywhere else are already accepted without the slightest hesitation?
Answer: Here, as everywhere, all men dispute what displeases them, or what they do not understand.
Question: Why do we see many good people withdrawn from public life?
Answer: Many good people have left Government service evidently because they found it advantageous to be in retirement.
Question: Why is everyone in debt?
Answer: They are in debt because they spend more than their income.
Question: Why are notorious and obvious good-for-nothings welcomed everywhere on the same footing as honest men?
Answer: Because they are not exposed in the law courts.
Question: In an era of legislative activity, why does nobody think of distinguishing himself in this field?
Answer: Because this is not everybody's business.
Question: Why in earlier times did buffoons, fools and jesters not hold official ranks, whereas nowadays they do, and very high ones?

Answer: Not all of our ancestors could read or write. N.B.: This question was born of a loose tongue, which our forbears did not have; if they had had, then for every instance of this sort today, you could have found ten in former times.

Question: Why are enterprises started among us with great zeal and enthusiasm, then abandoned, and often completely forgotten?

Answer: For the same reason that a man grows old.

Question: In what does our national character consist?

Answer: In acute and immediate understanding of everything, in exemplary obedience and in the root of all virtues given by the Creator to mankind.'

These replies were more than enough to show Fonvizin that offence had been taken in the highest quarter and that he had thoroughly overstepped the mark. Although he wrote an apologetic letter to the journal in an attempt to explain away his more embarrassing queries, the damage had been done. He was prevented from bringing out any new writings, and remained under a cloud until his death in 1792. Years later, a number of even more outspoken pieces of social satire were found among his posthumous papers, many of them attacking the abuses of serfdom no less energetically than Radishchev was to do. Had he been rash enough to publish these, no doubt he would have met with a similar fate to that of Radishchev, but he was discreet enough to keep most of them to himself. As a British observer expressed it: 'So accustomed has this Sovereign been to the Stile and Servility and Adulation that she can but ill brook the Language of Truth and Sincerity altho' it evidently conduces to Her own Happiness and to that of Her Country.'[1]

During the later years of her reign, even before the outbreak of the French Revolution, Catherine was coming to distrust the more radical manifestations of Western 'enlightenment'. When her position had been precarious and opposition to her usurped authority strong, the weapons of Voltaire's arsenal of propaganda had been useful adjuncts to her political armoury. At first, she had been at least partly sincere in soliciting advice from leading French reformers on how Russia might be refashioned on modern lines. By the time Diderot visited her in St Petersburg in 1773, the tide was beginning to turn; some years later, when Catherine saw some of Diderot's comments on her *Nakaz* or 'Instruction' to the legislative commission of 1767, she noted acidly: 'This piece is arrant babbling, in which one finds neither knowledge of the subject nor prudence nor insight; if my Instruction had been to Monsieur Diderot's taste, it would have been calculated to turn every-

[1] Public Record Office, F.O. Archives, *Russia*, vol. 65/19. Charles Whitworth to the Duke of Leeds, British Foreign Secretary, No. 52 of September 3, 1790.

thing topsy-turvy.'[1] In a conversation with the Prince de Ligne, she avowed that of all the learned French gentlemen whom she had welcomed in St Petersburg or corresponded with, the only one who had not bored her was Voltaire.

This estrangement between Catherine and the French *philosophes* was to some extent reciprocal. In Paris, a new generation of younger, more radical writers was growing up, and some of these were far from sharing Voltaire's old-fashioned respect for 'enlightened despotism'. Disappointed by Catherine's failure to follow up her projects with any genuine social reforms, even her old friend Diderot voiced misgivings as to her sincerity. The most vocal of Catherine's Parisian critics, however, was a close collaborator of Diderot's, the Abbé Guillaume-Thomas-François Raynal (1713–96), a vociferous opponent of autocratic rule, serfdom and colonial exploitation everywhere. Since it was Raynal's *Histoire philosophique et politique des deux Indes* which, more than any other literary influence, determined Radishchev to write and publish his *Journey from St Petersburg to Moscow*, it may not be out of place to give some account of this once renowned, and now almost forgotten author.

Born in the Rouergue district of the South of France, Raynal was destined for the priesthood and ordained, after which he came to Paris in search of fame and fortune. 'When I came to Paris,' he used later to say in his meridional patois, 'I started off by preaching and did not do too badly; but I had the very devil of an accent.' Soon Raynal, like other Abbés of the time, forsook preaching and joined the free-thinking society of Diderot, Helvétius and the Baron d'Holbach. As Garat comments in his memoirs, 'Having escaped rather late from the Society of Jesus, with which his principles and his character had so little in common, he had had time there to acquire a taste for an ordered life, for regular work, and for influence over the powers of this world.' These qualities Raynal put to practical use, and soon became one of the most successful journalists among the Encyclopedist group. He developed a special interest in questions of foreign trade, combined with an unbounded zeal for the cause of the negro slaves, for whose emancipation he campaigned with exuberance. Horace Walpole gives an amusing glimpse of the enthusiastic Abbé:

'The Abbé Raynal, though he wrote that fine work on the *Commerce des deux Indes*, is the most tiresome creature in the world. The first time I met him was at the dull Baron d'Olbach's [Holbach's]: we were twelve at table: I dreaded opening my mouth in French, before so many people and so many servants: he began questioning me, 'cross the table, about

[1] M. Tourneux, *Diderot et Catherine II*, Paris, 1899, pp. 519, 563.

our colonies, which I understand as I do Coptic. I made him signs I was deaf. After dinner he found I was not, and never forgave me.'[1]

The first edition of Raynal's 'philosophical and political history of the commerce and establishments of the Europeans in the Two Indies' came out anonymously in 1770, and had considerable success. The book contained data, much of it contributed by experts, on the overseas colonies of the European powers, the history of their conquest, and their present state and future prospects; it was seasoned with anti-clerical tirades calculated to attract public attention. As Horace Walpole remarked, it provided information about anything under the sun: trade, navigation, tea, coffee, porcelain, mines, salt, spices; about rice, and women who danced in the nude; about camels, gingham and muslin; about millions on millions of francs, pounds or rupees; about iron cables and Circassian beauties, and 'against all Governments aud religions'. A second edition appeared in 1774, and went through eight impressions in two years. The ambitious Abbé, however, was still dissatisfied. Bent on a *succès de scandale*, he paid Diderot ten thousand francs to reshape the work entirely, adding voluptuous descriptions and political diatribes calculated to cause a sensation. Diderot, who had just returned from his visit to Catherine the Great in St Petersburg, set to work with a will—with such gusto, in fact, that even Raynal was alarmed, and toned down some of the more outrageous passages.

The third, revised edition of Raynal's history was published at Geneva in 1780 in four quarto volumes, plus an atlas; as a result of Diderot's efforts, it is more violently anti-despotic and militantly anti-clerical than the earlier versions. Raynal had thrown caution to the winds, abandoned all attempt at anonymity, and reproduced a flamboyant portrait of himself as a frontispiece. The book was condemned by the Parlement of Paris as 'impious, seditious, blasphemous, tending to incite the nations against sovereign authority and to subvert the basic principles of civil order', burnt by the hangman, and personally denounced by Louis XVI. While its author fled the country, the book immediately became a best-seller. Though banned in France, many copies circulated there, as well as in other countries, including Russia, where Raynal's highly critical comments on the system of serfdom had much topical force.

Ironically enough, it was not for its 'philosophic' and political elements that Radishchev first had occasion to consult Raynal's book, but for its factual information on European trade with colonial territories in the West and East Indies. As deputy head of the Customs

[1] Walpole, *Letters*, ed. Toynbee, IX, 92: To the Hon. Henry Seymour Conway, November 12, 1774.

House at St Petersburg, he needed to know all about the production of spices, coffee, sugar, tobacco and other tropical products; Raynal's was one of the few works from which such data could be culled. But as he dipped into this outwardly respectable publication, Radishchev came upon many passages which struck a responsive chord in his own mind, and coincided with the ideas of civic liberty and the rights of man which he already held dear.

In the usual eighteenth-century fashion, special emphasis is laid by Raynal, partly under Diderot's influence, on the alleged role of religious superstition in establishing political tyranny. 'Religion,' we read, 'has everywhere been an invention by skilful and astute men who, failing to find within themselves the means of governing their fellows according to their taste, sought in heaven the strength which they lacked, and brought the terror of it down to earth.' Later on Raynal declares: 'Through superstition, cunning has shared dominion with force. When one of these has conquered and subdued all things, the other comes and promulgates laws in its turn. They work in unison: men bow their heads and permit their hands to be bound. If it happens that these two forces rise in enmity against one another, it is then that one sees the blood of citizens flowing in the streets.'[1] It is easy to detect the similarity between these sentiments, and the opening stanzas of the *Ode to Liberty*, parts of which Radishchev inserted in the *Journey from St Petersburg to Moscow*:

> The monarch's power preserves the faith,
> The faith supports the monarch's power;
> In unison they oppress society . . .

No less violent are the diatribes of Raynal and Diderot against absolutism and autocracy. 'All authority in this world has its origin either in the subjects' consent or the master's power. In either case it can legitimately be brought to an end. Tyranny has no claim against liberty.' The authors do not hesitate to recommend revolt, and the slaying of tyrants: they praise the natives of Ceylon for executing kings who do not abide by the law of the land: 'Before the law, as well as before God, all men are equal. The punishment of an individual avenges a simple breach of the law; but the punishment of a sovereign avenges contempt for it.' Discussing the state of China, Raynal demands: 'Have there been a large number of tyrants deposed, imprisoned, judged, put to death? Does one see on the public square a scaffold dripping continually with the blood of monarchs? Why is this not so?' Elsewhere the reader is informed:

[1] Page references for most of the passages cited from Raynal's *Histoire des deux Indes* are given in my article, 'Some Western Sources of Radiščev's Political Thought', in *Revue des Études Slaves*, XXV, Paris, 1949, pp. 73–86.

'It is only too true. The majority of nations are in fetters. The multitude is universally sacrificed to the passions of a few privileged oppressors. . . . Everywhere, extravagant superstitions, barbarous customs, antiquated laws stifle liberty. . . . Cowardly peoples! stupid nations! since the continuance of oppression imparts to you no energy; since you confine yourselves to useless moanings . . . obey! Tramp on, without pestering us with your complaints; and learn at least how to live in misery if you know not how to be free. . . . But liberty will be born from the bosom of oppression. She lives within every heart: she will pass by the medium of the written word into enlightened minds, and by that of tyranny into the spirit of the people. All men at last will feel—and the day of awakening is not far off—they will feel that liberty is the supreme gift of heaven, as it is the supreme seed of virtue. The instruments of despotism will become its destroyers, and the enemies of humanity, those who seem today to be armed only in order to exterminate it, will fight one day in its defence.'

All this boldly proclaimed in 1780, nine years before the taking of the Bastille! No wonder the eloquent ex-Jesuit was hailed a few years later as one of the prophets of the French Revolution. As Anatole Feugère, the authority on Raynal, remarks, his book was not lacking in texts whereby the legislators of 1793 could justify the right of popular insurrection.[1] When Radishchev begins his *Ode to Liberty* by hailing freedom—'thou blessed gift of Heaven'—and prophesying the imminent downfall of tyrants everywhere, we clearly detect the echo of Raynal's heady and grandiloquent tirades.

Another feature of the *Histoire des deux Indes* which impressed Radishchev was the zest with which Raynal, Diderot and their collaborators attacked both serfdom in Europe and colonial slavery on the plantations. The Russian Government in particular was urged to abolish 'this state of degradation', even at the expense of the propertied class: 'Never will the tyrants consent freely to the abolition of serfdom; in order to bring them to this order of things, it will be necessary either to ruin them or to exterminate them.' In sweeping terms, Raynal proclaims: 'Let us demonstrate in advance that there is no *raison d'état* which can authorize slavery. Let us not be afraid to denounce before the tribunal of eternal light and justice those Governments which tolerate this cruelty, or do not even blush to make it the basis of their power.' No Russian reader could fail to see that this applied with special force to the Empire of Catherine the Great.

Raynal repeatedly affirms the right of serfs and enslaved negroes to rise in revolt and massacre their masters:

[1] A. Feugère, *L'Abbé Raynal*, Angoulême, 1922, p. 408.

'If you think yourself entitled to oppress me because you are stronger than I, do not complain then when my vigorous arm rips open your breast to search out your heart; do not complain when you sense within your riven entrails the death which I shall have caused to pass thither with your food. . . . No, no, it is needful that sooner or later justice should be done. If it happened otherwise, I should address myself to the mob. I should say to them: O peoples whose roarings have so often made your masters tremble, what are you waiting for? For what moment are you reserving your flaming torches and the stones which pave your streets? Tear them up!—The subjugated nations are sighing for a liberator; the tormented peoples are groaning for an avenger; and for this avenger they will not have long to wait.'

In common with French public opinion generally, Raynal expressed sympathy with George Washington and the American colonists in their struggle against King George III, who was portrayed as the symbol of reaction and obscurantism. Speaking of the American War of Independence, Raynal declared:

'In any case, these great revolutions of freedom are lessons for the despots. They warn them not to count on too much patience on the part of the peoples, and on eternal impunity. . . . Such is the source of the lively interest which all wars of liberty arouse in us. Such is that which the Americans have inspired within us. Our imagination has been inflamed on their behalf. . . . I shall die without having seen the abode of tolerance, of morals, of laws, of virtue, of liberty. A fresh and sacred ground will not cover my ashes: but I shall have desired this; and my last words will be prayers offered to heaven for thy prosperity!'

These sentiments recur in very similar form in Radishchev's *Ode to Liberty*, stanza 46, where he follows Raynal in addressing an appeal to the land of Washington and his comrades in arms:

> To thee my soul in exultation strives,
> To thee, O land renowned,
> Where freedom lay trampled under foot
> And bent by oppression's yoke;
> Thou dost rejoice! but we here suffer . . .
> For that same thing we too do thirst:
> Thine example has revealed our goal.
> No share have I in thy glory—
> Yet grant, my spirit being undaunted,
> That thy shores my ashes at least may cover.

In the *Histoire des deux Indes*, Raynal and his collaborators made direct reference to the state of Russia. Diderot's visit had given him first-hand knowledge of conditions there, and he was able to draw on personal impressions when assisting Raynal in bringing out his new edition. The observations on Russia's rulers contained in this book are far less flattering than the fulsome letters which Diderot used to exchange with Catherine. Since he kept his co-operation with Raynal a secret, Diderot no doubt felt able to let off here some of the steam which he discreetly bottled up in his correspondence with the Russian Empress.

At all events, Raynal's book censures Peter the Great for riveting the fetters of serfdom firmly on to the wretched *muzhiks*. The apparent tranquillity of the Russian Empire was founded solely on 'superstition and despotism'. Peter bequeathed to his successors the 'atrocious and destructive idea that the subjects are nothing and the sovereign everything'. Liberty had always been held in contempt by Russia's Tsars, who lived in perpetual dread of revolt and destruction. The Russian nation was bound by a 'formless assortment of contradictory ordinances, successively dictated by the crassest ignorance', and without any regard for the customs of the country. (So much for Catherine's much vaunted *Nakaz*!) It was useless, concluded Raynal, for the Empress to squander her efforts on academies and schools while the mass of the people languished in stagnation and squalor.

Describing contemporary society under Catherine the Great, Raynal declared: 'Beneath her arbitrary laws, there lives in a state of ignorance a clergy once formidable, but now turned to docility since it was deprived of the possessions which superstition had lavished upon it and the million slaves which it formerly exploited. Then comes a class of aristocracy which holds in its hand the majority of the landed estates, and under its authority all the wretches who water them with their sweat. After these there comes the class of freemen. This category is so obscure that Europe was for a long time unaware of its existence. . . . Finally, the last class of the nation, if one can give it such a name, is made up of the slaves. . . .' The prime duty of the rulers of Russia, according to Raynal, should be to make their subjects happy; but this is impossible—'unless the form of Government there be changed'. Abetted by Diderot, Raynal criticizes Catherine's reckless imperialist policy, her mania for foreign conquests, her meddling in the political affairs of Western Europe. He exposes the inadequacy of the Russian mercantile marine and the errors of Russian commercial policy— subjects of direct interest to Radishchev as a customs official and a member of the Imperial Board of Trade. In spite of what he calls Peter the Great's 'blind predilection' for the city he created at St Petersburg, Raynal recommends the return of the capital to Moscow, remarking:

'The respect which is due to the memory of Peter I should not prevent one from saying that it was not vouchsafed to him to witness the complete establishment of a well constituted state. He failed to rise to the point of combining his people's happiness with his own personal grandeur. After his magnificent institutions, the nation continued to languish in poverty, servitude and oppression. He refused to surrender any portion of his despotic authority; he aggravated it perhaps, and bequeathed to his successors the atrocious and destructive notion that the subjects are nothing and the sovereign is everything. Since his death, this evil conception has been perpetuated. The authorities have refused to see that liberty is the first right of all men.'

Whereas the Empress Catherine is given credit for good intentions, Raynal points out that her legislative schemes were far too ambitious for Russia's backward condition. His verdict on her *Nakaz* or 'Instruction' is far from enthusiastic:

'It is impossible to doubt that Catherine has become fully conscious that liberty is the unique source of public welfare. Yet has she in fact abdicated her despotic authority? When reading attentively her instructions to the deputies of the Empire who were commissioned—in theory —to frame laws, does one detect therein anything more than a desire for a change in terminology, to be called monarch instead of autocrat, to call her peoples subjects instead of slaves? Blind though they are, will the Russians continue indefinitely to accept the name instead of the real thing? Will their character be exalted by this play-acting to that great energy which it was proposed to impart to them?'

In contrast to Russia, it is England which is singled out as the home of constitutional liberty:

'England is, in modern history, the land of great political phenomena. It is there that we have seen liberty most violently at grips with despotism, sometimes trampled beneath its feet, sometimes crushing it in its turn. It is there that a king, dragged by force of law to the scaffold, and another, deposed with all his line by a decree of the nation, have given a great lesson to the world. . . . It is there, finally, that after long and violent convulsions there has taken form that constitution which, if not perfect or free from drawbacks, is at least the one most happily matched to the country's condition—the only one, perhaps, since man has lived in society, in which the law has guaranteed to him his dignity, his personal liberty, his freedom of thought.'

These ideas are repeated by Radishchev in his *Ode to Liberty*, where he praises Cromwell for his share in the execution of King Charles I. In the closing stanzas of this ode, Radishchev puts forward a striking interpretation of world history, which also derives from that advanced by Raynal in the *Histoire des deux Indes*. According to Nature's immutable laws, says Radishchev, liberty and despotism are bound to succeed one another in cycles: freedom is born of tyranny, servitude in turn is born of freedom. This means that all tyrannies are doomed to perish sooner or later, and the human race need never despair of deliverance, for a time at least, from its bondage. But liberty must resign itself to being subsequently overwhelmed by the forces of reaction and to waiting long years again for a new dawn. The germ of this idea is surely to be found in Raynal, where he writes:

'Everywhere revolutions in government succeed one another with a rapidity which it is hard to follow. There are few countries which have not experienced all of these, and there is none which will not in time complete this periodic trend. All of them will follow more or less frequently a regular cycle of misfortune and prosperity, of freedom and slavery, of morals and corruption, of enlightenment and ignorance, of grandeur and weakness; each one of them will pass through all the stages of this fateful panorama. The law of Nature, which demands that all societies shall gravitate towards despotism and dissolution, that Empires are born and perish away, shall not be suspended for any of them.'

Particularly significant is the prediction made by Radishchev at the conclusion of the *Ode to Liberty*, namely that Russia will be convulsed by a revolutionary cataclysm and split up into a number of autonomous, federated States, an event which will bring about the reign of liberty. This is also Raynal's formula for the Russian Empire: 'In this condition of things, would the greatest good fortune that could happen to such an enormously extended country not be for it to be dismembered by some great revolution, and be split up into several small adjoining monarchies, so that good order established in some of these would spread into the others?'

These comparisons show that Radishchev was telling the truth when, after his arrest in 1790, he told the investigator Sheshkovsky that it was the eloquence of Raynal's *Histoire des deux Indes* which spurred him on to write his *Journey from St Petersburg to Moscow:* 'I may truthfully say that Raynal's style, drawing me on from delusion to delusion, led to the completion of my insane book.' The Empress Catherine, no mean student of the works of the French *philosophes*, had come quite independently to the same conclusion: on the margin of the chapter 'Krest'tsy' of Radishchev's book, she wrote that its author's reflections were 'culled from various half-baked sages of this century, such as Rousseau, the Abbé Raynal, and persons similar to that hypochondriac'. Against the chapter 'Khotilov', where Radishchev dilates on the depressed state of the *muzhiks*, Catherine commented: 'All this is mainly taken out of the Abbé Raynal's book.'

Radishchev could not know that his dependence on Raynal was, in Catherine's eyes, far from being an extenuating circumstance. From the first, she had regarded the truculent Abbé's remarks about Russia as a stab in the back, especially as they emanated from a school of writers whose good opinion she had sedulously courted. In April 1782, she complained to her Paris correspondent, Baron Grimm, about the 'vain declamations of the Abbé Raynal against us', adding that 'we are going on with our law-making without taking much notice of the Abbé Raynal's quackings and lies'. In July, she was as indignant as ever: 'As for the apostle Raynal, I absolve you from the duty of poring through him, as he is not worth bothering about.' But one should beware of dismissing Radishchev's courageous book as a mere literary compilation from Western radical writers; his nature, his upbringing, and his personal observations moved him to protest against the evil effects of serfdom and autocratic misrule on the people of Russia. It was simply that at a crucial phase in his life, when his heart and mind were already disillusioned, he happened to light upon a book—the *Histoire des deux Indes*—which expressed in terms more forthright than Radishchev had conceived possible that same zeal for progress and liberty which was already surging upwards within his consciousness.

The impression made on Radishchev's mind by Raynal's tirades is shown already in a pamphlet which he wrote in 1782, but did not publish until 1790. This brochure, entitled 'Letter to a Friend living in Tobolsk', was cast in the form of an epistle addressed to his old college friend Yanov, at that time serving as an official at Tobolsk in Siberia; it described the unveiling at St Petersburg on August 7, 1782, of Falconet's statue of Peter the Great, later the subject of Pushkin's celebrated poem, 'The Bronze Horseman'. The equestrian figure of the Tsar was erected on a huge rock, on which was set an inscription in letters of bronze by which Catherine staked her claim to the great reformer's heritage: *Petro primo/Catharina secunda/MDCCLXXXII*. After describing the triumphal celebrations which took place at the unveiling ceremony, Radishchev reflects on Peter's role in Russia's historical destiny, commenting ironically on the fact that only now, some sixty years after Peter's death, was it possible to comment frankly on his personality and achievements. During Peter's lifetime, he says,

H

the Tsar was surrounded by hypocritical sycophants and terrorized vassals, none of whom dared to tell him the truth; now, however, Peter can neither condemn anyone to death nor grant anyone a reprieve, and is in fact less powerful than any ordinary common soldier.

Radishchev goes on to interpret the symbolism underlying Falconet's execution of the figure of the great Tsar—the massive, rugged rock upon which the statue is set representing the obstacles Peter surmounted in his turbulent career; the old-fashioned, simple attire in which the monarch and his steed are arrayed betokening the conservative ways of old Muscovy; the laurel wrath signifying that Peter was renowned as a conqueror even before he won fame as a legislator, and so forth.—'By general recognition, Peter is surnamed the Great, and by the Senate, styled Father of the Homeland. But what entitles him to be termed great? Alexander, the ravager of half the world, is called great; Constantine, steeped in his offspring's blood, is called great; Charles I, the renewer of the Roman Empire, is called great; Leo the Pope of Rome, protector of the sciences and arts, is called great; Cosimo de Medici, Duke of Tuscany, is called great; Henry, the good King Henry IV of France, is called great; Louis XIV, the pompous and haughty King Louis of France, is called great; Frederick the Great, King of Prussia, is called great even in his own lifetime. All these monarchs, without making any reference to the many others to whom flattery has accorded the title of Great, have received this surname because they stood out from the ranks of ordinary men by their services to the fatherland, although they had great faults. . . . Even if Peter had not distinguished himself by the diversity of his institutions, which contributed to the public welfare, even had he not been the conqueror of Charles XII, he could still have been called great, because he gave the first impulse to that immense mass [i.e. the Russian State] which had previously been as immobile as primitive matter. Let me not sink in your estimation, O dear friend, if I sing the praises of so mighty an autocrat, who exterminated the last traces of his fatherland's wild liberty! He is dead, and to flatter the dead is impossible! I will add that Peter might have won still more glory and exalted both himself and his country if he had established individual freedom; but though we have examples of kings abandoning the purple to live in tranquil retirement—a decision arising not from magnanimity, but from satiety with their royal estate—yet there is no example, and perhaps until the end of the world there will be none, of a monarch voluntarily yielding up any part of his power so long as he sits upon the throne.'

Some years later, in 1790, Radishchev published this epistle on the private press which he installed in his home. By then the French Revolution was getting into its stride, and Radishchev added to the last sentence quoted a footnote: 'If this had been written in 1790, the example of Louis XVI would have inspired the author with different ideas.'

Unfortunately for Radishchev, a copy of this publication was filed away in the Government archives. After his arrest following the appearance of the *Journey from St Petersburg to Moscow*, Radishchev's sarcastic remarks about Peter the Great and other rulers were held by the Empress Catherine to constitute evidence that 'his mind has long been preparing itself for its chosen course'. From Radishchev's allusion to Louis XVI, and the concessions which that King had been forced to make to the Estates-General and the Paris mob, Catherine concluded: 'The French Revolution has determined him to become its first champion in Russia.'

In spite of Radishchev's preoccupation with the abuses of autocratic rule and serfdom in Russia, and in spite of the inflammatory effect which Raynal's book produced on his mind, it is just possible that he would have kept his thoughts to himself, had it not been for a personal tragedy which overtook him in 1783. In that year, his wife, to whom he was tenderly attached, died on giving birth to their third son, Paul. (In all, Anna bore six children, including three girls, of whom two died in infancy.) As he later said, 'The death of my wife plunged me into grief and desolation, and for a time distracted my mind from any form of occupation.' Anna Radishchev was buried in the Alexander-Nevsky cemetery. As an epitaph for her tombstone, Radishchev composed a few touching verses, beginning:

> O, if it be no lie
> That after death we live again;
> If we shall live, then feel we must,
> And if we feel, to love we must incline.

After one look at the first couplet, however, the sturdy guardians of Orthodoxy who watched over the cemetery concluded that Radishchev was not entirely convinced of the immortality of the soul. They withheld permission for the stone to be set up within their hallowed ground. Sadly, Radishchev took it away, and placed it in his garden at home as a monument to his departed love.

From this time onwards, though comforted by the affection of his sister-in-law and future helpmate, Elizabeth Rubanovsky, Radishchev was a saddened, often an embittered man. To make matters worse, his stipend as assistant director of the Customs House was not sufficient to provide for the needs of his four growing children. In spite of gifts of money and provisions from his father down in Ablyazovo, the burden of debt was added to the sorrow of bereavement. As so often happens in such cases, Radishchev sought refuge from personal misfortune in books and in writing. Perhaps he hoped to sublimate his own feelings by identifying himself with Russia's downtrodden millions. At all events, it is in the years immediately following the death of Radishchev's wife that his radical outlook becomes finally crystallized and takes on its definitive literary form, though it was some time yet before circumstances provided him with an outlet for publication.

CHAPTER 6

Before the Storm

✦❦✦ ❦❦ ✦

During the years immediately preceding his supreme gesture of defiance
—the publication of *A Journey from St Petersburg to Moscow*—Radishchev went on working as usual at his office in the Customs House. 'His
probity, pleasant manners, and social charm earned him general esteem
and affection.'[1] It was usual for leading customs officials to amass huge
fortunes by conniving at irregularities and accepting bribes, but Radishchev would have none of this. Since it was necessary to keep up appearances on his modest salary, the family continued to sink into debt.

For the time being, however, the Radishchev family enjoyed quite
comfortable circumstances. Radishchev's son Paul recalled in later years
that two or three years before his downfall, his father bought for six
thousand roubles a *dacha* or suburban estate on Petrovsk island, which
was registered in the name of his elder sister-in-law, Elizabeth Rubanovsky. He built there a small, two-storied wooden house, in which he
and all his family lived during the summer months. The rooms were
not large, except for the living-room in the centre, above which there
ran a gallery at first-floor level. Pleasant strolls could be taken through
the island, with its many copses, streams and little bridges. A broad
drive ran the length of the island, at one end of which was the Grand
Duke Paul's summer palace. It was out here that Radishchev was
arrested in 1790, after the publication of his famous book.

In the winter months, as Paul Radishchev also informs us, Radishchev
continued to live in St Petersburg on Dirty (now Marat) Street, not far
from the church of the Vladimir Virgin, and fairly near the Nevsky
Prospect. Facing the inner courtyard was the wooden house which had

---

[1] Masson, *Mémoires secrets*, II, 179.

belonged to his late father-in-law, Vasily Rubanovsky; Radishchev's own quarters were in a two-storied stone residence looking out on to the street. It was here that his private printing press was installed. Behind the house was a large garden with a pond in the middle. There were fruit trees, rose bushes, strawberries, and a large bed of asparagus. At the end of an alley of birch trees was a labyrinth, where Radishchev had set up the memorial to his dead wife, Anna.

The incorruptible arbitrator of many a tangled trade dispute, Radishchev was often the brains behind his chief at the Board of Trade, Count Vorontsov, for whom he drafted a number of commercial statutes and tariffs. Beneath the surface, however, other interests were stirring, other influences at work in the mind of the distinguished bureaucrat. We get a glimpse of this in a memorandum on the taxes of the St Petersburg province, drawn up by Radishchev between 1786 and 1788, at a time when the Government were striving to raise revenue to keep pace with inflated State expenditure. Amid cold figures and statistical data, Radishchev launches out in this memorandum into tirades like the following: 'O you who vaunt your expertise in methods of enriching the husbandman! You who think up [ways of increasing taxation] at a time when beneficent nature pressing out her breasts bestows, instead of ears of corn imbued with the sap of wheat, nothing but weeds; when on the threshing floor there issues from her sheaves, not corn, but tares and chaff—you should rather shudder at the prospect of having to fill men's veins, when empty of nourishing juices, with fodder intended for cattle, instead of with health-giving corn! Shame on your extortion! You should disdain to think of profit when the bony paw of hunger weighs down the peasant's shoulders. Give him work, but as well as work, payment also! Then shall he have food, his home will be warmed! his offspring shall not perish from nakedness or hunger.'[1]

This outburst was prompted by the severe famine which broke out in Russia in 1786–7, at the very time when the Government was seeking to augment peasant dues. In Moscow, swarms of beggars from the villages infested the streets of the city. The Governor of Moscow used ruthless methods to hustle all vagrants out of the way, so as to hide the true state of affairs from the Empress during her visit—methods which produced indignant, if unspoken reactions even in such onlookers as the old-fashioned courtier, Prince Shcherbatov. In areas normally fertile, the peasants were forced down to a bare subsistence level. From a document in the Vorontsov archives, we learn that the Governor of Orel sent round a circular to local police chiefs directing that the common people should not be allowed to eat pure wheaten bread. Flour should be adulterated with acorns, chaff, oats, barley, and even hemp

---

[1] Radishchev, *Polnoe sobranie sochineny*, III, 105.

and cotton-cake, before being sent to the bakers. The Governor further recommended the consumption of bread made from acorns only.

In foreign policy, Catherine and Potemkin still pursued their grandiose schemes. 'Whoever gains nothing is a loser,' the Empress would remark. Poland partitioned, the Ottoman Porte humbled, the Ukraine, Crimea and North Caucasian steppe swallowed up, the King of Georgia taken under Russian suzerainty, the Empress's grandson, Constantine, designated as Emperor of a restored Byzantium—these were only preludes to greater enterprises still to come. 'If I lived for two hundred years,' Catherine remarked to the poet Derzhavin, 'the whole of Europe would of course be subject to the Russian sceptre. I shall not die without driving the Turks out of Europe, subduing the pride of China and establishing trade relations with India.' In those years of her heyday, as Derzhavin commented, she was maintained by Potemkin in a state of ecstatic megalomania; intoxicated by the renown of her victories, she thought of nothing but the subjection of fresh Empires to her realm.[1]

Catherine and Potemkin finished by overreaching themselves. Their ambitious undertakings had alienated not only the principal Muslim powers, namely Turkey and Persia, but also Russia's former allies, Prussia and Great Britain, whose friendship had been sacrificed by the Russian Court in exchange for an intimate association with the Emperor of Austria. Foreign statesmen felt that Catherine could not be allowed to continue unchecked her triumphal progress round the Black Sea, through the Balkans and out into the Mediterranean and the Persian Gulf, to end one day in complete Russian hegemony in the Levant and possibly over the whole of Europe and Asia.

Boiling point was reached in 1787, when Catherine responded to Turkish demands for restitution of the Crimea by proceeding on a triumphal visit to her new Black Sea dominions, in company with Emperor Joseph of Austria. Cleverly stage-managed by Potemkin, this pantomime infuriated the Ottoman Government beyond endurance. In August, the Russian Ambassador at Istanbul was thrown into the Fortress of the Seven Towers, and Catherine and the Sultan were once more at war. Catherine had counted on a few more years of rearmament and leisurely economic consolidation, after which the Austro-Russian forces would launch their death blow at the Ottoman Empire. Now a conflict was thrust prematurely upon her. On the Russian side, scarcely anything was ready and for a time things went very badly. The Russian fleet, on its way from Sevastopol to Varna, was destroyed by a tempest. With British encouragement, King Gustavus III of Sweden declared

[1] G. R. Derzhavin, *Zapiski* ('Memoirs'), in *Sochineniya* ('Complete Works'), ed. Ya. K. Grot, VI, St Petersburg, 1876, pp. 606, 669–70.

war on Russia, launched an offensive from Finland and immobilized
the Russian Baltic fleet. In the east, Transcaucasia had to be evacuated,
leaving King Heraclius of Georgia at the mercy of the Shah of Persia.
Outside the Turkish bastion of Ochakov on the Black Sea, Potemkin
sulked jealously in his tent and for months did little except to hamper
the enterprises of his illustrious lieutenants, Suvorov and Rumyantsev.

Simultaneously, events equally damaging to the security of Russian
autocracy were taking place in France, where the rise of a new bourgeois
class, the inadequacies of the old social system, the spread of rationalism,
and growing economic difficulties all combined with the general effete-
ness of the Government of Louis XVI to lead the *Ancien Régime* to its
ruin. As the French Envoy at St Petersburg, Comte Louis-Philippe de
Ségur, commented, 'The truth is that from one extremity of Europe to
another, enlightenment, progressive thought and rational ideas having
made tremendous advances in the course of the last two centuries, with
the ideas of justice, order and liberty spreading everywhere and the
principles of morality and equity triumphing daily over prejudice, men's
minds were universally inclined to substitute the reign of law for that
of caprice and arbitrary power.'[1]

The fall of the Bastille and the Declaration of the Rights of Man
appeared to the world at large as the logical culmination of the propaganda campaign waged by Voltaire, the French Encyclopedists and
their disciples against the established order in Church and State. As
early as 1771, Diderot had declared in a letter to Princess Dashkov:

'Each age has its characteristic spirit. The spirit of ours appears to be
that of liberty. The first attack—that on superstition—has been fierce
and unmeasured. When men have once dared in any way to assault the
barriers of religion, the most formidable which exist, and the most
respected, then it is impossible to call a halt there. If once brought to
turn their proud gaze against the majesty of Heaven, they will assuredly
direct it the next moment against earthly sovereignty.'

Had not Diderot's friend, the Baron d'Holbach, looked forward with
relish from the comfort of his Paris mansion to the day when all the
mighty of this world and all the aristocrats would be 'hanged and
strangled with the entrails of the priests'?[2] Now that the mob was
howling in the streets, and Holbach's gory prediction was actually
coming to pass, not only the priests and nobles, but even many of the
freethinkers who had looked forward to the downfall of the *Ancien Régime*,
were appalled at the Frankenstein monster which had been unleashed.

[1] Ségur, *Mémoires*, in *Oeuvres*, Paris, 1824, III, 493.

[2] *Le Bon Sens* [*du Curé Jean Meslier*], first published in 1772. Though based
in part on Meslier's Testament, the book was written by Holbach.

In Russia, the fall of the Bastille was greeted with public rejoicing; people embraced each other and danced in the streets of St Petersburg. Inflammatory brochures by Carra and other French agitators were smuggled in, translated, and circulated clandestinely in manuscript copies. In Paris, to the dismay of the Russian Ambassador, young Paul Stroganov and his tutor, the Jacobin Gilbert Romme, were attending meetings of political clubs and taking an active part in the revolutionary campaign. The Russian semi-official Press followed events with horrified fascination. On August 7, 1789, the St Petersburg *Vedomosti* or 'News' carried a report of the sacking of the Bastille, adding that 'the hand shakes with dread when describing events characterized by such neglect of duty towards the monarch and towards humanity'. The Moscow *Vedomosti* likewise reflects the general mood of curiosity mingled with foreboding, describing the popular gatherings in the garden of the Palais-Royal, where the orators 'are stirring up the rabble to commit great outrages against the aristocratic class of the community'. In the spring of 1790, the Russian newspapers report from France that 'one section of His Majesty's subjects is exterminating the other with the most bestial tortures and assassinations. The mob is running amok throughout the provinces.' According to the Russian Court Chaplain, Samborsky, in St Petersburg itself, 'people are everywhere discussing the autocratic system in terms of great licence—the sentiments aroused by France's example forecast the most shocking bloodshed for our own beloved fatherland.'

From the beginning, Catherine was aware of the international implications of the French Revolution and its possible impact on Russian absolutism. She expressed the fear that like many other Paris fashions, the revolutionary mode might develop into a universal epidemic. To her correspondents, she dilated on 'the horrors of mob rule, the Empire of that most fearsome of tyrants, the domination of the rabble'. She lumped all French political groupings together under a common anathema, and termed Paris a 'hellish inferno', and the Constituent Assembly a hydra with twelve hundred heads; Mirabeau and Lafayette she abused in the same terms she was later to apply to Marat and Robespierre. She was irritated by the feeble behaviour of Louis XVI and his supporters, and declared that in no corner of Europe would she tolerate a Government controlled by a gang of cobblers. Instructing her envoy in Paris to give all possible assistance to the Royal cause, Catherine threw herself heart and soul into rallying the Courts of Europe for a crusade against rampant Jacobinism.

All this naturally led to a marked decline in official tolerance of even the most innocuous criticism. The authorities embarked on a regular drive against subversion and sedition. The spectre of Pugachev still haunted the Empress; widespread popular grumbling about conscription and the burden of taxation led her to apprehend that what she called 'fermentation of the scum' might spread from Paris into Russia itself. Any indiscreet freethinker was therefore liable to be labelled a 'Jacobin' and haled before the amiable Sheshkovsky, who often opened his interrogations by knocking out a few of his client's teeth with his walking stick.

Strangely enough, Radishchev seems to have remained almost impervious to the abrupt change in the climate of official opinion in Russia following the outbreak of the war with Turkey and Sweden, and the French Revolution. The German diplomat Helbig, who met Radishchev in St Petersburg about this time, wrote later: 'He would speak little, and seldom before a question was put to him. But when occasion presented, he expressed himself well and was very informative. Otherwise, he was always introspective, and looked like a man who takes no notice of what is going on around him, but is preoccupied with some absorbing problem.' In spite of his family responsibilities and his enviable position in the official hierarchy, Radishchev continued undeterred with his preparations for the launching of that most outspoken publication, *A Journey from St Petersburg to Moscow*, and in the meantime brought out several lesser works which showed clearly the direction in which his thoughts were tending.

For some time, Radishchev had been a member of an inoffensive St Petersburg literary club, founded in 1784, and called the Society of Friends of Literary Science. Some of its members were Freemasons; it included young literary men, army officers and Government officials. The Society produced a journal called *Beseduyushchy Grazhdanin*, or 'The Citizen in Conversation', the aim of which was declared to be the promotion of civic virtue: its general tone was pious and conservative. In 1789, Radishchev submitted to the editors an essay entitled 'Discourse on What is a Patriot'; since it was judged to be somewhat more controversial than the usual run of contributions published in the journal, its author was asked to go in person to the censorship to secure authorization for the article's inclusion—authorization which turned out to be readily forthcoming.

When one reads Radishchev's discourse, the editors' hesitations seem not surprising. 'Not all those born within the fatherland,' Radishchev exclaims, 'are worthy of the exalted title of son of the fatherland, or patriot. Those who live beneath the yoke of servitude are unworthy to be adorned with this title!' He goes on to say that there are only too many human creatures to whom avarice and cruelty have denied natural freedom, and to whom death alone can bring relief—unless, indeed, they themselves put an end to their own intolerable existence. They are not citizens, those poor serfs, not even men, but machines driven by their tormentors, beasts of burden, scarcely more than corpses! Since such poor wretches are not to receive the name of patriot, then to whom is it fit to be accorded? To the fashionable dandy with all his vices and dissipation? To the tyrant who revels in spurning fellow-citizens, and in whose presence no one dares pronounce the words 'humanity', 'liberty', 'honour'? Or to the glutton who wallows in brutish debauchery while thousands toil to satisfy his whims? Too long have so many human beings remained sunk in slavery and bestiality, the fault being that of tyrants who strive to stamp out mankind's high ideals. The true patriot, on the other hand, is a person of integrity, aspiring to the esteem of God and man. He is modest and honourable, a man of culture and understanding. In time of need, he will not hesitate to sacrifice his life for his country.

The Society of Friends of Literary Science did not long survive Radishchev's arrest and conviction in the summer of 1790. A fellow-member, S. A. Tuchkov, later noted in his memoirs that he returned from the war with Sweden later in that year, only to find that the police had closed down the Society's meeting place and forbidden it to assemble. This was, Tuchkov explains, because the 'spirit of liberty' was beginning to spread to Russia as a result of the French Revolution, and the police had received instructions to shut down all Masonic Lodges and even literary societies.

As if in answer to his own question: 'Who is worthy to be called a patriot?'—Radishchev also brought out in 1789 a biography of his old college friend Fedor Ushakov, who had figured so prominently in his intellectual and emotional life while the Russian students were at Leipzig University. Published anonymously, and dedicated to their common friend and comrade Alexis Kutuzov, Radishchev's *Life of Fedor Vasil'evich Ushakov* was one of the first intimate biographies of a private person ever published in Russia. In contrast to the tone of the official eulogy or Church panegyric—the sole forms of biography previously existing in Russia—the *Life of Ushakov* introduces into Russian literature the mood of Rousseau's *Confessions*: 'I seek in this my own consolation and would like to unfold before you, my very dear friend, the inmost recesses of my heart. For often in the image of the dead you will find traits which remain even yet within the living.'

The underlying idea of the *Life of Ushakov* is that although Fedor Vasil'evich died in his youth, before making his mark in the world, yet he was a finer patriot than the courtly favourites and sycophants who derive brilliant careers and enormous fortunes from pandering to a monarch's caprices. Radishchev tells of the arguments used by Ushakov's Court friends when trying to dissuade him from leaving St Petersburg to perfect his education; once ousted from the inner circle of influential courtiers, they point out, it is impossible for even the most talented to win promotion through sheer merit, owing to the intrigues of those who have a vested interest in monopolizing positions of influence for themselves and their cronies. Apart from its purely biographical interest, the *Life of Ushakov* contains a good deal of political theorizing, especially as Major Bokum's petty tyranny at Leipzig provokes Radishchev to indignant tirades against both large and small scale despotism. The human race is patient, he says, and can endure great afflictions without a murmur. But there is a limit to human patience, and this in itself may be the salvation of humanity. May God grant that the tyrants of this world continue wrapped in their folly and ignorance, until the desperation of mankind hurls them to their doom! While the rulers of nations glory in the wholesale murder which they call war, their dastardly example is followed by insolent subordinates, and the views expressed by the French thinker Helvétius on man's inherent trend towards despotism are continually being confirmed in practice. (The love of pleasure, Helvétius had written, leads selfish monarchs to enslave mankind in order to force it to minister to their desires. The entry to despotism is easy, but princes often fail to realize that in assuming arbitrary power they suspend a sword above their own head. Unfortunately, though tyrants are often assassinated, tyranny is seldom rooted out. Helvétius concludes that so long as princes remain ignorant of their true interests and those of their peoples, every Government will tend to drift towards despotism.)

In the tribute which Radishchev paid to the memory of his friend, he made it clear that Ushakov, the obscure rebel and freethinker, deserved greater honour than many famous men: 'Although it is not altogether possible to say about him what once Tacitus said of Agricola and d'Alembert of Montesquieu: "His end was grievous to us, a source of sorrow to the fatherland and even to strangers and those who knew him not", however I may justly say that all who knew Fedor Vasil'evich regretted his untimely death; anyone who will direct his gaze into the dim future, and reflect on the role which he could have played in society, will grieve over him for many a long day.'

In spite of its truculent tone, the *Life of Ushakov* did not bring any unpleasant consequences upon its author, though it aroused mixed feelings among the reading public. Alexis Kutuzov, to whom the book was dedicated without permission, expressed himself as out of sympathy with its doctrine; himself a Freemason and a mystic, he found the radical ideas attributed by Radishchev to their dead comrade quite uncongenial. In a private letter about the work, Kutuzov commented that its author 'expressed himself in a lively and audacious manner . . .

I confess that I found the majority of his propositions concerning religion and Government completely opposed to my own system. . . . The book caused a sensation. People began to cry: "What impertinence! Is it permissible to speak like that? etc. etc." But since on the highest level, no remark was made, all became silent beneath. There were even some impartial people who took the author's side, and it may be that the praise of those persons was the unintentional cause of what has befallen him. The sensation I have mentioned had not had time to die down before he appeared once more before the public with a new work: *Journey from St Petersburg to Moscow*.'[1]

A similar view of the biography in question was taken by Princess Dashkov, the sister of Radishchev's superior, Count Alexander Voront-sov. 'My brother, Count Alexander,' she says, 'employed in his Department of Trade and Foreign Commerce a young man named Mr Radishchev, who had been to Leipzig University, and of whom he was very fond.' One day while Princess Dashkov was at the Russian Academy, of which she was the President, the poet Derzhavin asked her whether she had read a stupid book by Radishchev concerning one of his deceased friends. Princess Dashkov told Derzhavin that she doubted whether the book could really be stupid, since its author was not, but when she had read the copy Derzhavin lent her, she changed her mind. 'I mentioned this to my brother the same evening, and he immediately sent a man off to a bookshop to buy the pamphlet for him. His protégé, I remarked, had the itch to write, though neither his style nor his ideas had been properly digested, and some of his thoughts and expressions were dangerous in the times in which we lived.

'A few days later my brother told me I had been too severe on Radishchev's little work; he had read it and found it merely useless, since the man whom it was about, Ushakov, had never said anything remarkable, and that was the end of it.

'I may have been a little severe in my judgment, I agreed, but as he was interested in the author, I thought it my duty to warn him of what I fancied I had seen in that silly little pamphlet. A man who had done nothing in his life but sleep, drink and eat could only find a panegyrist in someone with a mania for seeing himself in print. That writer's itch, I said, might one day induce his protégé to write something really reprehensible.' And referring to the publication in the following year of Radishchev's *Journey from St Petersburg to Moscow*, Princess Dashkov adds, 'And so in fact it turned out. . . .'[2]

This passage from the Princess Dashkov's memoirs is important,

---

[1] Radishchev, *Sochineniya*, ed. V. V. Kallash, Moscow, 1907, II, 480–1.
[2] *The Memoirs of Princess Dashkov*, trans. and ed. by Kyril FitzLyon, London, 1958, pp. 240–1. See also *Arkhiv Vorontsova*, V, Moscow, 1872, p. 223.

not only for the light which it throws on the reaction in aristocratic circles to Radishchev's literary efforts, but also as proof that he felt it prudent not to confide in his patron Vorontsov about them. This is significant, since efforts were later made to implicate Vorontsov, with Radishchev, in alleged activities directed against the régime. As it was, Vorontsov had not even received a copy of the *Life of Ushakov* from the author, and had to send out to a bookshop for one. One can only imagine what Vorontsov's reaction would have been had he known that his subordinate, taking advantage of the edict of 1783 permitting the installation of private printing presses, had actually bought one, and was busy setting up in print a book compared with which the *Life of Ushakov* appears inoffensive in the extreme.

*

For Catherine the Great, 1790 was a very trying year. This is borne out by a number of highly revealing and hitherto unpublished despatches addressed at the time by the young French chargé d'affaires at St Petersburg, Edmond Genet, to the Comte de Montmorin, the French Minister of Foreign Affairs.[1] In these reports, we are able to follow week by week the general situation in Russia and the prevailing mood of Catherine and her Court at the time when Radishchev was preparing to bring out his *Journey from St Petersburg to Moscow*. On January 1, 1790, speaking of the strain imposed upon Russia by the war with Turkey, Genet commented: 'Recruits are expected from all quarters of the Empire. Contingents are on the way from the depths of Siberia, from the banks of the Arctic Sea, from the Caucasus, from the Crimea and from Little Russia. A quarter of these wretches will perish from fatigue, hunger and misery on the high roads and another quarter in the hospitals. This depressing calculation is confirmed by long-standing experience; but no sovereign is deterred by this.'[2] On January 12, Genet described the critical situation in which Russia found herself in international affairs: 'Russia is therefore at the moment at war with Turkey and Sweden, threatened by Prussia and Poland, on the eve of being menaced by England and Holland, and possessing—apart from the [Austrian] Emperor—no other friends but France, on whom in any case she can count only in the distant future. . . . Never, certainly, has Russia's

---

[1] For permission to consult and quote these despatches, I am indebted to the authorities at the department of archives of the French Ministry of Foreign Affairs, Quai d'Orsay, Paris, where I was privileged to spend pleasant weeks in research.

[2] Quai d'Orsay archives, Paris, *Correspondance politique, Russie*, vol. 131, No. 1 of January 1, 1790, p. 12. The dates of Genet's despatches are according to the New Style.

position been more critical, never has her policy been subject to greater uncertainty; and yet, in the midst of so many hazards, surrounded by so many foes, Catherine II remains unshakeably attached to the system which she has embraced.'[1]

Later in the same month, Genet described to his Court the economic hardships which the policies of Catherine and Potemkin had imposed on the Russian people: 'The great landed proprietors are beginning to raise their voice in all seriousness, and it has been found necessary to despatch to Moscow Monsieur Sheshkovsky, Chief of the Secret Chancellery, to repress several of them; the people groan in every province to see the best cultivators being continually torn from the land and lamenting families being robbed of their sole means of support; money has completely vanished from circulation and it is evident that the Government, under the guise of banknotes, is manufacturing a veritable paper currency; the harvest has been bad, next year's is going to be even worse; no snow has fallen, it is freezing only at intervals, and the grain is fermenting and rotting in the bosom of the earth; the revenues of the crown lands have fallen; trade is languishing; the rate of exchange is sinking steadily; finally, everything proclaims that it is time to finish the war and repair the evils which it has occasioned. In so alarming a situation, if the Turks refuse to negotiate peace direct, if they put forward unjust demands, it will be necessary either for the Empress, deprived of our support, to throw herself into the arms of England, or else be crushed beneath the ruins of her Empire.'[2]

Genet's later despatches give a lurid account of the disorders and abuses prevalent in the Russian military administration—abuses which were carefully hidden from the Empress by Potemkin and his creatures. Completely ignorant herself of the science of war, 'she has an exaggerated notion of her forces'.[3] 'It is necessary to be here on the spot to realize the extent to which people delude this princess, and how easy it is to do this when one knows how to flatter her *amour propre*.'[4]

In May 1790, Genet reported that Gustavus III of Sweden was making great headway in his land and sea offensive, and threatening St Petersburg itself: 'The Russian army is badly paid, badly fed, and discouraged; the peasants are tending towards revolt and are ready to surrender to Sweden; the Generals are divided amongst themselves. . . . The Empress appears to despise the dangers which surround her, but I have learnt from a person belonging to her entourage that she has often been shedding tears, and that she has cried out in a moment of

[1] *Russie*, No. 3 of January 12, 1790, pp. 24–5.
[2] *Ibid.*, No. 4 of January 19, 1790, pp. 41–2.
[3] *Ibid.*, No. 9 of February 9, 1790, p. 92.
[4] *Ibid.*, No. 30 of April 27, 1790, pp. 266–7.

agony: "What have I done to Heaven for it to employ for my humilia-
tion an instrument so feeble as the King of Sweden?"—These words
are highly remarkable in the mouth of Catherine II.'[1] At that time,
naval engagements were taking place within earshot of St Petersburg.
On June 4, Genet wrote to his Government: 'For the last thirty-six
hours the Russian and Swedish navies have been locked in combat. We
have not ceased to hear the sound of cannon, the echoes have rever-
berated in Czarskoe-selo. . . . The city is in consternation, and the truth
itself would perhaps be less terrifying to the people than all the rumours
to which panic gives birth. . . .'[2]

A few days after this, the French diplomat chronicled raids by the
Swedish fleet against Russian positions near Viborg. The peasants were
welcoming the Swedish King as a liberator: 'There is not one of them
but burns with desire to enter beneath his dominion and shake off the
Russian yoke.'[3] A victory over the Swedish naval forces early in July
was followed by fresh Russian reverses. On August 17th, Genet reported
that a solemn Te Deum had been held to celebrate an alleged Russian
victory over the Turks on the Black Sea, commenting sardonically: 'It
is at least the twenty-fourth time since the beginning of this war that
we are summoned to the foot of the altar, to hear thanks offered up to
the Creator of mankind for the blood which has been shed for the conquest of useless deserts, or for the sake of dominion over the ocean's
volatile surface.'[4]

In spite of all the Government's attempts to raise popular morale,
confidence remained at a low ebb. 'They fear the great nobles, they
fear the people, they fear the Guards, they are afraid of everything in a
despotic régime. But it is principally since our revolution that this dis-
quiet has grown acute in all the Courts. It is to be feared for the sake of
humanity that this example [i.e. that of the French Revolution], instead
of contributing generally to the cause of liberty, may rather cause the
chains of slavery to weigh even more heavily upon many a nation.'[5]

These were the unpropitious times—to be precise, the month of
May 1790—chosen by Radishchev to launch his *Journey from St Peters-*

---

[1] *Russie*, vol. 132, No. 39 of May 31, 1790, pp. 76–8.
[2] *Ibid.*, No. 40 of June 4, 1790, p. 81.
[3] *Ibid.*, No. 42 of June 11, 1790, p. 94.
[4] *Ibid.*, No. 62 of August 17, 1790, p. 241.
[5] *Ibid.*, vol. 133, No. 70 of September 21, 1790, p. 43. The Russian Government eventually secured a copy of Genet's secret cypher, and intercepted and
read many of his despatches: extracts preserved in the Russian archives have
been published by S. Bogoyavlensky in the series *Literaturnoe Nasledstvo*
('Literary Heritage'), vol. 33/34, Moscow, 1939, pp. 25–48. For his sympathies
with the revolutionary cause, Genet ultimately became *persona non grata* at
St Petersburg, and was expelled in 1792.

burg to Moscow upon the reading public: a time when war fever was at its height, when the Swedes and Turks might any day deal some crushing blow to Russia's dispirited forces, when, above all, there loomed on the horizon the awful spectre of revolution, the plague of Jacobinism, spreading from France, so it seemed, to undermine and overthrow autocracy everywhere. Educated people called to mind the example of Cromwell and the English regicides, while the revolt of the American colonies against British rule was fresh in people's minds. Could it be that fifteen years after the execution of the Cossack insurgent Pugachev, the tocsin of civil war would sound again in Russia? Thus, in launching his protest against the abuses of Russian absolutism in the early summer of 1790, Radishchev inadvertently chose the very moment when his quixotic gesture was incapable of being interpreted as well-meant social criticism, but was fated to be taken for a criminal attempt to upset public morale.

I

CHAPTER 7

A Journey from St Petersburg to Moscow

PART I

The Sufferings of Mankind – A Sentimental Traveller – Bogus Pedigrees – Sweated Labour – A Narrow Escape – Promotion via the Oyster Bed – An Alarming Vision

One day in the spring of 1789—a few months, as it happened, before the Paris mob sacked the Bastille—the St Petersburg Chief of Police, Major-General Nikita Ryleev, received for inspection the manuscript of an anonymous work entitled *A Journey from St Petersburg to Moscow*, with the request for censorship permission for its publication. Hearing that it had been brought round by an official from the Customs administration, Ryleev contented himself with a perfunctory glance through the pages. Modelled in its literary form on Laurence Sterne's *Sentimental Journey through France and Italy*, the book appeared to consist of travel sketches and impressions collected on the road between the new and the old capital of Russia, concluding with a panegyric of the great scholar and scientist Lomonosov. After putting the manuscript on one side for a few weeks, the police chief, who was himself the official censor, appended his signature and returned the manuscript to the author ready for printing.

Had Ryleev been less of an ignoramus, some clue to the book's real purport might have been conveyed to him by the motto on the title-page: it is a line from the *Telemakhida*, an epic by the eighteenth-century poet Trediakovsky—'A monster gross, insolent, enormous, with a hundred barking jaws'. Now this quotation is taken from a passage in the poem where Telemachus is conducted through Hades and beholds the doom meted out to Kings who have abused their earthly power. A Fury is holding before them a mirror which reflects their disgusting vices, their vanity and idleness, their exploitation of their peoples, their selfish ambition and cruelty, so that they see themselves as more hideous than the Hydra or even Cerberus himself—'a monster gross, insolent', etc. (In the original, of course, Cerberus is correctly described as having only three jaws, but Radishchev has multiplied them for added effect.) This hundred-headed monster theme recurs later on in the *Journey from St Petersburg to Moscow* as a kind of *leit-motif*, symbolizing absolutism, serfdom and religious superstition. Thus, in the chapter 'Khotilov', serfdom is termed 'a hundred-headed evil' and again, 'a hundred-headed monster, devouring the nation's sustenance', while in the chapter 'Tver' it is the turn of organized religion:

> And lo, this monster horrible,
> Like the Hydra, hundred-headed,
> Suppliant and tearful constantly,
> But having jaws with venom filled:
> Worldly authority it supports
> And scrapes the heavens with its brow.
> 'Its home is there above,' it says,
> Phantoms and murk it spreads around,
> Expert in flattery and deceit,
> From all demanding blind belief.

The preface to the *Journey*, added after the book had been through the censorship, takes the form of a dedication to Radishchev's old college friend Alexis Kutuzov. In it, Radishchev utters those memorable words which stamp him as the father of the Russian intelligentsia: 'I looked around me—and my soul was afflicted with the sufferings of mankind. I turned my gaze into my inmost being—and I saw that man's misfortunes come from man himself, and often only because his view of the objects which surround him is out of focus. Can it be, I said to myself, that Nature has been so grudging to her offspring as to hide the truth from a humanity which has gone astray through no fault of its own? Can it be that this fierce stepmother has given us life solely that we should experience calamities, and never know bliss? My reason shuddered at this thought, and my heart cast it far away. I found for man a comforter within himself. "Remove the veil from the eyes of natural sensibility—and I shall be happy." This voice of Nature echoed loudly through my whole frame. I awoke with a jerk from the lethargy into which sensitiveness and compassion had plunged me; I felt within myself sufficient strength to combat error; and—happiness unspeakable! —I felt that every man may contribute to the well-being of his fellows.

—This is the thought which impelled me to sketch out what you shall read.'

Here surely is the keynote to Radishchev's life and work. Above all, he was a man with a mission, a reformer, a humanitarian. Sometimes we seem to hear the voice of a man of the eighteenth-century West, a man with the sensibility of Rousseau, the rational beliefs of Voltaire, the faith in human progress of Condorcet. At other times, we have a foretaste of trends of thought that were to be thoroughly characteristic of Russian progressive movements in the nineteenth century—including that form of hysterical philanthropy, often frustrated to the point of revolutionary protest, which inspired the *narodniks* or 'Populists' of the 1860s and 1870s. Above all, Radishchev stands out as virtually the first representative of that important group, the 'conscience-stricken gentry', a class obsessed with the idea that they were enjoying illicit privileges at the expense of the peasant masses, and anxious to atone and make reparation—a feeling which underlies the psychology of the Decembrists, of the young Turgenev, and of many others who were to make their mark in the political and literary history of Russia.

Radishchev chose to give his message literary form in the guise of a narrative of an imaginary trip between the two great cities of Russia, a narrative which superficially recalls the technique of Sterne's *Sentimental Journey*, from which several episodes are actually copied.[1] Both works, of course, contain a strong autobiographical element: Yorick is Laurence Sterne's *alter ego*, while the Traveller in Radishchev's book is simply a mouthpiece for his creator's comments on the Russian social scene. Indeed, this link between Radishchev's hero and Sterne's Yorick is brought out by the fact that at one point the Russian traveller is addressed by another character in the book, the nobleman of Krest'tsy, as *chuvstvitel'ny puteshestvennik* or 'Sentimental traveller'. Yet in social protest and political satire, Radishchev goes far beyond anything attempted by Sterne. The English writer makes his points by subtle touches, persiflage, intimate conversation with the reader; our Russian author harangues his audience with passionate conviction, virtually bludgeoning him into acquiescence. As Herbert Read has remarked, '*Sentiment* in Sterne is always set against *humour*, the sentimental is relieved by the humorous, the humorous is redeemed by the sentimental—two contrary principles that together give perfect equilibrium.'[2] Radishchev on the other hand was virtually devoid of anything resem-

[1] I have devoted an article to study of this point: see D. M. Lang, 'Sterne and Radishchev: An Episode in Russian Sentimentalism', in *Revue de Littérature Comparée*, Paris, 1947, No. 2.

[2] Introduction to *A Sentimental Journey*, Scholartis Press: London, 1929, p. xxix.

bling a sense of humour, and approached his theme, as he approached life generally, in a spirit of deadly earnestness. His subject was the iniquity of the Russian social system, and in denouncing it he offset sentiment, not with humour, but with indignation.

*

The Traveller quits St Petersburg. 'After a farewell dinner with my friends I got into the post chaise and lay down. The coachman as usual set off at full gallop, and in a few minutes I was already in the suburbs.' Our Traveller must have overeaten at his farewell celebration. He dozes into an uneasy slumber, and is in the throes of a nightmare when the carriage jolts over a rut and wakes him up. It draws to a halt in front of a three-storey house standing on its own by the roadside—the posting station of Sofiya. Silence everywhere. The coachman unharnesses the nags which have brought the Traveller from St Petersburg and demands his usual tip—'The price of a drink, Governor?' No signs of life, nor of fresh horses. So the Traveller, armed with his official movement warrant, goes into the coach house and scouts round for the man in charge. —'I came upon the station commissary snoring away and shook him lightly by the shoulder.—"What the devil's the hurry?" said he. "A plague on this craze for posting out of town by night! There are no horses, it is still too early. Pray go into the inn and drink some tea or go to sleep." When he had said this, Mister Commissary turned over towards the wall and began snoring even louder.

'What was to be done? I shook the commissary once again by the shoulder.—"To hell with you, I have already said there are no horses!" —and wrapping his head round with the counterpane, Mister Commissary turned his back on me. "If all the horses are out," I reflected, "then it is unjust for me to disturb the commissary's slumbers. But if there are horses actually in the stable . . ." And I determined to learn whether or not the commissary had told me the truth.'

A visit to the stable discloses a good score of horses—'although, truth to say, their ribs were sticking out through their sides, yet they would have taken me over the next stage all right'. So back to the commissary again, who starts up once more resentfully from his slumbers.—'A fine fellow you are,' he grumbles at our Traveller, 'it looks as if you got into that way of behaviour with old-time coachmen. People used to whack them with sticks, but nowadays times have changed.' And Mister Commissary is off to sleep again. Suppressing the temptation to resort to old-time methods of persuasion, the Traveller employs diplomacy, and finds that good results can be achieved with a few bronze copecks bestowed in the right quarter. Soon a willing ostler harnesses fresh horses, and the Traveller is again bowling along the highroad.

The driver intones a folk song which, like so many Russian melodies, seems to express the soulful yearnings of the Russian people. The Traveller is driven by this mournful ditty to reflect on the national character and temperament of his fellow countrymen.—'Look at an individual Russian: you will find him musing. If he wants to chase away boredom or, as he would put it, if he wants a spot of jollity, then he goes to the tavern. In roistering mood, he becomes impetuous, bold, truculent. If something chances to displease him, then he is quick to start a quarrel or a fight. A bargee who goes into a tavern with a hang-dog air, and emerges gory and blood-stained after a brawl, provides a clue to much that has seemed puzzling in Russian history.' And the Traveller drops off into a doze, giving thanks to God who has given to mankind sleep, the next best substitute for death to people like himself, who have no incentive to live.

An hour or two later, as he jogs along in the early dawn, the Traveller reflects on the atrocious condition of the road, which was last repaired many months before on the occasion of the Empress Catherine's tour to South Russia. In the original manuscript of the *Journey from St Petersburg to Moscow* Radishchev added some caustic reflections on the scandalous neglect of public highways in Russia, where the roads were only put into shape when the Empress herself was expected to travel over them. 'But in an autocratic régime, the monarch is like the sun in the realm of nature: where it shines, there life is found; where it is absent everything perishes. An autocratic sovereign is the only person in the State entitled to obey reason, all the rest have to obey orders. . . . What a bore! And that is why the road along which I travelled was so bad.' (This passage was deleted before Radishchev printed the book.)

On arrival at Tosna, thirty-six versts further on from Sofiya, a singular encounter awaits the Traveller. Entering the peasant hut which does duty as a coaching station, he finds seated at the rough table inside an old man busy sorting out a heap of ragged, moth-eaten documents. As he fumbles with his papers, the old man repeatedly urges the station superintendent to hurry up with the horses that are to take him on towards St Petersburg.

The Traveller enters into conversation with the old man, who tells him that the papers are the fruit of many years of toil as an archivist in the heraldry department of a Government bureau. He has employed his leisure hours in reconstructing ancient pedigrees for all the present-day noble families, tracing their descent a thousand years back to Rurik, Vladimir Monomachus, and other famed heroes of ancient Russia. Admittedly, Peter the Great had made service to the State the criterion for promotion into the ranks of the gentry and the higher aristocracy, and ancient titles of nobility were therefore at a discount. Lately, however, there has been a rumour that Catherine the Great was preparing to bestow the title of Marquis upon any noble who could trace his family back two or three hundred years, so the old archivist is hurrying to St Petersburg to cash in on the anticipated demand for genuine (and bogus) aristocratic pedigrees. Back in Moscow, he offered his genealogical wares to sundry sprigs of the nobility, but these had laughed at him for his pains. Nothing daunted, he is now going to the more enlightened atmosphere of St Petersburg, where such researches as his are better supported. The Traveller, responding to the old gentleman's hint, slips him a small gratuity, which is not refused. However, he advises him to sell his genealogical tables as waste paper to the rag-and-bone man, 'for imaginary marquisates might turn many people's heads, and be the pretext for reviving a vice which has died out in Russia of late—that of bragging about one's ancient lineage'.

A little way further on after leaving Tosna, near the village of Lyubani, the Traveller becomes weary of the jolting motion of his carriage and jumps out to stretch his aching limbs. It was summer time. 'A few paces from the road,' he says, 'I caught sight of a peasant ploughing the glebe. The weather was hot. I looked at my watch.—Twenty minutes to one.—I set out on a Saturday.—Today must be a Sunday.—So that peasant who is ploughing must belong to a proprietor who does not let him off with an *obrok* or commutation payment. The peasant is ploughing with great assiduity.—This field, obviously, cannot be part of the landlord's domain.—He turns the plough with amazing ease.' (The Traveller decides to pass the time of day with this countryman.)

—'God preserve you!' said I, approaching the ploughman. The latter completed without pausing the furrow which he had started.—'God preserve you,' I repeated.

—'Thank you, master,' replied the ploughman, shaking the ploughshare clean and shifting the plough on to a new furrow.

—'I suppose you are a *raskolnik* (dissenter), seeing that you plough on Sundays?'

—'No, master, I cross myself in the regular fashion,' he said, showing me three extended fingers. 'But God is merciful, He does not command us to die of hunger, so long as we have strength to work and a family to support.'

—'Do you mean to say that you have no time for work during the entire week, so that you cannot take a breather on Sunday, even at the hottest time of day?'

—'There are six weekdays, master, and we go six times a week to work for our lord; and towards evening we carry the hay that is left in the woods into the lord's grange, if the weather is good. And on holy days the women and girls go walking in the woods after mushrooms and berries. May God grant'—and here he crossed himself—'that we shall have a shower today by evening. Master, if you have peasants of your own, that is what they too ask of the good Lord.'

—'I own no serfs, my friend, and so there is no one to curse me. Have you a large family?'

—'Three sons and three daughters. The eldest is just on ten years old.'

—'How do you manage for bread if you have only Sunday free?'

—'Not Sunday only: the night too is ours. If you don't idle, you won't die of hunger. One horse is resting over there, do you see, and as soon as this one gets tired, I shall start off again with the other. Things keep humming!'

—'Do you work as hard as this for your master?'

—'No, sir, it would be a sin to work the same way. He has a hundred hands on his plough land for one mouth, but I have two hands for seven mouths, you can reckon that up for yourself. No matter how you sweat away working for the master, you get no thanks. The master won't pay your poll-tax for you; he won't let you off a single sheep, a single bit of cloth, a single chicken or a single pat of butter. Mind you, it is different when the master lets the peasant go away to work on the *obrok* system, especially when there is no bailiff around. It is true that sometimes even good masters take over three roubles a head, but anything is better than forced labour on the lord's fields. Nowadays it is the fashion to let out villages on lease, as they call it. But we call it putting our heads in a noose. The ravening tenant flays the hide off the *muzhik:* he won't even let us alone in the off season. In winter he won't let you earn money as a carrier or by working in town—it is toil, toil for him all the time, because he is paying the poll-tax for us. It is the most devilish idea to turn your peasants over to work for a stranger. At least one can complain about a bad bailiff, but who will give redress against a landowner's tenant?'

—'My friend, you are mistaken, the laws forbid people to torment others.'

—'To torment? That's as may be, but I warrant, master, that you would not change places with me.'—Meanwhile, the ploughman had hitched up the other horse to the plough, and as he started on a fresh furrow, he bade me farewell.

'The talk I had with this husbandman'—Radishchev's Traveller continues—'aroused in me a flood of thoughts. First of all, I reflected on the inequality of treatment as between the several categories of peasant. I compared the Crown peasants with those belonging to

private proprietors. Both classes dwell in villages; but one category
pays a fixed sum in dues, whereas the other must be ready to pay anything the lord demands. Peasants of the former category are judged by
their equals; but the others are dead in law, except perhaps for criminal
cases. A member of society has his existence recognized by the Government, his protector, only when he breaks out of the bounds of society,
when he turns into a criminal! This thought made my blood boil.
Beware, tyrannical landowner, on the brow of every one of your peasants
I see your condemnation written!' The Traveller goes on to reproach
himself for the occasions when he has been hard on his personal servant,
Petrushka.—'Remember the day when Petrushka was drunk, and did
not turn up in time to dress you. Recall the clout you gave him. . . . Who
gave you authority over him? The law. The law? And you dare to utter
blasphemy against that sacred word, wretch that you are!'—And tears
of shame trickle down the Traveller's cheeks as the post-horses draw
in to the next coaching station, Chudovo.

Before the Traveller has been many minutes at Chudovo, he is
joined unexpectedly by his old acquaintance Ch* (identified as Radishchev's college friend, Peter Chelishchev), who is quitting St Petersburg,
so he says, for ever. This decision, Chelishchev tells the Traveller, is
the result of a nerve-shattering incident which nearly cost him his life.
And Chelishchev goes on to relate how he and a party of friends went
for a summer evening row from Kronstadt to a seaside place called
Sisterbek (or Sestroretsk), on the Gulf of Finland some miles north of
St Petersburg. An unexpected storm blew up and drove their boat on
to a reef some distance from the shore, where they were in imminent
danger of perishing. Luckily, their head boatman, at great risk to himself, managed to scramble to shore, and rushed to the house of the
local commandant in the hope of organizing a rescue party. In the hall,
he encountered the duty sergeant and urged him to arouse the sleeping
commandant. 'My friend, I dare not,' was all the response he received,
and when the sailor protested, he was bundled out of the house. Fortunately, he found two small fishing boats nearby, with the aid of which
he succeeded in rescuing the shipwrecked party. A few minutes later,
their own vessel disintegrated and sank beneath the waves.

Arriving on shore, Chelishchev gave thanks to God for his deliverance. Then, he tells the Traveller, 'bitterness entered into my soul.
Is it possible, I said to myself, that in present-day Europe, near a capital
city, before the eyes of a great Empress, such inhumanity could take
place? I recalled the Englishmen imprisoned in the dungeon of the
Bengal nabob.' (Here Radishchev reproduces verbatim the Abbé
Raynal's account of the tragedy of the Black Hole of Calcutta, where
the dying victims ask for the Sultan to be told of their plight: 'He sleeps!'

was the answer given to the agonized captives, and not a man in Bengal conceived that for the sake of a hundred and fifty lives, the tyrant's sleep should be disturbed for a single moment.) Indignant beyond words, Chelishchev called at the commandant's house to lodge a complaint against the sergeant's callous attitude to the shipwrecked voyagers. To his amazement, he found that the commandant fully endorsed his subordinate's view of the matter: 'This is none of my business,' he replied calmly. Chelishchev, beside himself at this example of bureaucratic heartlessness, had difficulty in refraining from physical assault on the official. 'Back in St Petersburg,' Chelishchev concludes his story, 'I told various people about what had happened. They all sympathized with the peril I had run, they all condemned the commandant's callousness, but not one of them would undertake to rebuke him for it.—"If we had drowned, then he would have been our murderer."—"But in his official capacity, he had no orders to save you," said someone. So now I am bidding farewell to that city for ever. Never again will I enter that den of tigers. Their one delight is to gnaw at one another; their pleasure is to torment the weak to their dying breath and grovel before the powers that be. And it was your suggestion that I should settle down in that city! No, my friend,' exclaims Chelishchev, jumping up from the chair, 'I shall depart to places where no one treads, where man is unknown, where his name is never heard. Farewell.'—And he gets into his travelling carriage and drives away at a gallop.

Between Chudovo and the next posting station, Spasskaya Polest', the Traveller is overtaken by a heavy shower and takes refuge in a peasant's hut by the roadside, where he hangs up his drenched clothes to dry and settles down for the night. While dozing, he overhears a conversation between two other travellers, a legal official and his wife, who have sought shelter in the same hut. The husband is lamenting his bad luck. He has never won promotion in the civil service. What is more, having refused to share his haul of bribes with the ministry accountant, he has been denounced by that official and committed for trial. How different is the luck of a certain courier well known in Government circles! This man had the good fortune to be in the service of a famed gourmet who was ultimately promoted to be Viceroy of a mighty province. Now that Viceroy—and here Radishchev makes a topical dig at the great Potemkin—had a passion for oysters. Twice a year the trusty retainer, Sergeant N* by name, would be sent to St Petersburg, goodness knows how many times to Moscow, in order to collect the precious bivalves. Every journey, he received top priority treatment, all expenses paid, three post-horses waiting for him at every station to ensure the prompt passage of Courier N*, 'sent by His Excellency to St Petersburg with most essential despatches'. Finally, the great man

could no longer restrain his feelings of gratitude to that faithful servant.
—'Secretary, write an announcement for insertion in the *Gazette*: In
consideration of his efforts in various missions, and his most punctual
execution thereof, I award him promotion in official rank.'—'There
you are, my dear,' concludes the voice in the dark, 'that is how people
make their way up the ladder nowadays.' The voices die down, and
the Traveller again goes off to sleep.

Next morning, the Traveller sets off on his way towards Moscow and
falls in with a distracted individual who appears almost out of his wits
with grief. This man tells our Traveller an involved and (it must be
confessed) somewhat incoherent story about the disasters which have
befallen him because of the dishonesty of a business partner of his. It
turns out that this man, though himself innocent of any fraud, has been
falsely accused and convicted of conducting business while an undis-
charged bankrupt. The news of his impending arrest has caused the
unfortunate man's wife to have a miscarriage, from which both mother
and baby perished. As the police came to the front door to take him
into custody, obliging friends bundled him into a carriage standing at
the rear entrance. So now this luckless man, bereaved and penniless,
is fleeing the minions of the law in the hope of finding some obscure
refuge from injustice and oppression.

The fugitive's story fills the Traveller with indignation. 'Can it be,'
he says to himself, 'that under so benign a régime as we enjoy nowadays,
such ruthless deeds can be carried out? Is it possible that there are judges
so misguided as to rob people of property, honour, life for the benefit of
the Exchequer's bloated coffers?'—'I meditated on the possibility of
bringing this incident to the ears of the supreme authority. For I rightly
judged that in an autocratic Government, the supreme power alone
could afford to be impartial towards other organs of authority . . . O
Christ, Our Lord! Why didst Thou write Thy laws for such barbarians?
These people, though crossing themselves in Thy name, yet offer up
sacrifices to the demon of spite. Why wast Thou merciful towards them?
Instead of the promise of future punishment in store, it would have
been better if Thou hadst doubled their punishment in this life by
tormenting their conscience according to the measure of their misdeeds,
granting them no peace either day or night until their sufferings have
effaced the evil they have brought about.'—And in this embittered
frame of mind the Traveller continues his journey, until the swaying
of his carriage sends him to sleep.

As he slumbers, the Traveller has a vision. He dreams that he is 'a
tsar, shah, khan, king, bey, nabob, sultan, or holder of some such
dignity, sitting in regal power upon a throne'. His seat is of massive
gold, encrusted with precious stones, and on his brow he wears a laurel

wreath. All around are symbols of his majesty and might: a silver column engraved with scenes of naval and military victories, the sovereign's name in an inscription supported by an attendant Genius, sheaves made of gold in token of abundant harvests, books bearing the titles *Law of Mercy* and *Law of Conscience*, and a monstrous serpent of shining steel entwined around the foot of the throne to symbolize eternity. All round the throne, in respectful attitudes, stand the high officials of the realm. A little farther off can be descried a motley host of suppliants from the many nations and tribes of a far-flung empire, all anxiously awaiting the flavour of a glance from the almighty monarch.

Wearied by the monotony of such uncritical adoration, the King's jaws suddenly open wide in a vast yawn, at which consternation spreads over the attendant multitude. This is followed by an urge to sneeze, which the monarch tries to disguise with the semblance of a gracious smile. At this grimace, the courtiers' faces light up with joy. Everyone exclaims: 'Hail to our great ruler, may he flourish for ever!' One on-looker whispers: 'He has subdued his foes at home and abroad, extended the frontiers of the state, and subjugated thousands of different tribes to his sceptre.' Another exclaims: 'He has enriched the nation, increased internal and foreign trade, he loves the sciences and arts, and encourages agriculture and industry.' A throng of young people cry out in unison: 'He is merciful and just, his law is the same for all, he regards himself as its foremost servant. He is a wise lawgiver, a righteous judge, a zealous administrator, he is great above all monarchs, he grants liberty to all.'

These flattering utterances make a pleasing impact on the autocrat's ear. Turning now to his commander-in-chief, he bids him proceed with a countless host to conquer a land many thousand leagues distant. 'Your Majesty,' replies the Generalissimo, 'the renown of your name alone will subdue the peoples who inhabit that country. Terror will precede your arms, and I shall return bringing tribute offered to you by mighty chieftains.' The monarch likewise intimates his will to his Admiral, to his Lord Chief Justice, to his head architect, to the Chancellor of the Exchequer, all his suggestions being greeted with rapturous applause by the assembled crowd of courtiers, and instantly brought to a successful conclusion.

In the midst of this gratifying scene, the monarch catches sight of the austere figure of a woman, humbly dressed and leaning against a pillar. Alone among those gathered there, she keeps her hat firmly on her head; at every cheer which greets the King's pronouncements, her eyes flash with contempt and she gives vent to a sigh of displeasure. Ignoring this disconcerting apparition, the King adjourns the assembly in order to attend the revels arranged by the master of ceremonies. 'Stop!' commands the unknown beldame. 'Stay, and come to me. I am a physician sent to you and your fellows to make you see clearly. . . . I am Truth. The Almighty, moved to pity by the groaning of the common people, your subjects, has sent me down from the heavenly spheres to remove the dark veil which hampers your vision. This have I brought to pass: all things shall present themselves today to your view in their natural guise, and you shall penetrate the innermost recesses of men's hearts. . . . I appear once to each monarch during his entire reign, that he may recognize me in my true form; but I never abandon the abodes of the human race. My dwelling place is not within royal palaces.'

—'Never fear my voice,' the mysterious apparition goes on. 'If from the ranks of the nation there arises a man who denounces your actions, know that he is your sincere friend. Alien to all thought of gain, alien to servile timidity, he will proclaim my message to you in bold accents. Beware, and venture not to punish him as an instigator of popular insurrection. Call him to you, welcome him as a pilgrim. For everyone who censures a monarch in the fullness of his autocracy is a pilgrim in the land where all tremble before that king. Welcome him, I say, show him honour, that he may return to you again to tell you the truth more and more completely. But such intrepid hearts are rare; hardly will more than a single one appear in a century upon the world's arena. And in order that your vigilance may not be lulled to sleep by the delights of power, I give you this ring, that it may remind you of your unrighteousness, if any you venture to commit. For you must realize that you are capable of being the most dastardly murderer in the nation, the most dangerous robber, the most notorious traitor, the most damaging destroyer of the peace of society, the most uncompromising foe, stabbing the defenceless to the heart with the weapon of your spite. It will be your fault if the mother weeps over her son, slain on the field of battle, the wife over her husband; for even the prospect of being led into captivity can scarcely justify the murder which they call war. It will be your fault if the field becomes a wilderness, if the husbandman's offspring sinks into death upon its mother's breast, withering from lack of food. Turn now your gaze upon yourself and those who stand before you, observe how your commands are carried out; and if your spirit does not shudder with horror at what it sees, then I shall depart from you, and your palace shall be effaced for ever from my memory.'

At these words, the scales fall from the King's eyes. He sees his robes spattered with blood and drenched in human tears. His fingers are befouled with dead men's brains; his feet are sunk in filth. The souls and minds of his courtiers and the throng of subjects standing round are dominated by avarice, envy, cunning and hate. The Generalissimo sent to conquer foreign lands is revealed, revelling in luxury and self-indulgence, while the common soldiers are treated worse than cattle, and robbed by their corrupt paymasters of their pay and their rations. More than half the new recruits are dying through the negligence of their commanders, or the senseless rigours of military discipline. Even the most illustrious of the King's generals is exposed as a coward, owing his advancement and many decorations to the zeal with which he has pandered to the lusts of the supreme commander. The same applies to the royal fleet, the Lord High Admiral of which is now seen reclining on a couch, in full enjoyment of the embraces of a kept mistress.

A like disenchantment awaits the King when he turns his gaze upon home affairs. He finds that his ordinances have been evaded, and the royal prerogative of mercy turned into a source of bribery and corruption. Instead of enjoying a reputation for justice and mercy, the monarch learns that he is regarded as a deceiver, a hypocrite, a detestable play-actor. 'Keep your mercy to yourself,' thousands of voices cry out. 'Do not proclaim it to us in pompous language if you have no intention of putting it into effect. Do not aggravate insult with mockery, or oppression with the sensation thereof. We slept and were at peace, you disturbed our slumber; we had no desire to wake up, for there is nothing worth being awake for.' When he comes to survey the public edifices and new cities he has built, the King sees them as monuments of extravagance and architectural bad taste. Stained with the blood and tears of countless toilers, in their style of construction they are no whit superior to the uncouth buildings of the Goths and Vandals. In the academies of fine arts, the cult of the muses has fallen into decay. All his much advertised generosity and alms-giving has been in vain: the money which has poured from his coffers, instead of relieving the needy and rewarding the virtuous, has gone into the pockets of liars, murderers, traitors and harlots. Tears of rage and remorse pour down his cheeks, and he realizes that earthly honour is but dust and ashes. (Soon after this point, the Traveller's blood-pressure rises to such an extent that he wakes up in agitation.)

The chapter ends with a postscript from the author: 'Ruler of the world, when you read my vision, if you smile scornfully or wrinkle your brow in a scowl, then you may be sure that the pilgrim whom I saw has flown far away from you, and spurns your palace halls.'

The tale of the fairy Truth, who gives the King a ring which pricks his finger when he does wrong, is in the French *Cabinet des Fées*.[1] Another treatment of the theme occurs in a miscellany by the French

---

[1] *A Journey from St Petersburg to Moscow*, trans. L. Wiener, ed. by R. P. Thaler, Harvard, 1958, p. 263.

writer Louis-Sébastien Mercier, *Mon Bonnet de Nuit* (1784), in which there is a fantasy entitled 'De la Royauté et de la Tyrannie—Songe'. In this, the author, like Truth in Radishchev's vision, fancies himself entrusted with the mission of purging a monarch's mind from the lies and flattery implanted by courtiers.

In his own 'vision' at Spasskaya Polest', Radishchev has clearly taken pains to fit the details to the realities of the Russian scene under Catherine II. The topical allusions include obvious reference to Catherine's legislative projects, to her mania for building palaces, to her passion for foreign conquests. In his life of the Empress, the contemporary writer Castéra said that the dream of Radishchev's Traveller was widely interpreted as an attack on the régime of Catherine and her favourite, Potemkin.[1] Gustav von Helbig, a German diplomat then in St Petersburg, wrote that 'everyone who had the least knowledge of the conduct of affairs at that time could discover the allusions for himself, without the help of a key'.[2] Finally, a Russian observer, S. N. Glinka, states in his memoirs that Potemkin, who was Catherine's Generalissimo in the Turkish campaigns of 1787 to 1791, took the reference to the army commander wallowing in debauchery so much to heart that he pressed for Radishchev's condemnation to death.[3] When reading Radishchev's *Journey from St Petersburg to Moscow*, this is one of the sections which the Empress peppered most vigorously with indignant marginal comments.

It is obvious that poor Radishchev greatly fancied himself in the role of the candid adviser whom the mysterious woman in the vision commends to the King's benevolence—a man 'from the ranks of the nation', who was to proclaim the message of Truth 'in bold accents'. Here again, no doubt, Radishchev was carried away by the example of the Abbé Raynal, who grandiloquently informed the readers of his *Histoire des deux Indes:* 'I have told sovereigns the extent of their duties and of your rights. I have sketched out to them the baneful effects of an inhuman power which oppresses, or of an indolent or feeble authority which tolerates oppression. I have surrounded them with portrayals of your misfortunes, and their hearts must have trembled. I have warned them that if they averted their eyes from them, these faithful and terrifying scenes would be engraved upon the marble of their tomb, to call down curses on their ashes which posterity would trample under foot.' Where Radishchev went astray was in imagining that Catherine would tolerate from her own subjects the same advice which—for her own reasons—

[1] J. H. Castéra, *Vie de Catherine II*, Paris, 1797, II, 371–2.

[2] G. A. W. von Helbig, *Russische Günstlinge*, new edition, Stuttgart, 1883, p. 302. (First edition published at Tübingen, 1809.)

[3] *Zapiski* ('Memoirs'), St Petersburg, 1895, pp. 205–6.

she had accepted in good part from international celebrities like Voltaire and Diderot. He might have done well to heed the warning uttered in the *Gulistan* by the Persian poet Sa'di of Shiraz, 'It is proper for him to offer counsel to kings who dreads not to lose his head, nor looks for a reward.'

6 Country travel in Russia

7   The Shrine at Bronnitsy

CHAPTER 8

A Journey from St Petersburg to Moscow

PART 2

❧❧❧ ❧❧❧

Archaic Education – Great Novgorod and Ivan the Terrible – Sharp Practice – A Mystical Experience – Rustic Rape and Murder – Marriage à la Mode – A Prosy Paterfamilias – The Perils of Prostitution – Bath-house Beauties – A Monastery Amorist – A Sentimental Interlude – Projects for the Future

At Podberez'e, the next posting station after Spasskaya Polest', the Traveller gets out of his carriage to soothe his aching head with a cup of coffee. He encounters a seminarist from Novgorod on his way to visit an uncle living in St Petersburg. In conversation with the Traveller, the young student complains about the archaic form of education dispensed in such centres of learning as the Novgorod theological seminary, whence the metaphysic of Aristotle and the spirit of pedantic scholasticism have driven out all useful knowledge.—'Why,' asks the seminarist, 'do they not establish centres of higher education in this country, where the sciences could be taught in our national language, in Russian? Learning would become accessible to all, enlightenment would reach everyone with greater rapidity, and in a generation you would meet two hundred educated men for one Latin scholar existing nowadays. Then in every court of justice you would have at least one judge who understood the nature of jurisprudence or the science of law.'—And after further reflections on the ignorance of Russian judges and the need for increased University facilities in Russia, the seminarist proceeds on foot upon his way.

As he walks off, the student drops a paper, which the Traveller picks up from the ground and starts to read. It turns out to be an essay on the dangers of religious mysticism, with special emphasis on Free-

masonry. The fear is expressed that the Russian Freemasons, in particular the Moscow 'Martinists', would fain undo the good work of
Luther and Voltaire, and introduce into Russia a fanatical obscurantism
comparable to that preached by the Prophet Mohammed. In Voltairean
vein, Masonic ritual is compared with certain scatological refinements
discussed by Hebrew rabbis, on the basis of details culled from that
handbook of eighteenth-century rationalism, Bayle's *Dictionnaire
historique et critique*.—All this, of course, is simply an extension of the
arguments which the combative Radishchev used to have with his
college friend Alexis Kutuzov, the Freemason and mystic to whom the
Journey from St Petersburg to Moscow is dedicated. In face of social
injustice, should one agitate for reform and contribute to the spread of
rational ideas, as Radishchev attempted to do? Or should one, like
Kutuzov, take refuge in an ivory tower of metaphysical speculation and
secret ritual, shutting one's eyes to the harsh realities of the world
outside? This is the real issue underlying the rather obscure and
laboured essay which Radishchev's Traveller picks up out of the mud.

The next stage after Podberez'e takes the Traveller on to the ancient
city of Novgorod the Great, which lies on the River Volkhov close by
Lake Ilmen. As he drives towards this dull provincial town which was
once Russia's most thriving commercial centre, an outpost of the
Hanseatic League, and the capital city of an extensive republic, the
Traveller reflects sadly on the vicissitudes of human fortune. 'Where
are the wise laws of Solon and Lycurgus, which safeguarded the liberty
of Athens and Sparta?—In books.—Where is splendid Troy, where
Carthage?—Scarcely visible are the sites on which they proudly stood.
—Does smoke arise to the supreme being as the imperishable sacrifice
is offered up secretly in the renowned temples of ancient Egypt?—Nay,
rather, the grandiose remains of those temples serve as a refuge for the
bleating flocks at the time of noonday heat. Not with joyous tears of
gratitude to the Almighty Father are they sprinkled, but with the filthy
excreta of animals' bodies.'

As he approaches Novgorod, the Traveller notices the many
monasteries still standing round about the town.—'They say that all
these monasteries, even those situated up to fifteen versts from the city,
were once encompassed within its boundaries; that up to a hundred
thousand warriors could issue from its walls. It is known from the
chronicles that Novgorod had a republican Government. Although they
had princes, yet these exercised scant authority. All the power of
Government resided in the burgomasters and the captains of the people
(*posadniki i tysyatskie*). The people in its assembly, the *veche*, was the
real lord. The dominion of Novgorod extended in the north even beyond
the Volga. This free commonwealth stood within the Hanseatic League.

The ancient proverb—Who can stand against God and Great Novgorod?
—may serve as evidence of its might. Commerce was the cause of its
rise. Internal dissension and a predatory neighbour brought about its
downfall.' And Radishchev cites extracts from the Novgorod chronicle,
showing how the citizens achieved independent status for their city as
early as the year 997, after a struggle with their own Grand Prince
Yaroslav Yaroslavich, the city's privileges being written down in a
charter sealed with fifty-eight seals; how in 1420 the burghers of
Novgorod began to strike their own coinage; how they used to have a
bell which summoned the entire body of citizens to the assembly, for
the discussion of public affairs. Then, in 1478, Tsar Ivan III of Muscovy
subjugated the city, and took away from Great Novgorod its charter
and its bell, since when the town's annals have ceased to record any
deeds of note.

On the bridge over the Volkhov, the Traveller alights from his
carriage and looks over the parapet into the river waters beneath. He
calls to mind the story of how in 1570, Ivan the Terrible heard that the
men of Novgorod were plotting to throw off the yoke of Muscovy and
regain their ancient liberties, and so resolved to raze the city to the
ground. The Traveller visualizes 'that haughty, brutal but clever ruler'
standing with pole-axe in hand upon the bridge from which, according
to legend, he supervised the execution by drowning of the Novgorod
city elders. What right, demands the Traveller, had Ivan III and Ivan
the Terrible to crush the burghers of Novgorod and annex their city?
None at all! But when nation arises against nation, the will of the stronger
must prevail. Whoever succumbs is treated as the guilty party, and
against this verdict there is no appeal. International relations are
governed by the rule of the jungle: 'The example of all ages shows that
right without might has always in practice been regarded as an empty
word.'[1]

Some of Radishchev's modern commentators, curiously enough,
come out strongly against his views on Novgorod's patriotic struggle
against Muscovite aggression. The editor of one edition of Radishchev's
writings has this to say on the subject: 'Radishchev was mistaken in his
assessment of the Novgorod *veche*, the guiding force of which was the
ruling class of feudal landowners composed of *boyars* and substantial
merchants. Radishchev was inclined to idealize the *veche* as an organ
of popular democracy. In addition, he came to an erroneous judgment
regarding the necessary, historically progressive measures of the Musco-

---

[1] The late Lord Norwich expresses the same truth in his autobiography:
'International law has never existed in the full meaning of the words because
there has never been a sanction to enforce it.' (Duff Cooper, *Old Men Forget*,
London, 1953, p. 195.)

vite state, directed, as is well known, towards the suppression of the regional and separatist tendencies of the Novgorod princes, who opposed the unity of the Russian state.'[1] How interesting to find Ivan the Terrible dubbed 'progressive' and admitted into the Soviet pantheon! It is instructive also to find Soviet scholars preferring the political creed of Muscovite autocracy to that of the liberal Radishchev, and plumping heavily for the Bismarckian doctrine that might is right.

While in Novgorod, the Traveller takes the opportunity of calling on his old acquaintance, the former commission agent and finance broker Karp Dement'ich, who has not long ago retired from business. Karp Dement'ich is an astute old gentleman, as the Traveller knows to his cost. A few years previously, Karp bought up an I.O.U. for a thousand roubles made out to some long deceased creditor by the Traveller's grandfather fifty years previously. With the aid of a sharp lawyer, Karp collected from the Traveller the arrears of interest on the loan over the whole half century since the I.O.U. was issued. In this and similar ways —such as selling in advance non-existent consignments of hemp which never materialized—Karp made a comfortable fortune, all of which he laid by in his wife's name. Then he had himself declared bankrupt and retired from St Petersburg to Novgorod, where he had a nice house already built—in his wife's name, of course.

As things turn out, the Traveller has chosen a good day for his call, since Karp's son is being married and the Traveller is invited to join the wedding party. Down they all sit at table. The head of the family, Karp himself, makes a dignified figure with his grey beard over a foot long, his knob-shaped nose, his sunken eyes, his eyebrows still black as pitch; he strokes his beard all the time and addresses everyone as 'My very dear friend'. His spouse, Aksin'ya Parfent'evna, sixty years of age, has hair white as snow and cheeks as red as poppies; not liking to take on board too much vodka in front of the guests, she has fortified herself beforehand with a good glass full in the pantry. The happy bridegroom, Alexis Karpovich, has neither moustache nor beard; his nose is as red as fire. Trained as a shop assistant in St Petersburg, he is a past master in the art of giving customers short measure, on account of which he is the apple of his father's eye. At the age of fifteen, he asserted his manly nature by giving his mother a good slap in the face. Finally we come to the bride, Paraskov'ya Denisovna, a taciturn young lady with a pink and white complexion, and teeth stained black as was then the fashion among the Russian merchant class. Before her marriage, her one interest in life was to sit by the window making eyes at every man who walked past the house, while at eventide she would stand by the wicket-gate

[1] Radishchev, *Izbrannye filosofskie sochineniya* ('Selected philosophical writings'), ed. I. Ya. Shchipanov, Leningrad, 1949, p. 520.

looking out into the road. To cure her of this in good time, her new husband has already given her a black eye coming out of church.

At the wedding banquet, the conversation turns on Karp's financial *coups*. He recalls with pride how he made his clients pay in advance for goods that somehow never arrived, while Karp invested the cash in his wife's name. At his bankruptcy, Karp salved his conscience by paying his creditors fifteen copecks in the rouble and then withdrew from business. Now Karp's son is taking over. Already he is concluding deals for fifty thousand roubles worth of flax for the coming year, half the money to be paid over in advance by his customers. Probably this flax, like his father's, will 'develop a headache' and fail to materialize. This will give him time to transfer the deposits to his wife's name and build her a house too, before going bankrupt and retiring in his turn. Thus is business carried on in Holy Russia!

After this Dickensian interlude, the Traveller climbs into his carriage and is once more carried onwards by swift post horses, until he alights at the next halting place, Bronnitsy. Nearby is a lofty hill upon which, according to tradition, there stood in olden times a temple, where an oracle would utter prophecies concerning the destiny of the tribes that dwelt in those northern lands. As the Traveller clambers up the hill, he imagines himself transported back into an age before the Slavonic peoples had settled in those regions, and pictures himself asking the oracle for guidance on his own future. He seems to hear a voice of thunder crying: 'Madman! Why do you attempt to discover the secret which I have hidden from mortals with the impenetrable shroud of mystery? Why, O audacious one! do you thirst for that knowledge which only the mind eternal may attain? Know rather that your ignorance of the future is in accord with the frailty of your physical being. . . . What do you seek, unreasoning child? My divine wisdom has implanted all that is necessary within your reason and your heart. Appeal to these in times of grief, and you shall find them sources of consolation. Appeal to them in times of joy, and you shall find in them a curb to undue exultancy. Return into your home, return to your family; soothe your agitated thoughts, penetrate to your inmost being, and there you shall find my divine image, there you shall hear my prophetic utterances.'

Amid these daydreams, so characteristic of eighteenth-century deism, the Traveller climbs further up the slope until he reaches the summit. There, on the site of the ancient pagan temple, there now stands a small Christian shrine. As he surveys the scene, the Traveller meditates on the unity of all religions professed by mankind, and offers up a prayer to the Almighty. 'O Lord!' he cries out, 'behold this church of Thine, this tabernacle, as they call it, of the true, the only God. Upon this spot, where Thou art present at this time, they say a temple of error used to stand. But I cannot believe, Almighty One! that man ever offered up the prayer of his heart to any other being but Thee. Thy strong right arm, outstretched invisibly over all, compels even him who denies Thine omnipotent will to acknowledge a creator and a preserver of the world of nature. If mortal man in his delusion addresses Thee in terms strange, unseemly and barbarous, his veneration is nevertheless directed towards Thee, God Almighty, and he trembles before Thy might. Jehovah, Jupiter, Brahma; God of Abraham, God of Moses, God of Confucius, God of Zoroaster, God of Socrates, God of Marcus Aurelius, God of the Christians, O God of mine! Thou art one and the same everywhere. . . . The atheist who denies Thee, but acknowledges the immutable law of Nature, glorifies Thee by this very act, praising Thee more yet than we do in our hymns.' And in one manuscript draft of the *Journey from St Petersburg to Moscow*, Radishchev added the following sentence which does not appear in the printed editions: 'But what Thou art, where Thou art, what Thou art in us and we in Thee, I know not, Almighty; and tranquil in my ignorance I do not venture to lift the heavy veil which hides Thee from my mortal eyes.'

The Traveller concludes these pantheistic musings with an affirmation of faith in the eternity of the spiritual world. 'All that we see will pass away; all will be destroyed, all turn to dust. But a certain secret voice tells me that there is something which will live on for all eternity.' And in support of his belief in the immortality of the human soul, the Traveller quotes in Russian translation an extract from the tragedy of *Cato* by Joseph Addison, act V, scene 1:

> The stars shall fade away, the sun himself
> Grow dim with age, and nature sink in years;
> But thou shalt flourish in immortal youth,
> Unhurt amidst the war of elements,
> The wrecks of matter, and the crush of worlds.

At the Traveller's next halting place, the hamlet of Zaytsovo, he meets his old acquaintance Mr Krest'yankin. As mentioned in an earlier chapter, the character of Krest'yankin probably embodies certain echoes of Radishchev's own experiences in the St Petersburg Senate and on the staff of General Bruce. Krest'yankin had started his career in the military branch, but becoming disgusted with the brutalities of army life—'especially in time of war, where flagrant deeds of violence are committed under the cover of military law'—transferred to the judicial branch of the civil service, and became chairman of a provincial tribunal. There he hoped to find an outlet for his philanthropic instincts, but was soon disillusioned. Because of his attempts to adapt the punishment to fit the crime and to base his verdicts on a careful study of criminal psychology, he was laughed to scorn as a hopeless crank. His efforts to temper justice with mercy were simply taken as evidence that he was accepting bribes from the accused parties. Finally, one specific case brought the situation to a head and led to Krest'yankin's resignation.

In the province where Krest'yankin was serving as senior magistrate, there lived a certain landed proprietor of vulgar origins and evil disposition. This person had started life as a boiler-man, and had worked his way up the ladder of promotion until he was made a lackey and finally a wine steward. After fifteen years in this job, he obtained the official rank of ministerial assessor, which conferred on its holder membership of the gentry class. On the strength of this, he retired to his native district and purchased a village with some serfs. There, as Krest'yankin puts it, the assessor and his family led a life of debauchery to which only Hogarth's pencil could have done justice, while the peasants were robbed of their holdings and livestock and turned into full-time slave labourers, working for meagre rations doled out to them once a day. The squire went around beating up the peasants with a big stick or a cat-o'-nine-tails, while his hooligan sons roamed the fields looking for a chance to seduce the serf girls. The daughters of the house, having no suitors to sweeten them, worked off their frustration on the domestic servants, several of whom they tortured to the point of permanent mutilation.

One day the squire's sons picked on the fiancée of a certain young peasant on the estate. Not long before the wedding was due to take place, one of them lay in wait for the girl, bundled her into a nearby store room, and prepared to rape her while his brothers stood guard outside. As luck would have it, the bridegroom-to-be and his father came on the scene at this point. Seizing a wooden stake, the outraged peasant dealt his young master a mighty whack on the pate, which started bleeding copiously. These proceedings quickly reached the squire's ears. 'How dare you raise your hand against your master?' he shouted at the young peasant. 'Even if he had spent the whole night with your bride on the eve of your wedding day, you should have been grateful to him for that. Now you shall not marry her at all. She is going to remain in my house as a domestic servant, and you shall be punished.' And he told his sons to give the suitor and his father a good flogging with the cat-o'-nine-tails. The peasants took their beating manfully, until they saw the young man's bride being dragged off by force into the squire's house. At this, the younger peasant leapt from the hands of his tormentors, tore the maiden from the arms of her ravishers, and tried to make good his escape with her. Overtaken by the squire's party, the young peasant fought like a lion at bay, until the other serfs came to his aid, and a free fight ensued in which the squire and his three sons were battered to death. All the peasants involved were taken into custody and freely confessed their participation in the affair, pleading in exculpation the unbearable tyranny which had been exercised by their late master and his sons.

It fell to Krest'yankin to pronounce sentence of death on all the serfs who had taken part in the incident—a sentence which would in due course be commuted according to law to knouting, branding and forced labour for life. But as he read over the papers in the case, Krest'yankin could not bring himself to sign the judgment. The killing of the squire and his sons, he felt, was but the logical outcome of their own misdeeds. 'If as I walk along,' the magistrate reflected, 'a ruffian attacks me and, raising a dagger over my head, attempts to stab me with it, am I to be deemed a murderer if I forestall his crime and stretch him lifeless at my feet?' Krest'yankin's attitude appalled his fellow magistrates, who accused him of inciting the *muzhiks* against their lords and masters, and of accepting a bribe from the dead squire's widow, who naturally did not want all her serfs sent off as convicts to Siberia where they would be of no further use to her.

All this reached the ears of the Governor-General of the province, who gave instructions that the peasants were to be sentenced with the full rigour of the law. As Krest'yankin still held out, the Viceroy summoned him to Government House on levee day. (As Krest'yankin tells the Traveller, he normally refrained from attendance on such occasions: 'I never used to go in for those ridiculous bowings and scrapings which arrogance regards as a subordinate's duty, flattery considers to be a necessary procedure, but the wise man thinks of as an abomination and an insult to humanity.') When Krest'yankin turned up, the Governor-General started railing at him in front of the assembled company for his misplaced indulgence towards the accused *muzhiks*. Krest'yankin endured this patiently for a while, but finally lost his temper and launched out into an impassioned tirade on the rights of man, on human equality and on the principles of natural justice and the social contract. 'One man is born into the world in every way equal to another. We all possess the same limbs, we are all endowed with reason and will-power!' and so on. Krest'yankin finished his startling discourse by maintaining that if the law fails to provide the citizen—and within this designation he included the serfs—with protection against arbitrary oppression, then the individual is entitled to take the law into his own hands. 'By his bestial conduct, that assessor who was killed by his serfs had infringed their rights as citizens. . . . My heart justifies them on the basis of rational analysis, and the assessor's death, though violent, was well merited. . . . Into whatever condition heaven may have thought fit for a citizen to be born, he is and will always remain a man; and insofar as he is a man, the law of nature, that abundant fount of blessings, will never be dried up within him; and whoever ventures to injure him within his natural and inviolable rights commits a crime against him. Woe unto that aggressor if the civil law does not punish him! He will be branded by his fellow citizens with the mark of infamy, and may everyone who possesses sufficient strength wreak vengeance upon him for his evildoing!'

This diatribe, so much at variance with ideas current in an autocratic and serf-owning society, was received by the Governor-General and his guests with blank dismay. Little by little they all edged away from Krest'yankin, 'as from a person tainted with a deadly infection'. Disgusted at their mingled arrogance and servility, Krest'yankin withdrew from 'that assembly of sycophants' and submitted his resignation from the office of magistrate. Now, he tells the Traveller, he is retiring into private life, where he proposes to 'bewail the piteous lot of the peasantry' and seek solace in the enlightened conversation of like-minded friends.

And so Krest'yankin bears away his lost ideals, and our hero continues on his path to Moscow. But this is fated to be a bad day for travelling. The horses are skinny and always slipping out of their harness; finally the axle breaks and the Traveller is obliged to alight while a replacement is being fitted. Thinking of this and that, he sits on a stone by the roadside, tracing figures in the dust with his cane.

A touch of light relief is luckily provided by a friend who drives by and hands the Traveller a letter from a crony in St Petersburg. That young blade Baron Duryndin has just got married . . . at the age of seventy-eight. Who is his blushing bride? Why, one of the ornaments of St Petersburg society, Mrs Sh*, well known for her unfailing kindness to the younger generation. For many years, she used to offer her charms unstintingly to the highest bidder. Later on, finding these wane, she obliged her clients by procuring the charms of other damsels for a modest consideration. Now, at the age of sixty-two, she has amassed a fortune and feels it time to retire from business cares into the aura of rank and respectability. How nice to be promoted from *Madam* to *Madame la Baronne*! Obviously, in contemporary Russian society, even the Duryndins have their uses.

At the little town of Krest'tsy, the Traveller's next halting place, he witnesses the touching farewell of a local squire and his two sons, who are entering Government service. Radishchev takes advantage of this episode to launch out into a rather hysterical tirade against the moral dangers which confront young men brought up in an environment of innocence and virtue once they quit the family nest. 'You can bet a thousand to one that out of a hundred sprigs of the gentry class who enter Government service, ninety-eight are going to become reprobates', and a lot more in the same vein. From the Traveller's description of the squire of Krest'tsy, it is clear that we are face to face with one of those prosy paterfamilias types who keep turning up in Rousseau's novels and Diderot's plays and stories, not to mention Goldsmith's *Vicar of Wakefield*: 'The composed features of his face reflected the calm of his soul, inaccessible to the passions. A tender smile of tranquil content-ment, born of gentleness, furrowed his cheeks with dimples, so alluring in women; his gaze, when I entered the room where he was sitting, was directed upon his two sons. His eyes, eyes of sound understanding, seemed dimmed by a light film of grief, though this was pierced by rapid sparks of determination and hope.'

The squire's parting homily to his sons is a hotch-potch of ideas culled largely from Rousseau's *Émile* and from the writings of the German pedagogue Basedow, whom Radishchev greatly admired. The obligations of children towards their parents, says this enlightened father, must be founded not on duty, but solely on affection. Filial relationships must flow not from fear, but from love. This love he has done his best to foster in his sons' hearts by the system of education which he devised for them. By exposure to the weather, they have been made hardy and self-reliant and expert in all outdoor sports. They have learnt fencing—'that barbarous art'—solely for purposes of self-defence. Without burdening their infant minds with superfluous learning, he has encouraged them to use their brains and reason things out for them-selves, merely providing them with the necessary basic clues to lead them to a right judgment on the question of the nature of God and other fundamental problems of life. Among foreign languages, he has had them taught Latin and English, for these tongues are characterized by 'the resilience of the spirit of liberty', and help to train the mind in 'those firm principles so necessary in all administrative work'.

Nor has the moral training of the boys been neglected. Self-control in moments of anger, and self-restraint in the passion of love are essential for happiness. Useful pursuits and hobbies have been en-couraged, for it is impossible to predict the ups and downs of fortune: knowledge of a trade or handicraft might one day be the means of keeping them from starving. Neatness in clothing is desirable, though without foppish excess. 'Keep your body clean, for cleanliness promotes health, and physical slovenliness and filth often open up an unseen path to disgusting vices.' The lads should try to prepare themselves for their entry into married life, 'the sacred union of society'. In times of doubt, the old gentleman says, a man should always consult the dictates of his heart: 'It is good and cannot deceive you.' The squire concludes by stating that if in the prevailing corrupt state of society, his sons can find no refuge on earth from adverse fortune, they should not hesitate to take their own lives: 'Remember that thou art a man, remember thy greatness, seize the crown of bliss if they strive to take it from thee—and die. I leave you as an inheritance the words of the dying Cato.' (This defence of suicide, one of the first in Russian literature, may have been suggested by the chapter 'Du Suicide' in Holbach's *Système de la Nature*, where that writer describes self-destruction as sometimes the only solution to a person's hopeless situation: 'If he cannot endure his woes, let him quit a world which henceforth is for him no more than a fearsome desert. . . . When nothing is left to preserve within him the love of his existence, to live is the greatest of evils and to die is a duty for one who desires to escape from them.')

Much of the Krest'tsy squire's discourse strikes us nowadays as naïve and silly. But it retains a historical interest as one of the earliest Russian tracts on educational theory, embodying many ideas which have since become commonplace, but were novel and startling in eighteenth-century Russia.

And so, fortified by the squire's worthy precepts and virtuous example, the Traveller goes on his way, musing agreeably on the display of paternal affection he has just witnessed. His reverie is abruptly shattered when he arrives at Yazhelbitsy, thirty-eight versts further down the road. Passing by the local graveyard, he sees a coffin being lowered into the ground, while one of the mourners is tearing his hair and behaving like one demented. 'It is I who am the murderer of my beloved son,' he cries out, 'I alone cut his life short! At the outset of his existence I infected him with a poison which sapped his strength!' It turns out that in his youth, this bereaved father contracted venereal disease, which was then passed on to his offspring, with fatal results.

The Traveller reflects that he too is guilty in this respect, and attributes the bodily defects of his own children to his youthful escapades with prostitutes. (There is no evidence that Radishchev or his offspring suffered from syphilis or any kindred complaint; most probably, he is obsessed here with the terrible end of his friend Fedor Ushakov, who died from it in Leipzig.) The Traveller goes on to censure the administration for turning a blind eye to the evils of prostitution. He disputes the argument that its suppression would lead to an increase in rape and crimes of violence. He concludes by launching a violent attack on those writers who advocate State-regulated prostitution and Government brothels—with special reference to the French writer Rétif de la Bretonne, who had produced in 1769 a book entitled *Le Pornographe*, in which he set out what he termed 'the ideas of a respectable man on a projected set of regulations for prostitutes'. In opposition to Rétif, Radishchev demands that all prostitution be done away with, and a rigid code of morality enforced by law, thus flattering himself, so it seems, that he had solved a social problem which has exercised the ingenuity of moralists since the beginnings of human society.

Questions of sexual morals continue to occupy the Traveller's mind at the next posting station, the district centre of Valdai, a town dating, Radishchev recalls, from the reign of Tsar Alexis in the middle of the seventeenth century. The spot was peopled by that ruler mainly with Polish prisoners captured in the wars, and now 'this little town is memorable because of the amorous disposition of its inhabitants, and notably the unmarried women'. 'Who is there that has never been at Valdai?' the Traveller asks. 'Who does not know the cracknels of Valdai, and the well-rouged damsels of the town?' And he treats the reader to an account of the crafty technique used by these good wenches to assail the pocket and the chastity of the wayfarer. 'The public baths were and still are the scene of amorous celebrations. After making an appointment through the good offices of some obliging old woman or fellow, the wayfarer arrives at the premises where he plans to offer up sacrifice to the much venerated Lada.[1] Night has fallen. The bath is already prepared for him. The wayfarer undresses and enters the bath chamber, where he is greeted by the mistress of the house, if she be young, or else by her daughter or her kinswomen or neighbours. They massage his exhausted limbs and rub off the dirt. This they do after stripping off their own clothes. And thus they kindle within him an amorous flame, so that he spends the night there, losing money, health, and his valuable travelling time. In the old days, so they say, these lascivious wretches used to put to death any unwary traveller who succumbed through excess of amorous exercise and of wine, so as to seize his belongings. I know not if that be true, but it is a fact that the effrontery of the Valdai wenches has latterly become more restrained. Although they do not refuse even now to satisfy the wayfarer's desires, they have lost their former brazenness.' (The amorous proclivities of these Valdai damsels are also described by a contemporary French traveller, Count Fortia de Piles.[2] Though he found them brazen enough, this observer, more sophisticated than our Russian hero, did not think much of the uncouth charms of the Valdai Delilahs; to one accustomed to the Sirens of Paris, it appears that they presented little inducement to stray from the path of virtue.)

By Russian standards, the Valdai damsels must have been fairly alluring, for our Traveller goes on to relate that the place has not only its Sirens, but even a local Leander. Close by the town, he tells us, there is a lake with an island in the middle. On this island there stands a

[1] The Slavonic goddess of love and marriage.

[2] See *Voyage de deux Français au Nord de l'Europe*, Paris, 1796, III, 263–4.

cloister, the Iberian Monastery, built over a century before by the Patriarch Nikon. Once upon a time, one of the monks visited Valdai and fell for the daughter of a local citizen. His ardour was returned, and soon his amorous passion had nothing left to desire, except for the repetition of his joyous experiences. This presented difficulties; a monk could scarcely be seen calling on his lady friend in broad daylight, nor would the fair beloved have received much of a welcome from the monastery gatekeeper. And so our monastic lover was driven to swim a mile over the lake at night to spend a few hours in his beloved's arms. In one of the famed Valdai bath chambers he would taste felicity, before breasting the waves to reach his cell once more ere the bell rang out for Mattins. One night, alas, a wind sprang up as the intrepid lover was in the middle of the lake. In vain he struggled against the tempest, in vain tried to turn round and make for home. The waves overpowered him and the current sucked him under; in the morning his lifeless body was cast up on the shore. Did the Hero of Valdai long bewail her Leander? Did she cast herself into the waters to join her lover in the life beyond the grave? Probably not, for it is not the Valdai maidens' custom to die of love—except in a hospital bed. It is more likely that she philosophically stoked up her bath oven, in readiness for the next jaded traveller who might pass that way, and require the solace of her services.

In the following episode, which takes place in the village of Edrovo, we revert to an idyllic atmosphere more in harmony with that of Radishchev's literary model, Laurence Sterne's *Sentimental Journey*. Alighting from his carriage, the Traveller catches sight of a group of village women and girls doing their washing in a stream by the roadside. As he admires their bare feet and arms bronzed by the sun and the fresh air, their flashing white teeth, and their neat peasant costumes, the Traveller cannot help comparing them favourably with the spoilt beauties of the St Petersburg salons, with their wasp-waists and mincing ways. Our hero tries to enter into conversation with the most attractive of these rustic nymphs as she carries her bundle of washing down the road.

—'Don't you find it hard to carry such a heavy load, my dear?— Excuse me, I don't know your name.'

—'They call me Anna, and my bundle is not heavy. Even if it were heavy, sir, I should not want any help from you.'

—'Why so stern, Annushka my sweet? I do not wish you any ill.'

—'Very kind of you, I am sure: we often come across gay bucks like you. Just get along with you, if you don't mind.'

—'Anyutushka, I assure you I am not the man you take me for, and don't belong to the kind you are talking about. Those ones, I fancy, don't start off chatting with country maids in this way, but simply begin with a kiss; but even if I did kiss you, it would be like kissing my very own sister.'

—'Don't spin me a yarn, please; I have heard that line of talk before. If you are not up to any mischief, what is it you want from me?'

—'Annushka, my love, I wanted to know if your father and mother are still alive, what your circumstances are, are you well off or poor, do you enjoy life, have you got a suitor?'

—'What is that to you, sir? This is the first time in my life I have heard such ideas.'

—'That shows you, Anyuta, that I am not a scoundrel, I don't want to abuse you or get you into trouble.' And the Traveller launches into a dissertation on the virtues of country maidens, which quite disconcerts the simple Anyuta, who gapes at him in amazement.

Our author follows this up with a digression on the naughtiness of society rakes who make passes at peasant girls. He tells the story of one country squire, a nice, kind-hearted man really, who was nearly lynched by his serfs during the Pugachev rising for having seduced no fewer than sixty peasant girls on his estate. (This is evidently an allusion to a well-known case of the time, since the Empress later noted on her copy of Radishchev's book: 'That must be the story of Alexander Vasil'evich Saltykov!') Radishchev reflects that it is a pity that those serfs had no right, according to Russian law, to demand official sanctions against this immoral overlord: 'The peasant is dead in the eyes of the law, we have said.' But to this he adds a warning addressed to the governing classes: 'No, no, he is alive, or will be alive, if he so wills it!'

Meanwhile our Traveller has got on speaking terms with the coy Anyuta, who tells him the story of her life. She comes from a family of smallholders, and is fatherless, so she has to work hard to support her widowed mother and little sister. She has a difficult time of it. Not long ago, a rich neighbour tried to force her into marriage with his young son of ten—this being a common method in old Russia of securing the services of a strapping girl to do the housework in the daytime and share the master's bed at night. (The immoral aspects of this custom are commented on by several contemporary observers, such as William Coxe, Fellow of King's College, Cambridge, in his *Travels into Poland, Russia, Sweden and Denmark*, published in 1784, and William Tooke the Elder, who admits in his *View of the Russian Empire* that 'it is well-known . . . for a young lad to connect himself with a much older woman for the sake of bringing into the family one person more that is able to work'.) Anyuta would dearly love to be married to a man she could truly love and to have a sweet baby, like her girl friend who was married the year before: 'Her husband loves her, and she loves him so much that ten months after their wedding, she bore him a little son. Every evening she comes out to nurse him on the porch. She cannot take her eyes off him. It seems as if the little chap already loves his mother too. When she says to him, "Agoo, agoo," he starts chuckling. Every day I feel like crying. I would so love to have a tiny chap like that myself.'

At this point the Traveller is so overcome by emotion that he puts his arm round Anyuta and gives her a sympathetic hug. Anyuta, thinking he is being fresh, pushes him away. However, he reassures her by swearing that his embrace is a pure one, inspired solely by sympathy and respect. Eventually, the Traveller soothes Anyuta's indignation. She confides in him that she has indeed a fiancé, Vanya by name, a simple peasant like herself. Every evening he visits her cottage, and together they go to look at Anyuta's friend's baby, yearning for the day when they can have a child of their own. But there is one snag to their happiness. Vanya's father demands a hundred roubles before he will set his son free to marry and leave home. Anyuta cannot abandon her widowed mother and go and live on the smallholding belonging to Vanya's father. So her fiancé plans to seek his fortune in St Petersburg, and save up the hundred roubles he needs to set himself up on his own.

Our Traveller, well-meaning as ever, expresses the hope that Anyuta will not let her Vanya leave her for such a den of iniquity as St Petersburg, where he will surely learn to drink and go whoring, and cease to love his pure affianced bride. To avert this misfortune, the Traveller insists on calling upon Anyuta's mother in their modest abode, and offering as a gift the hundred roubles needed for the young couple's happiness. Vanya also happens to have dropped in at the time. He suspects the worst when the Traveller offers cash, which the family all take to be a bid for Anyuta's charms. It turns out that Vanya's father has relented after all, and withdrawn his opposition to the match, and the marriage ceremony is already scheduled for next Sunday. So our Traveller, sensing a coolness in the atmosphere, discreetly takes his leave. As he goes, he compares the disinterested simplicity of that poor yeoman household with the cynical and money-grubbing attitude of the husband-hunting mamas of St Petersburg society. And with his thoughts filled with Anyuta's pleasing image, the Traveller jolts on to the next posting station, Khotilov.

Alighting from his carriage, the Traveller catches sight of a sheet of paper lying in the dust. It turns out that this forms part of a whole bundle of documents, comprising draft projects for political reform, which have been accidentally left behind by a voyager who has lately passed through on his way to St Petersburg.[1] This first sheet bears the title 'Project for the Future', and is nothing less than a far-reaching scheme—of a type highly characteristic of that period—for a complete overhaul of Russian society.

Cast in the form of an official manifesto to be issued by some future Tsar of Russia, the plan lays special emphasis on the need to liberate the serfs. The imaginary monarch describes serfdom as 'the bestial custom of enslaving a man like oneself, which grew up in the tropical zones of Asia, a custom peculiar to savage peoples, a custom which denotes a stony heart and a complete absence of soul'. This baneful institution has spread far and wide over the face of the earth. 'And we Slavs, sons of *slava* ("glory"), we, renowned in name and deed among the generations of mankind, have been led astray by the darkness of ignorance into adopting this custom; and to our shame, to the shame of past centuries, to the shame of this enlightened era, we have retained it unaltered up to the present day.' Earlier Russian monarchs would willingly have liberated the serfs, had it not been for the opposition of the landed proprietors, to whom the Tsar now appeals in the name of God and of humanity to modify their heartless attitude.

The imaginary ruler proceeds to demonstrate (as Radishchev never tires of doing) that serfdom and domestic slavery as practised in Russia are repugnant to human nature, to natural law and to the social contract. Following Rousseau's formula, he reiterates that all men are born equal: men originally entered into organized society for their mutual advantage, and for protection against wild beasts and other foes of the human race. Since those primitive days, this primordial social bargain has been allowed to sink into oblivion, but it retains its validity to this day. To enslave one's fellows is a crime.

The institution of serfdom, the Tsar continues, is all the more criminal and unreasonable since it means that the husbandman whose labour feeds the nation has no title to the land he tills. 'In primitive society, he who was capable of cultivating a field had the title of its ownership, and he who ploughed it had the exclusive enjoyment of its product. Far indeed have we deviated from the original custom of society respecting land tenure. In our country, the man who possesses the natural title to the land is completely excluded from ownership of it. What is more, as he tills an alien soil he sees his own means of subsistence depending on another's whim. . . . Can a commonwealth be called fortunate where two-thirds of the citizens are deprived of their

---

[1] This is another literary trick freely adapted from Laurence Sterne: in the *Sentimental Journey*, Yorick's French valet brings him a pat of butter wrapped up in a piece of old manuscript. This turns out to contain a story about a henpecked notary, which Sterne weaves into the narrative.

8 *Above:* Russian
Costumes

1. Woman of Valdai
2. Woman of Moscow
3. Woman of Archangel

Right: Russian
Rustic types

9　Moscow: The Kremlin

Moscow: Cathedral of St Basil

claim to citizenship, and are to a great extent dead in the eyes of the law? Can one call happy the civic status of the peasant in Russia? Only a blood-sucking vampire could claim the serfs to be happy, for he has no conception of a better state!' A nation where order is maintained by repression and servitude, our Tsar continues, is like a regiment of soldiers on parade, who are little more than animated dolls; again, such a nation is like a crew of galley slaves chained to their oars and benches and rowing in unison, but with hearts full of torment and despair. 'Look always into the citizens' hearts. If within these you find peace and tranquillity, then you can say in all truth: these men are happy.'

After this, the reader is treated to a denunciation of the traffic in negro slaves and the wickedness of the European conquerors of America, with special attention paid to the scandals exposed by the Abbé Raynal in his *Histoire des deux Indes*. Then we have a pointedly topical paragraph on the Pharaohs: 'Even nowadays we marvel at the hugeness of the constructions of Egypt. The incomparable pyramids will continue to bear witness through the ages to the bold architectural gifts of the Egyptians. But why were such futile mounds of stone as these heaped up? For the burial of the haughty Pharaohs! In their thirst for immortality, those arrogant potentates desired even after death to be distinguished in external appearance from their people. And so the enormous size of those socially useless edifices provides clear proof of that nation's servitude.'[1] The implication here is, of course, that palaces and public buildings erected by autocrats of Radishchev's own time at the toiling masses' expense are no less futile than the monuments left behind by those ancient Pharaohs. The Tsar then turns to consider the careers of rulers who have sought renown through military conquests. He likens their victorious course to that of the famous balloons of the brothers Montgolfier—orbs of fragile fabric filled with gas, which rise up for a few minutes to thrill the spectator, and then fall back deflated down to earth. Here Radishchev displays a decided pacifist tendency. 'The fruit of your conquests'—the Tsar addresses an imaginary conqueror—'will be, have no illusion, nothing but murder and hatred. You will remain a tyrant in the memory of posterity. You will be punished through the knowledge that your new slaves loathe you, and have no other desire than for your death.'

After these digressions, we return to the matter in hand, namely the problem of serfdom. Having already demonstrated that this institution is repugnant to natural justice and to humanity, Radishchev's Tsar

---

[1] This passage is a paraphrase of a section from the French traveller and political writer Volney's *Voyage en Syrie et en Egypte*, 2nd edition, Paris, 1787, I, 250–5.

L

now shows it to be economically disastrous, since it deprives the labourer of all incentive to work hard. A man, being naturally moved by his own self-interest, will only give of his best when he is sure of gaining thereby. In Russia, where the field and its fruit belong to some-one else, the serf works languidly and without enthusiasm. In other countries, where the yeoman enjoys free possession of the land and its products, no effort is too great for him, and he will cheerfully brave all weathers and overcome all natural obstacles to cultivate and improve his soil, and derive the maximum harvest from it.

This section is of interest as containing an economic and psycho-logical argument which played an important part in securing the aboli-tion of negro slavery, and of serfdom in Western Europe. We find it expounded by the Physiocrat Dupont de Nemours: 'Slaves have no motive to perform the tasks which they are forced to undertake . . . with the intelligence and care which would guarantee their success; whence it follows that these labours produce very little.' Voltaire, in his *Diction-naire Philosophique*, article 'Propriété', says that 'it is certain that the possessor of a piece of land will cultivate his heritage much better than someone else's. The spirit of property doubles a man's strength.' The same argument occurs in Catherine the Great's *Nakaz*, paragraphs 295 and 296. In *The Wealth of Nations*, of which Radishchev possessed a French translation, Adam Smith declares: 'The experience of all ages and nations, I believe, demonstrates that the work done by slaves, though it appears to cost only their maintenance, is in the end the dearest of any. A person who can acquire no property can have no other interest but to eat as much, and to labour as little as possible.'

What is more, our manifesto continues, the low productivity of land tilled by serf labour directly obstructs the growth of population. This is one of the main causes of the dreadful famines which from time to time bring starvation to the Russian countryside. 'Where there is nothing to eat, there will soon be no eaters, for all will die of starvation. And so serfdom's fields, which fail to produce food in sufficiency slay those citizens whom nature intended to benefit by their abundance.'

Apart from the economic disadvantages of servitude, it has a de-moralizing effect on both master and slave. 'There is nothing more pernicious,' says Radishchev's Tsar, 'than the perpetual sight of serfdom and its attendant circumstances. On one side is born arrogance, on the other, faintheartedness. Brute force is the sole connecting link between them. . . . It seems that the spirit of liberty is so dried up in slaves that they not only feel no desire to put an end to their own sufferings, but are even irked to see others recover their freedom. They come to love their bonds, if it is possible for man to love his perdition.

I seem to see within them the snake which encompassed the fall of the first man.—Tyranny's symptoms are infectious.'[1]

At this point our manifesto assumes a decidedly threatening, prophetic tone. Addressing the landowners, the imaginary Tsar asks them whether they cannot foresee the doom awaiting them if they fail to lighten the burden of servitude which weighs upon the peasantry. 'When a torrent is dammed up in its onward flow, it derives still greater strength from the obstinacy of the barriers it encounters.' Now that the serfs have once tasted the delights of vengeance, as they did under that 'crude pretender', Emelyan Pugachev, there will be no holding them back when opportunity knocks again. 'They are waiting for the occasion and the hour. The alarum bell tolls. And behold, the bane of cruelty will spread with rapidity. We shall see around us slaughter and venom. Death and flames will be meted out to us for our cruelty and inhumanity. And the slower and more reluctant we have been to loose their bonds, the more violent will they be in their revenge. . . . Already Father Time, raising his scythe aloft, is waiting for the propitious moment. The first demagogue or friend of the human race who steps forth to stir those wretched beings into action will hasten its stroke. Beware!'

To prevent the catastrophe he sees looming up on the horizon, the author of the manifesto (who is of course Radishchev himself) puts forward a constructive plan for the liberation of the serfs by stages. This plan represents Radishchev's own considered prescription for the cure of Russia's social ills, and so deserves special attention. 'The first proposal relates to the separation of agricultural serfdom from domestic slavery. The latter is to be abolished first of all, and it is forbidden to turn peasants or anyone included in the village census returns into domestic bond-servants. Should a landowner take a peasant into his mansion for domestic service or other work, then that peasant at once gains his freedom. Peasants are to be permitted to get married without requiring their master's permission. No compensation money is to be payable to a landowner in respect of a serf girl leaving an estate on marriage. The second proposal relates to the peasants' property rights and personal security. They shall own individually the plot which they cultivate, for they pay the poll-tax themselves. Any property acquired by a peasant is to belong to him: no one shall deprive him of it by arbitrary caprice. The peasant is to be restored to the status of citizen.

[1] Compare Montesquieu, *De l'Esprit des Lois*, bk. XV, chapter 1: 'Slavery . . . is not beneficial either to the master or to the slave: to the latter, because he can do nothing by his own virtue; to the former, because he contracts all kinds of evil habits through his dealings with his slaves, becoming gradually accustomed to the lack of every moral virtue and growing proud, abrupt, harsh, ill-tempered, voluptuous and cruel.' Thomas Jefferson makes the same point in his *Notes on the State of Virginia* (1784).

He is to be judged by his equals in the lower courts, in which manorial peasants, among others, shall be chosen to serve. The peasant is to be permitted to acquire real estate, that is, to buy land. Freedom is to be granted without hindrance on payment of a fixed sum to the master for a deed of manumission. Arbitrary punishment without trial is prohibited.—"Let this barbarous custom of serfdom vanish away, let the tigers' power be crushed!" exclaims our legislator.—All this will culminate in the complete abolition of servitude.'

On this note Radishchev concludes his programme for solving Russia's peasant problem. Moderate and reasonable though his proposals seem to us today, they were sufficient, as we know, to bring down upon his head the full wrath of the Empress Catherine and her entourage. Not until seventy-one years later was the Tsar Liberator, Alexander II, to put into effect most of the proposals prophetically sketched out in Radishchev's forbidden book. By then it was far too late. The effects of the serf mentality on Russian society had gone so deep that two revolutions and untold suffering have not eradicated them to this day.

CHAPTER 9

A Journey from St Petersburg
to Moscow

PART 3

꩜

*Collective Farming – Jacobinical Reflections – Evils of Censorship –
Serfs for Sale – An Ode to Liberty – The Press-Gang at Work – A
Serf Intellectual – Grandees Unmasked – A Rustic Singer – Peasant
Squalor – A Forced Marriage – Faint Praise for Lomonosov –
Moscow at Last!*

The Traveller's next halt is at Vyshny Volochok, where he has a view
of the canal dug by Peter the Great to link the Baltic with the upper
reaches of the Volga and with the distant Caspian Sea. He sees a busy
procession of boats and barges carrying grain to St Petersburg from the
interior of Russia. But his exacerbated social conscience prevents him
from enjoying this bustling spectacle of trade and prosperity. He compares wheat grown by serf labour in Russia with the tropical products
imported from West Indian plantations on which negroes toil for their
brutal masters, and urges the inhabitants of St Petersburg to boycott
corn grown on the estates of squires who hold their peasants in bondage. 'Is not the earth on which it was grown fertilized by tears and
lamentations?' Morally speaking, says Radishchev's Traveller, there is
no difference between corn grown by serf labour on a Russian landowner's private estate, and the coffee and sugar produced by negro
slaves in America. All these products, he declares, 'have deprived your
fellow man of rest, and been the cause of toil exceeding his strength, of
his tears and groans, and of the punishments and outrages suffered by
him'.

The Traveller illustrates his point by citing the case of a certain
squire who set out to make a fortune by farming his estate on systematic

lines. Certain features of this proprietor's methods come uncomfortably
close to those practised in Britain by 'enclosing' squires of the eighteenth
century. This Russian landowner robbed his peasants of their own
small plots of land and forced them, their wives and their children to
work all day and every day on his own domains. Those who had families
received a daily portion of bread for their sustenance, while the bachelors
fed in Spartan fashion out of troughs in the yard, their diet being cabbage soup, bread and kvass, seasoned with periodic thrashings. By
cutting down on the peasants' rations and introducing large-scale
cultivation methods foreshadowing those of the modern collective farm,
our landowner soon made his fortune and gained quite a reputation as
a progressive agriculturist.

As a convinced advocate of peasant ownership of the land, Radishchev's Traveller refuses to accept such methods as legitimate. In his
view, the pauperization of the agricultural population is far too high a
price to pay for a few thousand more bushels of corn. A landlord
employing capitalistic methods of farming and exploiting his serfs as
full-time labourers is, in his view, on a level with a brigand or a public
hangman. Radishchev presses home this view with hysterical vehemence: 'Barbarian! You are unworthy to bear the name of citizen. . . .
Break the tools of his husbandry, burn his barns, sheds, granaries, and
sprinkle the ashes over the cornfields on which he exercised his tyranny,
brand him as a common thief, so that everyone who sees him may not
only be disgusted, but may flee his approach to avoid being contaminated
by his example.' No wonder that, reading these lines, Catherine the
Great considered Radishchev a rebel (*buntovshchik*) worse than
Pugachev!

At the next stopping place, Vydropusk, the Traveller settles down
to have another look at the bundle of papers he picked up at Khotilov,
from which he has already extracted the one containing the plan for the
liberation of the serfs. This time he finds a draft proclamation, in which
an imaginary Tsar of Russia decrees that Court appointments shall no
longer confer the same rank and precedence on the holder as equivalent
military and civil service posts. The manifesto is seasoned with some
decidedly 'Jacobinical' reflections. 'Dwelling amidst persons of such
limited minds and encouraged in their trivial outlook by the flattery
dished out by holders of hereditary dignities and offices, many monarchs
imagined that they were gods and that any object had only to touch
them in order to become radiant and transfigured. . . . In such daydreams of pomp and power, kings imagined that their slaves and
attendants, by standing every hour before their gaze, will themselves
take on a monarch's lustre. . . . Under this delusion, kings have set
up a class of palace waxworks who, like property gods in the theatre,

answer to the sound of a whistle or a rattle.' Our imaginary ruler goes on to denounce as a scandal the fact that his coachmen, valets and flunkeys, whose services are quite useless to the community at large, should be entitled to promotion up the official hierarchy simply because they contribute to the royal comfort. What is more, Radishchev's manifesto continues, adoration of pomp and power is symptomatic of a primitive, uneducated society. The need to impress the ignorant masses results in 'the pompous external display of the rulers of nations and the tribe of slaves who surround them'. In an enlightened community, no such regal mystique is required for good government.

Accordingly, the King proclaims that the sole criterion for promotion shall henceforth be bravery on the field of battle, zeal for the economic wellbeing of the country, life-long vigilance in the administration of justice, and public services of comparable nature. In this way, Radishchev's Tsar hopes to provide an example for remotest posterity of how authority and liberty may be combined together in the interests of the common weal. If poor Radishchev seriously imagined that this recipe would appeal to Catherine and her courtiers and favourites, he was a poor judge of human psychology.

This chimerical project occupies our Traveller until he arrives at Torzhok, a fair-sized township nearly forty versts further on towards Moscow. Here he meets yet another would-be reformer, this time an advocate of tolerance and the freedom of the Press. This question has, of course, always been a burning issue in Russia where strict censorship has, with insignificant intervals, always been imposed on both books and newspapers, both in Tsarist times and at the present day. The Traveller reminds this champion of free speech that by virtue of the decree of January 15, 1783, any citizen may install a printing press on his own premises. This does not satisfy his acquaintance, who demands complete abolition of preliminary censorship control over books and periodicals. In support of this, he launches into a discourse on the inhibiting effects of censorship on the minds of thinking men. 'The censorship has become the nursemaid of reason, wit, imagination, of everything great and fine. But where there are nursemaids, it follows that there are children going along in leading strings, from which they often develop bandy legs . . . and may grow up into complete cripples.' Censorship control is harmful to the development of the arts and sciences. 'It infects the atmosphere and stifles the breath. A book which goes ten times through the censorship before it reaches the light of day is not a book, but a counterfeit product of the Holy Inquisition.' In this connection, Radishchev inserts a long extract from the German philosopher Herder's treatise, *On the Influence of Government on the Sciences and of the Sciences on Government*. Especially futile is restriction of freedom of publication based on religious intolerance. 'If in his ramblings the fool says, not only in his heart, but even in a loud voice: "There is no God!" then from the lips of all fools rings out a loud and prompt echo, "There is no God, no God!" But what of that? Echo is but a sound. It makes its impact on the air, causes vibration, and vanishes. . . . God will remain for ever God, whose existence is felt even by the man who denies Him.'

Radishchev's propagandist strikes quite a modern note when he discusses the effect of pornographic literature on morals. He admits that amorous writings, filled with lecherous descriptions redolent of debauchery, every page of which bursts with enticing nude images, are harmful to immature minds. But such works, he thinks, are not in themselves the cause of immorality. 'In Russia, such works do not up to now exist in print, but on every street in both the capital cities we see painted whores. Deeds corrupt sooner than words, and example more than anything. Those roaming harlots, who surrender their hearts publicly to the highest bidder, will taint a thousand youths with poisonous contagion, and all that thousand's future posterity. But no book has yet given a disease to anyone. Therefore let the censorship concentrate on the prostitutes. It should have no concern with the productions of any brain, however dissolute.' The right of censorship belongs by right not to the Government, but to public opinion, which is quite capable of deciding whether to award a writer a laurel wreath or use his books for wrapping groceries.

As for personal libels, these are properly the concern of the individual who considers himself libelled, who should seek redress in the courts. To accuse a judge or official of being corrupt, deceitful or stupid may technically constitute libel. But if such charges are true, then this is fair comment on a matter of public interest, which the Government should not seek to suppress.

So strongly does our opponent of censorship feel on the matter that he has composed a tract entitled *Brief Account of the Origins of Censorship*, the manuscript of which he entrusts to our Traveller.[1] This turns out to be a dissertation on the Voltairean model, designed to show that censorship is a relic of the Roman Catholic Inquisition, and that 'priests have always been inventing fetters to burden the human reason at all epochs, that they clipped its wings to prevent it from soaring towards greatness and liberty'. The reader is conducted through a list of famous cases showing the baneful effect of intolerance on the spread of knowledge from ancient times onwards. From the hemlock administered to Socrates and the book burnings carried out by the Emperor Augustus,

---

[1] Radishchev culled factual material for this from J. Beckmann, *Beiträge zur Geschichte der Erfindungen*, Bd. 1, 2, Leipzig, 1786–8.

we progress through the reigns of Diocletian and Constantine the Great up to the Middle Ages and the establishment of the Holy Inquisition, which Radishchev regards as the first efficiently organized attempt to stifle science and literature by official restriction. The invention of printing served to encourage the Papal authorities in their efforts, and Radishchev quotes some fifteenth-century documents showing the operation of censorship regulations in Venice and cities in the German Empire. He condemns the Roman Catholic system of issuing an Index of prohibited books. 'The priests desired that only their own devotees should be educated, that the common people should regard learning as something of divine origin and surpassing their understanding, and should not dare to claim any share in it.' But what advantage is it in the long run to any authority, Radishchev asks, to rule over a tribe of ignoramuses instead of a nation of educated men? 'Spread darkness, and you will feel the fetters weighing down upon yourselves—if not always the fetters of sanctified superstition, then it will be those of political superstition, which may be less ridiculous but is no less pernicious.'

Then the operation of the Star Chamber in England is described, and the various measures taken to curb authors and printers until freedom was finally granted under King William III. Another paragraph reproduces statutes guaranteeing freedom of the Press in the American colonies of Pennsylvania, Delaware, Maryland and Virginia, as promulgated shortly after the Declaration of Independence. Coming to modern Europe, Radishchev recalls the severity of censorship in France under the *Ancien Régime* right up to 1789. Any writer bold enough to denounce the corruption of the French King's ministers was doomed to languish long years in the Bastille. Fortunately, Radishchev comments, the universal currency of the French tongue ensured that any work of merit banned in France would be promptly reprinted in the Netherlands, England, Switzerland or Germany and enjoy a wide circulation. Even the French Revolution had not resulted in complete freedom of the Press. Here Radishchev adds a topical allusion to proceedings lately taken by the French National Assembly against Marat, with a view to curbing the outspoken criticisms contained in his journal, *L'Ami du Peuple*. The great Lafayette, Commander of the National Guard, was detailed to arrest Marat. 'O France! thou dost still walk close to the abyss of the Bastille.'

Finally, Radishchev criticizes the half-hearted measures towards freedom of publication taken by Frederick the Great of Prussia, who tolerated many shocking books, but only those which happened to amuse him personally. 'It is hardly surprising that he failed to abolish the censorship: he was an autocrat, whose favourite passion was omnipotence.' The Prussian censorship had its funny side. When Frederick heard that his own edicts were to be collected and published, he appointed a couple of special censors to ensure that nothing unsuitable was included. Nor is even the liberal Joseph II of Austria spared. Radishchev reproaches him for going only part of the way in removing the restrictions imposed by his mother, the Empress Maria Theresa, and failing to abolish censorship altogether in Austria. 'But is that surprising? We repeat what we have said before: He was a monarch. Tell us, in whose head can there be more absurdities than in a monarch's?' As for the workings of censorship in Russia. . . . But here Radishchev draws a discreet veil, promising to talk about this another time. He leaves the reader in no doubt that his remarks would be the reverse of complimentary.

Thus ends Radishchev's courageous tract, directed against those who attempt to stifle free speech in the name of religious orthodoxy or reason of State. But he was fighting for a lost cause. Autocracy cannot function without censorship, and the Empress Catherine knew it. When she came to read Radishchev's ill-fated book, this chapter on the evils of censorship was vigorously marked with an indignant imperial blue pencil.

As his horses pull up at the next posting station, the village of Mednoe, our Traveller hears a group of country maidens singing a pleasing folk melody. There must be merry-making afoot, he says to himself. He is on the point of drawing near to enjoy the spectacle when he takes a look at another paper from the bundle left behind by the would-be reformer at Khotilov. He soon gets absorbed in this new document, which is a spirited attack on the auctioning of serfs and domestic slaves, who were commonly sold either separately or in whole families, and often without their land, during the reign of Catherine the Great.

Twice a week the St Petersburg and Moscow public is informed by the newspapers that some feckless individual has gambled, drunk or given away all his worldly goods, and is adjudged bankrupt. 'On such-and-such a day, at ten o'clock in the morning, his house will be put up for auction by order of the county court, and with it, the souls of male and female sex belonging to the proprietor. Potential buyers may inspect this desirable property, together with the domestic serfs, on the premises in advance.'

Our reformer gives a vivid description of one such auction of domestic serfs, the property of a retired army captain. Though offered for sale separately, they are members of a single family. The grandfather, a venerable figure leaning on a stick, was with his master's father on the Crimean campaign against the Turks fifty years before. Later he followed his present master into battle against Frederick the Great of Prussia in the Seven Years' War. At Kunersdorf he saved his wounded master's life and carried him on his shoulders from the battlefield to safety. Then he was governor and tutor to his master's young son, rescued him from drowning one day when he fell into the river, and even used his own savings to bail the lad out of prison when extravagant living as a Guards cadet landed him in debt. The old man's wife, eighty years of age, was once wet-nurse to her young master's mother, then governess to the lad, and housekeeper to the family for many years. The third serf up for sale is the aged couple's widowed daughter-in-law, a woman of forty, who nursed the master's son as a baby and then helped to bring him up. As the child's mother was occupied with society life, the serf nurse became the boy's second mother and felt quite as much affection for him as his real parents. Finally we come to the younger members of the family, a girl of eighteen, the old couple's grand-daughter, together with her little baby, and her husband, a young man of twenty-five. But this is not the idyllic family group it seems. The husband is a mere base accomplice of his master's immoral tyranny. Unsuccessful in his efforts to seduce the girl, the squire forced her into marriage with this young scoundrel, and then himself invaded her marriage bed. When thwarted in his stratagem, the master employed four ruffians to hold the girl down by her arms and legs while he raped her. Thus was conceived the pitiful infant whom the blushing girl carries in her arms. The baby is also included in the auction. And so this gentleman is putting up for sale, not only his nurse and his tutor, but even his own illegitimate son! What a commentary on the manners of the time!

As the auctioneer's hammer falls again and again, each member of the family is sold to a different bidder. Tears and sighs greet the news that they are to bid farewell to one another for ever. Overcome with emotion and disgust, the writer quits the room. On the stairs he meets a foreigner of his acquaintance, who has come to Russia from Western Europe.

—'What is wrong with you?' asks the foreigner. 'You are in tears!'

—'Go back outside,' cries our Traveller, 'and do not bear witness to this shameful spectacle. You once denounced the barbarous custom by which negro captives are sold in the distant colonies of your own father-land. Go away, and do not be a witness to our disgrace, for fear that you should proclaim our dishonour to your fellow countrymen when you tell them about our way of life.'

—'I cannot believe this!' replies his acquaintance. 'In a country where everyone is allowed to think and believe what he pleases, it is impossible that so infamous a custom should exist.'

—'Do not be surprised,' our reformer answers. 'The establishment of liberty of conscience injures nobody but the priests and monks, and they are more concerned with winning a sheep for themselves than one for Christ's fold. But freedom for the country folk, so they say, would offend against the rights of property. And all those who might assist in achieving that liberty are themselves great landowners, so that freedom cannot be expected from their counsels, but only from the oppressive nature of servitude itself.'—And with this phrase, with its prophetic ring of revolution, we leave the pathetic scene at the auction room, while the serf family, now sold off to various new owners, say to each other a last touching farewell.

The scene changes to the next place on the route, the ancient princely city of Tver (now Kalinin). In Tsarist times, Tver was the capital of an important province. Here the Traveller sits down to dinner in a tavern. His table companion is a poet, who treats him to a discourse on Russian poetry in the eighteenth century. Such exponents as Lomonosov and Sumarokov, Trediakovsky and Kheraskov, are weighed in the balance, with particular stress on technical questions of rhyme and metre, on which Radishchev was something of an expert. Though patriotic in his assessment of the merits of Russian bards, our poet shows catholicity of taste, declaring that Homer, Virgil, Milton, Racine, Voltaire, Shakespeare, Tasso and many others will be read until the human race perishes altogether.

The real reason for introducing this poet into the narrative is to give Radishchev the chance to publish extracts from an ode, *Liberty*, which he had composed some years previously, in 1781–3, under the impulse of the American Revolution and the Abbé Raynal's tirades against slavery and autocratic government. The poet tells our Traveller that his composition could not be published in Moscow. Some of the stanzas were judged obscure and patchy, and furthermore, the subject of liberty was not considered there as a suitable theme for poetry. He hopes for better luck in St Petersburg, especially as the subject of liberty was singled out for treatment in the Empress Catherine's own *Nakaz* or Instruction issued to the legislative assembly of 1767. In view of this, why should praise of freedom be taboo in modern Russia?

In the *Journey* as published by Radishchev, only certain selected stanzas of the *Ode to Liberty* are printed, the gaps being filled in by a brief connecting narrative. Perhaps Radishchev was conscious of the poetic shortcomings of some sections and intended to polish these up before publishing the complete poem. The fate of his book of course made this impossible, and the full text of the *Ode to Liberty* did not appear until as recently as 1906.

The ode opens with an invocation:

> O freedom, blessed gift of heaven,
> Thou source of every mighty deed;

> O liberty, thou priceless boon,
> Allow a slave to sing thy praise.
> Fill now my heart with ecstasy
> And with thy muscles' strong impact
> Turn serfdom's murk to freedom's light.
> Brutus and Tell call from their sleep;
> Arise in power and with thy voice
> Strike fear into the monarchs' breasts.

Enlarging on Rousseau's famous proposition, the poet recalls that all men are born free and equal. There follows a description of the idyllic state of primitive society, a utopian state where every man's desires contributed to the public welfare and the deity of justice, truth and righteousness held sway. The rule of law was everywhere observed and rewards and punishment were meted out without fear or favour. In justice people saw the image of God upon earth.

Now the idol of superstition makes its appearance, horrible in aspect, hundred-headed like the Hydra of old, and lending its support to the usurpations of despotic tyrants. Superstition obscures reason with a veil of darkness, robs man of his natural sensibility, and weighs him down with servitude and error. It teaches men to fear truth itself. The poet invites us now to direct our gaze upon those broad domains where stands the dismal throne of servitude. Religious obscurantism and political tyranny form an unholy alliance to keep the common man in subjection and deprive him of all rights as a citizen.

> Beneath the shade of servitude
> No golden fruit will grow;
> Where all things cramp the human mind
> No mighty deeds we know.

The results of serfdom and autocratic rule are careless indifference, indolence, base cunning, hunger and other kindred evils.

> Raising aloft his haughty brow
> The tsar an iron sceptre grasps;
> On massive throne he sits in might
> And scorns his folk as vermin base.
> His to decide man's life or death:
> 'The villain if I wish I'll spare,
> To him my power I can commit;
> Where I laugh loud, with mirth all shake,
> When I scowl fiercely all shall quake,
> And only breathe when I permit.'

But behold, there arises a mighty army of fighters for freedom, intent
on overthrowing the hated tyrant and his myrmidons:

> There surges up a warlike host,
> Each man's eager for the fray,
> And in the royal despot's blood
> Each speeds his shame to wash away.
> The sword's sharp blade all round I see:
> Death flies in varied forms about
> And circles round that cruel head.
> With joy the fettered nations shout,
> For Nature's great avenging hand
> Has dragged the tyrant to the block!

The victorious populace haul their dethroned ruler before the judgment seat and arraign him for his crimes. He has betrayed the trust his
people placed in him, failed to protect the rights of the individual, to
shield the widows and orphans, to avenge innocent blood and punish
lies and sin, to reward virtue and valour and to preserve honour and
purity. The community has enriched the monarch with its labour and
served him bravely in battle. What has it received in return? Imagining
that he and not the people is the source of sovereignty, the king has
squandered the nation's treasure on harlots and favourites, and made
heroes shed their blood on the battlefield for the sake of empty renown.
'Villain, most savage of villains,' cry the assembled citizens, 'die, die a
hundred deaths!' The poet conjures up the image of Oliver Cromwell:

> O mighty man and full of cant,
> You sacrilegious sycophant,
> In all the world no man but you
> So fine a model could provide.
> Cromwell, although your crime I blame,
> For having power within your hand,
> You freedom's stronghold overthrew—
> Yet you taught every race and age
> How nations can their wrath assuage:
> King Charles to death you did condemn.

Now the voice of freedom echoes through the land. The people troop
to the national assembly and destroy the tyrant's throne of iron, just as
Samson of old threw down the temple of the Philistines. In place of
arbitrary caprice they set up the rule of law as arbiter of their destinies.
'Great, great art thou, spirit of liberty! Full of creative power, like God
Himself!' In a group of stanzas omitted from this chapter 'Tver' of his

Journey, Radishchev chants the praise of Luther, who 'smashed the pillar of the church's power, raised aloft the beacon of enlightenment and reconciled heaven and earth'; of Christopher Columbus, 'coursing boldly through the watery deep to lands unknown'; and of Galileo, who achieved marvels of scientific invention in spite of every obstacle. Now, in the American War of Independence, every warrior is seeking a death of glory in the fight for freedom.—'O dauntless warrior, thou art and wert invincible, thou art the champion of freedom, Washington!'

We pass on to survey the ideal realm of liberty, where security, tranquillity, public welfare and moral grandeur are the characteristic features. But such idyllic conditions cannot last indefinitely. Human passions, self-indulgence, ambition, will bring discord into the body politic. Civil war may ensue, leading to re-establishment of absolutism. An example of this is the end of the Roman republic. Factional strife between Marius and Sulla pave the way for the Imperial rule of Caesar Augustus, followed by the degenerate tyranny of his successors. 'Such is the law of Nature: of tyranny is born freedom, of freedom, servitude.' Empires and republics are born, grow old, and perish. But what is so wonderful in this? Is not man himself born but one day to die?

Radishchev ventures a prophecy about the ultimate fate of the Russian Empire. In the end, territorial expansion will lead to disintegration. Russia will become too unwieldy to be controlled by any central power. One day, a fearful struggle will break out, in which autocracy will resort to ruthless measures to crush the spirit of liberty. These measures will fail. The Imperial structure will crack and fall apart. This will result in a free association of the peoples who formerly groaned beneath the Imperial yoke. This glorious consummation will not come to pass overnight. In a section of the ode omitted from the version published in the *Journey*, he affirmed:

> The fated time is not yet come,
> Not yet is destiny fulfilled;
> And far off still is that fair day
> When all men's woes will find relief.

But in the end, the forces of light will triumph over evil and darkness. The divine voice of liberty shall ring out in the land and the murk of ignorance and oppression vanish for evermore.

The prophetic vigour of Radishchev's ode is all the more remarkable when we recall that he composed it some seven years before the fall of the Bastille in France, under the impact of the American Revolution and the influence of French radical writers who extolled the colonists' struggle for independence. Yet the poem, which reflects Radishchev's own aversion to the workings of despotism in Russia, has a universal significance which transcends allusions to political events of his own time. It is a song of praise to liberty in the abstract, to the cause of freedom everywhere. It anticipates the ideology of the French revolutionaries of 1789 and that of the Russian revolutionary democrats of later times. Catherine the Great understandably regarded the extracts of the ode included in the *Journey* as 'quite flagrantly insurrectionary'. In spite of every effort to track down and destroy all printed copies and manuscripts of Radishchev's work, it circulated clandestinely. Even in its truncated form, the ode made an immense impression on Pushkin and his generation, including the leaders of the Decembrist conspiracy of 1825. Pushkin himself composed a poem on the same theme, in which he imitated certain of Radishchev's ideas and images, and alluded to the assassination of the mad Emperor Paul I. This poem, like Radishchev's, was vigorously suppressed, but Pushkin in later years counted it as one of his achievements that 'following Radishchev, I chanted liberty'.[1] Published in full for the first time after the Russian Revolution of 1905, Radishchev's ode remains a supreme example of the idealistic fervour of the eighteenth-century Russian enlightenment.

Muttering a hurried farewell to the poet of Tver, our Traveller hastens on to the next posting station, which is at the village of Gorodnya. A sound of wailing meets his ear. The recruiting officer and his staff have arrived to collect men for the army. Catherine and Potemkin's colonial wars and the campaigns against Turkey and Sweden were taking toll of thousands of soldiers every year. As the gentry were exempt from conscription, and the merchants could buy themselves off, the full burden fell, as usual, on the luckless peasantry. Here at Gorodnya, some of the recruits have been selected by lot from among the State serfs on the Crown domains in the neighbourhood; others have been handed over by individual landowners, who may send as recruits whichever of their serfs they choose to get rid of.

The conscripts take leave of their aged parents or their affianced brides, whom they may never see again, or at least not until their full twenty-five years' service is over. Some take their fate despairingly, others with philosophic resignation. One young man stands out among the rest. In contrast to the general gloom, he greets his lot with cheerfulness and composure. Learning that this recruit is a domestic serf-retainer belonging to a local landowner, the Traveller asks him why he is so pleased to be joining up.

—'Imagine, Sir,' the serf replies, 'a gallows set up on one side of you, and a deep river flowing on the other, so that you were standing between

---

[1] See Pushkin's poem, 'Ya pamyatnik sebe vozdvig nerukotvorny' ('A monument have I raised for myself not carved by human hands'), 1836, variant.

two forms of destruction. Suppose you were forced to go to right or to left, into the noose or into the water, which would you choose? I suppose anyone would prefer, as I have done, to cast himself into the river in the hope of escaping from peril by swimming to the far bank. Hard is a soldier's life, but better than the noose. It would not be so bad if that was the end of it, but to die a lingering death under the rods, under the cat-o'-nine-tails, in fetters, in a dungeon, naked, bare-foot, hungry and thirsty, subject to ceaseless abuse—good sir, while you may consider your serfs as your own private property, often treating them worse than beasts, yet, to their own bitter misfortune, they are not devoid of human feelings.'

The recruit tells the Traveller his life story. His father was serf-tutor to a wealthy landowner. In return for faithful service, the tutor's son was brought up together with the squire's own son, the future master of the estate. The boy serf and the boy squire had the same teachers and learnt the same lessons. The only difference between them was that the serf made the more able pupil. Then the old squire sent his son on the usual Grand Tour of Western Europe. The serf lad went too, not as a servant, but as his young master's travelling companion. The old squire promised to set him free when the party returned from abroad.

Before he could fulfil his promise, the old master died. His son and heir had always resented his serf comrade's superior attainments and now vented his jealousy on him. The young squire then got married to a haughty woman, who was indignant to think that her husband had lived on terms of intimacy with a mere slave. Starting on her wedding day, she set out to humiliate her husband's boyhood comrade, driving him from his place at the marriage feast and from his rooms in the mansion, to exist as best he could among the lowest of the domestic staff. She made him put on livery and wait at table as a lackey, taking pleasure in slapping and cursing him for the slightest fault.

One day it turned out that the young nephew of the mistress of the house had been making love to the parlourmaid, herself no novice in this kind of adventure. The girl was now in the family way. Her mistress had a bright idea. She would marry her off to her husband's former companion, now their lackey, and scandal would be averted. The ill-used young man angrily refused the suggestion and was punished on the spot with a sharp dose of the cat. Given another chance, he persisted in his contemptuous refusal. 'All right,' his mistress retorted, 'to the army with you!' Though she intended this as a punishment, her victim was overjoyed at the prospect of escaping from his mistress's persecution, to which he preferred any hardship or even death on the battlefield.

Nearby, the Traveller notices three dejected looking peasants fettered

M

with heavy leg irons and closely guarded. It turns out that these are men formerly belonging to a local squire in need of some ready cash in a hurry. The law forbids the sale of serfs during a recruiting drive, but the squire has got round this by certifying that he is granting the peasants their liberty voluntarily. He has then handed them over for a considera-tion to a village commune of State peasants who need some men to complete their quota of conscripts. Thus, these three individuals, officially free men, are being dragged off in chains to be forcibly enrolled in the army as 'volunteers'.

The sight of this flagrant abuse provokes Radishchev's Traveller to one of the most violent tirades in the book, a passage which can scarcely be matched in the whole of Russian eighteenth-century literature. 'Free men who have committed no crime, in fetters, and being sold like cattle! O, law of the land! Your wisdom exists too often in your wording alone! Is this not an open mockery of you? What is worse, this is a mockery of the sacred name of liberty. If only the slaves, weighed down by their heavy bonds, inflamed by despair, were to break our heads, the heads of their inhuman masters, with the iron which hinders their freedom, and crimson their fields with our blood! What would the country lose thereby? Soon from their midst would arise great men to replace the slain generation; but they would be inspired by a different attitude and have no right to exercise oppression. This is no fancy; my gaze pierces the thick curtain of time which hides the future from our eyes—I see through a whole century to come!'

This passage, with its uncannily prophetic ring, is one of the classic texts in the history of Russian revolutionary thought. At the same time, we detect an unmistakable echo of the famous invocation of the liberator of the negro slaves, contained in Raynal's *Histoire des deux Indes*—an invocation which found its response in the heroic career of Toussaint l'Ouverture, the Napoleon of St Domingo. 'Where is he?' demanded the Abbé Raynal. 'Where is that great man whom Nature owes to her vexed, oppressed and tormented children? Where is he? He will appear, let us have no doubt, he will show himself, he will raise the sacred standard of liberty. This venerated signal will rally around him his comrades in misfortune. More impetuous than mountain torrents, they will everywhere leave behind them the indelible traces of their just wrath. Spaniards, Portuguese, English, French, Dutch, all their tyrants will fall victim to sword or flames. The American plantations will become drunk with joy on the blood for which they have so long thirsted and the bones of so many wretched victims, heaped up over three centuries, will start up in exultation. The old world will join in applause with the new. Everywhere men will bless the name of the hero who will restore the rights of the human race, everywhere trophies will be set up in his honour.' It was this passage, a contemporary asserted, which helped to inspire Toussaint l'Ouverture in his struggle against the French and Spanish colonists in Haiti and St Domingo. 'He firmly believes that he is the man hailed by the Abbé Raynal—that man who is one day to arise and break the fetters of the negroes.'[1] It is remarkable that the same passage in Raynal's book which excited the ardour of the liberator of the West Indian negroes contributed also to inspire the great champion of the Russian serfs.

Moved to indignation by the sight of the poor fettered conscripts, Radishchev's Traveller goes up to try and help them in their plight.

—'My friends, do you realize that if you are not willing to enter military service, nobody can now force you to do so?'

—'Cut it out, good sir! Don't mock at poor folk like us. Even without your wisecracks it is hard enough for us to part, one of us from his infirm old father, another from his infant sisters, a third from his young wife. We know that our master has sold us as recruits for a thousand roubles.'

The Traveller starts to explain their legal rights, that they are now technically free men and entitled to take advantage of their liberty. But the recruiting agents soon bustle up and shove our well-meaning reformer out of the way. After another brief interlude—a chat with a French hairdresser who, after a brief career as tutor in a Russian family, he sold himself into the army for two hundred roubles—the Traveller continues on his way.

At Zavidovo, twenty-six versts further on towards Moscow, our voyager has an unpleasant encounter with a Very Important Personage and his retinue, for whom the Traveller's own post-horses are commandeered. Indeed, one of the VIP's minions starts flogging the post-station superintendent into prompt compliance with His Excellency's orders. When he finally succeeds in resuming his journey, our Traveller reflects resentfully on the vexations to which private citizens are subjected in Russia. 'Blessed are the grandees in autocratic régimes. Blessed are those adorned with ribbons and decorations. The whole of Nature submits to them. Even unreasoning animals fulfil their desires; to make sure that their yawning lordships do not suffer boredom on their journey, they race on, not sparing their legs or lungs, and quite often fall dead through overstrain. Blessed, I repeat, are those with an exterior which inspires awe in all they meet. Among those who tremble at the whip which is brandished over them, how many are there who realize that in his soul, the person in whose name they are threatened . . . is a highly disgusting individual; that deceit, treachery, treason, fornication, poisoning, theft, robbery, murder, mean no more to him

[1] Quoted by A. Feugère, *L'Abbé Raynal*, p. 419.

than drinking a glass of water; that his cheeks have never blushed with shame, but only with rage, or from a slap in the face; that he will curry favour with any palace boiler-man and ingratiate himself with even the meanest courtier. But to all those who fail to see through his baseness and servility, he behaves as a contemptuous tyrant. Lofty rank without genuine merit is like the sorcerers in our villages. The peasants all venerate and fear them, imagining them to be masters of the super-natural. Those tricksters lord it over them as they like. But as soon as some individual who despises their crude ignorance turns up amid their troop of worshippers, their fraud is shown up. Therefore they exclude such clear-headed men from the scene of their miracles. Similarly, anyone who dares to unmask the imposture of the magnates had better watch out for his skin.'

The next halting place on our Traveller's route, the little town of Klin, is the scene of a touching interlude in the sentimental vein of Sterne or Rousseau. An old blind singer is pathetically intoning a Russian folk ballad about Alexis, the Man of God. The Traveller, inclined as ever to prefer rustic innocence to urban sophistication, has no hesitation in preferring the old man's artless carolling to the colora-tura effects of the prima-donnas of the St Petersburg opera. 'How sweet is the gentle sensation of melancholy! How it refreshes the heart and its sensibility! . . . It seemed to me then, as indeed I have always thought, that the blessing of a responsive soul assists one along life's path and removes the thorns of doubt.' Overcome by emotion, our hero offers the singer a rouble. With simple dignity, the old man refuses a gift which, he declares, exceeds his modest wants. The Traveller prevails on him to accept a handkerchief with which to shield his throat from the cold winds. On this idyllic note, he hastens onwards on the last stages of his trip.

Less than sixty versts separate our Traveller from Moscow when, at the village of Peshki, he enters a peasant hut to eat a picnic meal of cold beef washed down with coffee from his flask. As he drinks 'the fruit of the sweat of the wretched African slaves' and munches his modest snack, he reflects that he would do better to join forces with some Russian General or even Colonel on campaign, since high-ranking officers always do themselves well even on the most hazardous expeditions— an obvious hit at Potemkin and his luxurious way of life in the Turkish wars.

The peasant mistress of the hut, seeing the Traveller produce some sugar, sends her little boy to beg a piece of this gentlefolk's food, as the child calls it.

—'Why gentlefolk's?' asks the Traveller, giving the child a lump. 'Do you mean to say that you can't afford any yourselves?'

—'It is a gentlefolk's dainty because we haven't the means to buy it, and the gentry manage to have it because they don't work for their living. It is true that our headman buys some when he goes to Moscow, but he too pays for it with our tears.'

—'Do you mean to say that whoever eats sugar makes you shed tears?'

—'Not everyone, but all our masters, the squires. Aren't you drinking your peasants' tears when they have to eat bread like ours?'—At this point the woman produces a sample of the bread the peasants live on, consisting of three parts chaff to one part wholemeal flour.—'And thank God we have as good as this, what with the crops failing this year. Lots of our neighbours eat even worse than this. What good does it do you nobles to eat sugar while we go hungry? The children are dying, the grown-ups too. What can we do about it all? You worry the whole time, and just have to do whatever the master orders.' And with that, she starts pushing her poor loaves into the oven.

The Traveller is taken aback by these reproaches, uttered as they are not in anger, but in a tone of anguished resignation. He looks around that humble peasant hut with eyes freshly opened to compassion. Four bare walls, half covered with soot and grime; a floor fissured with cracks and a couple of inches deep in muck; a stove without a chimney, belching out smoke into the room, though providing some protection at least against the winter cold; holes with dried bladders stretched over them to serve as windows; two or three pots to hold cabbage soup, when there was any going; wooden cups and spoons, and a table hacked out of a tree trunk. In the corner is a trough for the pigs and calves—if the household is lucky enough to possess any. The family sleep together with the livestock in a dense fug, through which the flame of a solitary candle flickers waveringly, as though in a mist. Their drink is kvass tasting like vinegar, their dress a rough, homespun smock, their usual footwear—bare feet or rags tied round the ankles.

The Traveller bursts into an indignant tirade against the system which inflicts such conditions on that very class of society which provides the nation's wealth. 'It is here that we see the cupidity of the gentry, our own extortion and tyranny, and the defenceless condition of the poor.—Rapacious beasts, insatiable leeches, what do we leave the peasant? That which we cannot take away—the air. Yes, nothing but the air alone. We often deprive him not only of the gifts of land, bread and water, but even of light itself.—The law forbids his life to be taken, you say.—Yes, instantaneously. But how many ways there are of taking it from him by degrees! On the one side—virtually absolute power; on the other—abject impotence. For in respect of his serfs, the landowner is lawgiver, judge, enforcer of his own verdict, and when he so desires, a prosecutor against whom the defendant dares say nothing in his own defence. Behold the fate of one fettered in irons, the fate of a captive in a noisome dungeon, the fate of an ox yoked to the plough!'[1] —And the Traveller concludes by denouncing the callous landowners for their indifference to the plight of their ragged and starving peasantry, for which they will one day have to answer before God Almighty.

At Chernaya Gryaz' ('Black Dirt'), the last posting station before Moscow, one last distressing spectacle meets our Traveller's eye, yet another 'flagrant example of the tyranny of the gentry over the peasants'. He sees a wedding ceremony in progress. But instead of joy and thanksgiving, he observes on the faces of the bridal pair nothing but sullen resentment. These two serfs are being joined in matrimony, not because they love each other, but because it suits their master's whim. The unworthy priest sees nothing wrong in making a mockery of this solemn sacrament. 'O! bitter fate of many millions!' Radishchev's hero cries out, 'thine end is still hidden from my grandsons' eyes. . . .'

As a final tit-bit, Radishchev slips into his *Journey* an essay entitled *Discourse on Lomonosov*, which is supposed to have been composed by that same poet whom the Traveller encountered at Tver earlier on in his trip. The writer wanders among the tombs and the evergreens of the Nevsky cemetery, and evokes the shade of the great pioneer of Russian science and literature. We are given a brief biographical sketch of the fisherman's son from Kholmogory, near Archangel, of his early struggles, his linguistic and philosophic studies, his pioneer scientific investigations and experiments. Tribute is paid to Lomonosov's work in developing the Russian language as a medium for poetry and to his studies of Russian grammar. With respect to the art of rhetoric, Radishchev points out, Lomonosov did not progress beyond barren theory; he cannot be compared with Demosthenes or Cicero in ancient times, or with Pitt, Burke, Charles James Fox and Mirabeau in the modern era. For the full exercise of the orator's faculties, active participation in great events is essential. To Lomonosov, who had 'surged up from among the popular masses', such facilities were denied under the absolutist régime of eighteenth-century Russia. Radishchev in fact goes so far as to reproach Lomonosov for chanting in his odes the praise of the Empress Elizabeth—a rebuke not without a hint of *lèse majesté*, as was duly noted by the Empress Catherine's vigilant pencil.

Later in the discourse one becomes aware that Radishchev is un-

[1] The wording of this diatribe derives in part from Raynal's *Histoire des deux Indes*, where the French writer deplores the lot of the Negro slaves on the plantations: 'I cannot kill my slave outright, but I can make his blood trickle drop by drop beneath an executioner's whip; I can burden him with pain, with toil, with privations. . . . It might be said that the law protects the slave against sudden death only to leave my cruel nature the right to make him suffer death every day.'

willing to subscribe to the official Russian view that Lomonosov equalled
and even surpassed the Western European scholars, scientists and poets
of his time. This attitude is, of course, quite at variance with the con-
ventional habit of extolling of Lomonosov as a sort of Russian Newton,
Galileo and Copernicus rolled into one, a tradition dear to patriotic
Russian hearts both in Tsarist and in Soviet times. In chemistry,
Radishchev places Lomonosov below his German forerunners Mark-
graf and Rüdiger, in the study of electricity, below Benjamin Franklin.
In this connection Radishchev quotes with approval the inscription
composed by Turgot to be set beneath Houdon's bust of Franklin, to
the effect that he had 'wrested lightning from the heavens, and the
sceptre from the hand of kings'.[1]—'Lomonosov knew how to generate
electric power and to deflect lightning flashes, but in this branch of
science Franklin is the architect, Lomonosov the handyman.' The
same disparaging note is struck when Radishchev turns to Lomonosov's
historical writings: 'Truth to tell, we shall not seek in Lomonosov a great
historian, we shall not compare him with Tacitus, Raynal or Robertson.'
Not even to Lomonosov's much admired odes and other poems can
Radishchev give unqualified praise, seeing that 'he failed to grasp the
principles of dramatic poetry and got bogged down in the epic, that in
his verse he was alien to sensibility, that he was not always perceptive
in his judgments, and that even into his odes he sometimes stuffed more
words than ideas'. Pushkin was probably right when he commented
sourly that Radishchev's aim in this essay was to deal a crafty blow at
the renown of the Russian Pindar.

But now our Traveller's coach is in sight of the towers and domes of
Moscow. Farewell, gentle reader! If the journey has not bored you,
perhaps we shall meet on the return trip. Coachman, drive on. Moscow!
Moscow!!

---

[1] 'Eripuit caelo fulmen, mox sceptra tyrannis.' Radishchev renders 'tyrannis'
as 'tsars', i.e. monarchs in general.

CHAPTER 10

The Reckoning

Suspicion Points to Radishchev – The Empress Acts – The Fortress of Peter and Paul – Sheshkovsky the Inquisitor – Sentence of Death – Diplomatic Repercussions – Peace with Sweden – Off to Siberia

From January and through the spring of 1790, Radishchev and one or two of his subordinates from the Customs House toiled away at the weary task of setting up the *Journey from St Petersburg to Moscow* in type on the private press at Radishchev's home, correcting the proofs, and printing off an edition of six hundred and fifty copies. In May, the book was ready for publication. Complimentary copies were sent to some of Radishchev's friends, including Alexis Kutuzov, to whom the book was dedicated. Several of these were later seized by the police. A copy was also sent to the poet Derzhavin, who entertained, as we have seen, no high opinion of Radishchev's literary talents. Count Alexander Vorontsov, Radishchev's patron, was not among the recipients.

To launch the work among the general public, twenty-five copies were delivered to a bookseller named Gerasim Zotov for sale in his shop. The book caused a sensation. Rumours spread swiftly through the city about this publication in which kings were threatened with the scaffold and the block, and serfs encouraged to revolt against their masters. The fact that it was issued anonymously further whetted public curiosity. Zotov sold out his copies and sent for more. The printer from whom Radishchev had acquired his press was also eager to take fifty or even a hundred copies to sell on his own account.

By this time, Radishchev was beginning to realize the extent of the challenge he had levelled at Tsarist autocracy. Pride of authorship was succeeded by anxious misgivings. His official position as head of the St Petersburg Customs would hardly protect him from the wrath of an incensed Empress. If he lost his job or even worse befell, what would become of his four children? So Radishchev declined to sell any more copies until he knew what the official reaction to his book would be.

Catherine was at her country residence in Tsarskoe Selo. It was some few weeks before an officious hand laid Radishchev's *Journey* upon her desk. But once she started to scan its pages, her response was swift. She felt herself a monarch defied and a woman scorned. We can follow her reactions day by day in the secret diary of her private secretary, A. V. Khrapovitsky, as well as in her marginal comments on Radishchev's book. On June 26, 1790 (Old Style), Khrapovitsky noted: 'Conversation about the book *Journey from St Petersburg to Moscow*: the French plague disseminated therein; revulsion from authority; the author is a Martinist;[1] I have read (she said) thirty pages. Suspicion points to Radishchev. Ryleev sent for.'

As we know, Major-General Ryleev, the St Petersburg police chief, had passed Radishchev's manuscript without reading it, though it is true that some controversial passages were inserted by the author later on. Summoned into the Imperial presence, Ryleev fell on his knees and begged for mercy. Now Catherine had a soft spot for poor Ryleev. At least he was loyal; in spite of his incompetence, he always tried to do exactly what she told him. 'If regimental officers have the least intelligence,' Catherine once remarked indulgently to Khrapovitsky, 'you can make decent police chiefs out of them. But I am afraid this poor fool here is past praying for!' However, it was not really Ryleev's fault that one of her subjects entertained such outrageous ideas about the Russian Government and social system. Catherine gave Ryleev a scolding and sent him off to arrest Zotov the bookseller and establish definitely the identity of the offending book's author. She also told her Secretary of State, Count Bezborodko, to approach Radishchev's chief, Alexander Vorontsov, with a view to giving the culprit a chance of confessing and pleading for the Imperial mercy. 'The affair,' Bezborodko told Vorontsov, 'is in a very nasty state.'

At this stage, Catherine had only had time to read part of the *Journey*. A few hours later, evidently, she reached the chapter 'Spasskaya Polest'', containing the allegory in which Radishchev makes his violent satirical attack on Catherine and her Court. This set her off into a regular tantrum. Bezborodko immediately notified Vorontsov that there was now no point in his interrogating Radishchev, since the Empress had decided to commit him for trial.

Vorontsov warned Radishchev of what was brewing. Friends offered to help him escape to Riga, and then to safety abroad. But he refused to abandon his family and his associates to the fury of Catherine's secret police. While awaiting the worst, he destroyed the remaining stock of his book. Then, on June 30th, a certain Lieutenant-Colonel

[1] That is to say, a member of the Russian masonic sect which Catherine held in particular detestation.

Goremykin arrived with a warrant for Radishchev's arrest, issued by his former chief Count Bruce, now Governor-General of St Petersburg. That night Radishchev was handed over in close custody to the Commandant of the Fortress of St Peter and St Paul, the political prison on the banks of the Neva. The investigation of the affair was entrusted to the dreaded Sheshkovsky, head of Catherine's Secret Chancellery.

On July 2, 1790, Khrapovitsky noted in his diary: 'Her Imperial Majesty continued to write comments on Radishchev's book, while he, so they say, has been handed over to Sheshkovsky and sits in jail.' These marginal notes by the Empress have been preserved. They form a highly interesting commentary on Radishchev's book, as well as on Catherine's philosophy of government. To start with, her remarks are relatively mild. 'He has quite a fund of learning and has read a lot of books.— Has a pessimistic temperament and sees everything in their blackest aspect, therefore is a man with a sombre, bilious constitution.' Some of her comments show robust common-sense. On Radishchev's story of the shipwreck and the sleeping Commandant at Sisterbek, she remarked, 'A sleeping man cannot be blamed because he was not woken up.' Again, there is much to be said for Catherine's viewpoint when she objects at one stage: 'The author says: Enquire of your heart; it is good. What it commands, that you should perform. And he tells us not to follow our reason.—This proposal can scarcely be reliable!'

As Catherine read the chapter 'Spasskaya Polest'', with its violent satire on royal pomp and corruption, her reactions became heated. This author is indeed filled with bitterness and spite! Can it be that he has himself been an unsuccessful candidate for the Imperial favour? Where Truth bids the monarch not to punish any of his subjects for proclaiming what is true, Catherine exclaimed sardonically, 'Our babbler has taken fright! If he were closer to the King, he would sing a different tune.' Against Truth's allusion to the monarch's being lulled into complacency by the delights of power, the Empress wrote indignantly, 'I do not know how much delight other rulers derive from their power. I do not get much out of mine.' Where Truth dilates on the futility of war and the King's responsibility for needless bloodshed, Catherine retorted 'Teaches his grandmother to suck eggs![1] There is malice in this spiteful man, but none in me.—"Murder which they call war", indeed!—What do they want, to be captured by the Turks or Tartars without a fight, or submit to the Swedes?' Later on, when the ruler wakes up to the appalling state of affairs in his realm, Catherine declared: 'Written with intent to foment insurrection. . . . The writer, so it seems, is the only person with any sense; the monarch alone is a complete fool.' Where Radishchev describes the contempt felt by the

[1] Literally: 'The fledgelings teach the mother bird.'

people for their sovereign, Catherine wrote: 'This page is covered with abuse and invective and malicious talk—this villainy spreads on to the succeeding pages.'

Herself a keen student of Russian history, the Empress read with interest Radishchev's account of Novgorod's annexation by Ivan III of Moscow and the repressions carried out there by Ivan the Terrible a century later.—'Speaking of Novgorod, of its free mode of government and of the severity of Tsar Ivan Vasilievich, he fails to mention the reason for these reprisals. The reason was that Novgorod had entered into union of faith with Rome and accepted the suzerainty of the Polish republic, consequently the Tsar was punishing heretics and traitors, in which, truth to tell, he overstepped the bounds of moderation.' Against Radishchev's reflections on international law and public morality, she commented, 'Raises those same issues for the sake of which France is at present being rent asunder.' Another note on this section throws light on the conservative political outlook of Catherine's maturity: 'Everything which is established in the world today has been settled through experience, in accordance with precedents laid down in ages past, and not according to blind caprice. If changes are made, they may be for the worse, because attempted improvements might destroy the good order at present prevailing. It is better to stick to what we know than to open up a path towards the unknown.'

Occasionally, Catherine tries to condemn Radishchev's ideas by reference to religious considerations. Reading his pantheistic musings at Bronnitsy, she exclaimed: 'These pages prove that the author is a complete deist—they are incompatible with Eastern Orthodox doctrine.' A curious reproach, as coming from a former pen-friend of Voltaire! Similar objections are made later on, with reference to the ethical homily delivered by the squire of Krest'tsy. She found it 'contrary to divine law, to the Ten Commandments, to holy writ, to the Orthodox faith and to the civil code'. From some of the squire's misanthropic remarks, Catherine concluded that the author 'was born with unbounded ambitions; aspiring to the highest station, he has so far failed to reach it, and so has everywhere given vent to his spleen against the established order and produced this particular theory, culled though it is from various half-baked sages of this century, such as Rousseau, the Abbé Raynal, and persons similar to that hypochondriac'.

The tale of the brutal assessor murdered by his serfs, as related by Krest'yankin to the Traveller at Zaytsovo, is described by the Empress as 'illegal talk', 'outpouring of the French poison', 'vain argument'. On Krest'yankin's harangue about the rights of man, delivered at the Governor-General's reception, Catherine commented, 'These pages advocate a point of view destructive of law and order. Ideas identical with these are turning France upside down. It would not have been surprising if the Governor-General had had our babbler arrested.'— The humane Krest'yankin resigns from the office of magistrate in disgust at the savage treatment meted out to the peasants. This produces the remark: 'Goes off to lament the pitiful fate of the peasantry, although it cannot be denied that there is no better lot in the whole universe than that enjoyed by our peasants with a good master.'

Later on in the book, the Empress's attention was arrested by the Traveller's idyllic encounter with the fair Anyuta at Edrovo, and his criticism of rakes from the city who try to seduce village girls. 'Here there is a sally concerning justice,' she observed, where Radishchev describes the under-privileged status of the serfs. 'At the end of this page are the words: No, no, he is alive, or will be alive if he so wills it. —These deserve attention as being a definite incitement to rebellion.' A like impression was produced on the Empress by the utopian 'Project for the Future', which Radishchev introduced in the chapter 'Khotilov'. —'Tends to inflame the peasants against the landlords, the armies against their commanders; the writer does not care for the words "tranquillity" and "calm". . . . Describes the condition of peasants who do not own any plough-land of their own, how they are worn out with toil, that slaves love their own fetters. All this is mainly taken out of the Abbé Raynal's book.' She added mockingly, 'He pleads with the land-owners to free their peasants, but nobody will listen!'

On Radishchev's plan to abolish the hierarchy of official ranks granted to Court servants, she remarked, 'Here the Tsar gets it in the neck. This bit ends with a discussion on how authority may be reconciled with liberty to mutual advantage. It looks as if he is alluding to France's present disgraceful example. This is all the more likely, since the writer everywhere seeks an occasion to pick a quarrel with the sovereign and his authority.' In his essay on the evils of Press censorship, Radishchev asked in whose head there could be more absurdities than in a monarch's. Catherine observed: 'Our writer does not love monarchs, and whenever he can diminish people's love and respect for them, he eagerly sets to work with unprecedented audacity.' The chapter 'Mednoe', with its painful description of the auction of a serf family, concludes with the statement that it is no use expecting liberation to result from the advice of the influential statesmen, who are themselves leaders of the serf-owning class, but rather from the very burden of serfdom itself—'that is,' Catherine deduced, 'he sets his hopes on a peasant uprising.'

The fragments of an *Ode to Liberty* inserted in the chapter 'Tver' brought Catherine's ire to fever pitch.—'Completely, utterly and flagrantly insurrectionary, where kings are threatened with the scaffold.

Cromwell's example is commended. These pages are of criminal intent, openly seditious.' She also took strong exception to the book's concluding chapter, consisting of a discourse on Lomonosov. 'He includes here a eulogy of Mirabeau, who deserves not one, but many gallows.— Here he is rude to the Empress Elizabeth Petrovna.—Here it is made clear that the author is no Christian. It looks as though he has set out to be the leader of a movement to wrench the sceptre from the hands of monarchs, either by writing this book or by some other means. As he could not do that by himself, this goes to show that he must have several accomplices.'

The Empress could scarcely believe that Radishchev had ever submitted the manuscript of his *Journey* to the censor at all. When convinced that Ryleev had in fact passed the book in draft without reading it, she seized eagerly on the fact that certain offensive passages had been added at a later stage. 'The intent of this book is visible on every page. Its author is filled and infected with the French mania, seeks out and seizes on every pretext to break down respect for authority and the powers that be and to arouse the people to indignation against their superiors and the Government. . . . Tell the author that I have read his book from cover to cover. As I read it, I wondered whether I could have done him any injury? For I do not wish to sentence him before hearing his excuses, although he himself condemns princes without listening to their defence. . . . We must find out whether many copies have been issued, and where they have got to.'

Catherine forwarded her comments to Sheshkovsky as a basis for his interrogation of Radishchev, and with a view to drawing up a formal indictment. The excellent Khrapovitsky jotted down on July 7, 1790: 'Notes on Radishchev's book sent to Sheshkovsky. She deigned to remark that he is a rebel worse than Pugachev, and showed me how at the end of the book he praises Franklin as a rabble-rouser, and sets himself up as another one. She spoke with heat and emotion.' When he received the Empress's notes, Sheshkovsky composed a long questionnaire concerning various objectionable passages in the *Journey from St Petersburg to Moscow*, to which the author was ordered to append his explanations.[1]

The renowned inquisitor was ready to press his enquiries with the 'knouting and bashing' technique in which he excelled. To save Radishchev from torture, the faithful Elizabeth Rubanovsky sold a house which she possessed, and gave presents to Sheshkovsky out of the proceeds. As it turned out, the sacrifice was unnecessary. As early as

[1] The documents in the case have been re-edited by A. S. Babkin, *Protsess A. N. Radishcheva* ('The Trial of A. N. Radishchev'), Moscow, Leningrad, 1952.

July 1st, the day after his arrest, Radishchev had already written an abject confession, giving details of the circumstances in which he had written, printed and distributed the *Journey*. He pleaded that he had been actuated by no criminal intent. The common people did not read such books as his. Radishchev's main object, he said, was 'to win renown as an author'; he had planned his book as a Russian imitation of Laurence Sterne's *Sentimental Journey*. For having altered some passages after the manuscript had been through the censorship he begged the Empress for mercy. The most offensive portions in the book were written under the influence of Raynal's *Histoire des deux Indes:* 'This work I can regard as the source of my present miserable condition. I began reading it in 1780 or 1781. His style appealed to me. I admired his rhetorical tone as eloquence, his audacious expressions I considered to be in excellent taste, and seeing him universally esteemed I wanted to imitate his technique. . . . And so I may truthfully state that Raynal's style, drawing me on from delusion to delusion, led to the completion of my insane book.' There is no reason to doubt his sincerity when he strenuously denied harbouring any feelings of personal hostility or disloyalty towards the Empress. Equally sincere was his avowal that 'for the peasants to be free, that was his desire'.

All Radishchev's disclaimers and pleas for mercy failed to save him from his fate. On July 13, 1790, Catherine wrote to Count Bruce, Radishchev's former chief and now Governor-General of St Petersburg: 'Not long ago a book was published here under the title *Journey from St Petersburg to Moscow*, filled with the most mischievous doctrines destructive of public order, diminishing due respect for authority, tending to arouse among the people indignation against their rulers and Government, and finally, containing insulting outbursts against the Imperial dignity and power. The author of this book was discovered to be the Ministerial Councillor Alexander Radishchev, who has himself confessed his guilt, admitting that after its censorship by the police authorities, he added many pages to the aforesaid book, which was printed on his own press. He was accordingly arrested. This crime of his we order to be investigated and judgment passed thereon according to legal procedure in the Criminal Court of the province of St Petersburg. When sentence has been passed, it is to be referred to our Senate for review.' Thus was Radishchev found guilty and condemned in advance of his trial.

In contrast with its usual dilatory methods, the St Petersburg Criminal Court now acted with extreme haste. Within two days of Catherine's letter to Bruce, preparations were set on foot. On July 17th, Radishchev was haled before the tribunal to answer a series of questions about his intentions in writing the *Journey*. He was encouraged to express penitence for his action. The most fantastic security precautions were taken, as if this mild-mannered Customs official had been some mass murderer or violent malefactor. He was brought in fettered and under heavy guard, and even the chancery clerks were sent out while extracts from his book were read out. Radishchev was granted no legal aid nor any opportunity of formulating a defence. Neither was he even told of what crime he was accused. This would have been difficult, seeing that he had committed no offence on the statute book which could justify the exemplary punishment demanded by the Empress.

The atmosphere surrounding the trial is conjured up in a letter written at the time, on July 16, 1790, by Count Bezborodko to one of Potemkin's factotums, Major-General Popov. 'Here in the Criminal Court a remarkable trial is now proceeding. Radishchev, the Director of Customs, though having plenty of business to cope with (which, truth to tell, he transacted competently and honestly) had the idea of devoting his spare time to philosophizing. Suffering obviously from the French infection, he brought out a book, *A Journey from St Petersburg to Moscow*, filled with the defence of peasants who butcher their proprietors, advocacy of equality and virtually of an uprising against the landowners, disrespect towards the powers that be, including a lot of venomous stuff. Finally, in demented fashion, he inserted an ode in which he ranted against kings and lauded Cromwell. The funniest thing of all is that the scamp Nikita Ryleev censored this book without reading it and, reassured by the title, inscribed his blessing upon it. The book started to become fashionable among a lot of the riff-raff; but luckily it was soon detected. The author has been arrested and has confessed, pleading that his only intention was to show off his literary talents to the public. Now they are trying him and naturally he has no defence to put up. What with the institution of free printing presses and the idiocy of the police, you have no idea what tricks they get up to!'

Further comments on the case are contained in a despatch written at the time by the Saxon diplomat and memoirist Helbig to the Court of Dresden. On July 6/17, 1790, Helbig reported from St Petersburg that recent Russian defeats in the war against Turkey had made the public nervous and restive. 'Owing to all these incidents, discontent among the Russians is visibly increasing and shows itself at every opportunity. The Customs Director Ratischeff, a man of great understanding and accomplishments, has written a brochure in Russian under the title *Journey from St Petersburg to Moscow*, printed the same in his own house and forthwith put it into private circulation. Therein he condemns many aspects of the present régime, subjects every branch of it to scrutiny, and without naming individuals, depicts them in such a way that they are not to be mistaken. He alludes also to many generally deplorable institutions and abuses: thus for instance the author describes the way in which serfs are sold here, and how without any regard for humanity, members of each family are put up for sale separately and the husband sundered from his wife, the mother from her infants in arms. . . . The writer also mocks at various rites of the Russian Church and in short makes fun of all manner of things. This action, reprehensible as it is in many ways, has however been brought to light and the author imprisoned in the castle. Every measure has been taken to suppress the copies, though many appear to be in circulation. It is remarkable how freely the Russians are discussing the work. They give many hundred roubles for a copy.'[1]

On July 24th, the St Petersburg Criminal Court pronounced the only sentence which, it was told, would satisfy the Empress: death. The verdict was conveyed in a lengthy judgment in which the magistrates strained their ingenuity to the utmost in order to clothe their verdict in some shreds of legality. All sorts of weird crimes were disinterred and laid to Radishchev's charge. Some were taken from the ancient code of Tsar Alexis: 'If any individual shall purposefully meditate an evil enterprise against the sovereign's health . . . such a one is to be punished with death. If any subject of His Imperial Majesty shall desire to seize the state of Moscow and be its lord, and in furtherance of this evil undertaking shall begin to collect an army . . . such a traitor is to be punished with death.' From the Naval Statute of Peter the Great: 'If anyone discovers that one or more individuals are plotting some harmful act, or possesses knowledge respecting spies or other suspicious characters lurking within the navy, and fails to report the matter in due time, then he shall be deprived of his life.' This ludicrous and almost incredible rigmarole goes on for sixteen pages.

The verdict of the Criminal Court was sent up to the Senate for confirmation, together with a report on the case by Count Bruce. It was in this same Senate that Radishchev had served as a promising young official less than twenty years before. The Senators duly confirmed the death sentence passed on Radishchev. They even added the proviso that he should meanwhile be sent off in irons to the penal settlement of Nerchinsk on the Chinese frontier, there to await the Imperial warrant for his execution. Radishchev was degraded from his official rank and his status as a member of the gentry, and struck from

---

[1] Saxon State Archives, Dresden: published by G. Sacke in his article, 'Radiščev und seine "Reise" in der westeuropäischen Literatur des 18. Jahrhunderts', pp. 46–7. Sacke was murdered by the Nazis in a Concentration Camp in 1945, and this article was published posthumously in *Forschungen zur Osteuropäischen Geschichte*, Bd. 1, Berlin, 1954.

the roll of knights of St Vladimir. For the next month, fettered and in chains, he was treated as a criminal under sentence of death.

Still wishing to maintain some façade of legality, Catherine now referred the sentence to her Imperial Council of State 'in order to avoid all semblance of partiality'. Its members were to be told, as Khrapovitsky noted in his diary on August 11th, 'not to pay any heed to the personal allusions to myself, since I disdain them'. The councillors included Radishchev's old chief, Count Bruce, Vorontsov's good friend Bezborodko, as well as Peter Zavadovsky, later a colleague of Radishchev on the legislative commission of Alexander I. They knew what was expected of them. On August 19, 1790, they announced that in their view Radishchev had broken his oath of allegiance to the sovereign, and merited the punishment decreed for him.

By now, Radishchev's case had turned into a regular *cause célèbre*. Its repercussions at Court and among the general public were being followed with keen interest by foreign diplomats in the Russian capital, who interpreted the appearance of the *Journey from St Petersburg to Moscow* as a sign of general discontent with the war policy of Catherine and Potemkin and with the autocratic system generally. This is made abundantly clear in a hitherto unpublished despatch from the British Minister, Charles Whitworth, dated August 5/16, 1790, and addressed to the Foreign Secretary, the Duke of Leeds.[1] After discussing the unfavourable course of Russia's campaign against the Ottoman Porte, Whitworth goes on: 'Amongst the many motives which should induce Her Imperial Majesty to turn her thoughts seriously to Peace, is one which certainly ought to have some effect upon her Mind. The spirit of reformation which seems to gain so rapidly in other parts of Europe, and which in some has been carried to such excess, manifests itself even in this; whilst other Countries are trampling upon all authority and order, this is measuring its strength by a freedom of speech unheard of in Russia, and even by (the natural consequences of such freedom) the publication of Libels; two or three have appeared lately, written with the utmost bitterness and rancour against the Person of the Sovereign, and her Government; both of which it must be confessed afford but too much cause of Animadversion. The Author of one of these Publications, in which the Empress has been treated with great Severity, has been apprehended, and is to lose his Head. This Person holds a considerable office in the Customs and has always been treated with great kindness and confidence by Monsieur Woronzow, Chief of that Department. Some suspicion has therefore fallen upon him also, as well as on his Sister, the Princess Dashkoff, Directress of the Academy

---

[1] Public Record Office, London: Foreign Office Archives, *Russia*, vol. 65/19, No. 47.

N

of Sciences, where it seems this Libel was printed.[1] The Princess, a few Days before the publication, set out to visit her Estates in a distant part of the Country. It is certain Monsieur Woronzow has not appeared in Council for a considerable Time, under a Pretence of Illness; but as this is generally the Pretext made use of to cover other Motives, it does not meet much credit from those who are acquainted with the Intrigues of this Court. I should have endeavoured to have procured a copy of this Paper, had I not judged it prudent, and most particularly so at this moment, to be cautious of giving the smallest Handle for Suspicions, which I fear, from the Malevolence of those who, on all occasions, endeavour to poison the Mind of the Empress, would but too easily have been adopted. . . .'

The French chargé d'affaires, Genet, also attached great significance to Radishchev's book and its impact on Russian public opinion. Like Whitworth, he laid stress on Radishchev's intimate connection with the Vorontsovs, who were known to be critical of Potemkin and his policies. On August 13/24, 1790, Genet wrote to the Comte de Montmorin from St Petersburg:[2] 'It is my duty to inform you, My Lord, of a very serious criminal case which is preoccupying the entire Court and may have important consequences. Monsieur Raditcheff, chief collector of Customs, upon whom favours were showered by the Empress and who was personally protected by Count Worontzow, brought out some time ago a satirical pamphlet directed against Prince Potemkin and the policies of the Court of St Petersburg. This man has been arrested. In his house have been found documents which compromise the most exalted personages and prove that he was merely the tool of a numerous faction. He has been condemned by the Secret Chancellery to have his head cut off. The Senate, to which the Empress referred the matter, has commuted his penalty and condemned him simply to the knout and forced labour. All those who have been implicated in this intrigue are under surveillance; the doings of French residents are supervised more closely than ever. There are at least ten thousand of them in Russia.'

Three days later, another secret despatch from Genet brought the French Court further news of Radishchev's book and its repercussions. The French Envoy wrote:[3] 'Count Woronzow, My Lord, does not appear at Court any more, and one sees officials of the Secret Chancellery frequently visiting his mansion. He is implicated in the Raditchef

---

[1] This is of course inaccurate: the *Journey* was printed on Radishchev's own press.

[2] Quai d'Orsay archives, Paris, *Russie*, vol. 132, No. 64 of August 24, 1790, p. 357, postscript (original in cypher).

[3] *Ibid.*, No. 65 of August 27, 1790, p. 265, postscript (original in cypher).

affair. The Minister of Commerce and Industry of Russia was bound
to be an enemy of Prince Potemkin, whose restless, ambitious and interfering spirit has brought upon this Empire a war which has retarded its
prosperity by more than twenty years. I sincerely hope that he will
vindicate himself; he is the only man of talent I know in the Russian
Government. What is more, he favours our interests since Monsieur
de Ségur converted him.'

*

When Radishchev was told that sentence of death had been passed upon
him, he made his will, which contained a final exhortation to his children. 'It is accomplished! If this testament, O my beloved ones, ever
reaches you, then listen with heart and soul to the words of your unhappy father and friend.—Remember, friends of my heart, remember
continually that God exists, and that we cannot take a single step or
think a single thought except beneath His almighty hand. Remember
that He is just and merciful, that He does not leave any good deed
without its reward, or any evil one without retribution. And every time
you embark on any undertaking, call upon Him for aid and have
recourse to Him with heartfelt prayers.' Radishchev, that 'rebel worse
than Pugachev', goes on to bid his sons be diligent in serving their
country, punctual in executing the orders of their superiors, and loyal
to their sovereign. In everything they are to follow the dictates of
virtue and justice. In place of himself and their dead mother, Radishchev's children are commended to the care of their aunt, Elizabeth
Rubanovsky. After sundry legacies, he bequeaths to his personal
servants their freedom, commits his family to the Empress's mercy,
and begs his parents for forgiveness if he has ever done anything to
offend them. This touching document, intercepted by the inquisitor
Sheshkovsky, never reached its destinatories.

   While awaiting the order for his execution, Radishchev was allowed
to occupy himself with his favourite pastime, that of literary composition. As he told his interrogator, Sheshkovsky, 'when engaged in
writing, the mind is more deeply absorbed than in reading. Even a
moment's oblivion makes it seem to me as if I were no longer in con-
finement.' The fruit of Radishchev's labours in his prison cell is an
unfinished moral tale about the holy Philaret, a worthy of mediaeval
Byzantium, whose biography is regularly included among those of the
saints of the Orthodox Church. 'I have rewritten it in some degree to
fit in with present-day ideas,' he wrote to Sheshkovsky, 'but without
in any way diverging from the authentic narrative, and I venture to
think that it may prove edifying to my children.' Into this life of Philaret,

Radishchev wove a number of autobiographical threads. The account of the holy man's student days in Athens with his comrade Probus, and his conversations with the learned Theophilus on philosophy, psychology and metaphysics, contain what seem to be reminiscences of Radishchev's life at Leipzig University with Fedor Ushakov and Alexis Kutuzov, and the lessons he learnt from the brilliant young philosopher Ernst Platner.

But Radishchev did not remain in his cell long enough to complete this edifying story. On September 4th, Catherine celebrated the conclusion of peace with Sweden by signing an order for Radishchev's reprieve. It is possible that influence brought to bear by Radishchev's patron Alexander Vorontsov had a part in this decision, as well as regard for public opinion both abroad and in Russia. It was also a convenient occasion for the exercise of Catherine's much vaunted clemency and magnanimity. Radishchev's death sentence was accordingly commuted into ten years' exile at the remote settlement of Ilimsk to the north of Irkutsk in Central Siberia. The French Envoy, Genet, reported to the Comte de Montmorin: 'On the occasion of the conclusion of peace, the Empress has spared Monsieur Raditchew the degrading punishment of forced labour, and he has been sent to Siberia for ten years. Count Woronzow has not yet reappeared at Court, but people aver however that he has exculpated himself.'[1]

Radishchev was taken in chains and under heavy guard from his prison cell to the St Petersburg Governor's office in the city. The Imperial decree exiling him to Siberia was read out to him. Already a sick and broken man, this desperate malefactor was placed in a clumsy open carriage for the first stage of his long journey into banishment. Count Vorontsov had sent three hundred roubles to the fortress so that provisions and clothing could be bought for him before he set out. However, the convoy left straightaway from the Governor's office, without giving Radishchev the chance to collect his belongings. Seeing him shivering in his thin summer coat, someone took a dirty sheepskin jerkin from one of the sentries and flung it over him.

According to Masson, the contemporary French observer, Radishchev was granted permission to bid farewell to his children and his sister-in-law, the devoted Elizabeth Rubanovsky. His carriage halted for a few moments on the banks of the Neva, opposite the fortress battlements. It was evening. His family were waiting for him at the gates of the castle of Peter and Paul, on the farther shore. At the moment when they saw him, the bridge had been drawn aside to give passage to a ship entering or leaving the harbour. Radishchev begged his guards

[1] Quai d'Orsay archives, Paris, *Russie*, vol. 133, No. 70 of September 21, 1790, p. 44, postscript (original in cypher).

to wait until the bridge was in place once more, or to give his family a chance to cross in a wherry. But all in vain. His custodians gruffly bade him get back into his carriage, while his dear ones with outstretched arms cried their farewells across the waters.[1] And so Radishchev, still in chains and covered with a filthy sheepskin, rumbled off into the gathering dusk.

The foreign Press soon got wind of the affair. A German paper called *Neueste Critische Nachrichten*, published at Greifswald, announced on October 2, 1790, that the head of the St Petersburg Customs House had published on his own private press a work on the liberty of man. In this book, the author encouraged his fellow countrymen to pay heed to the example of the French Revolution, and declaimed against the Empress's favourites. 'He has, however, lost his own liberty as a result of this.'[2]

When he heard of Radishchev's fate, Simon Vorontsov, the Russian Ambassador in London, wrote to his brother, Count Alexander, 'Radishchev's condemnation causes me extreme grief. What a sentence, and what a commutation, for a mere indiscretion! What will they do, then, for crime and for real revolt? Ten years in Siberia will be worse than death for a man with children, with whom he must part, unless he deprives them of education and employment by taking them with him. It makes one shudder.'

As the British and French Envoys had already reported, it was in-evitable that Radishchev's arrest and condemnation should have unpleasant repercussions for the Vorontsov family, with which his career was so closely linked. This was well known at the time. The German diplomat Helbig records in his book on Catherine's favourites that 'this incident also had some effect on Radishchev's protectors, Count Vorontsov and Princess Dashkov. Their connection with this man was known. They were accused of having collaborated in the book and had to justify themselves before the Secret Inquisition. They were not punished, but they lost their favour with the Empress and were forced little by little to retire from the Court and from public affairs.'[3] In her memoirs, Princess Dashkov gives her own version of the episode. After recalling that reading Radishchev's *Life of Ushakov* led her to foresee that he would one day 'write something really reprehensible', she says that in the summer of 1790, she was spending her holiday in

[1] C. F. P. Masson, *Mémoires secrets sur la Russie*, tom. II, Amsterdam, 1800, p. 181.

[2] H. Raab, 'Pervoe upominanie o dele A. N. Radishcheva v pechati' ('The first mention in print of the affair of A. N. Radishchev'), in *XVIII vek, Sbornik* 3 ('The Eighteenth Century, 3rd Collection of Essays'), issued by Academy of Sciences, Pushkinsky Dom, Moscow, Leningrad, 1958, pp. 538–9.

[3] Helbig, *Russische Günstlinge*, p. 304.

the country.—'I received a letter from my brother (Alexander Voront-sov) informing me that to his great distress my prophecy about Radish-chev had been fulfilled, for that man had published a work which, he was sorry to admit, could be taken for a tocsin to revolution; he had been denounced and banished to Siberia.—Far from being gratified at the correctness of my conclusions as proved by this catastrophe, I was greatly saddened by the fate of Radishchev, and even more by the distress which it caused my brother and was likely to cause him for a long time. I foresaw, too, that the favourite, who was no friend of Count Alexander's, would try to involve him in this affair. In fact he did, and under any sovereign other than the great Catherine he would have succeeded in doing him harm, but on her he made no impression. However, my brother was disgusted by his behaviour, which, joined to the intrigues of the Minister of Justice, upset him so much that he asked for a year's leave of absence, pleading ill-health which necessitated a period of rest and country air. He was granted his leave and went to live on his estate, while I remained in Petersburg, feeling quite alone among people who seemed to me more odious than ever.'[1]

Catherine's treatment of Radishchev shows how far her outlook had altered since the days of those old liberal flirtations with the ideas of Beccaria, Montesquieu, Voltaire, and other epigones of the Western Enlightenment. Then, she had proudly proclaimed the establishment of free speech in Russia, and contrasted her own mild and tolerant attitude with the benighted bigotry of Bourbon France. Three decades of success had wrought great changes in Catherine's habits of mind. Now, in 1790, criticism of the régime was made a capital crime. Long familiarity with the Russian character had no doubt contributed to this change of heart. Nearly thirty years spent in ruling this vast Empire, peopled as it was with ignorant peasants, turbulent Cossacks, re-calcitrant Poles, untamed Turcomans, and other unruly elements, had converted her to the traditional autocratic outlook of the Muscovite Tsars. For the system to work at all, the people must be ridden with a tight rein. Radishchev's crime was not simply that he preached the liberation of the serfs. It was rather that he had stripped the veil from the sacred shrine of Russian absolutism and revealed the sham which lay behind. He had poured scorn on the mystical adoration with which Russians were, and still are taught to worship their rulers. He had ventured to test the system by applying the criteria of practical utility and general wellbeing, and found it wanting.

Catherine was frightened. She knew, though she dared not admit it, that the Russian colossus had feet of clay. As she read Radishchev's

[1] *The Memoirs of Princess Dashkov*, trans. FitzLyon, p. 241, with a slight emendation kindly supplied to me by the translator.

Journey, she seemed to hear the Paris mob howling before the Bastille and to see the snarling face of the dead Pugachev. Who could tell when a Russian mob would howl before her own Winter Palace? She had herself been responsible for the death of two Tsars of Russia. Her turn might well come next. And so, *pour encourager les autres*, and to punish this renegade snake in the grass, Catherine staged the first of that long series of Russian mock-trials in which writers and thinkers have been condemned for holding and propagating opinions out of accord with those of the régime. To her and Sheshkovsky belongs the credit for evolving that effective 'brain-washing' technique perfected by their successors in our own day.

Can Catherine morally be blamed for the action she took? No doubt she acted according to her lights. Self-preservation is a primary instinct in all human beings. Free speech and abstract legality are luxuries which the people of Russia have rarely been permitted to enjoy. Catherine was a professional ruler, responsible for public order over a vast and largely uncivilized territory. In her eyes, Radishchev was a troublesome visionary, a malicious rabble-rouser. The French Revolution, the sight of the Swedish fleet before St Petersburg, had turned her into a tigress at bay, and those who bait a tigress must expect to be bitten. Could Catherine in 1790 have looked into the future and seen her son Paul I and two of his heirs, Alexander II and Nicholas II, strangled, blown up and shot by their own subjects, her adversary Gustavus III of Sweden murdered by Captain Anckarström, her 'royal cousin' Louis XVI haled to the guillotine, she might have claimed with some justice that therein lay the justification of her suppression of Radishchev and his revolutionary book.

Even here, she was not wholly successful. Radishchev might be relegated to remotest Siberia, his book hunted out and burnt by the police, but his ideas lived on. Witnesses interrogated preparatory to Radishchev's trial had testified to the 'great curiosity of the public concerning this book'; it was described as 'the book which everybody in town is talking about'. After it was banned, copies of the *Journey* were secreted away and read behind closed doors. The French eye-witness Masson knew Russian merchants who paid twenty-five roubles an hour for the privilege of reading Radishchev's book in secret.—'His courage has not been without value to his country. In spite of house to house searches by the despotic régime, copies of his work are preserved by a number of his fellow-countrymen; and his memory is dear to all rational beings and men of feeling.'[1] Numerous manuscript copies of the work were made and circulated: some thirty of these have come down to us. One such transcript was in the possession of the French

---

[1] Masson, *Mémoires secrets*, II, 180–2.

revolutionary Gilbert Romme, young Count Paul Stroganov's tutor, who was among those voting for the execution of Louis XVI. Another was found by Radishchev himself at the Mayor's house in the remote township of Kungur in the Urals, through which he passed in 1797 on his return from exile. A whole series of more or less obscure political writers and poetasters imitated the style and ideas of the *Journey*, and particularly the *Ode to Liberty*. Several of these audacious literati paid for their daring with a session with Sheshkovsky and his minions, and an uncomfortable sojourn in some grim fortress gaol.[1]

Not all who read the *Journey from St Petersburg to Moscow* took the author's side. Many of them, especially members of the landowning class, fully supported the Empress's action in suppressing the book and its author. The Russian Freemasons or 'Martinists', whom Catherine regarded with deep hostility and suspicion, found Radishchev's ideas as uncongenial as did the Empress herself. Writing to Alexis Kutuzov, to whom Radishchev dedicated the *Journey*, the Moscow Freemason I. V. Lopukhin declared: 'Furthermore, the condition in which he (Radishchev) now finds himself, however painful for the body, may perhaps be beneficial to his soul, as serving to enable him to discern his errors and turn back on to the path of Christianity. If he stood thereon, he could never commit such actions as that for which he is now suffering. Indeed, I definitely consider that he would not have acted thus had he been what they call here a Martinist.' In another letter, Lopukhin wrote to Kutuzov, 'Up to now I have been unable to procure Radishchev's book, in fact I am no longer really keen to read it. . . . In truth, such books are very pernicious. I think that the works of such writers as Voltaire, Diderot, Helvétius and all those anti-Christian freethinkers have greatly contributed to bring on France's present demented state.'[2]

Alexis Kutuzov was himself both displeased and alarmed by the fact that Radishchev had dedicated the *Journey* to him, without asking his permission. As a representative of the Russian masonic brotherhood in Berlin, Kutuzov was already suspect to the Russian authorities. Now that he was compromised in this affair, he foresaw that he too would be, like Radishchev, an exile from his native land, cut off from his family and every means of financial support. In a letter written during December 1790, Kutuzov recalled that he had tried in vain to dissuade Radishchev from airing his radical opinions in public; he had even quoted to Radishchev the lines spoken in the assembly of the Greek

[1] See V. Orlov, *Radishchev i russkaya literatura* ('Radishchev and Russian literature'), Leningrad, 1952.

[2] Ya. L. Barskov, *Perepiska moskovskikh masonov XVIII veka* ('Correspondence of the Moscow Freemasons in the 18th century'), Petrograd, 1915, pp. 15–16.

princes before Troy by the sage and prophet Calchas. With remarkable knowledge of English poetry, Kutuzov quotes these in the version by Alexander Pope:[1]

> For I must speak what Wisdom would conceal,
> And Truths, invidious to the Great, reveal.
> Bold is the task! when Subjects grown too wise
> Instruct a Monarch, where his Error lies;
> For tho' we deem the short-liv'd fury past,
> 'Tis sure, the Mighty will revenge at last.

It was indeed a pity, Kutuzov concluded, that Radishchev should have disregarded these prudent sentiments, while having no Achilles capable of protecting and sheltering him from the wrath of the mighty.[2]

Foreign journalists and commentators of the time, especially those critical of Catherine and her methods, naturally relished the element of scandal in the Radishchev affair. Thus Castéra, author of a *Vie de Catherine II*, noted with gusto how Radishchev had depicted in his *Journey* 'the despotism of Potemkin' and had 'even ventured therein to attack the Empress herself'. The well-informed Saxon diplomat Helbig devoted a whole chapter to Radishchev in his biographical sketches of Russian society, published under the title *Russische Günstlinge* or 'Russian Favourites'. On his journey from St Petersburg to Moscow, 'the author had a dream which he related. He spoke on this occasion with great boldness about aspects of the contemporary mode of government which were scarcely fitted to be made public in their true light. All the characters were concealed by other names, only in one context (and this may well have brought about Radishchev's downfall) was the Empress named, when Truth appeared veiled before her, removed her veil, and revealed to that princess her blood-stained countenance.—The book sold well, because it was written in a vivid, racy style. In a few days, a quantity of copies were sold.' Sheshkovsky got wind of all this, continues Helbig, and arrested the book's vendor, who revealed that its author was Radishchev. 'His house was searched, and it was found that he had printed the book himself. The astonishment of all who knew this man was as great as their compassion for the fate which awaited him. People found this undertaking quite out of keeping with his former well-known prudence. If only he had refrained from naming the Empress in this book, he could not have been convicted of any malicious intent.' As Helbig further notes, 'the book's confiscation did not prevent it from becoming well known. In Russia, manuscripts of

[1] Homer, *Iliad*, trans. Pope, bk. I, lines 101–6.
[2] Barskov, *Perepiska*, pp. 65–6.

it came into circulation, and some copies even crossed the frontier.'[1]

Taking the long view, Catherine's treatment of Radishchev may be viewed as an opening phase in the war which Tsarist autocracy waged against the liberal intelligentsia throughout the following century. This mutual antagonism, as is well known, rapidly reached the point where to support the régime was regarded in Russian intellectual circles as tantamount either to imbecility or to betrayal of a sacred cause. It was a situation which did the Imperial House immense moral and material harm. Essentially, Nicholas I and his gendarmes, Alexander III and the obscurantist Pobedonostsev were only following a path blazed for them by Catherine II and her tame inquisitor Sheshkovsky. By exiling Radishchev, snubbing and silencing the brilliant dramatist Fonvizin, persecuting and imprisoning the Freemason publisher Novikov, Catherine incurred the undying animosity of later generations of Russian writers. 'Catherine loved Enlightenment,' wrote Pushkin, 'but Novikov, who spread the first rays of it, passed from the hands of Sheshkovsky (the mild Catherine's domestic hangman) into a dungeon, where he remained until her death. Radishchev was exiled to Siberia; Knyazhnin died beneath the birch rods;[2] and Fonvizin, whom she feared, would not have escaped a like fate, had it not been for his tremendous fame.' Radishchev's fate was a salutary warning to all and sundry that, 'enlightened' or no, despotism would continue to be enforced in Russia by the knout rather than the statute book. And so it has continued up to our own day.

---

[1] For further references, see I. D. Smolyanov's article on 'Foreign comments of the 18th century on Radishchev's banishment' in *Radishchev: Stat'i i materialy* ('Radishchev: Articles and materials'), Leningrad, 1950, pp. 257–68.

[2] Yakov Khyazhnin (1742–91), eminent tragedian, author of *Vadim of Novgorod*, banned by Catherine for its alleged republican sentiments. Khyazhnin was probably not put to death, but died just before this tragedy was published.

CHAPTER 11

The Road to Exile

⤙⤙◈◈⤚⤚

Fetters Removed – To Moscow – Beyond the Volga – Picturesque Tribes – Shades of Yermak – Over the Urals – Life in Tobolsk – Siberian Manners – On to Irkutsk – Ilimsk at Last

Robbed, as she thought, of her last chance to bid farewell to Radishchev, Elizabeth Rubanovsky hastened to Count Vorontsov's mansion and told him how her brother-in-law was being transported to Siberia in fetters, like a common convict. Vorontsov heard the news with sympathy and indignation. The next day, he appeared at Court and pointed out to the officials there that Radishchev had been sentenced simply to banishment, and not to hard labour. He secured an order for an Imperial courier to be sent to overtake the convoy and have Radishchev's fetters removed, as well as arranging for him to receive money and clothing for his long journey.

But for Count Alexander's intercession, Radishchev would scarcely have survived even the first stages of his trip. Already in his book, *A Journey from St Petersburg to Moscow*, he had described the hardships endured by the traveller jolting along that uneven road, even when enjoying the luxury of a comfortable carriage, ample bedding and frequent stops for refreshment. Now he was being carted along that same route, shaking and shivering through the cool September night, with heavy irons round his ankles and a contemptuous orderly sergeant on guard by his side. Never a robust man, his health was impaired by ten weeks in the fortress casemate, by Sheshkovsky's relentless harrying, and by the strain of waiting for final sentence to be pronounced. At Novgorod, fortunately, the Imperial courier caught them up. Radishchev's chains were taken off. His escort was instructed to treat him with some respect and consideration. Things improved still further at Tver, the Governor of which city was an old friend of Vorontsov's. Money being received from the Count by special messenger, steps were taken to make Radishchev's onward journey tolerably comfortable. Nevertheless, Radishchev arrived in Moscow a sick man, and the authorities were forced to realize that he was in no shape to continue his long road for the time being.

Had Radishchev lived in Soviet times, he would have been sent on in a cattle-truck, to die conveniently on the way. But in Catherine's more civilized reign, some slight kindness was occasionally shown to political prisoners, especially when they enjoyed the protection of one of the most influential statesmen in the Russian Empire. Radishchev was allowed to stay under guard at his parents' house in Moscow for three weeks, until he was more or less restored to health. He had time to find out something about the spot where he was sentenced to spend the next ten years. Situated on the River Ilim, latitude 56.30 N, longitude 104.25 E, Ilimsk, according to reference books of the time, was a settlement of 107 houses, surrounded by a high wooden stockade with fortified turrets, and distant 5,894 versts, or little less than 4,000 miles from Moscow. 'The neighbouring country round the township consists of rocky hills and forests. There is no shortage of bread or of cattle. Game abounds, including bears, elks, deer, goats, foxes, squirrels, ermines, striped squirrels, martens, as well as sundry kinds of birds in plenty.' The prospect could have been worse. As Radishchev later wrote, 'From my childhood days, I longed passionately to set forth on lengthy journeys. For a long time I had been wanting to see Siberia for myself. My desire has been fulfilled, although in exceedingly harsh circumstances.' No voluntary tourist was he now, but one of those whom, as he wryly recalled, Laurence Sterne had referred to as travellers through necessity.

Finally all was ready and the day of departure arrived. In mid-October of 1790, Radishchev, together with his escort and several servants, drove out of Moscow by the Vladimir Gate, along a road familiar to generations of exiles. Thanks to letters sent by Count Alexander to officials in the principal towns on his route, Radishchev was everywhere treated as a gentleman on his travels rather than a disgraced exile. By the time he reached Nizhny Novgorod, his spirits were beginning to revive. 'My brain from time to time can find an active outlet,' he wrote to Vorontsov on October 20th. 'When I halt for the night, I get a chance to read. While I eat, I try to observe the siting of valleys, ravines, hills, rivers. In fact, I am making a practical study of the history of the earth, about which I used to read in books: sand, clay, stones, everything attracts my attention. You may hardly believe that after crossing the river Oka I scrambled with delight up a steep cliff and discovered some fossil sea shells in its clefts. . . . But what control can reason exercise over feeling? From my own experience, I now see that reason trails along after the emotions, or is even indistinguishable from them. According to the system of Helvétius, the mind revolves round one single idea, and all my reasoning, all my philosophy vanishes when I think of my children!' In a postscript to the same letter, Radishchev asked Vorontsov to send him a thermometer and a barometer with which to carry out certain meteorological experiments at Irkutsk, where he expected to find atmospheric conditions of special scientific interest.

From Nizhny Novgorod the party made haste to sail down to Kazan before the Volga iced up. To Kazan old Nicholas Radishchev came up from the manor at Ablyazovo to bid his son farewell. Radishchev's mother had to stay at home: the shock of her son's arrest and condemnation had brought on a stroke, and she was now partly paralysed. Then the party struck north-east towards Perm which lay on the route over the Urals to Tobolsk. Beyond the Volga, Radishchev's path took him over pleasant, undulating country, through Tatar, Chuvash, Marian and Russian villages and settlements. He started to keep a diary in which he jotted down many curious observations on the things he saw and the adventures that befell him[1].

—'November 11. At Kazan, then climbed up a hill, travelled through meadows, hollows, copses, as far as Biryul', a village belonging to a private landowner, where a whole crowd of tipsy peasants had collected for the feast of Michael the Archangel. Took a long time giving us fresh horses. The lady of the manor was being entertained by the priest thirty versts away.'

At Arsk, the next stop, Radishchev saw some old wooden towers, used for defence against marauders in days gone by, and a wooden church. The people made their living by arable farming and working as carriers. Farther on, he noted that the Tatars, Chuvash and Cheremiss (Marians) built their villages in the dales, the Russian settlers up on the hill-tops. However, the Chuvash huts were less stuffy and smelly than the Russian ones. The Chuvash and Cheremiss huts were black, but the Tatars painted theirs white. The Tatars hunted bears, wolves, foxes, hares, squirrels and martens in the forests. The party was ferried over the river Vyatka, 'as wide as the Neva at St Petersburg'. The Cheremiss peasants seemed poorer east of the river and less smartly turned out; they were languid in their manner, and many of them had some complaint, which Radishchev surmised to be of venereal origin, affecting their eyes. The Chuvash women were pretty and the Cheremiss girls had glossy black hair.

In a day or two they came to the country of the Votyaks, another people of Turco-Finnish origin. 'They have no barns for drying corn, they thresh it still damp, and after threshing, they dry it in ovens. A

---

[1] 'Zapiski puteshestviya v Sibir' ('Notes on a journey into Siberia') in A. N. Radishchev, *Polnoe sobranie sochineny*, III, 253–66.

timid and kindly folk . . . Votyaks are quite like Russians, many of them have married Russian women. Some of them have already painted their cottages white. . . . The Votyak women are ugly. The Votyaks sing as they drive along, like Russian coachmen do. Their character is inclined more to gaiety than to gloom.' At one place there was a small inn kept by a retired sergeant and his family. Further on, they spent the night at a place where popular festivities were in progress. 'All the damsels, women and menfolk go from house to house drinking beer. They kept going till dawn and drank themselves into a stupor. The women wear headdresses with fringes, embroidery and silver tassels.' On another halt, Radishchev stayed with the Tatar headman. These headmen were elected annually by the local folk to settle civil disputes and deal with petty larceny and other minor offences. Radishchev noted that in practice most criminal cases were judged summarily by the headman according to the Muslim law of the Koran, murders only being referred up to the regular Russian courts.

On November 19, 1790, Radishchev's party arrived at the town and provincial centre of Perm (later Molotov) on the River Kama. From here he wrote again to Count Alexander to thank him for a letter with money and several parcels which were now handed to him through the good offices of the local Governor. In this letter, Vorontsov renewed his assurances of unswerving friendship towards Radishchev and his family, while reminding him that he had only his own untimely zeal and indiscretion to thank for his present predicament. This was strictly true, since Radishchev had kept his literary activities secret from Vorontsov. But we shall never know how many of his more outrageous views on Catherine and her Court had been picked up in conversation with his disdainful chief. At all events, Vorontsov advised Radishchev to show genuine repentance for the offence he had given the Empress, in the hope that this might bring some further mitigation of his sentence. 'To reproach or utter complaints against anyone,' Radishchev wrote in response, 'I have no cause, as Your Excellency justly observes. It was I who procured my own downfall and I shall try to bear my punishment with patience, but how often this proves insufficient! I arm myself with hope and reason, but how painful it is to recall that I am living separated from my children! I have no reasoning faculty left, and hope itself is all but flown.' Yet unknown to Radishchev, this source of grief at least, through the devotion of Count Alexander and Elizabeth Rubanovsky, was soon to be assuaged.

After leaving Perm at the end of November, the party arrived at the curious old town of Kungur in the Urals. In the arsenal Radishchev was able to inspect some small cannon or falconets and other guns which had belonged to Yermak, that bold adventurer who laid the foundation of Russian rule over Siberia in the time of Tsar Ivan the Terrible. It was here, no doubt, that Radishchev conceived the idea of writing a saga on Yermak's life and career, and a history of the Russian conquest of Siberia—works which he began while in exile, but left unfinished at the time of his death. At Kungur, he was also shown some gruesome instruments of torture dating from the rule of the former military governors or *voevodas*: a great butcher's hook on which to impale condemned victims and hang them up by the ribs to die, large and small branding irons, and so on.

Leaving behind these relics, Radishchev pressed on towards Ekaterinburg (now Sverdlovsk). He passed near the famous Demidov copper and iron works and came down on the far side of the Urals. The peasants here grew but little corn, he noted, owing to the cold climate and stony ground on which rye alone would flourish. Many of them worked at the Stroganov iron foundries. For the most part they were not bond-serfs, but free, hired hands. They paid the usual taxes to the Government, but their most burdensome liability consisted in furnishing horses to travellers and escorts to passing convict gangs. Ekaterinburg on the River Iset' was reached on December 7th, an important industrial centre already, with its metallurgical industry, a Government mint, and flourishing trade in corn, fish, meat and other foodstuffs.

After a week at Ekaterinburg, Radishchev set out for Tobolsk, past quarries yielding pale grey stone speckled with white and red, and then over flat country among birch trees. At one small place he saw the ruins of a wooden fort and an empty arsenal, which had withstood an attack by Pugachev during the Cossack and Bashkir rising of 1773–4. The local people had beaten off the rebel hordes, as a reward for which their township had been granted municipal status. The peasants' cottages in this region had a black, weatherbeaten appearance. Radishchev found the people kindly and hospitable, though some of them were sallow from endemic fevers and went about in rags. As he entered Siberia proper, he recalled the words inscribed by Dante on the portals of his Inferno: 'Abandon hope, all ye who enter here.'

A few days before Christmas, Radishchev and his party arrived at Tobolsk on the Irtysh, the capital city of Western Siberia. There Radishchev was permitted to remain until the coming of spring made possible his onward journey to Ilimsk. Tobolsk society was used to the arrival of distinguished exiles from St Petersburg. Indeed, many of the chief residents had themselves come to Siberia under compulsion rather than from choice, and they were always eager to welcome newcomers bringing the latest scandal and political and literary news from the capital. The Governor, Deputy Governor and other officials received Radishchev in their homes and he was invited to dinner parties, recep-

tions and theatrical shows. The old rebellious spirit revived in this congenial milieu. Many years ago, the antiquary P. A. Efremov discovered
in an old album this short set of verses, composed by Radishchev in
reply to one of his Tobolsk acquaintances who enquired who he was
and whither he was bound:

> Who, what I am you wish to know, and where I go?
> I am the same I was and shall be all my life:
> No beast, no plant, no slave, but a human being!
> To blaze a trail where no man yet has trod
> For spirits bold and daring in prose as well as verse,
> To put fear into sensitive hearts and muzzle Truth,
> To Fort Ilimsk I go.

In his letters to Count Vorontsov, Radishchev gave a vivid and
picturesque account of life in Tobolsk in those lusty days of the late
eighteenth century, when European ways were fast superimposing
themselves upon the rugged customs of those parts. Much of the town
had been destroyed in a recent disastrous fire, but was being rebuilt on
more modern lines. The local burgesses, Radishchev reported, spent
their working time making money, their leisure in drinking tea and
snoring. Their greatest treat was to get drunk. In Holy Week, three
comedies were put on at the local theatre, including a farce called 'What
an Age!' written by Catherine the Great herself,[1] but outside the
Governor's box there were not fifty spectators in the place. A monthly
journal with the imposing title *Irtysh transformed to Hippocrene* strove
to impart to the Tobolsk public some elements of literary culture. Polite
society modelled its ways as best it could on those of Moscow and
St Petersburg, the tone being set by a number of distinguished exiles
banished thence and by the higher officials of Government headquarters.
Luxury and high living were restricted by the prudent reluctance of
local shopkeepers to grant credit. Until Governor Chicherin arrived in
1763, there had been no social life at all. Chicherin, so tradition had it,
used to force the local notables to attend his receptions willy-nilly and
so set in motion some beginnings of polite intercourse. Until Chicherin's
time, the magistrates used to preside over their assize court in sheepskin jackets and dressing gowns, while the sentries stood on guard in
shabby overalls. In those days, people at dinner parties would all drink
out of the same mug and eat out of a common dish. Even in 1790,
Tobolsk culture did not extend far down the social scale. 'As for the
common people, they are in no way surpassed in poverty and dissipation by the *lazzaroni* of Naples, whom they excel in sloth and drunken-
ness.'

[1] *O, Vremya!* (literally, 'O, Time!'), 1772.

In return, Vorontsov sent Radishchev the latest newspapers from Western Europe, including the *Mercure de France*, which enabled Radishchev to follow the day to day progress of the French Revolution. 'It seems (such is human nature) as if the printed sheet conveys me to the very scene of those events. At a distance of four thousand miles I can witness past events as though in the present, and just as if I were on the spot.' But even in a private letter to his indulgent patron, Radishchev was now discreet enough to keep his reflections on the French Revolution to himself.

Observant and curious as ever, the 'observer without spectacles', as Vorontsov called Radishchev, set to work on a geographical and statistical essay on the province of Tobolsk, with special reference to trade and agriculture. When it was complete, he sent it off to his old chief at the Board of Trade.[1] One of the main questions affecting the commerce of Tobolsk at that time was that of the Chinese trade route via Kiakhta, which had been closed for some time owing to Sino-Russian political tension. The Treaty of Kiakhta concluded between Russia and China in 1727 stipulated that trade between the two countries should be canalized via Kiakhta and Nerchinsk, but mutual suspicions and local frontier incidents often hindered the transit of merchandise, as at this time. This was causing loss and inconvenience to Tobolsk merchants, as well as a general shortage of tea. As President of the Board of Trade, Vorontsov wanted some accurate estimate of the effects of this situation on Siberia's economic progress, and Radishchev sent him his own views and observations in several private letters and a more detailed memorandum which he drew up later on.

Paul Radishchev says in his biography of his father that Radishchev was a 'great partisan of Free Trade', and some critics have sought to represent him as a disciple of Adam Smith and the English Free Trade school. But this is not borne out by study of his letters to Vorontsov. 'Just as I have often been a heretic in many of my opinions, in this instance too the evil effects of cutting off trade relations with China do not seem to me unlimited. I think that there is even some advantage therein.' Foreign trade, he thought, was only beneficial when it served to nurture commerce at home. In a large Empire like Russia, with abundant natural resources of her own, external trade can never be the main source of wealth. 'An item of merchandise which comes into the country and goes straight to the consumer is not and should not be regarded as something to be esteemed.' On the other hand, the unhindered circulation of home-produced commodities within the Empire should be encouraged by every possible means. In this connection, it was worth noting that the exclusion of Chinese textiles had encouraged

[1] Published in A. N. Radishchev, *Polnoe sobranie sochineny*, III, 133–42.

O

the growth of a Siberian flax and linen industry. Indeed, Radishchev shows himself markedly critical of Adam Smith's theories, even as applied to Western Europe. Speaking of tariff barriers, he wrote: 'England, with eight million inhabitants, by means of such regulations became one of the leading States of Europe. But the English now say and write that all obstacles to trade are harmful; for, so they say, commerce is inevitably bound to maintain itself automatically in perpetual balance.' It may be that countries such as Holland and the Hanseatic League cities made their fortunes by an unhindered transit trade, but Russia and Siberia could never profit in the same way. 'The prohibition on importing foreign manufactured products inevitably encourages industry at home, and without this measure, it may fall into decay.'

We must therefore agree with a Soviet economist, E. Prikazchikova, that 'Radishchev stands out as an advocate of the limitation of freedom of external trade, a supporter of protectionism'.[1] His views have certainly been endorsed by Russian Governments in modern times, notably the Soviet period. Under Nicholas I, a policy similar to that outlined by Radishchev was enforced by the Finance Minister Kankrin. In this connection, it is interesting to read a report from a British representative at St Petersburg, who wrote in 1826: 'England has flourished under a prohibitive system and persisted in it until she has amassed a capital which may enable her to dispense with it, or even render such a change profitable to her. But Russia is where England was 100 years ago. Whenever Russia shall have reached the point which England has now attained, she may perhaps adopt a similar system; but till then the prohibition of foreign manufactures for the protection of her own is considered by her governors as the only sound policy for Russia to follow.'[2] Thus Radishchev's study of the Russo-Chinese trade question is of interest as one of the first discussions of Adam Smith's economic theories as applied to Russian conditions. In their rejection, Radishchev foreshadowed Russian official policy for many years to come, although at the time his views did not carry weight, and the Chinese trade route via Kiakhta was in fact reopened in 1792.

With his usual prophetic vision, Radishchev clearly foresaw Siberia's future role in the economic and political destiny of Russia. 'What a rich country is this Siberia, with all its products, what a vigorous land! Centuries more are needed; but once populated, it is fated one day to play a great role in the annals of the world. When some driving force, some irresistible impulse has exerted a beneficial stimulus upon the

---

[1] *Ekonomicheskie vzglyady A. N. Radishcheva* ('A. N. Radishchev's views on economics'), Moscow, Leningrad, 1947, p. 116.

[2] E. C. Disbrowe, British Minister at St Petersburg, in F.O. Records, *Russia Correspondence*, 1825/8, vol. 182/2, No. 56 of 1826, p. 324.

drowsy denizens of these regions, we shall once more see the comrades of Yermak seeking out and opening up a passage across the supposedly impenetrable icy waters of the Arctic ocean; after establishing a direct link between Siberia and Europe, we shall see them rescue this country's immense agricultural potential from the stagnation in which it languishes. . . . If I had to drag out my life in this province, I would willingly volunteer to look for this passage, in spite of all the hazards attendant on these kinds of enterprise.'

Early in the spring of 1791, to Radishchev's unspeakable joy, he was joined in Tobolsk by his sister-in-law, Elizabeth Rubanovsky, together with his daughter Catherine, aged eight, and his youngest son, Paul, a boy of seven. His two eldest, Vasily and Nicholas, had been sent to live with Radishchev's brother, their Uncle Moses, at Archangel, where he had a job in the Customs House, also under Count Vorontsov's jurisdiction. Radishchev expressed his delight at his dear ones' arrival in another letter to Vorontsov. 'For the last few days, my heart, which had been as it were pierced through and through with sorrow, has seemed to blossom forth and open out once more to happiness; my languid spirit seems able to regain a little of its vigour. . . . So sudden a change in my being, a new life, I may almost say, this joy, to whom do I owe it? Solely to Your Excellency. You have made it your pleasure to shower with blessings a man whose only merit has been to fall into misfortune through an act of imprudence unforgivable at his time of life. What shall I say to you? What mark of gratitude can you expect of me? If to love you is enough . . . to adore you is still too little. . . . A tear shed before your portrait, which I have received from my dear friend's hand. . . . Be sensible to this tear of mine: it is all that I can send you.' Vorontsov also received the grateful thanks of Elizabeth Rubanovsky for all he had done to make their reunion possible.—'Allow me, Sir, to add here the sincere wishes which I cease not to offer for the preservation of your days, and be assured that the most profound respect and inviolable attachment which I have sworn you will end only with my life.' Of the heroism and self-sacrifice displayed by Elizabeth Rubanovsky in following Radishchev to Siberia and linking her life with his, one of her former schoolfellows at the Smol'ny Institute wrote, 'A skilled pen might compose a whole book about her virtues, her sufferings, and her constancy of spirit, which could be cited to many as an example to follow'.

Early summer came. Radishchev should officially have been well on his way to Ilimsk by now. Still he tarried, partly, it may be, in the vain hope that he might be yet spared the dreary solitude of Fort Ilimsk, and be allowed to stay in more congenial Tobolsk. To Vorontsov, who advised him to move on, Radishchev pleaded sickness, the state of the roads, delay over fitting up the necessary transport. Malicious busy-bodies commented to the authorities at St Petersburg on the length of Radishchev's stay, as if fearing that even Tobolsk might become infected with Jacobinism: the kindly Governor received a reprimand from Court.

Towards the end of July 1791, all was ready at last. The family set out along the banks of the Irtysh on the road to Tomsk. Rivers, bogs and forests they met in plenty, and also stretches of good black soil. They passed villages of prosperous peasants, old settlers who had had time to make good, and others inhabited by more recent arrivals, for the most part quite poor. There were colonies of Russian Old Believers, and others of Polish patriots captured by the Russians and banished by Catherine to Siberia after the partition in 1772. Poorer exiles who fell into debt were sent to work in the vodka distilleries, in company with squads of convict labourers. In old age, these more recent settlers suffered misery and privation. Owing to rainy weather and bad roads, the stretch from Tobolsk to Tomsk took the travellers three weeks. They were cordially received by the Commandant at Tomsk, a Frenchman named Thomas de Villeneuve, who was making a career in Russian service. As Elizabeth Rubanovsky had a bad attack of toothache, they stayed a fortnight, and then went on, through copses, pine forests, and birch woods, opening out beyond the River Kiya into fine meadow land dotted with oak trees, an excellent country for corn and cattle raising. The town and district of Krasnoyarsk, with the Enisey flowing through rugged cliffs, reminded Radishchev of pictures he had seen of the Alps. Later on, they passed by a deserted Buryat encampment or *yurt*, finally reaching Irkutsk on October 8th.

Here the Radishchevs were cordially received by the Governor-General of Eastern Siberia, Ivan Pil', an old friend of Count Alexander's. The Governor-General handed Radishchev a large sum of money sent by Vorontsov, together with the books and meteorological instruments for which he had asked his benefactor. The exiles were entertained frequently by Pil' at his home, while instructions were sent to Ilimsk for a comfortable house to be got ready for them. Radishchev continued to study Siberia's economic problems. He inspected the local schools: it is noteworthy that as early as 1791, there was already a Government school at Irkutsk, with several quite well qualified teachers; also a theological seminary, and a garrison school, where the soldiers' children learnt to read, write and do sums. In a letter to Vorontsov, Radishchev expressed the then somewhat revolutionary view that better results could be obtained by amalgamating all three classes of school: why should a priest's son not be trained as a soldier, or a soldier's son as a priest, instead of forming separate castes on their own?—And Radish-chev goes on to pay tribute to the advances in educational method produced in Western Europe under the influence of Jean-Jacques Rousseau's theories and the practical techniques evolved by the German pedagogue Basedow.

Before leaving Irkutsk, Radishchev addressed a letter to his old comrade Alexis Kutuzov, whom he was fated never to see again. 'Where are you, my beloved friend? If ever you believed that I loved you (and I do so still), then send me news about yourself, in the knowledge that a letter from you will be a comfort to me. Farewell, dear friend! . . . I am as resigned as it is possible for me to be, to the extent that human nature permits. Demand no more. . . .'[1] But Kutuzov too was an exile from home; his reply to Radishchev's letter, if it ever reached him, was not calculated to give much solace to his suffering heart. 'I cannot refrain,' Alexis wrote, 'from reproaching you for disregarding my friendly advice, and thereby condemning both of us to a fate which I find hard to bear.' However, Kutuzov continued, the earth was but dust and shadow. No doubt a spell of exile in Siberia would enable Radishchev to examine his own conscience, learn at the hard school of adversity, and perhaps even adopt the mood of pious resignation which Kutuzov and his fellow Masons recommended as the best solution for life's problems. Not many years after this, Kutuzov died miserably in a German debtors' prison. It was a wretched ending to an intimate comradeship which had lasted almost thirty years.

The only way of reaching Ilimsk during winter was by sledge. Preparations for the last stage of the journey took two months. The best plan would have been to wait for the River Angara to freeze over and then to have travelled over the icy surface. However, here in Irkutsk too the busybodies were active in criticizing the Governor-General for allowing this dangerous revolutionary to pollute the atmosphere, and there was even talk of a complaint being sent to St Petersburg. So Radishchev, Elizabeth Rubanovsky and the children, with a military guard, had to set forth on December 20th by another, more circuitous route, taking at first the main Yakutsk road which skirted the River Lena, and then branching off along a side track for the last hundred miles to Fort Ilimsk—a total of six hundred miles from Irkutsk. After a fortnight's journey through country sparsely inhabited by Russian settlers and Buryat and Tungus tribesmen, they arrived in January 1792, at the lonely outpost which was to be their home for the next five years.

---

[1] Radishchev, *Polnoe sobranie sochineny*, III, 408.

CHAPTER 12

In Siberia

Settling In – Amateur Medicine – Prospecting for a Mine – Siberian Witch-Doctors – Man's Mortality and Immortality – Catherine's New Favourite – Count Vorontsov Retires – More Family Cares – Bullying Officials – Death of an Empress – Returning Home

In the event, Ilimsk turned out to be even smaller and more lonely than Radishchev had been led to expect by the Russian gazetteers of the time. It had declined in importance since those turbulent days of the seventeenth century, when it served as the headquarters of one of the Cossack bands who completed the conquest of Siberia. The wooden stockade and watchtowers were decayed, and the former Commandant's house had been disused until the authorities had it repaired for Radishchev and his family. There were forty-six houses in the village, inhabited by Cossacks, peasants and small shopkeepers and traders, making a total of some two hundred and fifty souls. The Cossacks were governed by their *sotnik* ('centurion'), while the traders were headed by their burgomaster. There was a little church, and a depot of the Government vodka monopoly. But there was not a cobbler, a tailor, a tallow chandler nor a locksmith in the place.

The first few weeks were full of hardship. It was the coldest season of the year, with up to thirty-two degrees of frost. Elizabeth Rubanovsky and the children were often sick. Radishchev himself, apart from twinges of rheumatism, was exhausted by the long journey and downcast by the uncouth surroundings in which he now found himself. To take his mind off present cares, he picked up Voltaire's *Candide,* where that incurable optimist Dr Pangloss is introduced. 'Here we are, in the best of all possible worlds—said Pangloss to me in conversation last night. Pangloss, why cannot I adopt your philosophy? You are hanged, and you say it is all for the best!'

The family soon began to settle down. The children in particular grew quite accustomed to their new home. They had their own servants to look after them. Letters from Radishchev's elder sons in Russia and parcels of clothing from Count Vorontsov began to arrive. Thanks to Count Alexander, the family had plenty of money, and food was plentiful and cheap. To start with, they took over the former military Commandant's quarters, but soon carpenters arrived from Irkutsk to build them a new wooden house, cosy and warm. They kept a cow with its calf, a sheep, and a tame deer presented to Radishchev by one of the native Tunguses. In the morning, Radishchev gave reading lessons to his little son and daughter; in the afternoon, he took a short walk, and the rest of the day he would spend reading and writing. He was the only educated man for hundreds of miles around, and the only person with a medicine chest or any knowledge of anatomy or surgery, of which he had picked up the rudiments at Leipzig many years before. So people used to come to him with their ailments from outlying settlements. Many of them he managed to cure and saved several lives. He inoculated his own children and others against smallpox. These varied occupations at least prevented him from turning, as he once almost feared, into one of Jean-Jacques Rousseau's 'happy savages', and walking about on all fours.

With the spring, Radishchev's spirits revived. The non-commissioned officer and private soldier detailed to keep him under observation were tolerant souls, and did not hinder him from taking long walks into the surrounding country and boat trips down the Ilim and other rivers of the district. 'Promenades here are pretty monotonous. No meadows, except for narrow strips of grass land along the river bank. Dirty and gloomy woods. No trees but conifers: pines, firs and larches. . . . Nothing remotely approaching the descriptions which people give of the Alps and the Pyrenees.' However, Radishchev spent many happy hours studying local plant life, and also took up geology, especially as there were said to be some iron and silver mines in the neighbourhood.— 'When fate oppresses us with its heavy hand,' he wrote, 'and cuts us off from the society of civilized men, it leaves us instead the welcome resource of being able to study nature, to question objects deprived not only of reason, but even of sensibility and all semblance of life—stones and rocks. They give answer, yes, they reply, and often with more sincerity than is the case with human beings.'

The Russian settlers viewed Radishchev's attempts at prospecting with distrust, in case these attracted tax collectors or mining officials to the region. No such misunderstandings clouded his relations with the aboriginal Tunguses who lived a nomadic life in those parts. Little Paul Radishchev kept vivid memories of those simple folk, whom he recalled as tall and well-built people, with swarthy complexions and a Mongolian cast of features, not unlike the Kalmucks. Some of them, including the women, tattooed their faces, and they were fond of strong liquor. For Radishchev's benefit, they once staged a special demonstration by their Shamans or witch-doctors, adepts in the ancient pagan cults of the Siberian natives. 'If I were not afraid of being tedious,' Radishchev wrote to Vorontsov, 'I should have sent Your Excellency a description of the religious ceremony of the Tunguses, which they performed at my request when staying close to Ilimsk—the ritual known as Shamanism, which the common people believe to be an invocation of the devil, and which is ordinarily taken to be nothing but a mere mummery put on to fascinate the eyes of the credulous.' With a tolerance rare in that land and age, Radishchev added that for his part, he viewed this crude ritual as 'simply one of those widely differing ways of expressing consciousness of the supreme power of a Being whom we cannot know, and whose grandeur is proclaimed in even the most trivial things'.

The ways and dress of the local settlers and village folk also contained much to interest a student of Russian folk manners and national costume. The picturesque dress of the Ilimsk girls reflected the ease with which Chinese fabrics could normally be procured in that region of Siberia. They wore a kind of sleeveless padded jacket, called a *telogreyka* or 'body-warmer', whose ample folds concealed the waist line. The skirt was of nankeen, the long-sleeved chemise of yellow silk or of cotton, according to the wearer's social status. The girls had their hair bound round with a kerchief, but otherwise wore no head dress. Their popular dance (from which married women were excluded) somewhat resembled a minuet. Two girl dancers, facing one another, would go sideways in opposite directions, crossing their legs over towards the right. After going a certain distance, they would come back in the reverse direction, until they were again facing each other. According to Paul Radishchev, who watched this dance on many occasions, the effect was not particularly pretty or lively.

Radishchev employed many long evenings in his Siberian retreat in thinking out afresh the all-important problem of man's relationship to his Maker and to the world around him. The result of his meditations is a treatise entitled *On Man, his Mortality and Immortality*, the manuscript of which was treasured up by his sons and published by them some years after his death. It is a work which witnesses to Radishchev's enormously wide reading, to his powers of logical analysis and abstract reasoning, and to his literary talent. It embodies an epitome of German idealist thought in the tradition of Leibnitz, a critique of the extreme materialist position taken up by certain French thinkers of the eighteenth century, and an attempt at an original and independent solution of the problem of man's place in this life and the hereafter. According to Sir Isaiah Berlin, Russia has had plenty of prophets, thinkers, critics, publicists and revolutionary conspirators, but no philosophers worthy of the name—that is to say, no one to speak of who has engaged in a systematic enquiry into logical, epistemological and metaphysical questions.[1] To this rather devastating view Radishchev may be considered an honourable exception. His treatise has attracted increasing attention among historians of Russian philosophy, ever since Pushkin in his critical article 'Alexander Radishchev' accused him of being 'fonder of putting forward than of refuting the arguments of pure atheism'. Paul Radishchev, in his biography of his father, retorted to this: 'He revered Spinoza and Helvétius as virtuous and well-intentioned men who had thought profoundly, but he himself was never an atheist. Doubt is not in itself atheism.' Pushkin's *obiter dictum* makes a strong appeal to Marxist critics intent on claiming Radishchev as a forerunner. 'As the basis of an outlook on life,' says the Soviet scholar G. A. Gukovsky, 'materialism must, in Radishchev's view, remain unchallenged. It is another matter that Radishchev does not succeed in remaining at the summit of this principle; but this is in spite of himself and evidently unnoticed by himself.'[2] That kind of dialectic is not very fruitful or convincing, and it will be more helpful to turn to Radishchev's treatise and study what he has to say in his own words.

The treatise *On Man, his Mortality and Immortality* bears the heading 'Begun at Ilimsk, January 15, 1792', and the motto 'Le temps présent est gros de l'avenir: Leibnitz'. (This is a reminiscence of Leibnitz's *Théodicée*, paragraph 360: 'It is one of the principles of my system of universal harmony that the present is pregnant with the future, and that He who sees all, sees in what is what is to be.') In a dedication, 'To my Friends', Radishchev explains his purpose in examining whether man may cherish hope in a life to come. 'Forced to renounce, perhaps for ever, the hope of seeing you again, I wish to seize, if not the obvious and evident fact, at least the likelihood or even, it may be, the mere possibility that one day (I know not where) I may once more embrace my friends and say to them—in what tongue I cannot tell—I love you as before!'

In its general layout, Radishchev's book broadly follows the layout of a famous work by the German philosopher Moses Mendelssohn, *Phaedon, oder über die Unsterblichkeit der Seele*, which consists of a free elaboration of Plato's dialogue containing the last conversation of Socrates and his disciples before the great thinker drank the hemlock and met his death. Mendelssohn's *Phaedon* was published in 1767, at the time when Radishchev was in Leipzig, and was translated into

[1] Quoted by Eugene Lampert in *The Listener*, August 7, 1958, p. 194.

[2] This quotation is from the official Soviet *History of Russian Literature*, IV , pt. 2, Moscow, 1947, p. 556.

Russian ten years later. As explained in his preface, Mendelssohn did not hesitate to depart from Plato's own words, and to put into Socrates' mouth speculative arguments more typical of an eighteenth-century thinker than of an ancient Athenian philosopher. In book I, he treats of the definitions of life and death, and demonstrates that the human spirit cannot perish with the body; book II refutes common objections to belief in immortality; and book III treats of the nature of the life to come, and describes the death of Socrates. Radishchev in his *On Man* first considers man as a physical, social and intellectual being (book I), then gives the arguments against the spiritual nature and immortality of the human soul (book II); he proceeds to refute these arguments and defend the doctrine of immortality (book III), and finally to speculate upon the nature of man's future existence after life on earth (book IV).

From the outset, the writer emphasizes that he intends to adopt a completely impartial and dispassionate attitude towards the problem of man's mortal and immortal natures. 'Let us thrust from us all prejudice, all preconceived notions, and, guided by the lamp of experimental enquiry, attempt to gather a few facts which may lead us on in the knowledge of nature. . . . Weighing up as best we can both opposite extremes, I will leave it to you to choose, my dear ones, whichever solution is most probable and clear, if not completely obvious.' His own sympathies, he confesses, lie on the side of admitting the existence of a spiritual nature transcending the life of the flesh. 'Cut off from you as I am, my friends, I shall follow that opinion which gives solace to the grieving soul.'

How does a human being enter the world? Is there a soul already inherent in the embryo from the very moment of conception? In trying to find an answer to these questions, Radishchev uses biological data derived, so it appears, from such studies as the *Theoria Generationis* by K. F. Wolff (1733–94) and the *Vénus Physique* by Moreau de Maupertuis. He throws down the challenge to such crude advocates of materialism as La Mettrie, who had declared in his *L'Homme-Machine* that 'man is a machine and there exists throughout the entire universe nothing but one single substance with various modifications', and had in 1748 produced a pamphlet entitled *L'Homme-Plante* in which man was likened to the vegetable world. Radishchev for his part declares: 'We shall not say, like some thinkers—Man is a plant. For though there are great similarities, the difference between them is immeasurable.' Radishchev dwells on the exclusive properties of the human mind, which distinguish man from the brute creation; in this section he makes extensive use of the German philosopher Herder's *Ideen zur Geschichte der Menschheit*, one of the most influential books produced in the late eighteenth century.[1] He embarks on a reasoned critique of some of the conclusions advanced by Helvétius in his *De l'Esprit*, a work with which he had been familiar since his student days. The French writer had put forward the notion that everyone is born potentially equal in intellectual capacity, and that education and environment are the sole factors which determine the extent of a person's subsequent development. Radishchev takes Helvétius to task on this issue, pointing out the undoubted influence of hereditary factors on the individual mind and personality. Man is born with certain innate individual potentialities, which in a congenial environment will blossom out in due course. But great physical and mental disparities between members of the human family are clearly visible from the cradle onwards, and nothing can be done to eradicate these altogether.

In contrast to Helvétius and the Sensualist school of thought, Radishchev maintains that there are certain basic, inborn ideas, which can develop within the human brain independently of external stimulus or teaching. Among such innate ideas is belief in God. All men, Radishchev exclaims, feel instinctively that there exists some supreme almighty being—call it what you will. Hobbes and Spinoza felt this. God is everywhere. Men have only to open their eyes to see all around them the presence of the Father of mankind. This instinct is quite capable of existing in the absence of any form of religious instruction.

Radishchev now turns to criticize Jean-Jacques Rousseau's well-known ideas on the origins and abuses of human society. He disputes Rousseau's panacea for a regeneration of mankind through reversion to an idyllic state of nature in an imaginary Elysium. Despite the eloquence of the sage of Geneva, Radishchev maintains that man is born for society—a view which he also put forward in one of his letters to Count Vorontsov. Living isolated in remote Siberia, Radishchev declined to share Rousseau's faith in the advantages of a solitary, 'natural' existence, as preached with such vehemence in such writings as the *Discours sur l'Inégalité*. 'O Rousseau,' he asks, 'whither wert thou led by thy boundless sensibility?' More congenial to Radishchev, as a convinced advocate of peasant proprietorship of the land, were Rousseau's views on the concept of private property, as expressed in the same *Discours*. Radishchev was inclined to agree with Rousseau that any man's ownership of land should be confined to an area sufficient to feed the cultivator and his family, and should last just as long as he happened to dwell in any one place. As soon as anyone said: 'This plot of land is my property', he fastened himself to the earth and prepared the way for bestial autocracy, where people tyrannize over their fellow men.

[1] See the study by K. Bittner, 'J. G. Herder und A. N. Radiščev', in *Zeitschrift für slavische Philologie*, XXV, Heft 1, Heidelberg, 1956.

And for a moment Radishchev regrets humanity's primitive state of blissful ignorance. In a reference to Rousseau's *Émile*, he exclaims, 'The lad would be happy, as Rousseau says, if he reasoned not, knew nothing, was a stranger to rational thought!'

The first book of Radishchev's treatise ends on a note of optimism. Life extinguished is not annihilation. Death is at once destruction, transformation, and resurrection. Let hope of immortality be a reason for rejoicing! And at the opening of the second book, he recalls the example of Cato, who spends his last moments before committing suicide in meditating on the life to come. In Addison's tragedy, *Cato*, which Radishchev knew well, the hero cries out:

> 'Tis Heaven itself that points out an Hereafter,
> And intimates Eternity to Man.
> Eternity! Thou pleasing, dreadful, Thought!

And Radishchev draws the conclusion that man's inner conviction of immortality struggles with the evidence of decay and death in all created things around him, providing consolation to sufferers and the bereaved.

But what is the verdict of the scientist? Radishchev carefully examines the conclusions set out in Dr Joseph Priestley's *Disquisitions relating to Matter and Spirit*, published in 1777, but is driven to the realization that such questions as whether God exists or whether there is life after death lie beyond the scope of experiment and logical deduction. Scientists fall into absurdity when they venture outside their proper field into the realm of metaphysics. Even the judicious John Locke was misled into trying to explain the Creation of the world in terms of scientific speculation. 'Let us imagine an empty space,' Locke (or rather his French expositor, Coste) had written in the French version of the *Essay concerning Human Understanding*, 'and the Almighty addressing it and saying: Let it be divided and solidified.' What a ridiculous and pretentious fiction! What audacity to attempt to express the Eternal Thought in terms of words, sounds, vibration of the air! (Radishchev is here inadvertently unfair to Locke's memory, since the concept in question is ascribed by Coste not to Locke, but to Newton.) 'O philosophers,' Radishchev concludes, 'stick to experimental knowledge and derive benefit from it. Do not try to conjecture what you cannot know.'

The second book of Radishchev's treatise continues with an exposition of the extreme materialist point of view, according to which matter and spirit have no separate existence, thought being merely a function of matter. Several pages of this section appear in inverted commas, thus making it clear that Radishchev is quoting the views of someone with whom he does not necessarily agree. He is, in fact, introducing a 'man of straw', whom he can later demolish if he chooses, and the views expressed by this 'man of straw' bear a strong resemblance to those advanced by the Baron d'Holbach, author of the much-banned *Système de la Nature*. 'Does the soul not grow with the body, does it not mature and harden with it, and with it fade and grow dim? . . . Do you not receive all your ideas and thoughts from sensations? If you do not believe me, read Locke.' If bodily functions are upset by illness, indigestion or intoxication, the mind cannot operate effectively either; thus the brain must be a mere physical organ without any independent existence as a spiritual entity. 'And so, O mortal man! abandon the vain illusion that you are a portion of the Deity! You were a phenomenon necessary to the world as a result of eternal laws. Your end has overtaken you, the thread of your days is snapped asunder, time has ended for you and the hour of eternity has struck.'—Most of this is taken almost literally from Holbach's book.

But now Radishchev turns and rends the atheist. 'Cruel tyrant! You are worse than Tiberius, Nero and Caligula, whose power to torment mankind extended only to this brief earthly lifespan. But you seek to rob unhappy mortals of their sole comfort: eternal bliss in the hereafter. Are those who persecuted Socrates to suffer the same fate as he? Is annihilation to be the lot of virtuous and vicious alike?' No—the cold-blooded logic of the atheist must yield to the voice of the heart. And on the score of logic alone, the arguments of the atheist leave much to be desired. Even if ideas originate as sensations, how do we know that the spirit cannot feel and think even when the body has mouldered away? An Egyptian may spend his life beside the Nile, which never freezes, and therefore affirm that water can never solidify. How fatuous this would seem to an Eskimo in the Arctic! One should thus beware of sweeping assertions based on limited experience.

Radishchev's own view is that the human soul is an entity in itself, distinct from the body and imparting to the latter movement, life, feeling and thought. Death is nothing but a transition to a new and higher life, where the spirit can soar untrammelled by the infirmities of the flesh. Radishchev recalls the message of hope contained in Herder's *Ideen zur Geschichte der Menschheit*: 'From stone to man a gradual and awe-inspiring evolution is manifest—the staircase of creation, discovered long ago, upon which each species seems so little removed from the next that they may certainly be thought of as related, a staircase upon which the orang-outang and the aborigine appear as if born of the same womb. . . . O mortal man! You are tending towards perfection, and can become more and more perfect. What you are destined to become at last, you can but dream.'

Reverting to the plane of logical argument, Radishchev takes the war into the enemy's camp with vigour, roundly challenging the view held by Locke and Helvétius that all human ideas derive ultimately from sensations. What about complex mental operations involving comparison? To compare and contrast two sensations is something quite different from the simple impact of a single sensation on the organs of perception. Rousseau had already spotted this chink in the armour of Helvétius and his school. In a set of critical notes on the book *De l'Esprit*, Rousseau remarks that the comparison of yellow with red is neither the sensation of yellow nor the sensation of red: 'Apercevoir les objets, c'est sentir; apercevoir les rapports, c'est juger.'[1] Radishchev elaborates this objection further. Suppose a man sees a bell and hears it ringing; he receives two simultaneous impressions, visible form and audible sound. If he touches it, he can feel the bell to be an object endowed with solidity and extension in space. Three separate and distinct sensations are received by the organs of hearing, sight and touch respectively, yet the mind is able to form one joint concept, expressed by the word 'bell'. This mental synthesis can, in Radishchev's view, be achieved only by a spiritual, and not by any physical organ.

The arguments of the materialists, which fail to satisfy Radishchev on logical grounds, also seem to him ethically inadmissible. Are such qualities as magnanimity, honour and virtue products of 'sensations' or of crude self interest? Were Virgil, Milton, Michaelangelo mere automata of flesh and blood? Much has been made of the influence which the state of a man's body exercises over his mind. But what has the atheist to say of the effect of mind, spirit and willpower over the body? Every doctor knows that the will to recovery often saves the patient's body even when the malady seems desperate. Conversely, mental agitation can induce physical sickness. Thus, body and spirit, though closely linked, cannot be considered as merely two permutations of one single material substance.

The fourth and last book of Radishchev's treatise discusses the various possible forms which a future life might be expected to take. He considers the attractive doctrine of palingenesis, or the transmigration of souls. It is true that belief in reincarnation can be exploited by quacks and charlatans, but it is a consoling doctrine for those who find themselves frustrated by adverse circumstances or doomed to obscurity or a cruel death. 'We repeat: circumstances make the great man. Without his throne, Frederick II would have remained in the throng of mediocre poetasters and perhaps have achieved nothing else. . . . Propitious circumstances are essential. In their absence, John Hus perishes in the flames, Galileo is dragged off into a dungeon, and your friend (i.e.

---

[1] *Notes en réfutation de l'ouvrage d'Helvétius intitulé 'De l'Esprit'*, published posthumously in 1779.

Radishchev himself) languishes at Ilimsk. But time and preparation can remove all obstacles. Luther brought about great reforms, and Descartes likewise.' Thus it may be that the spirits of thwarted reformers are destined to fulfil their mission by reincarnation in a more favourable land and epoch.

The book closes with an eloquent vindication of belief in immortality. Death and resurrection are like the transformation of the humble caterpillar into a resplendent butterfly. To take a metaphor from Leibnitz, the caterpillar becomes a chrysalis, to all appearances dead: then there emerges a butterfly stretching its wings, radiant with every colour of the sunbeam. Like Socrates in his prison, Radishchev confidently announces his faith in the reality of a life to come. 'Where is the limit of the perfectibility of the spirit? O Man! Is it not clear that thou art son of the Deity, does not His boundless power dwell in thee? . . . Let us briefly sum up all that we have said: Man after death will be alive; his body will perish, but his soul cannot perish, for it is an essence simple and indissoluble. His aim on earth is perfection, and the same will be his goal after death. Believe, I repeat, believe, eternity is no illusion!'

Despite the special pleading of Marxist critics, it is clear that Radishchev in his treatise *On Man, his Mortality and Immortality* 'unequivocally defends the immortality of the soul'.[1] The bitterness of exile had served to strengthen his faith in a life to come. He found the arguments of the atheist as unconvincing to his reason as they were repugnant to his heart and his ethical sense. But he took great care to give both sides a fair hearing, and the whole book eloquently testifies to his stringent intellectual honesty. It would be a great mistake to dismiss it as simply a collection of snippets from various Western philosophers. Radishchev's *On Man* is both a synthesis of certain basic ideas dominating eighteenth-century metaphysics, and a critique of them. It is not too much to say that perusal of Radishchev's philosophical treatise convinces one of the onset of philosophical maturity in Russia, and the possibility of original achievement in the realm of metaphysics.[2]

*

On a rather different intellectual plane, Radishchev also completed the essay on the Chinese trade question which he had begun to study while staying in Tobolsk and Irkutsk. He sent the manuscript off to his old

[1] G. Shpet, *Ocherk razvitiya russkoy filosofii* ('Outline of the development of Russian Philosophy'), Petrograd, 1922, I, 66.

[2] V. V. Zen'kovsky, *Istoriya russkoy filosofii* ('History of Russian Philosophy'), Paris, 1948–50, I, 102.

chief Vorontsov for the information of the St Petersburg Board of Trade. But it arrived too late to be of much practical use. The Count's official position as President of the Board had become of late increasingly insecure. His disdain for Catherine's flamboyant paramours and his open patronage of the disgraced Radishchev had diminished his credit in Court circles. The all-powerful Potemkin—that 'scourge of Russia', as Vorontsov called him—died in 1791. If Vorontsov, Bezborodko and the other veteran administrators thought their hour of influence had come, they were sadly disappointed. Even before Potemkin's death, Catherine was sharing her bed with a self-satisfied young Guards officer named Platon Zubov. As soon as Potemkin was safely buried, Zubov was promoted General-Adjutant, created a Count, and presented with huge estates and swarms of serfs. The doting Empress told heads of Government departments to refer all important decisions on affairs of State to this insufferable upstart, and regularly upheld his rulings, however foolish they might be. Contemporaries felt that with Potemkin's death, the reign of Catherine had passed its zenith and was declining towards its end.

Under the stress of events in France, the prevailing mood at St Petersburg was one of violent hostility to anything that savoured of revolution, or even of liberal ideals. Catherine gave asylum in Russia to many French royalist émigrés, and her Court became a centre for the international counter-revolutionary crusade. The most innocuous activities of the Freemasons and other philanthropic bodies were treated as dangerous subversion, and punished as such. The censorship redoubled its vigilance. The Governor-General of Moscow, Prince Prozorovsky, sent in lurid accounts of the spread and influence of French republican propaganda, and urged Catherine to stamp out the unrest prevalent among the reading public. As a result of all this, the philanthropist and publisher Novikov was arrested on various trumped-up charges. After interrogation by the amiable Sheshkovsky, he was sentenced to fifteen years' imprisonment in the Schlüsselburg fortress.

'In the last years of Catherine II's reign, the atmosphere at St Petersburg was heavy and stifling; it was an atmosphere of old age, decrepitude, in which one sensed everywhere the presence of that elderly female libertine, the former disciple of the Encyclopedists, terrified now by the French Revolution into betraying all her convictions in the same way that she betrayed her lovers. Around the throne—a complete, an oriental hush. Somewhere or other were the Masonic lodges, the Martinists; she had already started persecuting them. Somewhere or other—sparks of liberalism, even an entire book, the splendid *Journey from St Petersburg to Moscow* by Radishchev, who preached the liberation of the peasants, and described the horrors of absolutism. She exiled the author to

Sorokonof del.   *C.Rustle sculpsit.*

Russian Gentleman in winter dress

...tonof del.   *R.Piccmr sculpsit.*

10   Russian with a sledge

11 Merchants on the road in winter

Siberia. And that is all; there was no concerted action, no logical policy, no union of forces, no organization.'[1]

Count Alexander Vorontsov had become more and more disgusted with the situation at Court, especially with what he called 'the favourites' pernicious influence'. His object in life, he declared, was to serve his country in a disinterested fashion, 'while preserving as much independence as one could retain in an absolutist and pretty immoral Government'. Vorontsov believed that 'in proportion to their personal qualities, men have an intrinsic worth which no despot has the power to take away from them'.[2] This was not an attitude which appealed to Catherine the Great.

Towards the end of 1791, Vorontsov fell ill. He applied for, and was granted a year's leave. When this period had elapsed, he asked for permission to retire permanently from official life. Catherine was happy to be rid of that wise, indomitable misogynist. 'Prepare a decree concerning Vorontsov's retirement,' she wrote to Count Bezborodko. 'I do not dispute that you esteem him, and that he has talents; but I have known all along, and now more than ever, that his talents are not apt for my service and that he is no servant of mine. The heart cannot be constrained, and I have no right to demand compulsory devotion from those who do not feel it. Estranged and separated shall we ever be, Devil take him.' And so Count Alexander departed to his estates at Andreevskoe, not far from Moscow, whence he could keep in touch with his many friends at Court, as well as with Radishchev at Ilimsk. But no longer did the official couriers of the Board of Trade bring the exiles large parcels of books and clothing from St Petersburg.

Meanwhile, Radishchev's family responsibilities were once more on the increase. His faithful sister-in-law Elizabeth Rubanovsky had thrown in her lot completely with him. While the ecclesiastical bar to marriage with a deceased wife's sister prevented their union from being consecrated by the Church, they lived together as man and wife during the six years they spent in Siberia. Elizabeth bore Radishchev three children: two daughters, Anna (named after Anna, his first wife) and Thekla, and a son, to whom they gave the Radishchev family name of Athanasius. This meant that Radishchev now had seven children to provide for: his two elder sons back in Russia, to whom Moses Radishchev and Count Alexander were acting as guardians, and the five children with him at Ilimsk. Since Radishchev had no job and no income to speak of, the family was entirely dependent on Vorontsov's

---

[1] Alexander Herzen, 'Études historiques sur les héros de 1825 et leurs prédécesseurs', in *Polnoe sobranie sochineny i pisem* ('Complete collection of writings and letters'), XX, Petrograd, 1923, pp. 211–12, 214–15.

[2] *Arkhiv Vorontsova*, V, Moscow, 1872, pp. 3–8.

P

unfailing generosity, however irksome this might be to one of Radish-chev's proud nature.

In July 1793, Radishchev wrote to his protector: 'Our time passes by amid routine pursuits and the pastimes of the summer season (mosquitoes permitting), mingled from time to time, as is inevitable in our insecure state, with a certain anxiety which, to cite the phrase of a Latin poet, sits behind us on the saddle.'[1] On occasion, the police chief from district headquarters at Kirensk, some three hundred miles distant, would come on a visit of inspection to Ilimsk. He knew that Radishchev was classed as a convicted criminal, an exile stripped of his privileges as a member of the gentry class. He also knew that Radishchev enjoyed the personal favour of the Governor-General in Irkutsk, which usually restrained such petty officials from indulging in their usual bullying insolence. But now and again, the police chief would get drunk and come reeling into Radishchev's home shouting 'Open up the money bags!' As Radishchev told Vorontsov, 'Intrigue, envy, perfidy, treachery, denial of all moral standards are only some aspects of the picture which is every day before our eyes. And if it is true that a man can attain to a sovereign contempt for the race of Adam (a sentiment laid to the charge of the late King of Prussia), there has never been a country more calculated to inspire this than the one where we are living. Do not start accusing me of mis-anthropy: you would be wrong. The more I advance in age, the more I feel that man is a social animal, and made to live in the society of his fellows.'

All unknown to Radishchev and his family, a new turn in their chequered fortunes was on the way. In November 1796, after a reign of thirty-four years, the shock of learning that the young King of Sweden, Gustavus IV, had abruptly broken off his engagement to Catherine's granddaughter, the Grand Duchess Alexandrina, proved too much for the sexagenarian Empress. Overstrained by those amorous delights of which she was still fond, Catherine fell down in a fit from the Polish royal throne which now served as her close-stool, and soon afterwards expired.

Her passing was sincerely mourned by many a prince, squire or army officer who owed advancement in rank and fortune to her. Russia had grown enormously in area, in population and in international prestige, while the upper classes had assumed, superficially at least, much of the trappings of European sophistication. 'The Empress Catherine,' wrote Prince Adam Czartoryski in his memoirs, 'who, when judged at a distance from her capital, possessed neither virtue nor even the decorum which befits a woman, succeeded in winning inside her country, especially within her capital, the veneration, even the love of her servants

[1] A reminiscence of the familiar ode by Horace.

and her subjects. During the long years of her reign, the army, the privileged classes, the administrators had their days of prosperity and of glory. It is beyond doubt that since her accession, the Muscovite Empire had gained in prestige abroad and in good order at home to a far greater extent than during the preceding reigns of Anne and Elizabeth. Men's minds were still filled with antique fanaticism and with vile adoration for their autocrats. The prosperous reign of Catherine confirmed the Russians still further in their servile ways, although some rays of civilization were by now penetrating to them.' The same observer adds that 'Catherine was ambitious, resentful, vindictive, arbitrary, shameless; but to her ambition was joined the love of renown. Although everything had to give way before her if her personal interests or her passions were involved, yet her despotism was far from being capricious. Her passions, however rampant they might be, were kept under control by her reason and her dexterity. Her tyranny was calculated. She committed no useless crime unprofitable to herself, and at times even consented to be just in unimportant matters when the resplendency of justice might enhance the lustre of her throne. Being moreover jealous of every form of glory, she aspired to the title of legislator, in order to acquire a reputation for equity at least in the eyes of Western Europe and of history. She knew only too well that monarchs cannot dispense, if not with being upright, at least with appearing so. She paid heed to public opinion and sought to win it over, unless it obstructed her designs, in which case she overrode it rough-shod.'

But Catherine had done nothing to resolve the stresses and anomalies inherent in the state of Russian society. She ensured that Russia was to enter on the nineteenth century burdened with a serf economy more appropriate to the Middle Ages. She ended by alienating the sympathies of the more liberal-minded, thinking members of that class—the gentry and aristocracy—which she was most concerned to win over. We have seen what Radishchev thought of her methods of government. His patron, Count Alexander Vorontsov, held views which approximated to those of Radishchev, though he refrained from couching them in such immoderate language. In 1801, Vorontsov told Tsar Alexander I that the régime of Catherine and Potemkin had produced abuses and evils which not only affected the armed services, but permeated all parts of the Russian Empire. 'It is impossible to deny,' he added, 'that the heart of Russia was drained by almost annual recruitment levies; to these were added taxes which Russia, in her immature condition, could not bear without being exhausted. . . . Immoderate luxury, indulgence in all forms of corruption, the avidity of self-enrichment and the ill-gotten gains amassed by the perpetrators of all these evils led people in 1796 almost to long for a rapid change—which, through the natural demise of that Empress, did in fact come to pass.'

Catherine was succeeded by her son, the mentally unbalanced Paul I, despite current rumours that the Empress intended him to be passed over in favour of her grandson, the future Tsar Alexander I. Like most rulers of Russia, including those of our own day, the Emperor Paul began by repudiating the excesses of the preceding reign and promising the Russian people a new and better era. Early in 1797, Radishchev wrote from Ilimsk to Count Vorontsov, 'News from St Petersburg begins to reach us out here. The Emperor is starting his reign with deeds of kindness. May Heaven prosper him in all his undertakings. People are already uttering blessings on his reign. Conscripts have returned to their homes. Those who groaned at being torn from their family's arms are transported with joy, and with a joy all the greater for being un-expected. Oh, how sweet it is to see again the spot where one was born! . . . Oh, how cruel it is to hope repeatedly in vain!'

For once, Radishchev's own hopes were not doomed to disappoint-ment. To be sure, Paul was no more a liberal than his late mother. But since he had never forgotten that Catherine and her lovers had mur-dered his father, Peter III, and excluded himself, the rightful heir, from power, all persons and policies dear to that Empress were anathema to Paul; conversely, victims of Catherine's malevolence could, within limits, count on Paul's favour. The much wronged Novikov, by now a broken man, was let out of his dungeon. Through the good offices of Count Bezborodko (one of the few high officials who remained in grace), Vorontsov secured an Imperial order permitting Radishchev to leave the lonely fastness of Ilimsk and return to Russia. There was no question of restoring him to his former status and professional position: Radishchev was to live in seclusion on his estates in the country. Un-beknown to Radishchev himself, orders were given that he should be kept under police surveillance, his letters censored and his visitors carefully scrutinized.

The good news reached the exiles at the end of January 1797. 'I know not to whom I owe this,' Radishchev wrote to Count Alexander, 'but I like to attribute all the good fortune which befalls me to that same person who has showered me with kindness for so much of my life. When I return home, I hope to be able to throw myself at your feet, to press you to my heart. Oh! find me words to express all that I feel at this instant and the full extent of my gratitude! I await that moment with boundless impatience, and that minute will be one of the finest in my whole life.' Within a few weeks, Radishchev had sold or given away his property and belongings and made ready for the long trail back. The local people and those same officials who had made themselves ob-noxious all imagined that the Tsar was going to make Radishchev a

Minister or a Senator. Their attitude changed overnight, and they hastened round with obsequious farewells. And so, late in February, without waiting for the bitter cold to cease and the spring thaw to set in, Radishchev and his family started out on their homeward trek.

One of those who shared Count Alexander's pleasure at the good news of Radishchev's partial reinstatement was his brother Simon Vorontsov, the Russian diplomatic envoy in London. From Richmond, Count Simon wrote: 'I learn that poor Monsieur Radistcheff is included among those who have been pardoned, which has caused me great pleasure: for I am convinced that he was never wilfully a criminal, and that his offence resulted solely from thoughtlessness and from being unaware of the consequences which his pamphlet might bring about.'

CHAPTER 13

Home and Ruin

*The Homeward Path – Fresh Bereavement – Down the River – A
Russian Robin Hood – Volga Boatmen – With Vorontsov Again – A
Mad Emperor – Cold Comfort Farm – Rustic Pursuits – Literary
Criticism – A Naughty Tale – The Muse of Poetry – Growing
Despondency – Tsar Paul Assassinated*

After the black reaction of Catherine's last years, it seemed to many
that a new era was dawning. Radishchev was anxious to play his own
modest part in bringing this to pass, so on this return trip there was no
dilly-dallying on the road. Without making the detour via Irkutsk to
the south, Radishchev and his family and escort struck straight across
country towards Krasnoyarsk. As on his outward path, Radishchev
kept a diary in which he noted down many characteristic observations
on Siberian life and manners.[1] He remarked with interest that many
ancient popular customs, expressions and words, which had vanished
in metropolitan Russia, were still preserved out here in Siberia. The
moralist and the reformer are never far away. At one village, he commented that the prevailing poverty was aggravated by 'idleness, negligence and such-like vices'. His humanitarian instincts are well to the
fore.—'Among the settlers are many orphans dressed in rags.'—'The
pitiful spectacle of aged and infirm paupers becomes much rarer. It may
be predicted that so long as the destructive hand of private exploitation
refrains from extending its ruinous sway, provided the conscription of
indentured labour to the factories (a system as pernicious as fire to the
country worker) does not spread to the folk of Baraba, then their prosperity will improve more and more.'

At Krasnoyarsk, Radishchev and his family were entertained by the
town Commandant. At dinner, an elderly Major regaled them with
reminiscences of the Seven Years' War and the campaigns fought by

[1] 'Zapiski puteshestviya iz Sibiri' ('Notes on a journey out of Siberia') in
Polnoe sobranie sochineny, III, 267–304.

the Russian Army against Frederick the Great. Further on towards
European Russia, Radishchev gained the impression that 'the Siberians
are becoming rather less hospitable. This is perhaps caused by the
great number of travellers passing through.' There was the usual
trouble with obstreperous coachmen and posting-station superinten-
dents. Sometimes the grooms were drunk and harnessed the horses all
askew, while making rude remarks about the powers that be. 'Obvious
bitterness against the gentry and the Government,' Radishchev commented at one place. They were ferried across a lake whose sulphurous
waters smelt of rotten eggs, which gave the local-brewed kvass a most
peculiar taste. At a place called Pokrovskoe, which they reached on
March 10, 1797, Radishchev encountered an old silversmith ninety
years of age. This venerable man had known Radishchev's grandfather,
Brigadier Athanasius, in days gone by.

They stayed at Pokrovskoe a whole day, because Elizabeth Rubanovsky had fallen sick. This was to be her last illness. Brave spirit that she
was, six years in Siberia had sapped her strength. A former pupil of the
most aristocratic school in St Petersburg, she had brought three children
into the world and endured every hardship in those primitive surroundings of Ilimsk, far from comfort and medical care. When now hope
dawned at last, with the prospect of seeing her old home, her relatives
and friends, even this happiness was snatched from her. The family
went on to Tobolsk by easy stages. At some halts, Elizabeth was too
weak to get out of her carriage, and tea was brought to her there. At
Tara, she made her confession to the village priest, and partook of the
Holy Communion in her room. When at dawn on April 1st, they
reached Tobolsk, Elizabeth was sinking fast, and the skill of the local
physicians were of no avail. Against the date of April 7th, Radishchev's
diary contains but one word: 'Death'. At Tobolsk Elizabeth had joined
Radishchev in exile, there she left him for ever. Her stepson, little Paul
Radishchev, imagined that his father was less grief-stricken at Elizabeth's death than he had been when Anna, his first love, died. Yet his
sorrow was genuine enough. 'Oh, how much pleasanter was my first
stay in Tobolsk!' Radishchev wrote. 'To be reunited in time of misfortune with those whom you love best of all on earth—then have to
bid farewell to them for ever. . . . This town will always have special
associations for me.' To Count Alexander, he exclaimed, 'Ah! why has
cruel fate not willed it that she who helped me to endure my misfortune
should share with me the sweet satisfaction I shall have in seeing you?
She looked forward to this as much as I.' To his elder sons, he wrote of
the sorrow they too would surely feel at the loss of 'this cherished
mother, who took care of our childhood—we have not been able to live
happy with her in our own homeland'.

Radishchev and the five children left Tobolsk with heavy hearts, to continue their homeward path. At a little place called Velizhanka, a girl was selling home-made gingerbread to passers-by—'like cracknels at Valdai,' Radishchev noted, recalling the episode of the complaisant damsels whom he had immortalized in his *Journey from St Petersburg to Moscow*. But the morals of these Siberian maidens were purer than those of the Valdai charmers.

Soon after entering the province of Perm, Radishchev met the Government courier distributing copies of the decree just issued by Tsar Paul, forbidding landlords to make their serfs work on Sundays and religious festivals, with the well-intentioned though not always effectual aim of restricting the exploitation of serf labour by individual proprietors.

At Perm, Radishchev and his family stayed with an old friend who held an important post in the local administration. Then they boarded a barge carrying pig-iron from the Ural foundries, and sailed for several days down the River Kama. It was May, the weather was fine, and at night as they lay down to sleep close to the river banks, they could hear the nightingales singing. At some places, the peasants were reluctant to sell even milk and eggs.—'They are afraid of the soldiers, who take everything without paying.' Near Elabuga, Radishchev got off the barge to visit an old ruin high on a hill, called the Devil's Castle.—'There was a young guide here, who related that this building was actually erected by the devil, in proof of which there existed some documents in the archives of the Church Commission. Once upon a time, this bastion was indeed besieged by a certain giant, who had a leg chopped off during the attack, this limb being still preserved in the church porch.'

As they approached Kazan, they had to be on the alert to ward off raids by bands of robbers infesting the river banks.—'It is worth noting that the bargees are acquainted with them and keep on good terms, and they do not attack the ones they know personally.' Still, Radishchev passed one or two sleepless nights on guard, in case the bandits took a fancy to his belongings. One of the brigands who infested the area in earlier times was a kind of Russian Robin Hood, so Radishchev was told. 'Story about the bandit Ivan Fadeev, how he used to plague the squires who tormented their peasants, but spared the good-natured ones. . . . They caught up with him at the home of a certain *muzhik*. Fadeev gave the *muzhik* five hundred roubles, and told him to set fire to his cottage, while he himself made off in a *troika*. When they overtook him, he started scattering banknotes along the road, and so they let him make his escape. He got away with about forty thousand roubles.' Despite these stirring yarns, Radishchev's party was not molested as they sailed down as far as Laishev. Thence they proceeded overland to

Kazan, which they reached on May 25, 1797. On the way, they encountered an ambassador from the Emir of Bukhara returning home
from St Petersburg, after delivering to Tsar Paul an elephant by way
of a gift from his sovereign.

Compared with the wastes of Siberia, Kazan seemed to Radishchev
like heaven. 'Walked round the city virtually in a rapture.' A fair was
being held all that week. Radishchev called on the Governor and
attended a dinner party at his mansion. He browsed in a bookshop and
avidly read the latest papers.

After this interlude, Radishchev and his family resumed their journey,
sailing up the Volga towards Nizhny Novgorod. The river was thickly
covered with boats passing up and down the river and bearing grain
for Moscow, metal from the Urals, merchandise from Nizhny. 'Lots of
midges and gnats on the Volga. . . . Saw many sick, retired boatmen.
They cannot get travel permits, and suffer much ill treatment. At Uslon,
I saw them flogging a bargee mercilessly because he had left his post.'
—'On a mud bank lie the oak planks of a Government vessel which the
pilot steered into the willow trees.' At one spot, people still pointed out
the oak tree under which Tsar Ivan the Terrible pitched his tent when
returning to Moscow following the capture of Kazan in 1552. On a
passing barge, in company with a load of pig-iron, Radishchev descried
a drunken army officer, who turned out to have been his own escort
from Perm to Tobolsk on his outward journey to Siberia in 1790: 'He
is accompanied by his wife, just as drunk as he.' There were the usual
brigand scares, but Radishchev concluded that since the times of
Catherine II, banditry had largely died out—either because life was
becoming more civilized in Russia, or else because so many officials
now demanded a rake-off that no ordinary brigand could cover his
professional expenses and show a profit!

Radishchev arrived in Nizhny Novgorod on June 24, 1797. Still
under escort and in semi-disgrace, he was however welcomed royally
by the Governor and leading officials of the city, who entertained him
to dinner and called on him in his rooms. Many had read or heard
about the *Journey from St Petersburg to Moscow*, and knew of its author's
fate. In fact, Radishchev was surprised to find himself a regular celebrity
—'I am like a rare bird,' he wrote in his diary.

From Nizhny, Radishchev proceeded by road towards Moscow as
far as Murom, where he was met by his brother Moses. 'Joyous reunion,
we had dinner and went on, I got into his carriage beside him.' Before
reaching Moscow, Radishchev made a detour to Count Alexander
Vorontsov's estate at Andreevskoe, near the town of Vladimir. It could
only be a brief visit, for Radishchev was still under the vigilant eye of
his escorting argus. 'Dined with the Count,' Radishchev entered in his

diary on July 9th; but just what those two old friends said to one another after seven years of separation we shall never know.

One thing can be safely conjectured, namely that Vorontsov impressed on his impetuous protégé the need for extreme discretion in his future conduct. By this time, Tsar Paul's true character was showing itself more clearly every day. The degenerate son of an unbalanced father, Paul seemed intent on working off without delay the frustrations of forty years, and the humiliations he had endured from his mother and her overbearing favourites. Some of Catherine's intimates were treated with the utmost ferocity. Count Vorontsov's sister, the elderly Princess Dashkov, who had helped to dethrone Paul's father, Tsar Peter III, was fortunate in being simply sent off to a remote village, where she had to live for a time in a crude peasant's hut. In his crazy way, Paul sought to make amends to Catherine's victims, and granted an amnesty to the Polish leader Kosciuszko and other patriots who had resisted Catherine's crimes against their country. Count Alexander and his brother, Simon Vorontsov, the Ambassador in London, were known as critics of the late Empress, and could have had the most exalted positions for the asking, but wisely preferred for the time being to stay as they were.

Many of Paul's intentions were good. He tried to suppress corruption in the civil service, and sporadically attempted to secure a fair deal for the peasants. But his mind was deranged. The intoxication of power brought on acute megalomania. He wanted to be the father of his people and to transact all public business himself; but since he had neither the time nor the brains to deal with the mass of papers daily set before him, his edicts grew more and more capricious and unpredictable. He was exasperated by what he could not understand, and imagined that everyone was conspiring to deceive him. He fancied himself in the role of Peter I or Frederick the Great, but turned into a latter-day Caligula. His secret police smelt out Jacobinism everywhere, and words like 'liberty', 'equality', 'citizen' were banned from the Russian language. Yet Paul was as much of a leveller as Robespierre and Fouquier-Tinville. He humiliated the gentry, on whose loyalty Catherine had built up her whole philosophy of government. He withdrew their exemption from corporal punishment and enjoyed sending gentlemen and even noble ladies to suffer stripped and quivering under the lash. He made no move to free the serfs. His entire policy, if such a name can be given to his whims, was to reduce the nation to a state of craven submission before the omnipotent, god-like autocrat.

To lie low, then, and wait for better days, was the advice which Vorontsov undoubtedly gave Radishchev. Leaving Andreevskoe, Radishchev went on now to Moscow, where he stayed four days to do

some shopping. He refrained from calling on any of his old friends for
fear of attracting the notice of the police. When at last he reached his
estate at Nemtsovo, a mile outside the town of Malo-Yaroslavets, it was
mid-July. Though still weighed down by the loss of his devoted Elizabeth, he felt an almost childish joy as he approached the end of his
Odyssey, 'for, I confess, perhaps to my shame, all the time I was on
the road and so long as I saw my sergeant escorting me, I fancied myself
back in Ilimsk'.

But when Radishchev looked round his estate, he received an unpleasant shock. Here indeed was Cold Comfort Farm with a vengeance.
Everywhere he saw traces of the villainy of his father's trusted land-
agent, a certain Morozov, who had plundered the farm right and left.
Radishchev wrote to his father, 'I have found Nemtsovo in great disorder, one might say, in downright ruin. Even the walls of the stone
mansion (though not all of them) have fallen down. I am living in a
shanty with water dripping through the thatched roof. Yesterday the
Lord narrowly saved us from a fire which broke out on top of the stove.
The fruit trees are all perished with frost, no fresh ones have been
planted, there is no fence. Nemtsovo is mortgaged and the seignorial
dues all have to be paid to the bank. All the crockery has been carted
off, the freshly erected outbuildings sold, even the new store-houses.
. . . I am writing in despair of spirit. In Ilimsk I lived on charity, but
what I am going to live on here I have no idea. Please God that I may
see you soon; then in spite of all this, your son's heart would be filled
with joy.'[1]

How competently Elizabeth Rubanovsky would have set about
putting the house into repair and reorganizing the domestic arrange-
ments! In his derelict cottage, Radishchev missed her more and more.
'Fine weather restores to my imagination more smiling vistas, but when
storms and rain coop me up beneath my thatch and largely cramp the
buoyancy of my mind, then melancholy invades my whole being.' To
make matters worse, the numerous debts which Radishchev had incurred before his arrest and exile now came home to roost, and long
forgotten creditors sent dunning notes demanding early settlement.
The begging letters which this proud spirit was forced to address to his
patron Vorontsov make painful reading.

In order to take his mind off all this, and to practise what he had
preached in his *Journey*, Radishchev threw himself heart and soul into
the role of the virtuous squire intent on improving the lot of his grateful
tenantry. He speedily learnt that there were more sides to the Russian
peasant problem than he had visualized from his armchair in St Petersburg. He made the first-hand acquaintance of the Russian peasant's

[1] Radishchev, *Polnoe sobranie sochineny*, III, 496.

native cunning. He learnt that the *muzhik* himself was often the first to oppose any change in his habits or condition. For instance, Radishchev forbade his serfs to marry their infant sons to grown-up girls, a device for recruiting unpaid domestic labour against which he had inveighed in his book, but found that the peasants themselves resented any attack on this cherished abuse. He tried to become a model rustic sage. In September 1797, he wrote to Count Alexander, 'As for my occupations, I read little, I write nothing at all, the mania for this has long since quitted me. I walk about, I go into a little wood close by my garden—in which, by the way, there is nothing but apples. I go into this wood, not to think, nor to shoot game (of which there is none), but—Your Excellency will certainly never guess it—to pick mushrooms. When I got here I was all eyes; in this respect I have been enjoying myself. I have watched the rye harvest, the spring corn gathered in, the threshing; I looked on, but did not indulge in any reflections. I have often recited Horace's noble ode *Beatus ille*, of which I know only the beginning, and it has often seemed to me that life can be enjoyed in various ways. On arrival, my eye was struck by the grey and yellow tints of the fields; towards autumn the grey changed into green. When I reached here, I saw the fields covered with a fine harvest, swayed by the wind in golden waves; the ears fell beneath the reaper's scythe, barren stubble now covers the countryside, over which herds of cattle and flocks of sheep can be seen roaming, while alongside the husbandman's green hope is already sprouting up. I repeat: I was quite alone, I was content. Once the summer work was done, I saw whole troops of rustic folk scurrying by me like wild geese and ducks: they are leaving their homes to seek a livelihood, just as the birds quit the north at the onset of the frosts. My heart was grieved. Does there exist then some other country which they find more abundant, more fruitful? Is its sky purer and more serene, are its dwelling places happier? No, the man of the people loves the spot where he was born. It is stark necessity which makes him abandon his home and everything a man is sad to leave; but he will return later on, loaded with the spoils which his industry will extract from folk simpler than himself, and gladness will return beneath his roof. A curse on whoever destroys his happiness!'

With a view to giving literary form to these musings, Radishchev started to assemble impressions, facts, statistics relating to peasant husbandry on his manor at Nemtsovo. These he worked up little by little into an essay, left unfinished at his death, entitled *Description of my Estate*. This is really a supplement to his *Journey from St Petersburg to Moscow*: in spite of Radishchev's outward recantation and submission to the powers that be, it becomes obvious that even a death sentence and years of Siberian exile had failed to damp the ardour of this doughty spirit, or shake his conviction that the iniquity of serfdom lay at the root of Russia's ills. Once more he shows himself a champion of peasant ownership of the land. Addressing the serfs, he exclaims: 'Happy and blessed would you be if only the whole fruit of your labours belonged to you! But—O grievous reminder!—the husbandman has been tilling the soil of another, and even his own body does not belong to him, alas!'

In another eloquent passage, Radishchev inveighs against the un-restricted power exercised by the individual landowner over his serf's goods and personal affairs. 'He can sell him wholesale or retail. This is not said as a joke: for circumstances may be such that the daughter is sold apart from her mother, the son apart from the father, and, it may be, the wife separated from her husband. . . . The master can force him to work as much as he requires, for the conditions of service of the peasant and the domestic serf are not defined. The master can punish him at his own discretion, he is his judge and the executioner of his own verdicts. The master is lord of his property and his children, he bestows and takes away as he likes. He arranges matches and unites in wedlock whomsoever he pleases; consequently, the peasant is in this respect a mere bond-slave.' With bitter irony, Radishchev qualifies this statement by conceding that the squire lacks only the right to exempt his serf from Government taxes and from punishment for criminal offences, or to force him to contract a marriage with a close relative or eat meat in Lent.

Radishchev had enough common sense to realize that such views as these had no more chance of winning acceptance under Paul than they had under Catherine. Indeed, a careful watch was still being kept on this potential Jacobin. Letters to and from Radishchev were intercepted, opened and copied out before being forwarded to their addresses. Many of these letters have in fact survived only in the form of copies kept in the archives of the Tsarist secret police, some of them with Tsar Paul's personal comments attached. Every effort was made to keep this censorship secret, but long delays in the post, broken seals and grubby finger marks told their tale.—'What do they expect to gain by opening my letters?' Radishchev asked Count Alexander. 'They have never contained anything in the least objectionable, nor will they ever do so.'

Apart from such minor annoyances, Radishchev was not actively molested by the authorities. His two elder sons, Vasily and Nicholas, who were in the army and stationed near Kiev, got leave to visit their father at Nemtsovo. He accompanied them as far as Kaluga on their homeward way, and was able to stay a couple of nights with his old college friend Yanov, who lived nearby. The Emperor's personal per-mission was sought and granted for a journey to stay with his old parents down at Ablyazovo. Radishchev found his blind father and partly paralysed mother in a pitiful state. Truth to tell, they disapproved of Radishchev's union in Siberia with his sister-in-law Elizabeth—a union unblessed by the Church—and were reluctant to welcome his offspring by this second marriage. The atmosphere, as he confided to Count Alexander, was depressing down at Ablyazovo, but all the same he and the children stayed there from the spring of 1798 until the January of the following year.—'I am putting on weight, as my waistcoat warns me each day!'

Returning to Nemtsovo, Radishchev began to cultivate a muse for which he had long felt an attachment—that of poetry. But now, instead of the fiery calls to revolution contained in his *Ode to Liberty*, he chose more innocuous themes. In the chapter 'Tver' of the *Journey from St Petersburg to Moscow*, he had already sketched out some ideas on the theory and practice of Russian versification, with special reference to the innovations made by the much ridiculed Trediakovsky in his *Telemakhida*, an epic devoted to the adventures of Telemachus, first published in 1766. Radishchev now returns to this theme in a work, part parody, part literary essay, in which for the first time in Russian literary criticism due tribute is paid to Trediakovsky's pioneer work in departing from the hackneyed iambic metre, and endowing Russian poetry with new tonal values and rhythmic beauties.

The title given by Radishchev to this literary excursus was 'Memorial to a Dactylo-Trochaic Champion, or Dramatico-Narrative Conversations of a Young Man with his Tutor, illustrated in the course of the prose narrative by fragments from the heroic poem by N.N. (i.e. Trediakovsky), a man famous in the World of Learning.' Radishchev imagines that the egregious family of bumpkins immortalized in Fonvizin's comedy *The Minor* have moved to a new estate, called Narengof (from German *Narrenhof*, or 'Fools' Farmyard'). Radishchev gives Mitrofan, the hobbledehoy hero of the play, a younger brother, Faliley. Mrs Prostakov ('Simpleton'), the mother of Mitrofan and Faliley, turns out the tutors Kuteykin, Tsyfirkin and Vral'man, who feature hilariously in Fonvizin's comedy, and entrusts Faliley's education to the trusty old serf Tsymbalda. This worthy man is very fond of Trediakovsky's *Telemakhida*, which he quotes on every relevant or irrelevant occasion, affording an opportunity for good-natured burlesque.

Later on, Radishchev switches to a serious discussion of Trediakovsky's place in the history of Russian literature. This takes the form of a dialogue between two critics, in the course of which one of them declares that Trediakovsky had the misfortune to begin his literary career before Lomonosov had completed his task of purifying the Russian literary language. 'He was proceeding along an untrodden path, with only his native wit to guide him. As a result, Trediakovsky was unable to re-educate himself. He had an excellent knowledge of versification and, being conscious of the discordant quality of the poetry of Simeon of Polotsk and Kantemir, he wrote in the same type of metre as the ancient Greeks and Romans, that is, in a metre completely new to Russian ears. As he knew Virgil's tongue better than his own, he imagined that the same metaphors could be created in Russian as in Latin. His misfortune was that while being a man of learning, he had no taste.' And Radishchev compares the *Telemakhida* with Klopstock's sacred poem, the *Messias*, concluding that 'in the *Telemakhida* there are a few excellent lines, a few good ones, many mediocre and weak ones, and so many absurd ones that even if it be possible to count them, no one would set out to do so. And so let us say that the *Telemakhida* is the creation of a man proficient in versification, but without the slightest rudiments of literary taste.'

Some thirty-five years after Radishchev wrote these lines, Pushkin singled out his critical assessment of Trediakovsky for high praise. 'Being in his soul an innovator, Radishchev tried to reform the techniques of Russian poetry. His essay on the *Telemakhida* is outstanding.' —'The study of Trediakovsky,' added the great poet, 'is of more benefit than that of our other old writers. Sumarokov and Kheraskov are certainly not in the same class as Trediakovsky—*habent sua fata libelli*.'

A point which Radishchev had already made in his *Journey from St Petersburg to Moscow* was that blank verse would be well suited to the genius of the Russian language, although up to the time of writing (i.e. 1788–90), 'Parnassus is girded about by iambics, and rhymes stand everywhere on sentry duty.' This recipe he now sought to try out in a satirical mock-heroic saga about the adventures of Bova Korolevich (Bova the King's Son), a character dear to Russian folklore and popular literature. Incredible though it may seem, this Bova is really that same Sir Beves of Hamtoun who figures in early French and Middle-English romance. The tale seems to be a composite work, made up of Anglo-Norman, Celtic, Oriental and Germanic sources. The versions in French and Middle-English go back to the early thirteenth century, if not earlier, and there are also Dutch, Cymric, Irish, Yiddish and Norse adaptations.[1] Later on, the worthy Sir Beves gained fame in Italy, his name being turned into 'Bovo d'Antona'; other characters featuring in the legend received Italianate names like Druxiana, Pulicane, Soldan

---

[1] There is a large literature about the Beves romance. See, for example, E. Kölbing, *Studien zur Bevissage*, Halle, 1894; also *The Romance of Sir Beues of Hamtoun*, ed. Kölbing, London, 1885–94; L. A. Hibbard, *Medieval Romance in England*, New York, 1924.

de Sadonia and Lucaferro, and the story was elaborated according to Italian literary tastes. By the seventeenth century, 'Bovo d'Antona' and his exploits were becoming familiar in Serbia, Rumania and White Russia. From the Balkans, our hero's fame spread through the Russian lands. Under the name of Bova Korolevich, Sir Beves became thoroughly acclimatized in this Slavonic milieu, in which his foreign antecedents were quickly forgotten. The details of his eventful career were modified bit by bit to accord with the Russian scene, while the names of subsidiary characters took on a Russian garb, Lucaferro becoming Lukoper, Pulicane becoming Polkan, and so forth.

The tale of Bova Korolevich circulated in the form of simple chapbooks, as well as being passed down orally by village story-tellers. As he recalls in the introduction to his poem, Radishchev had himself heard the tale from his peasant tutor, Peter Suma, in days gone by. 'I will tell you a story of those years of long ago which I heard from my dear old *dyad'ka* Suma. Peter Suma, come and help me, and enliven my tale with a stream of sweet eloquence.'

For this mock-heroic ballad, Radishchev used an eight-syllable trochaic metre, the so-called *Russky sklad*, which is much the same as that which Longfellow employs in *Hiawatha*. Only the introduction and first canto survive. A prose framework gives us clues to the contents of the other sections, which, if actually completed, were lost or accidentally destroyed. After the surviving portion, in which Bova is pictured sitting on a ship telling the sad story of his evil fate and the cruelty of his wicked mother, Radishchev intended to make a storm overtake the vessel. The sailors, who believe Bova to be the bringer of their ill-luck, cast him overboard. Washed up on an island, Bova at first thinks himself in paradise. Then the mirage vanishes, leaving nothing but a barren wilderness. Bova saves a beautiful sylph from her rival's clutches, and receives in reward a magic mirror, which is to guide him through every peril. Taken prisoner by a local king, Bova falls in love with his captor's daughter. He conquers all the princess's rival suitors, including Lukoper, son of the Khan of the Volga Bulgars. The mother of the princess makes indecent advances to Bova, who rebuffs her. The spurned Queen prevents the lovers from marrying. Bova is sent to fetch magic water from a mountain spring at the far end of the world. On the Taurus mountains he overcomes the giant Polkan, sent by the wicked Queen to kill him. Bova passes on to Isfahan in Persia, only to find that his enemy Lukoper is now master of that city. Bova kills Lukoper, after escaping from a dungeon into which his rival, aided by a wicked wizard, has cast him. Meanwhile, Bova's intimacy with his beloved princess has become known. She flees from her evil mother and gives birth to twins. In spite of the gloomy prognostications of Bova's old *dyad'ka*, the two lovers are at last reunited, and live happily ever after.

How does the Bova story as sketched out by Radishchev compare with its Western prototype? In spite of five centuries of telling and re-telling in many lands and tongues, study of the Middle-English Beves romance reveals that many episodes are reproduced more or less faith-fully in the Russian framework which Radishchev intended to use for his treatment of the theme. Both Beves and Bova have a wicked mother who ill-treats them. Beves rescues his lady love from the advances of Brademond, King of Damascus, just as Bova saves his from Lukoper, Prince of the Bulgars. Beves is later captured by Brademond, Bova by Lukoper. Beves and his bride have two sons, so have Bova and his princess. Both stories take place in the same bizarre, exotic world of giants, monsters and supernatural events.[1]

Faithful though he was to his subject-matter, Radishchev treats it in an ironic, sophisticated vein quite alien to the technique of the village story-teller. He was, of course, a confirmed disciple of the 'Age of Reason', which regarded the naïve romances of the Middle Ages as fit butts for wit and travesty. Bova must needs be decked out with all the trappings of the French comic mock-epic, of which Scarron and Voltaire were the prime exponents. In fact, Radishchev frankly announces his intention of imitating Voltaire's burlesque skit on the life of Joan of Arc, *La Pucelle*: 'O Voltaire, O most renowned of men! If only Bova could remotely resemble Jeannette, that valiant maiden of whom you sang, or be worth but her little finger; if it could be said that Bova was even a dim shadow of her, it would be enough—then he would be the shadow of Voltaire, and my faded image would be installed in the Panthéon.'

In the first and sole surviving canto of *Bova*, imitation of Voltaire's more scabrous mood is much in evidence. Our hero sits on board ship lamenting his misfortunes. The ship's cook, a decrepit hag, 'tender in heart and spirit, for all her grey hairs, could not look with indifference upon that young fellow as he shed scalding tears'. She leads him off to the cookhouse, gives him a hug and bids him confide his woes in her sympathetic ear. (Perhaps this episode was suggested to Radishchev by the realistic novel by M. D. Chulkov entitled *The Comely Cook, or Adventures of a Depraved Female*, published in 1770.) Bova's heart is melted. As Radishchev puts it, 'If that glorious knight Robert could tenderly caress an aged witch and in her disgusting embrace emerge victorious and win the shrivelled blossom—Robert was expert in love and knew how to fulfil his marital duties without a hitch: he held his nose, screwed up his eyes, and cut the Gordian knot, like the hero of

---

[1] See J. E. Wells, *Manual of the Writings in Middle English, 1050–1400*, Yale, Oxford, 1916, p. 22.

Q

Macedon, with one slash—then why should not Bova make love to a senile hag? Bova, we know, is an artless lad and sees no snag; he answers caress with caress and kiss with kiss. No riddle had he to solve like Robert had when he shared the beldame's couch.'

The allusion here is to Voltaire's verse tale *Ce qui plaît aux Dames*, in which a poor and noble knight named Robert is condemned to die unless he can discover what it is that women like best of all. In search of the answer to this riddle, Robert meets the prototype of Radishchev's aged cook, 'a toothless crone, sooty of complexion, short of stature, bent in two, holding on to a stick; her pointed nose touches her blunt chin.' The old hag tells Robert the solution to his riddle: a woman likes best of all to be mistress in her own home. In return for this authentic information, she demands that Robert take her to wife. When he gallantly performs his nuptial duties, his ugly bed-fellow is transformed into a beautiful nymph, and they live happily ever after.

The only other point of interest in the first canto of *Bova* is a grotesque treatment of the suicide motif which runs through a number of Radishchev's writings. The fair princess Meletrisa decides to die rather than marry Gvidon, the suitor forced on her by her father. 'No, do not imagine that I shall enter Gvidon's embrace! Rather let my odious existence be ended.' And the distressed damsel looks round for some lethal instrument. 'Almost frantic in the darkness, she wanders searching everywhere for the longed-for weapon, which is to end with a swift death the existence of a grieving, desperate creature whose life has become hateful.' But all she can find is a wooden coat-peg, an arshin long or more, which is set up above her mother's bed. We do not know whether Meletrisa carries out her fell intent, since the old cook interrupts Bova at the crucial moment. But the prevailing tone of the poem is such that the coat-peg is more likely intended as a phallic symbol than as an instrument of self destruction.

Radishchev's *Bova* inspired Pushkin to begin a satirical mock-epic with the same title. Pushkin pays handsome tribute to his forerunner. 'Can I vie with Radishchev?' he asks. But in the article 'Alexander Radishchev' which he wrote many years afterwards, he judged Radishchev's poem rather severely, remarking that there was none of the folk element essential in this genre. 'But then Radishchev meant to imitate Voltaire,' concluded Pushkin condescendingly, 'because he was always imitating someone or other.' Apart from the involved eroticism and tasteless boutades about the excreta of the Dalai Lama, Radishchev's *Bova* makes quite amusing reading, especially as it has a racy style and a light touch rare in our author's prose works.

Another poetic work of this period is Radishchev's 'Songs sung at Contests in Honour of the ancient Slavonic Deities'. This composition, also incomplete, was inspired by the celebrated *Lay of Prince Igor*, which created a sensation when published at Moscow in 1800. The scene is set by an invocation in prose. 'Bard of glorious years of old, bard of the age of Vladimir, whose fame has been borne in the thunder clouds to the very Hellespont—Boyan, sweetest of singers, whose voice was like the nightingale's and did ravish so tenderly the ears of thy contemporaries—lay, O Boyan, thy melodious fingers on thine animated, thy lively strings; send down to me thy song from the heavenly palace of light where, with Homer and Ossian, thou dost celebrate the triumph of antique heroes or the glory of the gods; send down thy song, and may its sound be heard in all lands inhabited by the scions of the Slavonic race.'

The poet describes the gathering of the tribes on the banks of the Dnieper, as they assembled to worship their Deities, Perun, Svyatovid, Veles, Chornobog and other reputed gods of the ancient Slavs, many of them invented by zealous latter-day mythologists. Ten chosen bards stand on the river bank, each with a falcon attached to his right hand. A band of wild musicians goes to rouse the swans of the Dnieper with raucous strains of trumpets, flutes and cymbals. As the startled birds fly past, the bards release their falcons. The one whose falcon first seizes its prey is the first to sing. This is young Vseglas, from the shores of Lake Ilmen. He describes the creation of the world by almighty Perun, and the mysteries of the Slavonic pantheon. He tells of the victories of the Slavs over the Celtic invaders. Part of his lay is told in the words of the priest of Perun, the prophet Sedglav, as he blesses his son who is departing on a campaign against the enemies of the Slavs. 'Thou art still young, O my son! O Veleslav, thou art young. But thou wast the witness of war's dread horrors and disasters.—It was a year ago and more when the abounding Celtic tribes united their strength in one contingent, from the cape which juts out into the distant sea, from the remote ends of the earth, through northern Ullin and Thule and Morven and the Isles of the Hebrides and all the shores of vast Scandinavia, and they advanced as far as those same low and marshy shores where the quiet Neva draws its deep waters from Lake Ladoga. . . .' (With place-names like Ullin and Morven, we are of course projected straight into the bogus Celtic twilight of Ossian and Fingal, as made fashionable by the forger James MacPherson, whose productions were translated into Russian at an early stage.)

Sedglav goes on to tell how the Celtic hordes under their leader Ingvar descended on the city of Novgorod, founded by the great Ratomir close by the shores of Lake Ilmen. The Celts murdered a hundred maidens of the city, and abducted Veleslav's betrothed, the fair Charomila. But now revenge is at hand. 'See, many bands of Slavs gather already from every side. Listen to their cheerful cries: Death, they shout, doom to the enemy! Countless boats are ready to carry these valiant warriors over the billows of the Varangian sea. The Slavonic people remembers all the merits of thy fathers, of my fathers, and knows how gracious towards me is almighty Perun, how dear to him is his high priest. All the tribes of one accord have named thee as their leader. Onward into battle and boldly to the fray: scourge and destroy the foe, avenge upon his person all the wounds he has dealt thee and me and our nation. Carry fire and sword through the Celtic villages, and let gore flow in streams!'

Calling upon Perun for inspiration, Sedglav utters a curse on the Celtic race: 'O nation hateful to the Slavonic people! Behold, death, opening a hundred black jaws, will sink its savage fangs into your breast and heart! You will weep and sob: there will be no salvation for you at all. . . . But alas! revenge alone, sweet revenge shall we taste, and nothing more. Our enemy shall not be wiped out. . . . Long, long, O stubborn race, will you continue hostile to us. . . . A mist covers my sight, and hides the future from my eyes.' Now the Slavonic warriors raise their voices in a parting anthem to Chornobog, while Sedglav intones: 'O Perun, O almighty Deity! Be thou their champion in battle, be their refuge in disaster. O nation, most glorious nation! Your remote scions will surpass you in glory with their splendid valour, their godlike courage, the marvel of all the universe. With their powerful hand they will break down all barriers, all ramparts. They will conquer Mother Nature herself. Before their mighty glance, before their face lit up by the triumph of great victories, kings and realms will fall prostrate. . . . O posterity!'—At this point, the reader is happy to note, a thunderclap interrupts the seer's rhapsodies, and Sedglav is silent. And so Radishchev's *Ancient Songs* come to a premature end.

When one recalls the vigour with which Radishchev had earlier attacked the warlike policies of Catherine and Potemkin, it is something of a shock to find this disciple of the 'Age of Reason' succumbing so readily to the pinchbeck patriotism fostered throughout Europe by early Romanticism. But around 1800, no one could foresee that this cult of Russia's glorious past was to play much the same role in encouraging militaristic Chauvinism under later Tsars as Wagner's operas were to play in fostering German nationalism under Imperial Prussia. The wars of the French Revolution and the incredible exploits of Suvorov in Italy and the Alps had stimulated Russian national pride, and brought to the fore that innate contempt for the West which lurks beneath the surface of the Russian mind. Sensitive as ever to the spirit of the age, Radishchev produced this work which is basically a hotch-potch of Ossian and Prince Igor, and foreshadows to a remarkable extent the resurgence of national ardour which was to culminate in Borodino and the great Patriotic War of 1812. So often a 'Westerner' in his political outlook, Radishchev appears here almost as a precursor of the mystical adepts of nineteenth-century Slavophilism.

The third and last of these ambitious poems which Radishchev began in the last years of his life, *Song of History*, is conceived as a broad survey of the progress of humanity from ancient times. The surviving portion of the work, which breaks off at the death of Marcus Aurelius, treats the history of mankind from a distinctly rationalistic, 'enlightened' viewpoint. Like the French *philosophes*, Radishchev regarded the Prophet Moses as a superstitious fanatic, not unlike Mohammed, whom he portrays as a bloodthirsty impostor. World history before classical times is dismissed summarily. 'Troy, Tyre, Sidon, Carthage, the ancient Chinese and Indians and peoples unknown pass by, shrouded in the mist of obscurity.' Like Diderot or Voltaire, Radishchev finds a few kind words to say about Zoroaster and Confucius, who were looked on as tolerant and progressive. Some space is devoted to Cyrus the Persian. Are we to believe the 'veracious story' of Herodotus, with the grisly details of how Tomyris, Queen of the Massagetae, cut off his head, and threw it into a bag filled with human gore, so that he might satiate himself, as she put it, with blood? Or should we give credence to the idealized picture presented by the modern writer Ramsay in his *Voyages de Cyrus*? After some discussion, Radishchev plumps for Herodotus.

An account of the exploits of Hercules is succeeded by a brief history of Athens and Sparta, following in many points the book by Mably which Radishchev had himself translated into Russian many years before. Like Mably, Radishchev accords high praise to Lycurgus, and echoes his views of the characters and careers of Alcibiades, Philip of Macedon and Alexander the Great. From Greece, we pass on to survey the founding and early history of Rome under Romulus, Numa Pompilius and Tarquin, and then, the exploits of Brutus, Scaevola and Cincinnatus under the Republic. The story of the Punic Wars and Hannibal's campaigns is followed by the grim spectacle of the civil strife of Marius and Sulla, which led up to the final destruction of Rome's liberty. When discussing the fall of the Republic and the elevation of Octavian to the Imperial throne, Radishchev acknowledges his debt to Montesquieu, whose *Considérations sur les Causes de la Grandeur des Romains, et de leur Décadence* may be regarded as a laconic prologue to Gibbon's *Decline and Fall*, and had been widely acclaimed since their publication in 1734. Many parallels between Montesquieu and Radishchev can be detected if the *Song of History* is compared with the *Considérations*, as has been done by a Russian scholar.[1]

In addition, some lurid details about Tiberius, Nero and Domitian derive from the *Annals* and *Life of Agricola* by Tacitus. Of the reign of Domitian, Radishchev writes: 'So vile an age was this—thus speaks Tacitus—that there was neither voice nor hearing. Rome became dumb, speech vanished; and even memory would have perished if mortal men could lost their memory through silence.' Again, Radishchev's account of Tiberius on Capri owes much to Tacitus: 'He abandoned himself to vile lechery, the shameful form of which, or even the memory of it alone, arouses disgust. There he indulged his lust amidst a troop of boys, inventing new vices and new names for them. Thence his base menials constantly sought everywhere for fresh victims for his filthy concupiscence.' As a contrast to these gloomy pictures, Radishchev recalls the verdict of Tacitus on Trajan's reign: 'Happy century of ours, where men can think what they will, and utter what they think.'

It is interesting to find Radishchev drawing an analogy between the tyranny of Sulla and the Age of Terror in France under the Revolution. Describing Sulla's maniacal blood-lust, Radishchev exclaims: 'No, nothing can equal him in savagery, scarcely even Robespierre in our own time.' This attitude towards the high priest of the guillotine is not what one would expect from the sanguinary revolutionary which Radishchev is sometimes alleged to have been—especially by Bolshevik apologists anxious to claim him as one of themselves.

However, there is little doubt that parts of the *Song of History* were intended by the author as a veiled commentary on Russian absolutism and its baneful consequences. On the ignominious end of Tiberius and the accession of Caligula, Radishchev comments, 'Alas, is this the fate of mortals, that even the doom of the savage tyrant does not save them from calamity? . . . The ruler falls, the personality changes, but still the yoke exists. As if to mock the race of man, the new tyrant will be gracious and mild. But not for long—for but a moment; after this, he will redouble the savagery of his rage and spite, and vomit hell into all men's souls. Such a one was Caius Caligula—merciful, but only to start with.' This is surely an allusion to the liberal declarations with which Russian Tsars were accustomed to begin their reigns, only to resort subsequently to the ruthless methods favoured by their forerunners. Perhaps Radishchev even had in mind Paul I, who had begun by recalling so many exiles from banishment, but finished up as a more oppressive tyrant than Catherine had ever been.

The pessimistic tone, the sombre fatalism one detects in Radishchev's

---

[1] See V. V. Miyakovsky's article in *Zhurnal Ministerstva Narodnogo Prosveshcheniya* ('Journal of the Ministry of Public Instruction'), February 1914.

Song of History is symptomatic of the growing despondency and weariness of soul which overtook that brave spirit as the eighteenth century drew to a close. It was ten years now since his great gesture of defiance had made him a marked man. It is true that Siberia was now a memory. But here he was among the rustics of Nemtsovo, no nearer than ever to resuming his place in the world of intellectual and practical affairs for which he yearned. He was subject to hysterical changes of mood. 'You must admit that man is a pretty comical, ludicrous, odd creature,' he wrote in 1797 to Count Alexander, 'weeping in the morning, laughing in the evening, without any change in his situation, sometimes without altering his position, sunk in an armchair in bonnet and slippers. Yes, I have myself been in this very same case, having wept in the morning and laughed in the evening just like an idiot. And yet since leaving Tobolsk, I have not laughed once in a lighthearted way, since my separation from my beloved helpmate, although the kindness of our gracious Emperor gives me every reason in the world to be more cheerful.' To his brother Moses, Radishchev wrote from Nemtsovo, 'I find it so tedious living here, it gets more boring every day, in fact (though I can hardly credit it myself), even more boring than at Ilimsk.' He had aged and grown grey. 'If you caught sight of me somewhere in a crowd, you would never recognize me,' he remarked to one of his relatives. When asking the Tsar for permission to visit his parents, Radishchev wrote: 'For my part, though only about to enter my fiftieth year, I cannot count on a long extension of my days, for bitterness and sorrow have undermined my natural strength. Anyone who looks at me can tell how old I have grown before my time.'

In 1800, the term of ten years' banishment should rightly have expired. With great deference, Radishchev addressed a petition to the Emperor, asking for a permit to revisit St Petersburg, and giving as an excuse his desire to see two of his sons stationed on military service there. This request was never even acknowledged, and it seemed as if his disgrace was to last indefinitely.

It was doubtless a merciful providence which prevented Radishchev from returning to St Petersburg in the last months of the reign of ill-fated Paul. The unbalanced Tsar was reeling crazily towards his predestined fate. His rule now resembled the capricious tyranny of some Ottoman Sultan or Mongol Khan, rather than the government of a European autocrat. Loyal officers were flogged to death on mere suspicion of uttering words disrespectful to the Emperor. Illustrious Suvorov and famous Admiral Chichagov were alternately insulted and fawned on by the Imperial maniac, according to the impulse of the moment. A curfew was in operation every night. In the daytime, anyone whose carriage came in sight of the Tsar's had to alight and kneel prostrate in snow, slush or dust. With his known views about the evils of despotism, Radishchev would probably not have remained unmolested in the capital, even if he had not invited reprisals by some indiscreet utterance or gesture.

The vagaries of Paul's policies precipitated the final débâcle. After Suvorov's brilliant operations against the armies of the French Directory, Paul suddenly broke with the English alliance and declared for an alignment with his idol, Napoleon, the new master of France. The English Ambassador was expelled from St Petersburg, and Paul made crack-brained plans for a Franco-Russian invasion of the British dominions in India. He gave his whole devotion to the hard-headed adventurer Pahlen, while loyal servants of the Crown like Arakcheev and Rostopchin were banished from the city. Suspicious and nerve-ridden like all tyrants, Paul sought refuge from his terrors by entrenching himself in the grim Michael palace and redoubling his already stringent security precautions. But the gentry, the higher aristocracy, the Guards regiments, even the Imperial family, had endured more than enough. On the night of March 11/12 (New Style, 23–24), 1801, Pahlen gave the signal, the conspirators advanced on the palace and made common cause with the Guards on duty, the Tsar's bed chamber was invaded, and, after a scuffle, Paul's brief reign came to an end.

The Last Months:
Radishchev and Alexander I

⊰⊶⊘ ⊱⊷⊰

The news of Paul's murder spread like wildfire through the Empire. In
St Petersburg, crowds thronged the streets, strangers embraced one
another, and all gave thanks for deliverance from the tyrant. The new
Tsar, Alexander I, had long been the idol of the younger generation—
a generation which had grown up under the heady influence of French
revolutionary ideology and Western liberal ideas, however rigorously
these trends had been discountenanced in Russia during the preceding
decade. The peasants looked to him for deliverance. At the same time,
the nobility and gentry, whose rights had been brutally trampled on by
Paul, greeted with approval the announcement that Alexander proposed
to rule in all respects 'according to the spirit and the heart of his illustrious grandmother', that is to say, with a proper regard for the privileges
of the upper classes.

Within a few weeks, a series of proclamations were issued, abolishing
the vexatious excesses of the previous reign. Officers and civil servants
dismissed by Paul were invited to apply for reinstatement; restrictions
on foreign commerce were eased; political prisoners and exiles were
pardoned; provincial and municipal institutions suppressed by Paul
were restored; the police were directed to respect the rights of the
individual citizen; the frontiers were reopened to private travellers;
importation of foreign books was again permitted; the decree allowing
people to instal printing presses (rescinded in 1796) were reintroduced;
Catherine's 'Charter granted to the Nobility' and 'Charter granted to

the Towns' were again put into force; the secret political police was suppressed; the clergy were exempted from corporal punishment; the use of torture in criminal investigations was abolished.

For Russia, the nineteenth century now commencing seemed blessed with bright auguries. Radishchev himself, in an eloquent poem entitled 'The Eighteenth Century', wrote an epitaph on the epoch which closed with the death of Paul, and gave voice to the general feeling of optimism about the future.

Time's urn pours out the hours like drops of water:
    The drops have gathered into streams, the streams to rivers grown,
And by the distant shores they pour forth foaming waves
    Of eternity into the ocean, where neither boundaries nor banks can be
        seen;
No island rises therein, no bottom can the plumb-line fathom;
    The centuries have flowed into it, there all trace of them disappears.
Made now for ever illustrious with its blood-stained torrent
    With a roar of thunder our century rushes to find an outlet there;
At journey's end the ship which bore our hopes
    Is shattered and swallowed up in the whirlpool when already near its
        haven,
Happiness, virtue and freedom are devoured by the wild, watery abyss:
    See, still in the torrent fearsome wreckage floats.
No, you shall not be forgotten, century insane and wise,
    Accursed will you be for ever, for ever glorified by mankind.
In gore steeped in your cradle, for lullaby the thunder of battles:
    Ah, soaked in blood are you, as you descend into the tomb.
But see, two crags arise amid the blood-stained torrents:
    Catherine and Peter, children of eternity, and the Russian people.
Dark shadow behind them, in front of them the sun;
    Its radiant brightness reflected in the solid rock. . . .
O century unforgettable! you endow joyful humanity
    With truth, liberty and light, a constellation for ever bright;
Tearing down the pillars of mortal wisdom, you raised them up again;
    Kingdoms perished at your hand, like a ship hurled on a reef:
Kingdoms you do create; they shall flourish and fall again in ruin;
    Whatever mortal man shapes, all that shall be destroyed and return to
        dust.
But you were a creator of ideas, and these are the work of God;
    And they shall never perish, even if earth itself be shattered;
Boldly with expert hand you drew aside the curtain of creation,
    And gazed on nature's secrets in the remote sanctuary of things.
From the seas arose new nations and new lands,
    From depths of black night, new metals at your call.
You count the stars like a shepherd his sportive lambs;
    With guiding thread, you lead the comets back to earth;

The solar rays you have divided, and called new suns into being;
 New moons from distant murk you have conjured up before us;
You have urged on stubborn nature to bear new children;
 Even the flying steam you have harnessed to your yoke;
Heaven's lightning flash you lured into iron bonds upon earth,
 And carried up mortal men into the sky on wings of air.
Manfully have you destroyed the phantoms' iron gates,
 And cast down to the ground the idols which men revered on earth.
You burst the bonds which hemmed in our mind, that towards new truths
 It might soar like winged lightning, rushing ever farther into immensity.
Mighty and great were you, O century! The soul of ages past
 Fell prostrate and silent in admiration before your altar,
But your strength did not suffice to expel all the spirits of Hades
 Which squirt flaming venom throughout eternal ages;
You had not power to vanquish the rage and bitterness which with iron
 heel
 Trample underfoot the flowers of joy and wisdom within us.
On the sacrificial altar, mortals are still steeped in gore by rapacious hands,
 Still is man transformed into the savage tiger's shape.
The torch of battles, see, whirls along there on hills and plains,
 In peaceful valleys, through the meadows, it roars on its rampant course.
Behold its black companions! Terrible are they! Ever onward they advance
 Like nightmare phantoms—savagery, uproar, famine, plague!
Is peace, which gives joy to the nations, never again to be seen?
 Or is humanity to sink yet deeper into the mire?
From the depths of the century's tomb, the voice of comfort resounds:
 Down with despair! Mortal man, have hope, God lives!
He who commanded the spirit of storms to whip up the mutinous waves
 Holds still in his mighty hand the chain of time:
The spirit of storms shall not sweep mortals away, though mere creatures
 of one day they be,
 Which blossom forth at sunrise, and with the twilight fade away. . . .
The dawn of the new century has appeared to us still stained in blood,
 But already the light of day chases off night's grim darkness;
Higher and higher towards the sun soar up, thou Russian eagle,
 Bring down its radiance to earth, but leave behind the deadly lightning
 flash.
Peace, justice, truth and liberty from the throne shall flow,
 Which Catherine and Peter raised up, that Russians might prosper.
Peter and thou, Catherine! your spirit lives with us still.
 Look down on this new era, gaze on this Russia of yours.
O Alexander, remain for ever with us, as our guardian angel.

These ecstatic lines are typical of the spirit of those first heady months, when Russia celebrated its release from the mad despot Paul. If the revolt of Pugachev had implanted in a few thinking men the conviction that sooner or later serfdom must go, the reign of Paul had shown the ruling classes how fragile was the basis even of aristocratic privilege, and underlined the lack of any constitutional safeguard against autocratic caprice. Nothing could have been more sincere than the ardour with which educated Russians at least awaited the signal for an advance towards the new and better order for which they longed.

Yet that signal never came. The pattern of Alexander's reign is well-known. A few years of liberal idealism—endless consultations with the Emperor's 'Confidential Committee' of young reformers and statesmen; the foundation of ministries and universities; the sponsoring of Speransky's administrative and constitutional projects. And then the long duel with Napoleon; Speransky to the wolves; the Great Patriotic War of 1812; the mystic maunderings of Baroness Krüdener; the 'Holy Alliance'; Arakcheev and his infamous Military Colonies; the growth of political secret societies in the army and among the young aristocracy; the final decline into pietistic obscurantism, political reaction—and a premature death at Taganrog in 1825.

There is something enigmatic about Alexander's character. Some writers have ascribed the scanty achievement of his reign to weakness of the will, which made the Tsar bend before the pressure of vested interest. But it is not certain that Alexander was ever ready to embrace liberalism, if it meant the end of autocracy. He had phases of genuine idealism, when he would talk of giving up his Imperial destiny and retiring to some romantic castle on the Rhine. At other times, he was the parade-ground pedant, jealous of any encroachment on his absolute authority. Like his grandmother, he was a self-willed person, though endowed with charming manners and a great fund of diplomacy and dissimulation. He understood the need for keeping up appearances, and for adapting his policies to the spirit of the age. Brought up by a Swiss republican, Laharpe, and a pious, anglophile cleric, Samborsky, he had to manoeuvre adroitly between his grandmother, Catherine, and his father, Paul, who loathed each other, but both adored Alexander. Not for nothing did Napoleon nickname Alexander the 'Talma of the North', a handsome tribute to the Tsar's diplomatic ability and acting talents.

In the climate of opinion of 1801, Alexander could not have treated Russian society as Paul had done, even if he had been so minded. As a reaction against the murky atmosphere of the last decade, liberalism was in the air. There was everything to be said for aligning Russian autocracy with this mood as long as it lasted. In any case, Alexander, like most thinking Russians, was well aware of the real deficiencies of the system. But this did not mean that he was ready to destroy the system altogether. He was like a young man taking over a rambling, dilapidated family mansion. Of course the place must be spring-cleaned, redecorated, possibly the roof mended and modern plumbing installed. But if the builders suggested knocking the place down altogether, while the proprietor went to live in a service-flat, then they would soon be made to feel who was the master of the house. We find an apt character-ization of Alexander in the memoirs of Prince Adam Czartoryski, who wrote: 'The Emperor loved the outward forms of liberty just as one loves theatrical shows; he enjoyed the sight of the externals of a free government, and his vanity was thereby gratified. But he desired only the forms and externals, and had no intention that these should be transformed into reality. In a word, he would gladly have consented for all the world to be free, on condition that everybody voluntarily carried out his will and nothing else.'[1]

But in that spring time of 1801, Radishchev and all the others who had incurred the wrath of Catherine and Paul were too filled with joy and relief for misgivings of this kind to enter their heads. One of Alexander's first acts had been to publish a decree, declaring an amnesty for those imprisoned or living under surveillance as a result of pro-ceedings instigated by the Secret Chancellery, which was itself abolished. One hundred and fifty-six persons were released from arrest or police supervision, restored to their former rank and status, and declared free to proceed wherever they liked. Radishchev's name came sixth on the list.

As soon as he heard the news, Radishchev hastened to St Petersburg. At last, he thought, his hour had come. Now surely he would be enabled to put into practice the conviction which he had expressed in the introduction to his *Journey*, namely that 'every man may contribute to the well-being of his fellows'.

Another of those whom Alexander's accession encouraged to return to the capital was Radishchev's old protector, Count A. R. Vorontsov, who had prudently remained aloof throughout the reign of the un-predictable Paul. He was cordially welcomed in Court circles, although to some, this elderly bewigged figure from the age of Louis XV seemed to embody the spirit and manners of a bygone era. Vorontsov was at once named a member of the Council of State.

Much of the real power during those first feverish months lay with the four personal friends who made up Alexander's so-called Con-fidential or Intimate Committee. They were the impetuous Paul Stroganov, pupil of the revolutionary Gilbert Romme and at one time librarian of the Jacobin Club in Paris, an ardent champion of the liberation of the serfs; the cautious, middle-aged N. I. Novosil'tsev, who had resided for some years in London, and was later identified with repressive Russian policy in Poland; the brilliant young administrator Victor Kochubey, who had already been Vice-Chancellor of the Empire

[1] *Mémoires du Prince Adam Czartoryski*, Paris, 1887, I, 345.

under Paul, and was to hold many other ministerial offices; and, most oddly of all, the Polish Prince Adam Czartoryski, who was for a time Foreign Minister of Russia, before embarking on a long career of resistance to Russian rule over his native land. Flitting about in the background were other semi-accredited advisers, such as the mercurial, hair-brained Ukrainian Karazin, who fancied himself as the Tsar's 'Marquis Posa', affected to be the life and soul of every progressive movement, and for a short time really did exercise some influence over the Emperor's mind. It is also worth mentioning the quizzical, outspoken Admiral Mordvinov, whose enlightened views on such questions as land reform and the abolition of corporal punishment, expressed in terse and witty form, later won him the sympathy of the Decembrist revolutionaries. At the same time, Alexander remained in close touch with his military aides-de-camp, men of diehard stamp drawn from the ranks of the higher aristocracy, and inclined to deplore the 'Jacobinical' leanings of the Tsar's young friends on the Confidential Committee. Finally, there were the elderly worthies on the Senate, some of them by no means hostile to reform on moderate constitutional lines, while others were slaves to sloth and bureaucratic routine.

Amid these sometimes conflicting groups, Count Alexander Vorontsov occupied a dignified and conciliatory position. He was particularly acceptable to the younger men on the Confidential Committee. Indeed, Victor Kochubey recommended him to the Emperor in warm terms. 'Count Alexander Vorontsov will be a suitable man, and there is no need to fear that he will take up an unco-operative attitude . . . since he is very far from being a supporter of despotism; he was even accused under Catherine of democratic leanings, for having extended his protection to Radishchev.'[1] Prince Adam Czartoryski also reckoned that the Confidential Committee found a welcome ally in Vorontsov's person. 'He was reputed in Russia to be a statesman of the highest calibre.' Czartoryski goes on to say that Count Alexander's constitutional principles were shared and in part inspired by his brother Simon Vorontsov, the Russian Ambassador in London. 'Count Simon had acquired friends in England by his noble, positive and frank character. He had taken root in the country, he was devoted to England as it then was, more devoted even than the most convinced Tories could have been, and he ecstatically adored Mr Pitt. . . . The Tory views of Count Simon were extremely liberal by Russian standards, and could not fail to influence the sentiments of his brother. . . . Count Alexander himself was by no means hostile to certain liberal ideas. . . . He had retained certain characteristics which recalled that old Russian aristocracy which

[1] Cited in G. P. Makogonenko, *Radishchev i ego vremya* ('Radishchev and his times'), Moscow, 1956, p. 585.

attempted to impose restrictions on the power of the Empress Anna when it invited her to occupy the throne.'[1]

One of the great ambitions of Counts Alexander and Simon Vorontsov was to see that bureaucratic body, the Russian Senate, transformed into the equivalent of the English House of Lords—a legislative assembly, capable of exercising a power of veto over the whims of the autocrat. In the meantime, Alexander Vorontsov drafted a 'Charter for the Russian People', which he hoped the Tsar would consent to promulgate at his coronation in Moscow in the autumn of 1801. It has been thought by some that Vorontsov invited Radishchev to help him draft the Charter, but this has been denied by a scholar who has made the most thorough study of the question.[2] At all events, this is a document of great historical interest, reflecting the ideas then current among moderate political thinkers at the opening of Alexander's reign. The Charter begins by asserting that nations are not created for the sake of monarchs, but rather monarchs for their people's welfare. The privileges of the gentry should be secure from the encroachments they had suffered under the dictatorial Paul. The personal security of every Russian subject should be guaranteed, together with enjoyment of his possessions without interference. 'We repeat, affirm and establish that the right to own movable and immovable property is the right of a Russian citizen, to the extent that it is appropriate to each class of the nation by virtue of the law.' (It is not clear whether this excludes the serfs.) Clause 8 of the Charter was to safeguard freedom of thought, conscience and speech 'in so far as they are neither contrary to the laws of the nation, nor offensive to any private person'. Subsequent paragraphs betray Vorontsov's admiration for the laws and liberties of England. Thus, articles 13 to 20 provide that an accused shall be presumed innocent until and unless pronounced guilty by due process of law; an accused should be tried by his own peers—thus implying introduction of the jury system; the defendant might choose counsel to defend him; he could claim the removal of judges appointed to try him, if he had reasonable grounds for so doing; no one should molest or detain a Russian citizen without proper authority, and every arrested person must be released after three days if no specific charge had by then been brought against him; no man might be tried twice for the same offence. Finally, it was declared that no taxes were to be levied without the authority of the Senate; the Emperor would pledge himself to observe all existing laws and—most important of all—to submit all necessary changes or new measures to the Senate for ratification.

[1] Czartoryski, *Mémoires*, I, 300–3.

[2] Georg Sacke, *Graf A. Voroncov, A. N. Radiščev und der 'Gnadenbrief für das russische Volk'*, Emsdetten, 1938.

It is revealing to see that in this document, as it turned out, the veteran Vorontsov had gone far beyond what even Alexander and his youngish advisers had bargained for. When the draft Charter came up for discussion in the Confidential Committee, Novosil'tsev remarked that it would be highly dangerous for the Emperor to renounce any portion of his absolute powers. Nor should the Government be committed to principles which it might fail to live up to, and would probably have to discard to maintain public order and carry on the day to day business of administration. Such a Charter, it was felt, might arouse exaggerated hopes among the common people and lead to riots and disorder. The Confidential Committee advised Alexander to wait until plans for reforms were worked out in detail before announcing any such far-reaching programme as this. Alexander followed the Committee's advice; Vorontsov's draft Charter was put on one side, and not published at the Emperor's coronation after all.

This does not mean that all Alexander's 'young friends' had decided to ally themselves unreservedly with the party of reaction. Thus, Paul Stroganov was in favour of strict control of the powers of landlords over their serfs. The Confidential Committee discussed this question on November 18, 1801, when certain members expressed the fear that any change in the situation might cause upheavals in country districts. Stroganov's retort to this objection was worthy of Radishchev himself. 'What could give rise to any such dangerous upheaval? Either the activities of factions, or else of discontented individuals. What elements of this kind exist in this country? The people, and the gentry. What is this gentry class, what is its composition, its spirit? The gentry of this land is made up of a host of persons who have become members of the gentry solely by virtue of promotion in Government service, people who have received no education at all, whose entire cast of mind is conditioned to conceiving of nothing loftier than the power of the Emperor; neither considerations of equity nor law, nothing could arouse in them any idea of tendering the slightest resistance. This is a social class of the most ignorant and insignificant character, in its outlook, downright obtuse—there you have a rough picture of the majority of our rustic squirearchy. As for those who have received anything like a comprehensive education, these are few in number, and are for the most part quite disinclined to oppose any measure undertaken by the Government. Those nobles who are receptive to present-day notions of justice will sympathize with the measure envisaged; the remainder, while constituting the majority, will not dream of doing anything at all apart from mere chattering. Most of the gentry who are in Government service, alas, try to feather their own nests in the process of administering the Government's orders; very often, they swindle as they serve, but they do not put up any resistance. So you have one section of our gentry class who live in their villages, sunk in crassest ignorance, and the other, those in State service, who are imbued with a spirit quite inoffensive. As for the great magnates, there is nothing to be feared from them. What is left, apart from these? Where are the elements of dangerous discontent?'

As for the serfs themselves, Paul Stroganov was confident that they would greet with loyal enthusiasm any measure tending towards ultimate emancipation. 'They are all gifted with sound common sense, to an extent which amazes those who have come to know them at close quarters. From their childhood days, they are filled with loathing for the squires, their oppressors. The common people are always faithful to the Government. They believe that the Emperor is ready at all times to protect them. If there comes into force some vexatious measure, they attribute it not to the sovereign but to his ministers, who, as the people say, abuse the Emperor's confidence, because they belong to the aristocracy themselves and are striving to further their own private ends. If anyone should think of making the slightest attempt against the prerogatives of the supreme power in the land, then the peasants would be the first to come to its defence, since they deem it to be a bulwark against their natural foes.'[1]

Notwithstanding Stroganov's eloquent pleading, Alexander's advisers could not bring themselves to recommend any general measure of peasant emancipation. The only measure taken in this direction was the decree of February 20, 1803, which permitted any landowner to free his peasants on terms mutually acceptable: each family or commune which was liberated must be given the chance to acquire a reasonable portion of land in freehold possession for its own use. Only forty thousand peasants were freed on these terms during the whole of Alexander's reign. It is fair to add that this was partly due to the obstinate refusal of most serfs to accept personal liberation without land. This was offered by many landowners, who would willingly have switched to the system of husbandry by hired agricultural labourers. But the conservative Russian peasant clung tenaciously to his little plot, however much this, and his own person too, might be at the mercy of his master. One squire who offered freedom without land was told, 'Let's stay as we are, master: we belong to you, the land belongs to us.'[2]

*

[1] M. I. Bogdanovich, *Istoriya tsarstvovaniya Imperatora Aleksandra I i Rossii v ego vremya* ('History of the reign of Emperor Alexander I, and of Russia in his time'), I, St Petersburg, 1869, pp. 51–2.

[2] I. D. Yakushkin, *Zapiski* ('Memoirs'), Moscow, 1926, pp. 34–7.

R

Alexander's accession had brought Radishchev restitution of his personal rights and dignity. He was once more a Ministerial Councillor, and a Knight of the Order of St Vladimir to boot. But there the Government's magnanimity ended. There was no question of compensation for all the sorrow, hardship, and financial loss which he had endured over the past ten years. Nor was there any question of unseating the present Director of the St Petersburg Customs House, and giving Radishchev his old job back again. He had sold his house on Dirty Street. Here he was, without a salary, with a large family to support, and forced to look round for furnished rooms in the most expensive residential area of all Russia.

To the rescue once more came his old protector Vorontsov. There existed in St Petersburg a body called the Commission for the Drafting of Laws. This had been set up by Paul I to carry out the task which Catherine's great assembly of 1767 had left undone, namely to produce some coherent body of legislation for Russia. The three members who had survived from Paul's reign were veteran civil servants, expert in citing the numbers and dates of Imperial *ukazes*. They were given a new chairman in the person of Count Zavadovsky, a former favourite of Catherine the Great, who was among the Senators who signed the verdict condemning Radishchev to death in 1790. Alexander, it was said, placed great faith in Zavadovsky, who was 'noted to all and sundry for his idleness and addiction to wine'.[1] For all his faults, Zavadovsky was an amiable and obliging man, and a great friend of Alexander Vorontsov. The latter easily persuaded him to appoint Radishchev to his Commission, with the rather meagre stipend of fifteen hundred roubles a year.

When Radishchev took his seat on the Legislative Commission, he found his colleagues hard at work copying out passages from various *ukazes*, statutes and earlier codes, and trying to fit them into a coherent whole. This was an unrewarding business. As Zavadovsky later explained to the Emperor, most of these old laws dated from ancient, barbarous epochs; they conflicted with one another, and with all modern notions of equity. In spite of this, the Commission had no general mandate to start from first principles with a view to drafting a new code, as was being done in France under Napoleon (*Code civil*, 1804; *Code pénal*, 1811). They were merely trying to produce a digest of existing legislation, bad as much of it admittedly was. They had also been told to devise ways of promoting efficiency in the civil service and the law courts by simplifying the cumbrous bureaucratic procedures of those days—a task in which scant progress was made.

[1] Grand Duke Nikolay Mikhailovich, *Graf P. A. Stroganov*, St Petersburg, 1903, I, 101.

Radishchev was not the sort of man to get absorbed in a mass of futile detail. One of his colleagues on the Commission, N. S. Il'insky, recorded that Radishchev 'had no particular sections of the code to compose, and worked quite on his own'.

In one branch of the Commission's activities he took an active interest. In addition to its main function, the Legislative Commission also served as a final Court of Appeal, to which the Senate could refer dubious cases not covered by existing laws. The low standards prevailing among the Russian judiciary gave added importance to this function. 'If you knew what an advocate, or a man of law is here,' wrote Dumont, the editor of the French version of Jeremy Bentham's *Theory of Legis-lation*, 'you would blush for the honour of the profession. . . . And the judges! In England you could have no notion of the state of things.'[1] To the discussions on cases sent up for consideration by the Legislative Commission, Radishchev brought all the fire and reforming zeal of the author of the *Journey from St Petersburg to Moscow*. His candour alarmed the other members. 'When we used to review cases sent up by the Senate and write down our verdicts according to the laws, he used to expound his personal views on each decision without agreeing with us, but basing himself solely on philosophic free-thinking. He considered everything in the way of established practices, customs, rights and edicts as of small account, and viewed them as idiotic and burdensome to the people.'[2]

Even though Radishchev often found himself to be in a minority of one, his judgments, two of which have been preserved, are outstanding for their humanity and common sense. One of these relates to the accidental killing of a serf by another belonging to a different proprietor. How much money should the master of the serf responsible pay to the owner of the dead man? The question had been discussed in the Senate purely in terms of the market price of serfs. No thought had been given to the interests of the dead peasant's family, who had presumably been left destitute through the death of their breadwinner, which had taken place no less than thirty years previously! Radishchev felt that the emphasis in this case was all wrong. In terms reminiscent of the *Journey*, he burst out: 'What price can be laid down for the life of a faithful servant, what interest payment for loss of services where an accident has occurred bringing about the death of one who looked after his master in infancy, in childhood, as a young man? What price is to be paid for a woman who nourished her master with her breasts and became a second

[1] Dumont to Romilly, from Russia, 1803. Quoted by C. K. Ogden, *The Theory of Legislation*, by Jeremy Bentham, London, 1931, p. xxxiii.

[2] N. S. Il'insky, in *Russky Arkhiv* ('The Russian Archive'), 1879, No. 12, p. 416.

mother to him? We shall not enter into an enumeration of such prices nor set down a tariff for landowners in respect of the killing of persons belonging to them. The price of human blood cannot be measured in cash.' Radishchev goes on to point out that compensation ought to be paid to the relatives of the deceased, not to his owner. 'The dead person may be a father, a son, a husband, or else a mother, a wife, a daughter, and so on. . . . Who can be unaware of the loss which a peasant may suffer in his husbandry if his family is deprived of working hands?' From this, Radishchev concludes that in such cases, there is no reason for the serf-owning proprietor to be paid for loss of his chattel, but that dependants of the slain person must be properly cared for by the town or village in which they dwell.[1]

In the second minority judgment delivered by Radishchev during his work on the Commission, we find him insisting on the right of defendants in criminal cases to demand the removal of judges whom they may suspect of partiality. This was already permitted by Russian law in civil actions, and Radishchev remarked that this rule was all the more necessary to be observed in proceedings where life, liberty or honour were at stake. He advocated that the accused should have the right to nominate his own defending counsel, and that two-thirds of the bench, and not a simple majority, should be required to establish a conviction. In putting forward these recommendations, which were quite radical by Russian standards, Radishchev referred to Catherine's *Nakaz*, as well as to the ancient maxim of jurisprudence, 'It is better to acquit a hundred guilty men than to cause one innocent man to suffer.'[2]

Apart from his day to day work on the Commission, Radishchev was engaged in drawing up his own individual schemes for legislative reform. This had nothing to do with the routine activities of his colleagues, who spent their time copying out bits and pieces from antiquated statutes, and trying to knock them into shape. Radishchev's memoranda, on the other hand, were cast in schematic form, and incorporated some of the ideas already put forward in his *Journey from St Petersburg to Moscow* and other controversial works of his earlier period. They were drafted not for the eyes of his staid colleagues on the Commission, but for those of his patron Vorontsov, now on the way to becoming Chancellor of Russia, and of the Emperor himself. This is made clear by the fact that copies were handed to the Tsar's confidant, the volatile Karazin, who either suppressed or accidentally mislaid them (this on the evidence of Radishchev's sons, who tried in vain to recover the documents from Karazin); copies of the memoranda have more recently come to light

[1] Radishchev, *Polnoe sobranie sochineny*, III, 246–8.
[2] *Ibid.*, 249–50.

among the papers in the Vorontsov family archives.

In one of these memoranda, 'On Legislation', Radishchev described the preliminary research which needed to be undertaken before a new and adequate set of laws for the Russian Empire could be drafted.[1] This outspoken document is not without touches of satirical humour. Radishchev stresses the need for keeping the spirit and the letter of the law up to date, to accord with the relative degree of barbarism or of enlightenment typical of the people who are to be governed. He expresses regret that Peter the Great never found time to draw up a unified code. Half a century later, Catherine II came to the throne, at a time when Frederick of Prussia was giving the world an example of how a philosopher should reign; Montesquieu had published his immortal works; Beccaria was still actively working; Blackstone was spreading throughout Europe the renown of English jurisprudence; Voltaire 'was preaching tolerance until he was hoarse, wielding a scourge against superstition, and putting vain idolatry to flight by means of the devastating weapon of mockery; and his tongue, with razor-edge precision, was destroying the fragile fabric of delusion'. In this atmosphere, Catherine composed and published her *Nakaz*, which, in Radishchev's view, did her great honour, in spite of certain errors due to exaggerated respect for the views contained in Montesquieu's *De l'Esprit des Lois*. However, the *Nakaz* never bore fruit; towards the end of her reign, Catherine in many cases abandoned her liberal principles. (A wry reflection on Radishchev's own personal case?) The enthusiasm of youth was succeeded in her case by the suspicious caution of old age. In the same way, Radishchev reflects, the young and ardent Louis XIV who took over the reins of government on the death of Cardinal Mazarin was a different man from the middle-aged fanatic who revoked the Edict of Nantes in the bedchamber of the superstitious Madame de Maintenon.

During Catherine's long reign, intellectual standards and public opinion generally had made great strides, but the administration of justice had remained dilatory, corrupt and barbarous. 'From our breast there bursts forth a sigh of woe as we see one single righteous judge or governor languishing amidst a troop of debauched, venal, rabid, shifty characters, frustrated in his vocation, and hearing his voice ring out without effect in the judgment hall, and his good intentions reduced to naught.' And Radishchev goes on to attack with his usual verve what he calls 'the almost universal abuse of power' among Government officials of his day. This was aggravated by Peter the Great's 'Table of Ranks', which encouraged functionaries to concentrate on securing dignities and titles, and encouraged arrogance and inefficiency. It would be a good thing to apply to such persons the custom of ancient Persia,

[1] 'O zakonopolozhenii', in Radishchev, *Polnoe sobranie sochineny*, III, 145–65.

where a courtier was appointed to remind the King every day that he too was but a mortal man.

'The principle of all legislation, a principle which should always be regarded as an axiom, is that it is better to prevent crimes than to punish them.' To this end, educational facilities must be improved. Brothels and taverns must be supervised. Radishchev quotes from Catherine's *Nakaz* the sentence 'Agriculture cannot flourish where no one possesses private property.' Instead of remaining serfs, the peasants should become independent smallholders. This would give them a stake in the country, and an incentive for hard work. The birth-rate would rise, and Russia's vast expanse would be filled by a race of industrious inhabitants. Within the Empire, all restrictions on commerce should be removed: it should not be 'limited or encumbered by tariffs or tolls or any Customs formalities or inspections which, unless accompanied by strict honesty and saintly solemnity, always resemble knavish tricks or, as in the case of the censorship, an offshoot of the Inquisition or the Secret Chancellery.'

Fiscal policy is discussed with special reference to inflation. Radishchev inveighs against the issue of worthless paper money, as practised in revolutionary France, and to some extent in Russia itself. One day, perhaps, the value of such currency will be less than that of the paper on which it is printed. 'Then the hour of doom will strike, the hour of sudden bankruptcy, and he who today reckoned his capital resources in terms of millions will be a poor beggar, nourished by the alms of the haughty, or else he will have recourse to the ultimate refuge of the unhappy—suicide.'

Throughout the memorandum 'On Legislation', the emphasis is on the need for statistical data about the economic state, the trade, manners, and local institutions and conditions prevalent in all parts of the Russian Empire. In addition, Russian lawgivers should copy the ancient Greeks and Romans, and travel abroad to widen their outlook by study of the best foreign models. To read foreign law books was not enough. What made laws effective was the climate of public opinion in the countries where they operated. This could only be gauged by personal visits. It would be useful, for instance, to visit Pennsylvania and investigate the humane system of the Quakers there, who had abolished capital and even corporal punishment. People said that their model prisons had remarkable success in reforming the criminals, who came out as changed men. Experts should travel to England and study the renowned jury system. (Indeed, according to his son Paul, Radishchev was anxious to go himself, and would have done so but for his tragic death a few months later.) Finally, Radishchev makes a discreet allusion to political upheavals resulting from the French Revolution, and from the third and final Partition of Poland. Venice, Milan, Bologna and Ferrara, he said, were now under new régimes, and it would be instructive to see whether the change had brought greater wellbeing to the people. Nearer home, Poland had been carved by Russia, Austria and Prussia into three portions, each of them ruled by a different sovereign. This gave the legislator an opportunity of seeing which system of rule was the more beneficial to those under its authority.

Another product of this preliminary work is Radishchev's 'Project for the Classification of the Russian Code'.[1] This brief document defines such concepts as fundamental and State laws, the rights and duties of citizens, civil and criminal laws, and categories of crimes, offences and misdemeanours. It examines the purpose of punishment, as well as possible methods of educating public opinion, 'that most solid rampart of all human legislative measures', to uphold and respect the rule of law. Of interest is the paragraph about the rights and duties of the Emperor in ensuring peace and security at home, and in the conduct of foreign policy. In judging criminal offences, the establishment of motive is of paramount importance. The true ends of justice are to prevent crime and correct the offender. 'Revenge is always odious,' says our reformer. The death penalty is unnecessary, mutilation is savage and ineffectual as a punishment. 'The value of corporal punishment is (for me at least) far from being proved. It produces its effect by means of terror. But terror is not salvation, and it produces only a momentary effect.'

The most extensive of these memoranda which Radishchev drew up during the last months of his life is entitled 'Project for a Civil Code'; the manuscript came to light among the papers of Count Alexander Vorontsov, whose arms were stamped on the cover in which it was bound.[2] The 'Project for a Civil Code' is not in itself a series of laws, but rather a plan for their future drafting. It covers the following subjects:

1. General definitions: law in general; obligation; individual and collective persons; property; actions; responsibility for actions; criminality.

2. Consent and authorization: forms and conditions of authorization; consent obtained by false pretences; contracts; obligations arising from the causing of hurt, damage, or loss.

3. Property and ownership: rightful and wrongful ownership; acquisition, loss, and defence of property; who can acquire property;

---

[1] 'Proekt dlya razdeleniya ulozheniya Rossiyskogo', in Radishchev, *Polnoe sobranie sochineny*, III, 166–70.

[2] 'Proekt grazhdanskogo ulozheniya', in Radishchev, *Polnoe sobranie sochineny*, III, 171–245.

rights arising from the concept of property; various categories of property; goods and chattels.

4. Direct acquisition of property:

a. Initial entry into possession of things previously without ownership, e.g. metals, minerals exploited by mining.

b. Entry into possession of things abandoned and found.

c. Treasure.

d. Chase and venery.

e. Plunder and booty.

f. Emblements, accession, confusion.

g. Rewards.

h. Inheritance.

i. Non-claim and prescription.

5. Acquisition of property through intermediary: purchase or sale; barter; cession; gains from insurance, lottery or bets; loans, usury, gifts, etc.

6. Wills and legacies.

The preamble of Radishchev's 'Project for a Civil Code' is based on the familiar theory of the contractual origin of society. The law, says our author, considers man from two points of view: firstly, as Nature created him, and secondly, as society formed him. 'The law is merely the confirmation of what Nature has bestowed on man. From this it follows that if a man on entering society yields to it some portion of his rights, then it is obliged to compensate him for them. Consequently every man living in society is entitled to demand from it defence and protection. The law in relation to man is like Nature: . . . before it, all are equal.'

In another passage, Radishchev writes: 'Property is one of the objects which man had in mind as he entered into society. Property thus became so essential an adjunct of the citizen that to diminish his rights to it would be a real breach of the primitive social contract. The free and unrestricted enjoyment of it is simply a consequence arising from the original contract.'

The influence of Rousseau's *Du Contrat Social* may be detected in these two passages. This theory of an original pact can, of course, be traced well back into the seventeenth century at least, where its eminent exponent was John Locke. The *Second Treatise: of Civil Government* lays the same emphasis on the inviolable nature of property as does Radishchev in the above paragraph and in his book, *A Journey from St Petersburg to Moscow*. Blackstone in his *Commentaries*, a work familiar to Radishchev, held a not dissimilar view of the origin of human society, though he warned against the fallacy of imagining that the Social Contract was anything more than a convenient fiction to illustrate the nature of society, as a free association of individuals banding together for their common advantage.

Radishchev's statement that before the law, 'all are equal', is significant; it shows that he hoped to modify by legal reform the disabilities suffered by the Russian serfs.

He defines as follows the actions over which the law's jurisdiction extends: 'Every action is preceded in man by will, intention. Where there exists no will nor intent, there exists in law no action. Where there is no freedom of action, the law does not judge. . . . The law can judge only outward actions, in so far as the will is expressed in free action; but decisions of the mind, will and intention are not subject to the law's jurisdiction.'

He emphasizes the law's benevolent and protective role in the life of a citizen: 'In relation to a person's natural condition, the law receives man under its protection before his birth and in this state determines his rights; it follows him at birth, determines his sex, follows him in infancy, childhood, maturity, old age and senility, and takes into account his mental and physical powers, their weaknesses or perfection. It surveys his life and is inseparable from him at death; it lives with him when he is resident in his civic sanctuary, his home: here the law combines with nature to determine his happiness, the highest happiness, domestic bliss; and the law confirms all family relationships according to the dictates of Nature herself.'

Radishchev's exalted idea of the importance of individual liberty and freedom of speech, which he had earlier stated with vigour in the chapter 'Torzhok' of the *Journey*, also finds expression in the following paragraph: 'But if anyone should have so little good sense as to consent to have some obligation laid upon himself hampering his freedom of thought, his freedom of faith, his freedom of action or his personal security, the law does not recognize such acts of consent as legitimate and deems them null and void because they destroy what is the very nature of a citizen.'

Typical of Radishchev's independent approach towards ecclesiastical questions are his views on church vows. To the enforcement of such vows under Canon law he applies the doctrine expounded by Blackstone: 'A *nudum pactum* or agreement to do or pay anything on one side, without any compensation on the other, is totally void in law: and a man cannot be compelled to perform it.' Since church vows are not contracts, but simply promises, they are not, in Radishchev's view, legally enforceable. No human being has the right to say 'God has entrusted me with the enforcement of His rights.'

In his recommendations for drafting the laws of tort, Radishchev bases himself again on the concept of the Social Contract and shows much concern for the interests of the common people who, he says, are too often treated with disdain by the aristocracy and wealthy classes. 'Inasmuch as the aim of life in society is the advantage of all, inasmuch as all are equal before the law, it follows that no one may cause hurt, damage or loss to another, and that whoever has caused anyone hurt, damage or loss, or been the cause of it, is obliged to make reparation. Although he will be liable to punishment for this (since punishment is reparation to the law for the prevention of similar harm in the future), however, this will not compensate the sufferer. Compensation for harm is a consequence of the original social pact. If the guilty party is reduced through punishment to a state where he cannot make reparation for the damage which he has caused, then society as a whole is under an obligation to do so.'

One humane measure proposed by Radishchev was that a seducer should be obliged by law to go through a form of marriage with his victim. Divorce should be automatically pronounced after the ceremony, but the woman would bear his name and be entitled to claim alimony from him.

In discussing property and the rights of self-defence, Radishchev repeats the doctrine which he had already expounded in the *Journey*. 'To the rights of a proprietor and owner belongs also the demand for legal protection to be afforded by the Government in the preservation of his property or possessions. For man entered into society solely in order to enjoy lawful defence in the rights appertaining to him. But if society delays its assistance and he is likely for this reason to suffer irreparable harm or loss, then he has the right to undertake his own defence, and ward off force by force.' (Compare Blackstone's *Commentaries*: if a man 'be forcibly attacked in his person or property, it is lawful for him to repel force by force'.)

The right of the State to confiscate a citizen's property is contested by Radishchev—even if he should be convicted of grave criminal offences. This applies, of course, to wholesale confiscation, not to imposition of a fine. However, Radishchev allows a guarded exception to this rule: people may be obliged to give up their possessions 'for the public good, but receiving compensation for them'.

The 'Project for a Civil Code' contains provisions designed to protect the children of a testator from capricious disinheritance. A man's right to dispose freely of his estate by will and testament should be regulated in inverse proportion to the number of his offspring: thus, with two children, he would dispose of a fifth part of his possessions; with three, of a seventh part, and so on. Only the most outrageous conduct on the children's side should constitute grounds for disinheritance.

This survey of Radishchev's Project may be concluded with some of his aphorisms on legislation in general:

> A sure sign: if it is possible to break a law with impunity while observing the prescribed forms, then that law is bad.
> To govern much, to govern constantly, is the same as being incapable of governing.
> In order to govern the multitude, it is sensible to assume that the worst citizens are better than they really are.
> It is better to abolish a law altogether than once to give occasion for a flagrant breach of it.

The formal evidence of these memoranda may be supplemented by the testimony of Radishchev's son, Paul, to whom his father's ideas were of course familiar. In his reminiscences, Paul Radishchev sums up some of his father's views as follows:

1. All classes of society should be equal before the law, and therefore corporal punishment should be done away with.

2. The 'Table of Ranks' should be done away with.

3. In criminal cases, interrogations of an inquisitorial nature should be abolished. Justice should be administered by public tribunals complete with the jury system, otherwise there could be no real justice.

4. Complete freedom of religion should be established, and everything which cramped liberty of conscience eliminated.

5. Freedom of publication should be introduced, with clear definitions of the degree of legal liability incurred by authors and publishers.

6. Manorial serfs were to be freed, and the sale of men as recruits for the army forbidden.

7. The poll tax should be replaced by a levy on landed property.

8. Liberty of commerce should be established.

9. The severe laws against money-lenders and insolvent debtors should be rescinded, and something on the lines of *Habeas corpus* written into the law of the land.

According to Paul Radishchev, his father had in fact gone farther than this, and advocated the setting up of constitutional government on the lines of the British monarchy. When Paul was preparing these memories of his father for publication in the journal *Russky Vestnik* ('The Russian Messenger') in 1858, the censor cut out this particular passage, as too dangerous for printing in autocratic Russia. However, discovery of Paul Radishchev's original text enables us to fill the gap. 'Radishchev said that in her provision for the election of representative officers by the gentry, Catherine II had laid the basis for a future constitution of Russia. He proposed that unlimited monarchical power in Russia should be abandoned, and democratic institutions introduced.

Let the Tsar still be great, but let Russia be free, like England.'[1] One must allow for Paul Radishchev's desire to make out his father to be a forerunner of the liberal thinkers of his own day, for he was writing in the reign of Alexander II, over half a century later. However, such utterances are thoroughly characteristic of Radishchev, and there is no reason to doubt their general tenor.

To understand Radishchev's state of mind during the last year of his life, it is instructive to turn again to the account of his colleague on the Legislative Commission, Il'insky. Very much the regular civil servant, Il'insky regarded the *Journey from St Petersburg to Moscow* as a highly dangerous work, though he admitted that in it 'besides the satirical element, there is much good material, and this shows the goodness of his heart, which could not tolerate abuses'. One day, Radishchev was talking to Il'insky about his life in Siberia, where he admitted that he had been well treated and had enjoyed personal freedom. Il'insky asked him what could have induced him to write a satirical attack on the Government, as he had done. Radishchev in reply denied that his *Journey* was intended as a satire at all, any more than the German jurist Puffendorf's renowned book on the duties of the citizen, *De officio hominis et civis*, which was translated into Russian by order of Peter the Great. This work by Puffendorf outlined the duties and obligations of the sovereign, the nobility, the judges and so forth, just as he had himself tried to do in the *Journey from St Petersburg to Moscow*. Love of truth and sincerity alone had impelled him to write and publish that book, which he saw no reason to retract now. If such writings had been tolerated and even encouraged by Peter the Great, why should they now be treated as criminal libels?—From all this, Il'insky rightly concluded that to the end of his life, Radishchev remained unswervingly devoted to the radical, 'free-thinking' principles which he had expounded in his ill-fated book.[2]

Radishchev's friends and colleagues perhaps failed to allow sufficiently for the fact that after all his ordeals, he was still a frustrated, insecure, melancholy man, weighed down by debt and the threat of material want, and over-sensitive to any slight, real or imagined. The young rebel had turned into a middle-aged visionary, while his ideas retained all their uncompromising vigour. The trouble was that in spite of all the high-sounding projects in the air, the mentality of Russian officialdom had changed scarcely at all. Autocracy remained something sacred. Nor

---

[1] See R. P. Thaler, 'Radiščev, Britain, and America', in *Harvard Slavic Studies*, IV, The Hague, 1957, p. 75. Text in *Chteniya* ('Readings)' in the Imperial Society of Russian History and Antiquities at Moscow University, bk. 241, 1912, 'Miscellany', p. 22.

[2] *Russky Arkhiv*, 1879, No. 12, pp. 415–16.

were courtiers and Government officials any more ready under Alexander than they had been under Catherine to put up with being described as 'debauched, venal, rabid, shifty characters', revelling in 'almost universal abuse of power' (see Radishchev's memorandum 'On Legislation', quoted above). As the months wore on, Radishchev's candour and reforming zeal became something of an embarrassment to the Legislative Commission's easy-going chairman, Count Zavadovsky. One day, so it appears, Zavadovsky asked him whether his earlier banishment had not taught him a lesson. 'Tut, tut, Alexander Nikolaevich, still babbling on as usual. Was not one dose of Siberia enough for you?' Even Radishchev's old friend and protector Vorontsov, now an important member of the 'establishment', advised him to be more discreet in future.[1]

For Radishchev, this was the last straw. For a year, he had been toiling single-handed over his cherished legislative projects, while beset by personal and family problems. Now that his house was sold, he had no fixed home, but was reduced to wandering from one set of furnished rooms to another. 'For the last month I have been ill,' he wrote to his old parents in August 1802. 'Although I am a bit better now, I am still very weak. The lawsuit against Kozlov is not making any progress, goodness knows when they will announce their verdict. God grant that you may live to see its conclusion. I keep on moving from one flat to another. It is terrible not to have a house of one's own. . . . Farewell, my beloved ones, and give your blessing to your devoted and obedient son.'[2]

In one of his fits of melancholy, Radishchev said to his sons: 'What will you say, children, if they send me back to Siberia again?' Every day he became more downcast. The doctor administered tonics and sedatives, but none of them did any good. Radishchev began to ponder once more over the words which he had put into the mouth of the squire of Krest'tsy in the *Journey from St Petersburg to Moscow*: 'If thy virtuous nature can find no refuge upon this earth, if, driven to desperation, thou art left without any shield against oppression, then remember that thou art a man, remember thy greatness, seize the crown of bliss if they strive to take it from thee—and die.'

Radishchev paid his last visits to the Legislative Commission on September 1 and 2, 1802. On the eleventh of the month, he awoke with a feeling that he had reached the end of his tether. His eldest son, Vasily, had prepared a glass full of nitric acid to clean up and polish some old, tarnished officer's epaulettes of his. Wandering round the apartment,

---

[1] G. P. Makogonenko, *Radishchev i ego vremya*, Moscow, 1956, pp. 629–30.

[2] Radishchev, *Polnoe sobranie sochineny*, III, 535, 657, where details are given of the Radishchev family's unsuccessful lawsuit with Senator Kozlov.

Radishchev caught sight of this glass, raised it to his lips on a sudden impulse, and swallowed the contents at a gulp. Then he seized a razor and tried to cut his throat. Vasily saw what was happening, hurled himself towards his father, and wrenched the razor from him. 'My agony will be long,' Radishchev said, and asked for a priest to be brought. As it happened, there was a priest at the door of the house. Radishchev confessed himself like a good Christian, and kept on repeating, 'O Lord, receive my soul.'

By now, the poison was taking effect, with vomiting and other horrible symptoms. A doctor came and prescribed an emetic. An hour later, Dr James Villiers, the Emperor's Scottish physician, arrived from Court, where the news of the tragedy had already become known. Villiers shouted, 'Water, water!' and ordered another medicine which, he felt sure, would counteract the effect of the acid. He asked Radishchev what had led him to this desperate pass. The sick man's answer was delirious and rambling. Villiers said, 'Here clearly is a man who has been greatly unhappy.' In the evening another doctor came, but there was already little hope left. At one o'clock in the morning of September 12th, Radishchev died. His son Paul added: 'And the heavenly bodies were not darkened, nor did the earth shake.' Radishchev was buried in the Volkov cemetery. Time has effaced his gravestone, and no one now can tell where he was laid to rest.

CHAPTER 15

The Legacy of Radishchev

❧ ❧❧ ❧❧❧

'Posterity will Avenge Me!' – Pushkin and Radishchev – 'How can one forget Radishchev?' – The Censorship at Work – Herzen and the 'Journey' – Lenin and Radishchev – A Forerunner of Communism? – Radishchev and Russian History

In the *Ode to Liberty*, Radishchev had a vision of a youth in years to come visiting his grave and crying out: 'Born beneath the yoke of tyranny, and bearing gilded fetters, this man was the first to proclaim freedom unto us!' And shortly before his death, in a moment of despair, he wrote: 'Posterity will avenge me!'

And yet, however lonely and persecuted Radishchev may have felt, it is not true to say that he died unappreciated by his contemporaries in Russia. During that last year in St Petersburg, his flat had been one of the meeting places of a group of young literary men of liberal leanings, who formed a society called 'The Free Association of Lovers of Literature, Science and the Arts'. Of this society, Radishchev's sons, Vasily and Nicholas, were members. Also prominent in its activities was Ivan Pnin, an illegitimate son of Prince Repnin, who had edited a rationalist periodical, *The St Petersburg Journal*, which appeared under the patronage of the future Tsar Alexander I. Pnin's *Essay on Education applied to Russia* (1804) expounds a form of social Utilitarianism, and uses many of Radishchev's arguments to attack the institution of serfdom.[1]

Pnin composed an elegy on Radishchev's death, which clearly shows the esteem and affection in which he was held by the younger generation of those days.

> And so Radishchev is no more!
> My friend, within the grave he lies!
> Cold is that heart which virtuous beat

[1] See D. M. Lang, 'Some Forerunners of the Decembrists', in *The Cambridge Journal*, I, No. 10, July 1948, pp. 632–4.

Now that inexorable fate has struck.
Those lips which spoke the truth,
Alas!—must ever be silent,
Extinguished is his mind's bright torch;
This friend of man, this friend of nature,
Who strove for bliss by freedom's path
Has left us for eternity!

He left us, and found peace at last.
So let us bless his ashes now!
He who thus sacrificed his all
Not for himself, but for mankind,
A faithful son to his own land,
A citizen, a model father
Who boldly stood and spoke the truth,
Who never bowed his knee to man,
Nor deigned the mighty to cajole—
That man, I think, has ripely lived.

Another member of that literary group, the poet Ivan Born, composed an epitaph on Radishchev, part in verse, part in prose, which appeared in an almanach called 'Scroll of the Muses' which the Free Association of Lovers of Literature brought out in 1803.

'Blessed,' exclaims the poet, 'is the man whom the satrap's halls cannot lure, who knows the true value of life, whose ardent heart embraces the whole world and every race of man; blessed is he who is not afraid of false authority, who boldly proclaims the truth, and fears not to disturb the grandee's slumbering ear nor to rend his stony heart! —But the fate of truth is to be persecuted, many of you will say. In our own land, the cult of truth and virtue has its martyrs, while in countries afar off, Socrates the sage, the benefactor of mortals, was done to death, and patriots in exile still drink a hundred times the cup of death. What is the use of virtue then?—This, I declare, is a question fit for slaves who drag out their lives in gilded fetters! Truth will stay alive for ever, worshipped by every mortal endowed with virtue.'

Such, Ivan Born continues, are some of the thoughts inspired by news of the death of Radishchev—'a man well known to you all, and whose loss is serious from more than one standpoint in a philosopher's eyes, serious too for humanity at large'. And Born speaks of Radishchev's unselfish life at Ilimsk when in exile, and how he cured local people of the goitre and other ailments. 'When they heard that their teacher, their father, their guardian angel, was leaving them grateful folk streamed in to see him from five hundred versts around. Each one brought some gift out of heartfelt gratitude; the tears of each were mingled with those of that honourable man, now vindicated. O moments worthy of eternity! Who among the grim scourges of humanity—those bloodthirsty conquerors who devastate flourishing lands, and chain free citizens with the fetters of slavery—who among these, I say, has ever enjoyed such moments?' Born recalls that he himself when in Siberia had chanced to visit the house at Tara where Radishchev and his family stayed for a week on their homeward path from Ilimsk. 'The master of the house could not find words enough to praise his goodness of heart, his kind nature.'

'Radishchev is dead,' exclaims the poet, 'and his end, they say, was violent, abrupt. How can we reconcile this action with that unshakable resolution of a philosopher who had triumphed over adversity, and devoted himself to caring for his fellow men even in banishment, in exile, in misfortune, when sundered from the circle of his relatives and friends?—Or did he come to recognize the vanity of human life? Or did he despair, like Brutus, of virtue itself? Let us set a seal upon our lips, and mourn for the destiny of the human race. Friends! Let us offer up a tear from the heart to Radishchev's memory. He loved sincerity and righteousness. His ardent affection for mankind yearned to enlighten all his brethren with the unquenchable flame of eternal truth, he longed to see wisdom seated upon the throne of the whole world. He saw around him naught but weakness and ignorance, deceit behind the mask of virtue—and he is gone into the grave. He was born to spread enlightenment, he was persecuted in his life-time—and is gone into the tomb. Within the hearts of grateful patriots let a monument be erected that shall be worthy of him!'

The passionate words of those two young writers set the tone for the veneration accorded to Radishchev's memory by generations of liberal thinkers. The Decembrists in their rebellious, idealistic schemes found inspiration in Radishchev's *Journey*, which continued to circulate in printed and manuscript copies in defiance of the censorship ban. Thus, Nicholas Turgenev, the future conspirator, would muse on Russia's history during the age of Catherine and Potemkin, and ponder on the vision in Radishchev's book where Truth appears to the sovereign in his palace and exposes the corruption and wickedness of the régime. The young Pushkin, of course, was intimate with the Decembrists, and as fiery a democrat as any of them. Following Radishchev, he too wrote an *Ode to Liberty*, which the authorities found highly objectionable. Pushkin counted it as one of his claims to renown that 'in Radishchev's steps I sang of liberty, and chanted the praises of clemency'. To a critic who omitted Radishchev from an article on the art of letters in Russia, Pushkin wrote: 'In an essay on Russian literature, how can one forget Radishchev? Whom then shall we remember? This omission is unpardonable.'

S

In his mature years, the great poet tried to reconcile himself more or less to the parade-ground rule of Nicholas I and his gendarmes. In 1833, Pushkin began to write a sequel to the *Journey from St Petersburg to Moscow*, under the title *A Journey from Moscow to St Petersburg*. In this uncompleted work Pushkin joined issue with Radishchev on a number of points, especially where he felt that the earlier writer had acted unpatriotically by painting Russian life in excessively sombre hues. Later on, Pushkin wrote an article about Radishchev for a literary journal, *The Contemporary*, in which he criticized his 'cult of half-baked enlightenment' and 'his blind zeal for innovation'; at the same time, he paid tribute to Radishchev's exceptional mental gifts, and considered that his action in publishing the *Journey* showed 'amazing self-sacrifice and a kind of chivalrous sincerity'. But even the severely critical tone of Pushkin's article could not save it from the indiscriminate ban placed by the Tsarist authorities on anything which might arouse public interest in Radishchev's life and work, and the ideals for which he had stood. Prohibiting the publication of Pushkin's essay, the Minister of Education wrote: 'I find it inconvenient and completely superfluous to recall to mind a writer and a book which are completely forgotten, and deserving of oblivion.' Pushkin's essay could therefore appear only when the poet had been dead for twenty years.

There was no question of reprinting the *Journey from St Petersburg to Moscow* during the half century which followed Radishchev's death. His sons, it is true, managed to take advantage of the relative liberalism of parts of Alexander I's reign to bring out a collection of Radishchev's works, but without the *Journey* itself; the *Life of Ushakov* was mangled by the elimination of controversial passages. This edition, in six little volumes, came out in Moscow between 1807 and 1811, but was largely destroyed in the great fire of 1812. The *Journey*, meanwhile, circulated in manuscript copies, which passed secretly from hand to hand and commanded high prices.

It was not until 1858 that the stormy petrel of Russian radicalism, Alexander Herzen, brought out in London the first reprint of Radishchev's *Journey*, which he coupled with an edition of Prince Shcherbatov's searing discourse, *On the Degradation of Morals in Russia*. 'A. Radishchev looks into the future,' Herzen wrote in the preface, 'he was imbued with the heady influences of those last years of the eighteenth century. Never was the human breast more filled with hope than in those great spring days of the 1790's. Everyone awaited with beating heart some superhuman event. A holy impatience disturbed men's minds, and turned the most sober thinkers into visionaries. When he heard of the proclamation of the French Republic, Immanuel Kant took off his hat, his heart overflowing with emotion at these great events, and uttered the *Nunc dimittis*. Permeated with the rapturous ideals of those days, it was Radishchev's fate to live in Russia: tears, indignation, compassion, irony—our own national brand of irony, the irony of consolation, of vengeance—all this is poured out into his superb book. . . . Radishchev does not stand like a Daniel in the antechamber of the Winter Palace, he does not confine his world to the three upper classes of society, he has no personal feeling of bitterness against Catherine. He goes along the high road, he sympathizes with the sufferings of the masses, he chats with coachmen, domestic servants, recruits to the army, and in every word of his we find hatred of tyranny combined with thundering protest against the system of serfdom. . . . His humour is entirely fresh, completely sincere, and remarkably lively. And in whatever he wrote you hear those same familiar chords which we have grown used to hearing in the early poems of Pushkin, in the *Meditations* of Ryleev,[1] and in our own heart.—What his convictions were, that he demonstrated after his return from exile. When summoned personally by Alexander I to take up work again, he hoped to give force of law to some of his ideas, above all, his thoughts on the liberation of the peasants. And when he realized, fifty-year old dreamer as he was, that it was no use entertaining any hope of this, he took poison and died! . . . How terrible is all this! How can we fail to cherish that martyr's memory in our breast?'

The events which followed the death of Tsar Nicholas I in 1855, culminating in the abolition of serfdom six years later, gave the subject of Radishchev and his *Journey* added topical appeal. At last the reforms for which Radishchev had fought and suffered were to be effected. The belated publication of Pushkin's article on Radishchev, followed by the appearance of the reminiscences of Paul Radishchev, gave a curious reading public the first reliable information about this literary classic of a bygone age. But still the ban of 1790 remained in force. Even Radishchev's likeness was to be blotted out. On a page of engraved vignettes of eighteenth-century writers, published in 1856, Radishchev figures along with Lomonosov, Sumarokov, Derzhavin, Fonvizin and Novikov—but alone of all these, Radishchev's portrait appears on the page anonymous and without a superscription, a stranger at the feast.

Even after serfdom had been abolished in 1861, the authorities kept up their cat and mouse game. Autocracy, it was felt, had not altered its basic nature. What Radishchev had said about the Tsarist system of 1790 might by malicious spirits be applied with equal force to the régime existing in 1890. White-bearded bibliophiles smuggled passages from the *Journey* into their antiquarian publications, and one edition did

[1] The great poet and revolutionary idealist, executed for his part in the abortive Decembrist rising of 1825.

S*

appear in print, but with three of the most outspoken chapters cut out. In 1868, the censors publicly lifted their ban. However, an edition printed in 1872 was seized by the police on special orders from the Council of Ministers, and reduced to pulp; then two expensive limited editions managed to get through; as late as 1902, another edition was burnt by Government order. Yet the diehard Tsar Alexander III actually sent a telegram of congratulation and good wishes to a group of descendants of Radishchev and admirers of his work, who opened a Radishchev Museum in Saratov, the capital of the writer's native province!

After the 1905 revolution, it was no longer possible to maintain the official ban. Several editions of the *Journey* appeared in rapid succession, with a spate of articles on Radishchev's life and writings. In Soviet times, Ya. L. Barskov brought out in 1935 a photolithographic reproduction of the original edition of 1790; a three volume definitive edition of Radishchev's complete works was published between 1938 and 1952 by the Soviet Academy of Sciences.

Like the Decembrists, the liberals, the radical intelligentsia and all other foes of Tsarist absolutism, the Bolsheviks too were quick to claim Radishchev as their spiritual ancestor. Lenin expressed pride that even the Russia of 'tsarist hangmen, nobles and capitalists' could produce freedom-loving men of Radishchev's calibre. This theme was taken up by the leading article in *Pravda* of August 31, 1949, celebrating the bicentenary of Radishchev's birth. The paper's readers are exhorted to look on Radishchev as a materialist, an active fighter against autocratic tyranny, a veritable forefather of Bolshevism. 'The Bolshevik party, which is the heir and continuator of all the best elements in the teaching and the struggle of the revolutionary democrats, was the first in history to bring to fulfilment the people's age-old yearnings for liberty.' This is the spirit with which are inspired many recent publications on Radishchev emanating from the Soviet Union, in which he is hailed as an active promoter of revolution, a political thinker superior to Rousseau, Montesquieu and all other Western European writers of the eighteenth century. Those who see in Radishchev an outstanding representative of the European libertarian, radical tradition, a man steeped in the ideology of the Age of Reason, are denounced with declamatory, chauvinistic vigour.

On reflection, it is hard to see what Radishchev's ideas have in common with present day Communism as practised in Russia. The keystone of his philosophy was the sacredness of the personal liberty, the human dignity of every man or woman, and the value of each individual human life. The good Communist, on the other hand, does not hesitate to kill or to imprison without trial whenever he thinks the end justifies the means. Radishchev's life-long concern was with the peasantry, with each man's right to possess and work his own plot of land without being forced to toil for a master. In Communist Russia, every effort has been directed towards abolition of individual ownership of land, and towards enforced collectivization of the peasantry. For Radishchev, to criticize the Government was the right of every citizen. In Soviet Russia, every citizen is called on to support the Communist Party Line. Radishchev viewed as obnoxious every form of censorship of books or control over the Press. In the Soviet Union, the State controls every organ of publication, and nothing can appear without the *imprimatur* of a Party official. Radishchev attacked every form of dogma and superstition, either religious or political. The Soviet citizen is indoctrinated from birth with a brand of philosophy and political doctrine which he questions at his peril, doubt or 'deviationism' being a criminal charge. Radishchev abhorred militarism, and stood for non-violence and the renunciation of warlike and colonial aims. Soviet Russia maintains an enormous standing army and holds down many countries by force of arms. Radishchev believed in free speech. In the Soviet Union, an unguarded word has sent many a person to his doom. Radishchev strove for fair administration of justice, without regard for political or class ends. In Soviet Russia, the law is viewed as a legitimate weapon in the class struggle. Almost the only issue on which Radishchev and the Soviet rulers are at one is on the need to suppress sexual licence and enforce strict morality. But Radishchev advocated this in order to enhance the sanctity of family life and stamp out venereal disease, whereas the Soviet rulers (in defiance of the classic Communist doctrine of free love) have chosen for their own reasons to foist upon their subjects a drab and uniform brand of puritan ethics.

To debate whether Radishchev and his writings and ideas are to be treated as a distinctive Russian phenomenon, or as a product of the European Age of Reason, is beside the point. In his immense compassion and his conscience-stricken care for the underdog, in his intuitive sympathy for country folk, in his sometimes impractical idealism, in his capacity for living on two levels—that of the conscientious public servant, and that of the vehement, protesting reformer —there is something very Russian about Radishchev's personality. And yet by his education and convictions, he was a true son of the Western Enlightenment, a humanitarian who had the misfortune to live under a régime dominated by serfdom, autocracy, and despotic caprice. Many were those in Russia who professed themselves adepts of European rationalism, 'Voltaireans' as they were indiscriminately dubbed. But the originality of Radishchev, the justification for regarding him as the first Russian radical, lies in the fact that he was virtually the first disciple of the Enlightenment in Russia to draw the inexorable conclusions suggested by his readings and reflections. Not for him the wit of the salon and the cynicism of a spoilt aristocracy. Surveying the reality of Russian everyday life, he came to the conclusion that here were the concrete results of the irresponsible despotism against which the precursors of the French Revolution were inveighing. Radishchev was the first Russian writer to invoke the ultimate moral law, the rights of man, holding a pistol to the heads of the Russian gentry, and warning them of the reckoning in store if they did not take heed in time.

Fonvizin the satirist, Novikov the Freemason and philanthropist, Radishchev the champion of the serfs and the critic of autocracy, these are three intellectual giants of Catherine's reign. Their contribution to literature and the formation of public opinion in Russia was enormous. Historically, their ideas stand out as the reflection of a growing *malaise* among educated people, among members of the privileged gentry class itself. Peter the Great had attempted to create an educated squirearchy to further his great plans for the country. But the St Petersburg *imperium*, remote from the people, set its face against social reform and became identified more and more with the worst features of the absolutist system. In the meantime, Russians had been enabled to think for themselves, and there were already a few who were no longer content to carry out blindly the *ukazes* of the despot. Radishchev's *Journey* is the first manifestation of this new intellectual independence on the part of Russian-thinking people. The book was a sign that not everyone was clinging obediently to Catherine's apron strings. There is nothing more deadly to autocracy than doubt. That is why Catherine could never forgive Radishchev for his gesture of defiance.

Had the Empress and her successors heeded Radishchev's prophecies, and the growing chorus of those who felt social reform in Russia was overdue, then the course of Russian history would no doubt have been different. But the St Petersburg autocrats lacked the will or the means to take action in time. The Decembrist conspirators of 1825 were doomed after one heroic, futile demonstration to die or languish in exile. The peasants remained enslaved until 1861; the feeble beginnings of constitutional government were forced on a reluctant sovereign by the military defeat and revolution of 1905. By then, the ruling classes were losing the will and the moral authority to govern. Wave after wave of discontent, together with economic and social dislocation, had cracked the foundations of the Imperial structure. Finally, in 1917, it fell. It was not Radishchev and those thinkers who came after him who destroyed the Russian monarchy, but the defects in a system which could not bring itself to move with the times.

Radishchev's voice still rings clear to us down the years. A visionary, if you like, a hysterical crank, perhaps. But he was above all a reformer, a crusader for humane government and the rule of law, a man who championed with religious fervour the cause of the downtrodden and the rights of the individual citizen against the totalitarian State machine. From Alexander Radishchev to Boris Pasternak stretches the line of writers who have fallen victim to Russian official intolerance. It is one of the saddest features of Russia's history that never have conditions existed there in which the idealist, the candid seeker after truth, can be allowed to think, to speak, even to live in peace.

BIBLIOGRAPHY

1. PRINCIPAL WORKS BY RADISHCHEV

(a) BELLES-LETTRES AND SOCIAL THOUGHT

1. *Razmyshleniya o grecheskoy istorii, ili o prichinakh blagodenstviya i neschastiya grekov*, 1773. (A translation of the Abbé G. Bonnot de Mably's *Observations sur l'Histoire de la Grèce, ou des causes de la prospérité et des malheurs des Grecs*, 1766.)

2. *Dnevnik odnoy nedeli* ('Diary of One Week'), 1773 or later.

3. *Pis'mo k drugu, zhitel'stvuyushchemu v Tobolske po dolgu zvaniya svoego* ('Letter to a Friend living in Tobolsk through the duties of his profession'), 1782.

4. *Zhitie Fedora Vasil'evicha Ushakova, s priobshcheniem nekotorykh ego sochineny* ('Life of Fedor Vasil'evich Ushakov, with the addition of a few of his writings'), 1789.

5. *Beseda o tom, chto est' syn otechestva* ('Discourse on What is a Patriot'), 1789.

6. *Puteshestvie iz Peterburga v Moskvu* ('A Journey from St Petersburg to Moscow'), 1790.

—— German translation by A. Luther, Leipzig, 1922.

—— English translation by L. Wiener, edited by R. P. Thaler, Harvard, 1958.

7. *Filaret Milostivy* ('The Holy Philaret'), 1790.

8. *Zapiski puteshestviya v Sibir'* ('Notes on a journey into Siberia'), 1790-2.

9. *Pis'mo o kitayskom torge v Kiyakhte* ('Letter on the Chinese trade at Kiakhta'), 1792.

10. *O cheloveke, ego smertnosti i bessmertii* ('On Man, his Mortality and Immortality'), begun in 1792.

11. *Zapiski puteshestviya iz Sibiri* ('Notes on a journey out of Siberia'), 1797.

12. *Opisanie moego vladeniya* ('Description of my Estate'), 1798-1800.

13. *Pamyatnik daktilokhoreicheskomu vityazyu* . . . ('Memorial to a Dactylo-Trochaic Champion, or Dramatico-Narrative Conversations of a Young Man with his Tutor, illustrated in the course of the prose narrative by fragments from the heroic poem by N. N., a man famous in the World of Learning'), 1799-1800.

(b) POETIC WRITINGS

1. *Vol'nost'*, *Oda* ('Ode to Liberty'), 1781-3.

2. *Tvorenie mira, Pesnoslovie* ('The Creation of the World, A Cantata'), before 1790.

3. *Bova. Povest' bogatyrskaya stikhami* ('Bova. A Heroic Tale in Verse'), 1799-1800.

4. *Pesni petie na sostyazaniyakh v chest' drevnim slavyanskim bozhestvam* ('Songs sung at Contests in Honour of the ancient Slavonic Deities'), 1800.

5. *Pesn' istoricheskaya* ('Song of History'), about 1800.

6. *Os'mnadtsatoe stoletie* ('The Eighteenth Century'), 1801.

(c) CORRESPONDENCE AND LEGISLATIVE PROJECTS

1. Letters to Count Alexander Romanovich Vorontsov, 1782–1800.

2. *Opyt o zakonodavstve* ('Essay on Legislation'), 1782–9.

3. *O dobrodetelyakh i nagrazhdeniyakh* ('On Virtues and Rewards'), before 1790.

4. *Zapiska o podatyakh Peterburgskoy gubernii* ('Memorandum on the taxes of the St Petersburg province'), 1786–8.

5. *O zakonopolozhenii* ('On Legislation'), 1801–2.

6. *Proekt dlya razdeleniya ulozheniya Rossiyskogo* ('Project for the Classification of the Russian Code'), 1801–2.

7. *Proekt grazhdanskogo ulozheniya* ('Project for a Civil Code'), 1801–2.

(d) MAIN EDITIONS

1. *Puteshestvie iz Peterburga v Moskvu*, printed by Radishchev in his own home, St Petersburg, 1790.

2. *Sobranie ostavshikhsya sochineny pokoynogo Aleksandra Nikolaevicha Radishcheva* ('Collection of the remaining works of the late A. N. Radishchev'), edited by Radishchev's sons, 6 vols., Moscow, 1807–11. Does not include the *Journey* or *Pis'mo k drugu* . . . .

3. *Puteshestvie* . . . , edited with an introduction by Alexander Herzen, London, 1858.

4. Collected Works, edited by V. V. Kallash, 2 vols., Moscow, 1907.

5. Collected Works, edited by Borozdin, Lapshin and Shchegolev, 2 vols., St Petersburg, 1907–8.

6. *Polnoe sobranie sochineny* ('Complete collection of works'), edited by specialists of the Soviet Academy of Sciences, 3 vols., Moscow, Leningrad, 1938–52.

2. ORIGINAL SOURCES AND CONTEMPORARY WORKS

ADDISON, Joseph. *Cato. A Tragedy*, London, 1713.

BAYLE, Pierre. *Dictionnaire historique et critique*, Rotterdam, 1697.

BECCARIA BONESANA, Marquis Cesare. *Dei Delitti e delle Pene*, Milan, Monaco, 1764.

BECKMANN, Johann. *Beiträge zur Geschichte der Erfindungen*, Bd. 1, 2, Leipzig, 1786–8.

BLACKSTONE, Sir William. *Commentaries on the Laws of England*, Oxford, 1765–9.

CASTÉRA, J. H. *Vie de Catherine II, Impératrice de Russie*, Paris, 1797.

CATHERINE II, Empress of Russia. *Nakaz* and Correspondence with Voltaire, in *Documents of Catherine the Great*, ed. Reddaway, Cambridge, 1931.

—— *O, Vremya!* ('What an Age!'), a comedy, 1772.

CHAPPE D'AUTEROCHE, Abbé J. *Voyage en Sibérie*, Paris, 1768.

COXE, Rev. William. *Travels into Poland, Russia, Sweden and Denmark*, London, 1784.

CZARTORYSKI, Prince Adam. *Mémoires*, Paris, 1887.

DASHKOV, Princess Catherine Romanovna. *The Memoirs of Princess Dashkov*, translated and edited by Kyril FitzLyon, London, 1958.

DERZHAVIN, G. R. *Zapiski* ('Memoirs') in *Sochineniya* ('Complete Works'), ed. Ya. K. Grot, VI, St Petersburg, 1876.

DIDEROT, D'ALEMBERT, etc. *L'Encyclopédie*, Paris, 1751–65.

FONVIZIN, Denis I. *Nedorosl'* ('The Minor'), a comedy, 1782.

GENET, Edmond. Manuscript despatches to the Comte de Montmorin, in Archives of the French Ministry of Foreign Affairs, Quai d'Orsay, Paris, *Correspondance politique, Russie*, vols. 131–3.

GLINKA, S. N. *Zapiski* ('Memoirs'), St Petersburg, 1895.

GRIBOVSKY, A. M. *Vospominaniya i dnevniki A. M. Gribovskogo (1767–1834), Stats-sekretarya Imp. Ekateriny Velikoy* ('Memoirs and diaries of A. M. Gribovsky, 1767–1834, Secretary of State to the Empress Catherine the Great'), Moscow, 1899.

HARRIS, James, First Earl of Malmesbury. *Diaries and Correspondence*, London, 1844.

HELBIG, G. A. W. von. *Russische Günstlinge*, Tübingen, 1809.

—— Reprinted, Stuttgart, 1883.

HELVÉTIUS, C. A. *De l'Esprit*, Paris, 1758.

HERDER, J. G. von. *Vom Einfluss der Regierung auf die Wissenschaften und der Wissenschaften auf die Regierung*, 1780.

—— *Ideen zur Philosophie der Geschichte der Menschheit*, 1784–91.

—— *Über die Seelenwanderung*, 1785.

HOLBACH, Baron Paul Thiry d'. *Système de la Nature*, 1770.

—— *Le Bon Sens [du Curé Jean Meslier]*, 1772.

IGOR, Prince. *Iroicheskaya pesn' o pokhode na Polovtsov . . . Igorya Svyatoslavicha* ('Heroic lay of the campaign against the Polovtsians of . . . Igor, son of Svyatoslav'), edited by Count A. I. Musin-Pushkin, Moscow, 1800.

IL'INSKY, N. S. *Zapiski* ('Memoirs'), in *Russky Arkhiv* ('The Russian Archive'), 1879. No. 12.

JOSEPH II, Emperor of Austria. *Gesetze und Verfassungen*, 1781–9.

KARAMZIN, N. M. *Letters of a Russian Traveller, 1789–90*, translated by Florence Jonas, New York, London, 1957.

KASHIN, N. P. 'Novy spisok biografii A. N. Radishcheva' ('A new manuscript of the biography of A. N. Radishchev'), in *Chteniya* ('Readings') in the Imperial Society of Russian History and Antiquities at Moscow University, bk. 241, Moscow, 1912, 'Miscellany'.

KHRAPOVITSKY, A. V. 'Pamyatnye zapiski' ('Diary notes'), in *Chteniya*, 1862–3.—Also published as *Dnevnik* ('Diary'), ed. N. Barsukov, St Petersburg, 1874.

KLOPSTOCK, F. G. *Der Messias*, Halle, 1749.

LA METTRIE, J. O. de. *L'Homme-Machine*, Leyden, 1748.
—— *L'Homme-Plante*, Potsdam, 1748.
LEIBNITZ, G. W. von. *Essais de Théodicée*, 1710.
LOCKE, John. *An Essay concerning Human Understanding*, 1690.
—— *Two treatises of Government*, 1690.
MABLY, Abbé G. B. de. *Le Droit Public de l'Europe, fondé sur les Traités*, The Hague, 1746.
—— *Entretiens de Phocion*, The Hague, 1764.
—— *Observations sur l'Histoire de la Grèce*, Geneva, 1766.
MASSON, C. F. P. *Mémoires secrets sur la Russie*, Paris, Amsterdam, 1800–2.
MAUPERTUIS, P.-L. Moreau de. *Vénus Physique*, Paris, 1745.
MENDELSSOHN, Moses. *Phaedon, oder über die Unsterblichkeit der Seele*, Berlin, Stettin, 1767.
MERCIER, L.-S. *Mon Bonnet de Nuit*. Neuchâtel, 1784–5.
MONTESQUIEU. *Considérations sur les Causes de la Grandeur des Romains, et de leur Décadence*, Amsterdam, 1734.
—— *De l'Esprit des Lois*, Geneva, 1748.
NOVIKOV, N. I. *Truten'* ('The Drone'), St Petersburg, 1769.
—— *Zhivopisets* ('The Painter'), St Petersburg, 1772–3.
—— *Koshelëk* ('The Purse'), St Petersburg, 1774.
PILES, Count Fortia de. *Voyage de deux Français au Nord de l'Europe*, Paris, 1796.
PLATNER, E. *Philosophische Aphorismen*, Leipzig, 1776–82.
PRIESTLEY, Joseph. *Disquisitions relating to Matter and Spirit*, London, 1777.
RADISHCHEV, N. A. 'A. N. Radishchev', in *Russkaya Starina* ('Russian Antiquity'), VI, 1872, no. 11.
RADISHCHEV, P. A. 'Aleksandr Nikolaevich Radishchev', in *Russky Vestnik* ('The Russian Messenger'), XVIII, 1858, no. 12.
RAYNAL, Abbé G. T. F. *Histoire philosophique et politique des établissements et du commerce des Européens dans les deux Indes*, Amsterdam, 1770.—3rd., enlarged edition, Geneva, 1780.
RÉTIF DE LA BRETONNE. *Le Pornographe*, London, The Hague, 1769.
ROUSSEAU, Jean-Jacques. *Discours sur l'Inégalité*, 1755.
—— *Du Contrat Social, ou Principes du Droit Politique*, 1762.
—— *Émile, ou de l'Éducation*, 1762.
—— *Notes en réfutation de l'ouvrage d'Helvétius intitulé 'De l'Esprit'*, 1779.
SBORNIK IMPERATORSKOGO RUSSKOGO ISTORICHESKOGO OBSHCHESTVA ('Collected Works of the Imperial Russian Historical Society'), X, St Petersburg, 1872.
SÉGUR, Comte Louis-Philippe de. *Mémoires*, in *Oeuvres*, Paris, 1824, vols. 2, 3.
SHCHERBATOV, Prince M. M. *O povrezhdenii nravov v Rossii* ('On the Degradation of Morals in Russia'), London, 1858.
SMITH, Adam. *The Wealth of Nations*, London, 1776.
STARTSEV, A. I., and SHLIKHTER, B. A. 'Volneniya russkikh studentov v Leyptsige v 1767 godu' ('The disturbances among the Russian students in Leipzig in 1767'), in *Zapiski otdela rukopisey* ('Publications of the Department of Manuscripts'), no. 18, Moscow, 1956.
STERNE, Laurence. *A Sentimental Journey through France and Italy*, London, 1768.

TOOKE, William, the Elder. *View of the Russian Empire*, 2nd edition, London, 1800.

TREDIAKOVSKY, V. K. *Telemakhida* ('The Adventures of Telemachus'), an epic, St Petersburg, 1766.

TUCHKOV, S. A. *Zapiski* ('Memoirs'), edited by K. A. Voensky, St Petersburg, 1908.

VOLNEY, V.-F. Chasseboeuf, Comte de. *Voyage en Syrie et en Égypte*, 2nd edition, Paris, 1787.

VOLTAIRE. *La Henriade*, 1723; *La Pucelle*, 1755; *Candide*, 1759; *Contes de Guillaume Vadé*, 1764; *Épître au Roi de Danemark, Christian VII, sur la Liberté de la Presse, accordée dans tous ses États*, 1771.

VORONTSOV. *Arkhiv Knyazya Vorontsova* ('Archive of Prince Vorontsov'), edited by P. E. Bartenev, Moscow, 1870–95. (See especially vols. V, X, XII, XIII.)

WHITWORTH, Charles, later Earl Whitworth of Adbaston. Manuscript despatches to the Duke of Leeds, in Foreign Office Archives, Public Record Office, London, *Russia*, vol. 65/19.

WOLFF, K. F. *Theoria Generationis*, Halle, 1759.

YAKUSHKIN, I. D. *Zapiski* ('Memoirs'), Moscow, 1926.

3. OTHER WORKS

ACADEMY OF SCIENCES OF THE U.S.S.R. *Literaturnoe nasledstvo* ('Literary Heritage'), tom. 9/10, 33/34, Moscow, 1933, 1939.

ACADEMY OF SCIENCES, PUSHKINSKY DOM. *XVIII vek. Sbornik 3* ('The Eighteenth Century, 3rd Collection of Essays'), Moscow, Leningrad, 1958.

BABKIN, A. S. *Protsess A. N. Radishcheva* ('The Trial of A. N. Radishchev'), Moscow, Leningrad, 1952.

BARSKOV, Ya. L. *Perepiska moskovskikh masonov XVIII veka* ('Correspondence of the Moscow Freemasons in the 18th century'), Petrograd, 1915.

—— 'Knigi iz sobraniya A. N. Radishcheva' ('Books from the collection of A. N. Radishchev'), in *Dela i Dni* ('Deeds and Days'), I, Petersburg, 1920.

—— *Materialy k izucheniyu 'Puteshestviya iz Peterburga v Moskvu' A. N. Radishcheva* ('Materials for the study of A. N. Radishchev's *Journey from St Petersburg to Moscow*'), in *Puteshestvie*, Academia edition, Moscow, Leningrad, 1935.

BECKER, Carl L. *The Heavenly City of the Eighteenth-Century Philosophers*, eleventh printing, New Haven, 1957.

BERDYAEV, Nicholas. *The Origin of Russian Communism*, London, 1937.

—— *The Russian Idea*, London, 1947.

BITTNER, K. 'J. G. Herder und A. N. Radiščev', in *Zeitschrift für slavische Philologie*, XXV, Heft 1, Heidelberg, 1956.

BLAGOY, D. D. *Istoriya russkoy literatury XVIII veka* ('History of eighteenth century Russian literature'), 3rd ed., Moscow, 1955.

BOGDANOVICH, M. I. *Istoriya tsarstvovaniya Imperatora Aleksandra I i Rossii v ego vremya* ('History of the reign of Emperor Alexander I, and of Russia in his time'), I, St Petersburg, 1869.

BOGOLYUBOV, V. N. I. Novikov i ego vremya ('N. I. Novikov and his times'), Moscow, 1916.

DOBROLYUBOV, N. A. 'Russkaya satira ekaterininskogo vremeni' ('Russian satire in the time of Catherine II'), 1859, reprinted in Sochineniya ('Collected works'), 5th ed., St Petersburg, 1896, vol. I.

ENGELMANN, J. Die Leibeigenschaft in Russland, Leipzig, 1884.

EVGENIEV, Boris. Alexander Radishchev. A Russian Humanist of the 18th century, London, 1946.

FEUGÈRE, A. Un précurseur de la Révolution Française: L'Abbé Raynal (1713–1796), Angoulême, 1922.

GRIGOROVICH, N. Kantsler Knyaz' A. A. Bezborodko v svyazi s sobytiyami ego vremeni ('Chancellor Prince A. A. Bezborodko in connection with the events of his time'), St Petersburg, 1879–81.

GUKOVSKY, G. A. Ocherki po istorii russkoy literatury i obshchestvennoy mysli XVIII veka ('Studies in the history of Russian literature and social thought in the 18th century'), Leningrad, 1938.

—— Istoriya russkoy literatury ('History of Russian literature'), vol. IV, pt. 2 (edited by G. A. Gukovsky and V. A. Desnitsky), Moscow, 1947.

HAUMANT, Émile. La culture française en Russie, 1700–1900, Paris, 1910.

HERZEN, A. 'Études historiques sur les héros de 1825 et leurs pré-decesseurs', in Polnoe sobranie sochineny i pisem ('Complete collection of writings and letters'), XX, Petrograd, 1923.

IVANOV-RAZUMNIK, R. V. Istoriya russkoy obshchestvennoy mysli ('History of Russian social thought'), 2nd ed., St Petersburg, 1908.

KIZEVETTER, A. A. Istoricheskie ocherki ('Historical essays'), Moscow, 1912.

KLYUCHEVSKY, V. O. A history of Russia, translated by C. J. Hogarth, London, 1911–31.

KÖLBING, E. Studien zur Bevissage, Halle, 1894.

KUZ'MINA, V. D. Radishchev v russkoy kritike ('Radishchev in Russian literary criticism'), Moscow, 1952.

LANG, David Marshall. 'Sterne and Radishchev: An Episode in Russian Sentimentalism', in Revue de Littérature Comparée, 1947, no. 2.

—— 'Radishchev and the Legislative Commission of Alexander I', in American Slavic and East European Review, VI, 1947, nos. 18–9.

—— 'La légende de Radiščev au Panthéon', in Revue des Études Slaves, XXIV, 1948.

—— 'Some Forerunners of the Decembrists', in The Cambridge Journal, I, no. 10, July 1948. (Reprinted in The Making of Modern Europe, ed. H. Ausubel, I, New York, 1951.)

—— 'Some Western Sources of Radiščev's Political Thought', in Revue des Études Slaves, XXV, 1949.

LAPSHIN, I. I. Filosofskie vzglyady A. N. Radishcheva ('The philosophical views of A. N. Radishchev'), Petrograd, 1922.

LARIVIÈRE, Charles de. Catherine II et la Révolution Française, Paris, 1895.

—— La France et la Russie au 18me siècle, Paris, 1909.

LASERSON, Max M. The American Impact on Russia—Diplomatic and Ideological, 1784–1917, New York, 1950.

LÉGER, Louis. Russes et Slaves, 3me sér., Paris, 1899.

LENINGRAD STATE UNIVERSITY. Radishchev: Stat'i i materialy ('Radishchev: Articles and materials'), Leningrad, 1950.

T

LITERATURNY ARKHIV. *A. N. Radishchev. Materialy i issledovaniya* ('A. N. Radishchev. Materials and researches'), Moscow, 1936.

LUPPOL, I. K. *Istoriko-filosofskie etyudy* ('Historico-philosophical studies'), Moscow, 1935.

LYASHCHENKO, P. I. *History of the national economy of Russia to the 1917 revolution*, New York, 1949.

MAKOGONENKO, G. P. *Radishchev i ego vremya* ('Radishchev and his times'), Moscow, 1956.

MARTIN, Kingsley. *French liberal thought in the eighteenth century*, 2nd ed., London, 1954.

MAVOR, James. *An economic history of Russia*, London, 1914.

MCCONNELL, A. 'Radishchev's Political Thought', in *American Slavic and East European Review*, XVII, 1958, no. 4.

MILYUKOV, P. N. *Ocherki po istorii russkoy kul'tury* ('Studies in the history of Russian culture'), St Petersburg, 1899–1901.

MIYAKOVSKY, V. V. *'Pesn' Istoricheskaya* A. N. Radishcheva i *Considérations* Montesquieu' ('Radishchev's *Song of History* and Montesquieu's *Considérations*'), in *Zhurnal Ministerstva Narodnogo Prosveshcheniya* ('Journal of the Ministry of Public Instruction'), pt. 2, February 1914.

MOHRENSCHILDT, D. S. von. *Russia in the intellectual life of 18th century France*, New York, 1936.

MORNET, D. *Les origines intellectuelles de la Révolution Française*, Paris, 1933.

NAVILLE, P. *Paul Thiry d'Holbach et la philosophie scientifique au XVIIIe siècle*, 6th ed., Paris, 1943.

NEZELENOV, A. I. *Literaturnye napravleniya v ekaterininskuyu epokhu* ('Literary trends in the time of Catherine II'), St Petersburg, 1889.

NIKOLAY MIKHAILOVICH, Grand Duke. *Graf Pavel Aleksandrovich Stroganov*, St Petersburg, 1903.

ORLOV, A. S. *XVIII vek. Stat'i i materialy* ('The Eighteenth Century. Articles and materials'), Moscow, 1935.

ORLOV, V. *Poety-Radishchevtsy. Vol'noe Obshchestvo Lyubiteley Slovesnosti, Nauk i Khudozhestv* ('The Poets of Radishchev's School. The Free Association of Lovers of Literature, Science and the Arts'), Leningrad, 1935.

—— *Radishchev i russkaya literatura* ('Radishchev and Russian literature'), Leningrad, 1952.

—— *Russkie prosvetiteli 1790–1800-kh godov* ('Russian protagonists of Enlightenment of the 1790's and 1800's'), 2nd ed., Moscow, 1953.

PAVLOV-SIL'VANSKY, N. *Ocherki po russkoy istorii XVIII–XIX vekov* ('Studies in Russian history of the 18th and 19th centuries'), St Petersburg, 1910.

PLEKHANOV, G. V. *Istoriya russkoy obshchestvennoy mysli* ('History of Russian social thought'), Moscow, 1918.

POKROVSKY, S. A. *Gosudarstvenno-pravovye vzglyady Radishcheva* ('Radishchev's constitutional views'), Moscow, 1956.

POKROVSKY, V. I., edit. *A. N. Radishchev: ego zhizn' i sochineniya* ('A. N. Radishchev: his life and writings'), St Petersburg, 1907.

POPEL'NITSKY, A. 'Vnov' otkrytaya zapiska A. N. Radishcheva o zakono-datel'stve' ('The newly discovered memorandum by A. N. Radish-chev on legislation'), in *Golos Minuvshego* ('Voice of the Past'), 1916, no. 12.

PRIKAZCHIKOVA, E. V. *Ekonomicheskie vzglyady A. N. Radishcheva* ('A. N. Radishchev's views on economics'), Moscow, Leningrad, 1947.

PUSHKIN, A. S. *Puteshestvie iz Moskvy v Peterburg* ('A Journey from Moscow to St Petersburg'), 1833–5.

—— 'Alexander Radishchev', 1836.

PYPIN, A. N. *Istoriya russkoy literatury* ('History of Russian literature'), IV, St Petersburg, 1898–9.

—— *Russkoe masonstvo* ('Russian Freemasonry'), Petrograd, 1916.

ROBINSON, Geroid T. *Rural Russia under the Old Régime. A History of the Landlord-Peasant World and a Prologue to the Peasant Revolution of 1917.* Second printing. New York, 1949.

SACKE, G. *Graf A. Voroncov, A. N. Radiščev und der 'Gnadenbrief für das russische Volk'*, Emsdetten, 1938.

—— 'Radiščev und seine "Reise" in der westeuropäischen Literatur des 18. Jahrhunderts', in *Forschungen zur Osteuropäischen Geschichte*, Bd. 1, Berlin, 1954.

SAKULIN, P. N. *Pushkin i Radishchev* ('Pushkin and Radishchev'), Moscow, 1920.

SEMENNIKOV, V. P. *Novy tekst 'Puteshestviya iz Peterburga v Moskvu' Radishcheva* ('A new text of Radishchev's *Journey from St Peters-burg to Moscow*'), Moscow, 1922.

—— *Radishchev. Ocherki i issledovaniya* ('Radishchev. Essays and studies'), Moscow, Petrograd, 1923.

SEMEVSKY, V. I. *Krest'yane v tsarstvovanie Imperatritsy Ekateriny II* ('The peasants in the reign of Catherine II'), revised edition, St Petersburg, 1901–3.

SHPET, G. *Ocherk razvitiya russkoy filosofii* ('Outline of the development of Russian Philosophy'), Petrograd, 1922.

SHTRANGE, M. M. *Russkoe obshchestvo i frantsuzskaya revolyutsiya 1789–1794 gg.* ('Russian society and the French Revolution of 1789–1794'), Moscow, 1956.

SKABICHEVSKY, A. M. *Ocherki istorii russkoy tsenzury 1700–1863* ('Studies in the history of the Russian censorship, 1700–1863'), St Peters-burg, 1892.

SOLOVEYTCHIK, G. *Potemkin. A Picture of Catherine's Russia*, London, 1938.

SOPIKOV, V. S. *Opyt Rossiyskoy Bibliografii* ('Attempt at a bibliography of Russia'), new edition, revised by V. N. Rogozhin, St Petersburg, 1904.

STARTSEV, A. I. *Universitetskie gody Radishcheva* ('Radishchev's Univer-sity years'), Moscow, 1956.

STINTZING, R., and LANDSBERG, E. *Geschichte der deutschen Rechtswissen-schaft.* München, Leipzig, 1880–98.

SUKHOMLINOV, M. I. *Issledovaniya i stat'i po russkoy literature i prosvesh-cheniyu* ('Researches and articles on Russian literature and educa-tion'), I, St Petersburg, 1889.

SVETLOV, L. B. *Izdatel'skaya deyatel'nost' N. I. Novikova* ('The pub-lishing activities of N. I. Novikov'), Leningrad, 1946.

SVETLOV, L. B. *Aleksandr Nikolaevich Radishchev. Kritiko-biografichesky ocherk* ('Alexander Nikolaevich Radishchev. A critical and biographical study'), Moscow, 1958.

THALER, R. P. 'Radiščev, Britain, and America', in *Harvard Slavic Studies*, IV, The Hague, 1957.

TOMPKINS, Stuart Ramsay. *The Russian Mind, from Peter the Great through the Enlightenment*, Norman, 1953.

TOURNEUX, M. *Diderot et Catherine II*, Paris, 1899.

VERNADSKY, G. 'Reforms under Czar Alexander I. French and American Influences', in *Review of Politics*, IX, January 1947.

VESELOVSKY, A. N. *Iz istorii romana i povesti* ('From the history of the novel and the tale'), St Petersburg, 1888.

—— *Etyudy i kharakteristiki* ('Studies and literary portraits'), 2nd ed., Moscow, 1903.

—— *Zapadnoe vliyanie v novoy russkoy literature* ('Western influence in modern Russian literature'), 4th ed., Moscow, 1910.

VOGEL, Julius. *Goethes Leipziger Studentenjahre*, 4th ed., Leipzig, 1923.

WHITFIELD, E. A. *Gabriel Bonnot de Mably*, London, 1930.

ZEN'KOVSKY, V. V. *Istoriya russkoy filosofii* ('History of Russian philosophy'), Paris, 1948–50.

—— *A History of Russian Philosophy*, translated by G. L. Kline, London, 1953.

INDEX

GEORGE ALLEN & UNWIN LTD
London: 40 Museum Street, W.C.1

Auckland: 24 Wyndham Street
Bombay: 15 Graham Road, Ballard Estate, Bombay 1
Calcutta: 17 Chittaranjan Avenue, Calcutta 13
Cape Town: 109 Long Street
Karachi: Metherson's Estate, Wood Street, Karachi 2
New Delhi: 13–14 Ajmeri Gate Extension, New Delhi 1
Sao Paulo: Avenida 9 de Julho 1138–Ap. 51
Singapore, South East Asia and Far East: 36c Princep Street
Sydney, N.S.W.: Bradbury House, 55 York Street
Toronto: 91 Wellington Street West

KINO

A History of the Russian and Soviet Film

JAY LEYDA

It is primarily in the Soviet Union that the film has been used with a consciousness of its persuasive powers, and this history gives a full account of the film's development as an art in the service of that society.

Concluding with the problems of the present, this first comprehensive history of the film in Russia begins with the Lumieres' filming of the last tsar's coronation in 1896. For the first time full attention is given to the large and important Russian film industry before the revolutions of 1917, and to its many links with the emerging Soviet film. The Russian film's continuing history is set against the connected background of Russia's social and artistic progress of the past fifty years.

The author's three years of work in Soviet film schools and studios gave him the opportunity to examine all Russian and Soviet films of importance, many never seen abroad, and his personal acquaintance with the leading film-makers of all Soviet nationalities makes his account of their careers colourful and authoritative.

The history's appeal is to the general reader as well as the specialist. It is fully documented, both with newly translated statements by creators and critics, and with rich illustrations, many published for the first time.

Illustrated. Small Royal 8vo. About 42s net

DOSTOEVSKY

E. H. CARR

'So excellent. . . . There can be no doubt that this biography supersedes all others.'—TIMES LITERARY SUPPLEMENT

'For the first time Dostoevsky is shown life-size, and in such a sane light that the man, his work, and his complicated career fit together into a unity as understandable as it can possibly be to the onlooker. . . . In addition to this fine historical presentation, Mr Carr has also analysed the novels and collated them with the poet's life, proving himself to be as sane a literary critic as he is a historian.'—NEW STATESMAN

'The first complete biography and the best: a masterly book full of new material and close analysis.'—DAILY TELEGRAPH.

Second Impression. Demy 8vo. 15s net

GEORGE ALLEN & UNWIN LTD